CHAMBER

Dictionary of

Idioms
and
Catch Phrases

CHAMBERS

Dictionary of Idioms *and* Catch Phrases

Edited by
Betty Kirkpatrick

CHAMBERS

CHAMBERS
An imprint of Larousse plc
43-45 Annandale Street
Edinburgh EH7 4AZ

First published by Larousse plc 1995
Based on *Chambers Idioms*, edited by
E.M. Kirkpatrick and C.M. Schwarz.

10 9 8 7 6 5 4 3 2 1

A CIP catalogue record for this book
is available from the British Library

ISBN 0-550-18301-9 (Paperback)
ISBN 0-550-18307-8 (Hardback)

Typeset by Tradespools Ltd, Frome, Somerset

Printed in England by Clays Ltd, St Ives plc

Contents

Preface

Terms like 'idiom' and 'idioms' are bandied about quite freely, and it would be as well to clarify what this book is about. It is less concerned with *idiom* – the characteristic ways in which words are put together to form natural language – than with *idioms* – phrases that are wholly or partly fixed, are usually rich in metaphor or allusion, and cannot be understood from the usual meaning of the individual words they contain. English is exceptionally rich in idioms, and this alphabetical survey will be as invaluable to native speakers as to learners.

The book also includes a generous coverage of catch phrases, which carry a particular association or resonance like *elementary, my dear Watson*, and proverbs, which state a general truth or proposition like *two blacks don't make a white*. Idioms are arranged under key words contained in them, so that **hide one's light under a bushel** is entered at **light**. Cross-references are provided when this seems helpful, as in this case at **bushel**. This arrangement was chosen because idioms are capable of many minor variations in use, and because it seemed helpful and illuminating to show which words tend to be most used as a basis for forming idioms. Example sentences are given in some cases, to help further clarify meaning and usage. These are marked with the symbol •.

The origins of many idioms have been obscured with time, but some of the more colourful idioms are associated with particular circumstances that are now largely forgotten in themselves but are of considerable linguistic interest, as users will find, for example, at **make the grade** and **break the mould**. Notes on origins are marked with the symbol ⓘ.

Idioms help to enliven language, but it is often difficult to bring to mind the precise phrase that is wanted in a particular context. To help users further, we have added an index of key topics, so that an idiom associated with a particular theme such as happiness, money, or courage can be readily found at the key word referred to, bringing colour and variety to written and spoken communication.

Users will find this an enjoyable book to browse in as well as an informative and authoritative source of information on an aspect of language that is arguably the most rich and vivid and certainly the most productive.

Abbreviations used in this book

arch	archaic
Brit	British
c	*circa*, about
C	century
derog	derogatory
eg	for example
esp	especially
etc	et cetera, and so on
euph	euphemistic
facet	facetious
fig	figurative
ie	that is
inf	informal
interj	interjection
liter	literary
neg	negative
NY	New York
RAF	Royal Air Force
sl	slang
US	United States
usu	usually
vulg	vulgar

A

A

from A to B
from one point or place to another
• *He regards a car just as something to get him from A to B*

from A to Z
very thoroughly and completely

A1

A1
informal of the highest quality; very good
Ⓘ A1 is the highest grading in the scale on which the condition of a ship and its cargo is rated for Lloyd's Register

ABC

ABC
the simplest and most basic knowledge

about

month, week etc **about**
every alternate month, week

above

above board *see* **board**

above someone's head *see* **head**

be/get a bit above oneself
to have or acquire too high an opinion of oneself; to be or become very conceited

be above suspicion *see* **suspicion**

absence

absence makes the heart grow fonder
when people or things are not present we tend to view them with more affection since we are not constantly being made aware of what we consider their bad points

leave of absence *see* **leave**

accident

accidents will happen
things can go wrong unexpectedly in anyone's life

an accident waiting to happen
a situation that is so dangerous that it is bound to result in a disaster of some kind at some point
• *The blind bend in that road is an accident waiting to happen*

a chapter of accidents *see* **chapter**

accidentally

accidentally on purpose
giving the appearance of being done unintentionally but actually being done deliberately and often maliciously

accord

of one's own accord
of one's own free will

with one accord
formal everybody in agreement

according

according to one's lights *see* **light**[1]

according to Hoyle
in keeping with the established rules or procedures
Ⓘ From Edmond Hoyle (1679–1769), the writer of various treatises on card games, which became established authorities

account

bring someone to account
formal to make sure that an offender is punished

by all accounts
in the opinion of most people

call someone to account
formal to demand an explanation for their actions

give a good account of oneself
rather formal to do well

on my etc **account**
because of me or for my sake

on no account
not for any reason, or in any circumstances

take something into account/take account of something
to include it as relevant to a problem or issue one is considering

turn something to account/good account
to use a situation or opportunity to one's advantage

ace

an ace in the hole
informal a hidden advantage kept in reserve for emergencies
Ⓞ From a card in stud poker, called a 'hole card'

an ace up one's sleeve
a secret or hidden advantage that can be used to defeat an opponent
Ⓞ From cheating at cards

hold all the aces
informal to be in a position of total power or control
Ⓞ From card games

within an ace of
very near to
Ⓞ An idiom from the game of dice

Achilles

an Achilles' heel *see* **heel**

acid

the acid test
a test which will prove or disprove something beyond doubt
• *His leg appears to be completely well again, but the acid test will be the tennis tournament tomorrow*
Ⓞ From a method of testing for gold by using acid

across

across the board *see* **board**

get something across
informal to be or make something understood

put one across on someone
slang to deceive them or play a trick on them

act

an act of God
a totally unexpected natural happening which could not have been foreseen or prevented
Ⓞ Strictly a legal term, identifying events for which one can expect no legal compensation

act the goat *see* **goat**

act up
informal to behave or act badly or wrongly

catch someone in the act
to discover them while they are doing something wrong

get one's act together
informal to get oneself organized

get in on the act
informal to join or copy someone in doing something successful or fashionable, especially in order to share in the success

a hard act to follow
someone or something that sets such a high standard that others will find it difficult or impossible to meet
Ⓞ From acts in music-hall and variety shows

put on an act
to make an elaborate pretence

action

actions speak louder than words
what people do is more important and effective than what they say

action stations
a state of readiness for activity
• *Action stations! It is time to line up for the race*
Ⓞ Literally, positions taken up by soldiers in readiness for a battle etc

actress

as the actress said to the bishop
an expression used to point out a sexual double meaning in a seemingly ordinary remark
• *He couldn't get it out — as the actress said to the bishop*

Adam

Adam's ale
facetious water

not to know someone from Adam
not to recognize them; not to have any idea who they are
Ⓛ Presumably because Adam, the first man according to the Bible, is both the ultimate person one would not know and the archetype of all men

the old Adam in us
the tendency towards wrongdoing or evil that is in all human beings
Ⓛ From *Adam*, the first man according to the Bible, who disobeyed God

add

add fuel to the fire *see* **fuel**

add up
informal to seem sensible or logical
• *I don't understand his behaviour – it simply doesn't add up*

Adonis

an Adonis
a beautiful young man
Ⓛ In Greek myth, Adonis was the beautiful youth loved by Aphrodite and killed by a boar while hunting

advantage

have the advantage of someone
formal to recognize them without being recognized oneself
• *She stared blankly at the young man who had addressed her and said 'You have the advantage of me'.*

take advantage of someone or **something**
to make use of someone or something in such a way as to benefit oneself

to advantage/best advantage
formal so that the good points are easily seen
• *Put the picture on the long wall so that the colours can be seen to best advantage*

aegis

under the aegis of someone
formal with their moral or financial support
• *under the aegis of the British government*
Ⓛ *Aegis* is a Greek word for the shield or armour of Zeus or Athena

after

be after someone
to be pursuing them

be after something
informal to be looking for or hoping to be given something

aftermath

the aftermath
the situation etc resulting from an important, especially unpleasant, event
Ⓛ This term means literally 'second mowing' and was applied to the new grass that grows in summer after the hay has been cut

against

be up against it
informal to be in a position where one has to deal with very severe, often apparently impossible difficulties

age

act/be one's age
to behave in an adult or sensible way; not to be childish

the age of consent
the age at which a person may legally agree to have sexual relations

come of age
to become old enough to be considered legally an adult: in Britain aged eighteen or over

a/the golden age *see* **golden**

of a certain age *see* **certain**

a ripe old age *see* **ripe**

under age
too young, especially legally

agony

the agony column
informal the part of a newspaper or magazine where letters setting out readers' problems are printed along with advice from a member of the magazine's staff

agreement

strike an agreement *see* **strike**

ahead

ahead of one's time *see* **time**

be streets ahead *see* **street**

aid

aid and abet
to provide help and encouragement in some bad or illegal activity
Ⓞ Originally a legal term

what is something in aid of?
Brit informal for what reason or purpose is something being done etc?

air

airs and graces
derogatory behaviour in which a person acts as if they are better or more important than others

clear the air
to make a situation simpler and less tense

go up in the air
informal to become very angry or excited

hot air *see* **hot**

in the air
informal in existence; current

in the open air *see* **open**

make the air turn blue *see* **blue**

on the air
broadcasting regularly on radio or television

put on airs/give oneself airs
to behave as if one is better or more important than others

take the air
old or facetious to go for a walk

thin air *see* **thin**

up in the air
uncertain; undecided
• *Our holiday plans are still rather up in the air*

walk on air *see* **walk**

Aladdin

Aladdin's cave
a place full of valuable or desirable objects
• *The toy department is an Aladdin's cave to children*
Ⓞ From the tale in the Arabian Nights in which *Aladdin* gained access to a cave full of treasure with the help of the genie from his magic lamp

alarm

alarms/alarums and excursions
confused activity, especially disorganized arguments etc
Ⓞ From a stage direction in Shakespeare's history plays calling for a vague representation of the edge of a battle

a false alarm *see* **false**

albatross

an albatross round one's neck *see* **neck**

ale

Adam's ale *see* **Adam**

alert

on red alert *see* **red**

on the alert
vigilant and watchful
• *We must all be on the alert for trouble*

alive

alive and kicking
in a strong or healthy condition

all

all and sundry *see* **sundry**

all chiefs and no Indians *see* **chief**

all in
informal
1 exhausted
• *After a morning's tennis we were all in and ready for lunch*
2 with everything included
• *Is that the price all in?*

all in all
considering everything
• *All in all, it's a fair result*

all is fair in love and war *see* **fair**

all my eye *see* **eye**

all out
using the greatest effort possible
• *They were obviously all out to win*

all singing, all dancing *see* **singing**

all systems go *see* **system**

all that glitters is not gold
appearances can be deceptive and many things that appear attractive or valuable are worthless

all there
informal completely sane; having an alert, intelligent mind and good ideas
• *He may be a bit vague at times, but he's all there when it comes to making decisions*

all told *see* **tell**

be all ears *see* **ear**

be all over someone
derogatory to treat them with great or excessive friendliness and affection

be all things to all men *see* **thing**

it is all up with someone
there is no hope left for them

when all is said and done
considering all the facts

allowance

make allowances for someone
to judge them less severely, or require them to do less well, because of particular circumstances

alma

alma mater
one's old university, college or school
• *She is attending a reunion at her old alma mater*

alpha

alpha and omega
the beginning and the end
Ⓞ From the names of the first and last letters of the Greek alphabet

also

an also-ran *see* **run**

Amazon

an Amazon
sometimes derogatory a woman who is strong, energetic or warlike
Ⓞ From a legendary race of warrior women believed by the Greeks to live in Southern Russia and said to have had their right breasts removed to enable them to draw their bows better

amends

make amends
to do something to improve the situation after doing something wrong, stupid etc
Ⓞ From the Old French word *amendes* for a monetary fine

American

the American dream
the hope of achieving success and prosperity through hard work

amiss

come amiss
to be unwelcome or unwanted
• *Some extra help would not come amiss*

take something amiss
formal to be upset or offended by something
• *He took it amiss that I had not consulted him before signing the contract*
Ⓞ The original meaning of this phrase was 'to be in error about' — literally 'to miss-take'

amount

any amount of *see* **any**

analysis

in the final/last analysis
rather formal when the problem or situation has been simplified so that only the essentials are left to be considered

anchor

an anchor-man
a person on whom the success of an activity depends, especially, on television, the person responsible for the smooth running of a discussion between other people etc
Ⓞ Literally, the man at the back of a team competing in a tug-of-war

ancient

ancient history
informal something that happened long ago and is no longer of importance
• *Their love affair is ancient history*

the Ancient of Days
God
Ⓞ A Biblical epithet for God — Daniel

7:9 — first used in English in the Geneva Bible of 1560

the ancients
people who lived in ancient times

angel

an angel of mercy
a person who appears when they are particularly needed, bringing help, comfort etc

angel's visits
visits that are rare and short but very pleasant

entertain an angel unawares
to meet and talk to someone whose fame or worth is unknown to one

fools rush in where angels fear to tread *see* **fool**

on the side of the angels
basically agreeing with accepted ideas of what is good and bad

angry

an angry young man
a young man who disapproves of the way his parents' generation have run the country etc and makes his feelings known
Ⓛ A term which became popular after being applied to John Osborne, whose play *Look Back in Anger* was first performed in 1956

answer

answer back
to give an impertinent or aggressive answer to someone in authority

the answer to a maiden's prayer
exactly what one desires and has been searching for
Ⓛ The answer to a maiden's prayer was traditionally thought to be an eligible bachelor

know all the answers
often slightly derogatory to be in complete command of a situation and perfectly able to deal with any developments, especially if too proud of this ability

ant

have ants in one's pants
informal to be very restless

any

any amount of
informal a great deal of

anybody's guess *see* **guess**

any day
in any circumstances
• *I would rather employ you than her any day*

any old how
informal without any special care
• *Her desk is always terribly untidy — she just throws papers and letters into it any old how*

anything for a quiet life
an expression indicating that someone will agree to any conditions as long as they are assured of a trouble-free existence

like anything
informal very strongly or energetically; very much; intensely
• *They argued like anything all evening*

not to get anywhere
informal to make no progress

apart

be poles apart *see* **pole**

take someone or **something apart**
slang to deal with or criticize someone, a plan etc severely

tell apart
usually with can, cannot etc to recognize the difference between; to distinguish between

apology

an apology for something
informal a poor-quality example of something
• *That's rather an apology for an essay — do it again!*

appearance

keep up appearances
to behave in such a way as to hide the truth, especially something bad or unpleasant from other people

put in/make an appearance
to attend a meeting, party etc usually only for a short time

to/by all appearances
rather formal judging by, or basing one's opinion on, what can be seen etc

appetite

whet someone's appetite *see* **whet**

apple

an apple of discord
formal or literary something which causes jealousy and fighting
Ⓛ From the golden apple inscribed 'for the fairest' which according to Greek mythology was thrown among the gods by Eris, goddess of discord, and was claimed by Aphrodite, Athene and Hera

the apple of someone's eye
a person or thing that is greatly loved by someone
Ⓛ Originally a term for the pupil of the eye

an apple-pie bed
a bed made up as a joke in such a way as to be impossible to get into because the top sheet is doubled

bad/rotten apple
someone who is likely to have a bad influence on the rest of a group of which they are a member
Ⓛ From the fact that a rotten apple quickly rots other apples with which it comes into contact

in apple-pie order
informal neat and tidy, with everything in its correct place
Ⓛ Origin unknown

upset the applecart
informal to spoil plans, obstruct progress etc

April

April showers bring forth May flowers
adversity is often followed by good fortune

apron

tied to someone's apron-strings
derogatory ruled by and dependent on a woman, especially one's wife or mother

argue

argue the toss *see* **toss**

ark

like something out of the ark
extremely old-fashioned
• *her hat was like something out of the ark*
Ⓛ From *Noah's Ark* in the Bible

arm

armed to the teeth *see* **teeth**

the long arm of the law
informal the power or authority of the police force

be up in arms
to be very angry and make a great protest about something

chance one's arm *see* **chance**

keep at arm's length
to avoid becoming too friendly with someone

lay down one's arms
to surrender; to stop fighting or opposing other people

someone's right arm
someone's main help and support

a shot in the arm *see* **shot**

take up arms
to become actively involved in a dispute, argument etc

twist someone's arm
informal, often facetious to make them do something
• *'Do you want a drink?' 'Well, if you're twisting my arm, I'll have a whisky.'*

with one arm tied behind one's back
with no difficulty whatsoever
• *I could do that with one arm tied behind my back*

with open arms *see* **open**

armour

a chink in someone's armour *see* **chink**

a knight in shining armour *see* **knight**

around

have been around
informal to have a great deal of experience of life

ash

the Ashes
the trophy, originally imaginary, for which Australia and England compete at cricket
• *Having won the first two Tests, Australia is now almost certain to retain the Ashes*

ⓘ In 1882 the Australian cricket team had a very successful visit to England, and the *Sporting Times* published a mock 'In Memoriam' notice announcing the cremation of the body of English cricket and the taking of the ashes to Australia. Thereafter, English teams were anxious to 'bring back the ashes' by defeating the Australians

rise (like a phoenix) from the ashes
to develop and flourish after experiencing ruin or disaster
ⓘ In Greek legend a phoenix was a mythical bird which, after a certain number of years, set fire to itself and was then reborn from the ashes

ask

ask after someone
to make enquiries about their health and well-being

be asking for it/trouble
informal to be behaving as if inviting something unpleasant

someone's for the asking
something that a person may have quite easily or readily

asleep

be asleep
informal said of a person's arm or leg: to be numb, usually because of pressure on a nerve

assured

rest assured *see* **rest**

attack

attack is the best form of defence
in certain situations it is better to be aggressive and tackle an issue of dispute with someone rather than wait for them to accuse or blame one

attendance

dance attendance on someone *see* **dance**

Attic

Attic salt
dry, delicate and refined wit
ⓘ A term coined by the Roman writer Pliny

attitude

strike an attitude *see* **strike**

auction

a Dutch auction *see* **Dutch**

aunt

Aunt Sally
a person or thing that is subjected to general abuse or criticism
• *The press is often treated as an Aunt Sally by the public*
ⓘ Traditionally an *Aunt Sally* was a model of a woman's head which was mounted on a pole and at which people threw balls to try to win a prize

avail

of no avail/to no avail
formal of no use or effect

awake

be awake to
to be aware of

away

do away with *see* **do**

the one that got away
an opportunity which someone failed to take advantage of
ⓘ A reference to a common angling story in which a supposedly very large fish escapes from an angler who then tells exaggerated stories about it

axe

get the axe
informal
1 to be dismissed from a post
2 said of a project etc: to be abandoned or got rid of

have an axe to grind
to have a personal, often selfish, reason for being involved in something or for wanting a particular answer or solution
ⓘ Originally US, stemming from a story told by Benjamin Franklin of how a man had once asked him to demonstrate how his father's grindstone worked — and had then produced an axe which he wanted to sharpen

B

babe

a babe in arms
an innocent, inexperienced person

babes in the wood
people who are naive and trust others unduly
Ⓛ From a traditional story in which two children go into the woods with people who intend to murder them

baby

be left holding the baby
to be the person who has to deal with a problem, organize something etc because everyone else has abandoned it

throw out the baby with the bathwater
to be so enthusiastic about changing or reorganizing things and getting rid of old ideas etc that one destroys or disposes of things that are essential

back

answer back *see* **answer**

backbiting
criticizing and speaking evil of a person when they are not present

a back-handed compliment *see* **compliment**

a backhander
informal a bribe

back number
someone or something that is no longer of importance or use
Ⓛ From a back or out-of-date issue of a magazine

the back of beyond
informal derogatory a very remote place
Ⓛ Originally Scottish and Northern English

backpedal
to reverse one's opinion or course of action
Ⓛ Literally, to turn the pedals of a bicycle backwards, which on many early models operated the brake

backscratching
derogatory doing favours for other people in return for favours which they do for you

a back-seat driver
a passenger in a car who gives unwanted advice on how to drive it

back the wrong horse *see* **horse**

back to the saltmines *see* **salt**

a backwater
usually derogatory a place not affected by what is happening in the world outside, usually because of its isolation
Ⓛ Literally, a stretch of water connected to a river but not now in the line of the main flow

backwards in/at coming forwards
informal shy; reluctant to draw attention to oneself

behind someone's back
informal without their knowledge or permission

bend over backwards *see* **bend**

break the back of something
to complete the heaviest or most difficult part of a task etc

fed to the back teeth *see* **fed**

get off someone's back
informal to stop annoying or harassing them

get one's own back *see* **own**

go back on *see* **go**

have one's back to the wall
to be in a very difficult or desperate situation
Ⓛ From someone involved in a fight who

can retreat no further and is forced to turn and fight from a defensive position

know backwards *see* **know**

lean over backwards *see* **bend**

like the back end of a bus *see* **bus**

make a rod for one's own back *see* **rod**

put one's back into something
informal to do something with all one's strength

put someone's back up
informal to anger them
Ⓛ The image is of a cat, which arches its back when angry

put/place something on the back burner
to set something aside to be attended to at a later time
Ⓛ From putting a pan on the back burner of a stove

stab someone in the back *see* **stab**

take a back seat
to take an unimportant or unnoticed position
• *At these discussions he always takes a back seat and listens to others talking*

talk through the back of one's head/neck
informal to talk complete nonsense

bacon

bring home the bacon
informal to complete a job, task etc successfully

save someone's bacon
informal to cause them to escape unharmed from a difficulty, danger etc

bad

a bad egg *see* **egg**

bad blood *see* **blood**

a bad hat *see* **hat**

bad language *see* **language**

badly off for something
not having much of it, especially money

be in someone's bad books *see* **book**

feel bad about something
to be sorry about it; to regret it

give something up as a bad job *see* **job**

go bad
said of food: to decay, to become rotten

go from bad to worse
to get into an even worse condition etc than before

go to the bad
to become immoral; to behave in a way of which people in general disapprove

hit a bad patch *see* **patch**

in bad odour *see* **odour**

in a bad way *see* **way**

make the best of a bad job *see* **best**

not bad
informal quite good; acceptable

too bad
informal unfortunate

with a bad grace *see* **grace**

bag

bag and baggage
with all one's belongings, equipment etc
Ⓛ A military phrase originally describing an orderly retreat in which neither personal belongings — *bag* — nor army equipment — *baggage* — had to be abandoned

a bag of bones
informal a very thin person

a bag of nerves *see* **nerve**

a bag of tricks
informal all the equipment etc required for doing something or connected with something

bags of something
informal plenty of it

in the bag
informal as certain as if done or completed (in the desired way)
• *Your appointment as director is in the bag*
Ⓛ From the bag used in hunting to carry what one has shot etc

let the cat out of the bag *see* **cat**

a mixed bag *see* **mix**

pack one's bags
to get ready to leave

bait

rise to the bait
to do what someone has been trying to make one do by means of suggestions, hints, attractions, etc
• *I could see he was trying to make me angry, but I didn't rise to the bait*
Ⓘ A fishing term

baker

a baker's dozen
old use thirteen
Ⓘ It was once customary for bakers to add an extra bun, loaf etc to a dozen to be sure that they were not giving short weight

balance

in the balance
formal in an undecided or uncertain state
Ⓘ From *balance* — a pair of hanging scales

on balance
having taken everything into consideration

strike a balance *see* **strike**

throw someone off balance
to cause them to be disconcerted or confused

bald

as bald as a coot
extremely bald
Ⓘ A coot is a bird with a spot of white feathers on its head

ball[1]

the belle of the ball
the most attractive or best-dressed woman present at a gathering of some kind
Ⓘ *Belle* means beautiful woman and is derived from French

have a ball
slang to have a good time; to enjoy oneself

ball[2]

have the ball at one's feet
to be in a position to become successful; to have an opportunity
Ⓘ From football

have the ball in one's court
to be responsible for the next development in a situation
Ⓘ From racket sports such as tennis

on the ball
informal quick, alert and up to date
Ⓘ From football

play ball with someone
informal to work or act together with them

start/set/keep the ball rolling
to start or keep something going, especially a conversation

ballgame

a different ballgame/a whole new ballgame
informal a completely different situation, an entirely different matter
Ⓘ The term originated in America, *ballgame* meaning simply a game played with a ball, such as football, baseball and basketball, each game having a different set of rules and conditions

balloon

when the balloon goes up
informal when the trouble starts; when something unwelcome occurs
Ⓘ From military observation balloons

ballpark

in the right ballpark
informal roughly accurate, more or less correct
• *I think the price is in the right ballpark*
Ⓘ *In the ballpark* is a baseball term meaning 'within certain limits'

bananas

be/go bananas
slang to be or become violently angry

slip on a banana skin
to do something that causes one humiliation or public embarrassment
Ⓘ Cartoons often show people literally slipping on banana skins while other people laugh at them

band

beat the band
slang to be especially loud, strong, good or remarkable
• *The baby was howling to beat the band*
Ⓘ Originally US

look as though one has stepped out of a bandbox
to have a neat, elegant appearance
Ⓞ From a lightweight box once used for carrying small articles such as hats

bandwagon

jump on the bandwagon
derogatory to take part in something, or show an interest in something, because it is fashionable or because it is going to be of some financial advantage to oneself
Ⓞ A *bandwagon* was a large, elaborate, horse-drawn vehicle capable of carrying the band in a circus procession etc and thus figuratively any group of people which was showy, popular and successful

bang

bang goes something
informal that puts a sudden end to hopes, plans etc
Ⓞ From a bursting bubble, balloon etc

bang one's head against a brick wall *see* **head**

bang on
informal exact or exactly; precisely
• *It was just a guess, but it proved to be bang on*
• *They arrived bang on time*

go with a bang
informal to go well; to be very successful

bank

bank on something or **someone**
informal to rely on them
Ⓞ Originally US, meaning 'to use a sum of money etc to start a bank in a card game'

break the bank
to leave oneself or someone else without any money
• *The price of a cup of coffee won't break the bank, even if we can't afford a meal*
Ⓞ Literally, to win all the money which the management of a casino is prepared to pay out in one night

baptism

baptism of fire
a first experience of something difficult, frightening etc
Ⓞ Originally a theological term

bare

the bare bones *see* **bone**

bare one's soul to someone
to tell all one's private feelings or worries to someone

with one's bare hands *see* **hand**

bargain

drive a hard bargain
to try to get the deal that is most favourable to oneself

into the bargain
in addition; besides
• *They were all penniless, and drunk into the bargain*

strike a bargain *see* **strike**

bargepole

not touch something with a bargepole
informal to refuse to have any contact with something or to be involved with it in any way

bark

someone's bark is worse than their bite
informal they sound angry but are harmless or ineffectual
Ⓞ The reference is to a dog

bark up the wrong tree
informal to attempt to do the wrong thing, or to do something in the wrong way or from the wrong direction
Ⓞ Originally US — from raccoon-hunting, in which dogs are used to locate raccoons up in trees

barking

barking mad
completely insane, extremely foolish

barrel

have someone over a barrel
to be in a position to get whatever one wants from them
Ⓞ A 19c US expression

not exactly a barrel of laughs
informal boring, not at all amusing or entertaining
Ⓞ From the phrase *more fun than a barrel of monkeys*, meaning 'extremely entertaining' and derived from the fact that monkeys often get up to amusing antics

scraping the bottom of the barrel
derogatory making use of something or someone of very poor quality because it is all that is left or available

base

get to/make first base
to complete the first stage of a process
Ⓞ Literally, in baseball, to complete the first of the four sections of a run

basket

put all one's eggs in one basket *see* **egg**

bat[1]

off one's own bat
informal completely by oneself, without being told to do something or being given any help
Ⓞ A phrase from cricket

bat[2]

blind as a bat
completely blind

have bats in the belfry
informal, often facetious to be slightly but harmlessly crazy or eccentric

like a bat out of hell
informal with extreme or violent speed or effort
• *After the game they left the ground like bats out of hell*

bat[3]

not to bat an eyelid *see* **eyelid**

bated

with bated breath
in anxious expectation; apprehensively
• *We waited with bated breath for the football results*

batten

batten down the hatches *see* **hatch**

battle

battle royal
a fight or dispute in which many people get involved, a free-for-all
Ⓞ Origin uncertain: perhaps from medieval jousting tournaments in which each side was led by a king, or perhaps a reference to a cockfight in which a number of birds were left to fight until there was only one survivor

be half the battle
to be the largest or most important part of a difficult task

bay

bay at the moon *see* **moon**

hold/keep something or **someone at bay**
to prevent them from attacking; to keep some threat from harming one
Ⓞ A French phrase, originally a hunting term

be

the be-all and end-all
the final aim apart from which nothing is of any real importance
• *This job isn't the be-all and end-all of existence*
Ⓞ A Shakespearian phrase, from *Macbeth*, I viii

beady

keep one's beady eye on someone or **something** *see* **eye**

beam

broad in the beam
informal wide in the hips
Ⓞ Literally used of a ship and meaning 'wide in proportion to its length'

off the beam
informal off course or target; inaccurate
Ⓞ An aeronautical idiom from the radio beam used to bring aircraft in to land in poor visibility

on one's beam ends
informal short of money, and in difficulties because of it
Ⓞ A nautical term describing a ship lying over on its side and thus in danger of capsizing completely

beans

full of beans
informal full of energy; very cheerful
Ⓞ Probably a reference to a horse fed on beans, which are an effective energy-producing food

know how many beans make five
informal to know quite a lot about life and therefore be able to take care of oneself

not to know beans about something
informal to know absolutely nothing about a subject
• *He is always talking about sailing but he doesn't know beans about it*
Ⓛ Originally US

not have a bean
informal to have no money

spill the beans
informal to reveal secret or confidential information
• *By Monday it was evident that someone had spilled the beans to the newspapers*
Ⓛ Originally US

bear[1]

bear down on someone
to approach them quickly and often threateningly
Ⓛ A nautical term, meaning to sail towards another ship with the wind behind one, and thus with some force

bear fruit
formal to produce results
• *I hope your hard work will bear fruit*

bear in mind *see* **mind**

bear something out
formal to support or confirm an argument or proposition
• *The latest figures bear out your budget forecast*

bear the brunt of something
to suffer the worst or greatest part of some kind of misfortune
Ⓛ Originally *brunt* meant the main force of an attack by an enemy army

bear up
to remain brave, strong etc, especially under a strain

bear with someone
formal to be patient with them, especially during a temporary difficulty

bear[2]

bear garden
a noisy and disorderly place or assembly
Ⓛ From a public place that was used for bear-baiting, in which dogs were made to attack bears and make them angry for public amusement

like a bear with a sore head
informal in a very bad mood and easily angered

beard

beard someone in their den
formal to face them openly or boldly; to confront them
Ⓛ Probably a quotation from Sir Walter Scott — *Marmion*, XI xiv

bearing

find/get one's bearings
to find out the details of one's position or situation

lose one's bearings
to become uncertain of where one is, what one is doing etc
Ⓛ Literally, with reference to establishing one's position by means of a compass and a known landmark, etc

beat

beat about the bush *see* **bush**

beat a path to someone's door *see* **path**

beat a retreat *see* **retreat**

beat one's breast *see* **breast**

beat the band *see* **band**

beat the drum *see* **drum**

beat the living daylights out of *see* **living**

beat someone to it/to the draw
to manage to do something before someone else can
Ⓛ From drawing a gun

if you can't beat them, join them
a proverb, meaning if you can't persuade your opponents to change their ideas the most sensible thing to do is to change yours

it beats cock-fighting *see* **cock**

off the beaten track
away from main roads, centres of population etc

take some/a lot of beating
to be of very high quality and therefore difficult to improve on

beautiful

the beautiful people
the wealthy, glamorous section of society that follows the latest trends and fashions
• *The holiday resort is a favourite of the beautiful people*
Ⓞ A term originating in the mid 1960s

beauty

beauty is in the eye of the beholder
a proverb, meaning that everyone decides individually whether something is beautiful or not, and implying that things or people which are considered beautiful by one person are not necessarily beautiful to others

beauty is only skin-deep
a proverb, meaning that physical attractiveness is only the most immediately obvious form of attractiveness and there are other deeper, less obvious, but more important and longer-lasting forms

beaver

beaver away at something
informal to work very hard and busily at it
Ⓞ See below

eager beaver
someone who is very enthusiastic or industrious

work like a beaver
to work very hard and busily
Ⓞ Beavers are traditionally held to be very hard workers

because

because it's there
a catch phrase, and a stock reason for doing something that other people find foolish or excessively dangerous or difficult
Ⓞ The term was first used by mountaineers to account for their interest in climbing high peaks. It was used by George Leigh Mallory (1886–1924) and by Sir Edmund Hillary (1919–) of Mount Everest

beck

at someone's beck and call
always ready and waiting to carry out their orders or wishes
Ⓞ *Beck* is another form of *beckon*

bed

a bed of nails
an extremely difficult situation which one has brought upon oneself
Ⓞ From the spiked bed used by Indian fakirs

a bed of roses
informal an easy or comfortable place, job etc

get out of bed on the wrong side
to start the day in a bad mood

have made one's bed and have to lie in it
to be obliged to suffer the disadvantages of a situation one has caused oneself

put something to bed
informal to send a newspaper or magazine to be printed

reds under the bed *see* **red**

bee

as busy as a bee *see* **busy**

have a bee in one's bonnet
to have an idea which has become too fixed in one's mind

make a bee-line for something or **someone**
to take the most direct way to them; to go with determination to them
Ⓞ Bees are reputed to fly back to their hives by the most direct course

think one or **someone is the bee's knees**
informal, often derogatory to have an inflated opinion of oneself or of someone else
Ⓞ 1920s US slang

beef

beef something up
informal to strengthen or add to its size or bulk
• *They've asked us to beef up our report with a bit more detail*

beer

not all beer and skittles
not consisting only of pleasure, but frequently involving something difficult or unpleasant

small beer
formal something unimportant
ⓘ The figurative use of this phrase — literally, 'weak beer' — probably derives from Shakespeare's *Othello*, II i

beetle

beetle off
informal to hurry away
ⓘ From the insect

before

before you can say Jack Robinson *see* **Jack**

beg

beg, borrow, or steal something
to obtain it by any means possible

be going begging/a-begging
informal to be unclaimed, unsold, or unwanted

beg the question
formal to take for granted the very point that needs to be proved
• *Discussing what we should invest our money in begs the question of whether we will have any money to invest*
ⓘ From Latin *petitio principii*, the technical name for this device in medieval logic

beg to differ
formal to disagree

beggar

beggar description
formal to be so great in some way that no words can adequately describe it
• *Her beauty beggared description*
ⓘ A quotation from Shakespeare — *Antony and Cleopatra*, II i

beggars can't be choosers
a proverb, meaning that if one is in need one must accept whatever one is given whether or not it is what one would have chosen

beginning

the beginning of the end
the event which eventually leads to the end or ruin of something

behind

behind someone's back *see* **back**

behind the scenes *see* **scene**

behind the times *see* **time**

fall behind with something *see* **fall**

put something behind one
to think of something, usually an unpleasant experience, as being in the past or finished

belief

to the best of one's belief
formal as far as one knows; to the extent of one's knowledge

believe

believe it or not
although it may seem unlikely or extraordinary it is true
• *Believe it or not our team won*

make believe
to pretend that

not be able to believe one's ears/eyes
to find it difficult to believe that one has actually heard/seen correctly something which is surprising, shocking, startling etc

bell

as clear as a bell
very easy to hear

as sound as a bell
undamaged and in very good condition

bell the cat *see* **cat**

bells and whistles
informal additional features that are decorative rather than necessary or functional

give someone a bell
slang to telephone them

ring a bell
to cause a vague memory of having been seen, heard etc before, but not remembered in detail

saved by the bell
often as an exclamation rescued from an unpleasant or difficult situation by something which brings the situation suddenly to an end
Ⓞ From the bell which signals the end of a round in a boxing match

belle

the belle of the ball *see* **ball[1]**

belt

below the belt
said of a method of fighting, attacking, competing etc: unfair; not following the accepted rules of behaviour
Ⓞ A phrase from boxing, where a blow below the level of the belt is against the rules

belt and braces
a term used of a system with its own back-up facility which leaves little to chance
• *Their security system is belt and braces: an electronic alarm, nightwatchmen, and guard dogs*

belt something out
slang to sing, shout, or play it loudly and enthusiastically

tighten one's belt
informal to make sacrifices and reduce one's standard of living

under one's belt
firmly secured and in one's possession for future use

bend

bend someone's ear
informal to force someone to listen to one at great length

bend/lean over backwards
to take great trouble to do something, especially mistakenly or without results

on one's bended knee
in a very humble and submissive manner
Ⓞ *Bended* is an old form of *bent*

round the bend
informal; not usually serious mad
Ⓞ Originally naval slang

benefit

give someone the benefit of the doubt
to assume that someone is innocent or is telling the truth because there is not enough evidence to be sure that they are not
Ⓞ A legal term

berry

as brown as a berry
extremely sun-tanned

berth

give someone or **something a wide berth**
to keep well away from them or avoid them
Ⓞ A nautical idiom — a *berth* is the amount of space necessary for a sailing ship to manoeuvre safely

beside

be beside oneself with anger, excitement, etc
to be in a state of uncontrolled emotion such as anger, excitement, etc
• *He was beside himself with jealousy when his brother got married*

be beside the point *see* **point**

best

all the best!
used as a toast, as a farewell etc: I hope that you may be happy, successful etc

at the best of times
when the situation is as favourable as possible — and better than at the time referred to

the best-laid schemes ...
plans, however carefully worked out, often go wrong
Ⓞ A shortened form of 'The best-laid schemes o' mice an' men gang aft agley' from 'To a Mouse' (1786) by Robert Burns

the best of British
the best possible luck
Ⓞ Short for 'the best of British luck'

the best part of something
most of it; nearly all of it

the best/greatest thing since sliced bread *see* **bread**

do one's (level) best
to try as hard as possible

for the best
likely or intended to have the best results possible for a particular situation

have the best of both worlds
to benefit from the best features of two different sets of circumstances

make the best of it/a bad job
to do all one can to turn a failure, disaster etc into something successful

past one's best *see* **past**

put one's best foot forward *see* **foot**

six of the best *see* **six**

to the best of one's belief *see* **belief**

with the best of them
good or well enough to compete with people who are older, stronger, healthier, more experienced etc

with the best will in the world *see* **will**

bet

bet one's boots *see* **boot**

bet one's bottom dollar *see* **bottom**

hedge one's bets
to do something in order to protect oneself from possible loss, criticism, etc
• *We don't know which of them is going to be made manager so we'd better hedge our bets and be nice to both of them*
Ⓛ Literally, to make sufficient bets on both sides to make sure of not losing anything either way

you bet!
slang certainly

better

someone's better half *see* **half**

better late than never *see* **late**

better off
richer; happier in some way

the better part of something
most of it

better safe than sorry
a proverb, meaning that it is better to spend time and effort taking precautions than to risk the consequences of not taking them

for better (or) for worse
formal whatever the result may be
Ⓛ From the wedding vow in Christian marriage

get the better of someone
to overcome them; to win against them

go one better than someone
to surpass them noticeably in what they have done, achieved, etc
Ⓛ Originally US, literally 'to bid one more unit than someone' in an auction or a card-game

have seen better days
often facetious to be in a worse condition or situation than in the past
• *My coat has seen better days, but it is very warm*

know better *see* **know**

no better than she should be
not very moral, promiscuous

think better of *see* **think**

between

between a rock and a hard place *see* **rock**

between Scylla and Charybdis *see* **Scylla**

between you and me (and the cat, bedpost, gatepost etc**)/between ourselves**
facetious in confidence

in between times
at intervals between other events

beyond

beyond compare *see* **compare**

beyond one's ken *see* **ken**

beyond price *see* **price**

beyond the pale *see* **pale**

bid

bid fair to do something
formal to seem likely to do something

bide

bide one's time *see* **time**

big

be big of someone
slang, usually facetious to be a generous action or speech on their part, usually implying that they are not in fact being generous at all

Big Apple
New York

Big Brother
a catch phrase, meaning an apparently benevolent but in fact oppressive leader or organization thought to be constantly watching and controlling people's actions
Ⓘ From a dictator in George Orwell's book *Nineteen Eighty-Four* (1949)

the big C
informal cancer

a big cheese *see* **cheese**

big deal! *see* **deal**

a big fish *see* **fish**

the bigger they are the harder they fall
a proverb, meaning the more important people are the more dramatic is their fall from power

the big guns *see* **gun**

a big noise *see* **noise**

a big shot *see* **shot**

the big screen *see* **screen**

the big stick *see* **stick**

the big time *see* **time**

the big white chief *see* **chief**

go over big with someone
slang to have a great effect on them; to impress them

have a big mouth *see* **mouth**

in a big way *see* **way**

Mr Big
informal the leader or organizer of a group, especially one who controls its affairs from a distance

too big for one's boots
informal conceited; thinking too highly of one's own importance

bike

on your bike!
informal an instruction given to someone to go away, usually in order to do something active or constructive rather than doing nothing

bill

fit the bill
informal to be suitable; to be exactly what is required
Ⓘ Originally US, referring to a handbill or public notice

foot the bill
to pay, usually for something expensive
Ⓘ Originally US, probably from the custom of signing a bill as a promise to pay

top the bill/be top of the bill
to be the most important and highly-paid performer in a show at a theatre

billy

like billy-oh/billy-o
informal vigorously; enthusiastically
• *They were clapping like billy-oh*
Ⓘ Origin uncertain

bird

a bird in the hand is worth two in the bush
a proverb, meaning that it is not worth giving up something one already has for the possibility of getting something better

as free as a bird
absolutely free, with no restrictions on one's freedom

the bird is/has flown
the person or thing that one is looking for has gone
Ⓘ Originally meaning that a prisoner had escaped from jail or a criminal from a hiding-place

the birds and the bees
facetious basic information about sexual activity and reproduction
Ⓘ A popular 19c euphemism

a bird's-eye view
a view, photograph, etc taken from high up

birds of a feather
people of similar interests or personalities, from the proverb *birds of a feather flock together*, which means that such people usually enjoy each other's company

an early bird *see* **early**

eat like a bird
to eat very little

for/strictly for the birds
informal only acceptable to people who are more stupid, weaker, etc than oneself; hence, unacceptable
Ⓛ Originally US

give/get the bird
slang to send or be sent away in a very definite manner and usually rudely
Ⓛ A theatrical idiom, from the custom of audiences hissing like geese at performers who do not please them

go like a bird
usually said of machines, especially motor cars: to run fast and smoothly

kill two birds with one stone
to achieve two of one's aims at once by means of the same action

a little bird told me
I found out in a way that I do not intend to reveal

birthday

in one's birthday suit
facetious naked

biscuit

take the biscuit
ironic to be much worse than everything else
• *His latest piece of impertinence really takes the biscuit*
Ⓛ A British variant of US *take the cake*, which is probably from the giving of cakes as prizes at rural competitions

bit[1]

a bit off
informal in bad taste; rude
• *It was a bit off to criticize her husband in front of her*

bits and pieces
informal miscellaneous objects

do one's bit
informal to take one's share in a task

not a bit of it
not at all

thrilled to bits *see* **thrill**

bit[2]

champing at the bit
impatient and frustrated with eagerness to start something
Ⓛ Literally, of horses, 'to chew the bit', ie with impatience

take the bit between one's teeth
to go ahead and act on one's own, ceasing to follow instructions, advice, etc from others
Ⓛ From a horse's method of escaping from the rider's control

bite

bite someone's head off *see* **head**

bite off more than one can chew
to try to do more than, or something more difficult than, one can manage

bite (on) the bullet *see* **bullet**

bite the dust *see* **dust**

bite the hand that feeds one *see* **hand**

bite one's lip *see* **lip**

the biter bit
the person who has tried to cheat someone or do wrong to someone has suffered from the consequences of their own actions

have two bites at the cherry *see* **cherry**

once bitten, twice shy
a proverb, meaning that if something one has done or experienced has turned out badly, one is likely to be more cautious another time

put the bite on someone
slang to try to extort money from someone

what's biting you?
informal what is the matter with you?

bitter

a bitter pill (to swallow)
formal something difficult to accept

until/till/to the bitter end
up to the very end, however unpleasant etc
Ⓛ Probably a nautical expression — 'the bitter end' was the inboard end of an anchor rope or chain, attached in such a

way that it could be taken in or paid out as the tide rose or fell. When the chain was paid out to the bitter end, however, no further adjustment was possible

black

as black as ink *see* **ink**

as black as the ace of spades *see* **spade**

blackboard jungle
the educational system, the teaching profession
Ⓞ From a novel by Evan Hunter (1954), made into a film in 1955, dealing with the disadvantages of the US state educational system

a/the black dog
a bout of depression
Ⓞ Used by Winston Churchill, but the expression was known by the 19c as in 'The black dog is on his back'

as black as pitch *see* **pitch**

be as black as one is painted
to be as bad etc as others say

be in someone's black books *see* **book**

black and blue
bruised

black out
to lose consciousness

a black sheep
a member of a family or group who is unsatisfactory in some way
Ⓞ An old proverb held that 'a black sheep is a biting beast'

in black and white
in writing or print, and therefore definite and verifiable, and in some cases legally binding

in the black
informal making a profit; not in debt
Ⓞ From the use of black ink to make entries on the credit side of a ledger

the pot calling the kettle black *see* **pot**

two blacks don't make a white
a proverb, meaning that even if someone else has behaved badly in doing you an injury etc, you will only make things worse if you also behave badly

blank

a blank cheque
permission to do what one feels necessary with complete freedom
Ⓞ Literally, a signed cheque on which the sum to be paid has not been entered

go a complete blank
to be unable to think of anything appropriate
• *my mind went a complete blank when I saw the exam paper*

draw a blank
informal to be unsuccessful in a search, enquiry, etc
Ⓞ Literally, to be given an unsuccessful ticket in a lottery

blanket

on the wrong side of the blanket
used in the context of family relationships, illegitimately
• *He is descended from Charles II — on the wrong side of the blanket, of course*

a wet blanket
informal, derogatory a person who spoils other people's enjoyment by being dreary or pessimistic

blast

at full blast
at full power, speed etc

blaze

blaze a trail *see* **trail**

bleed

bleed like a pig
informal to bleed profusely

bleed someone white
informal to get them to spend all their money on one, often by coercion or bribery

bleeding

bleeding heart
derogatory a person who is constantly trying to help others, often in a self-righteous way

blessing

a blessing in disguise
something that has proved to be fortunate after seeming unfortunate

① A quotation from a poem by the 18c poet James Hervey

count one's blessings
to be grateful for what one has, rather than unhappy about what one lacks

a mixed blessing *see* **mix**

blind

blind alley
a situation or activity that offers no prospects of success or advantage
① From a street that has only one entrance or exit

blind as a bat *see* **bat[2]**

the blind leading the blind
one inexperienced or incompetent person helping another to do something or telling another about something
① A Biblical reference, to Matthew 15:14 — 'And if the blind lead the blind, both shall fall into the ditch'

a blind spot
any matter about which someone always shows a lack of understanding
① Literally, the one point on the retina of the eye where there are no visual cells

blind someone with science
to explain away something in a deliberately confusing way by using technical terms that the hearer is unlikely to understand

not take a blind bit of notice of someone or something
not to pay any attention whatsoever to someone or something

turn a blind eye *see* **eye**

blink

on the blink
informal usually of an electrical appliance, not working properly
① From the characteristic flickering lights of a piece of faulty apparatus

block

put one's head on the block *see* **head**

blood

bad blood
ill-feeling
① From an old misconception about the cause of angry feeling, resentment, etc

be after someone's blood
to have the intention of punishing someone severely, originally of killing someone

blood and thunder
a term applied to novels, plays, films, etc that are melodramatic and violent

blood is thicker than water
a proverb, meaning that one should have more loyalty to people who are related to one than to other people

blood, sweat, and tears
the maximum amount of effort

bloody but unbowed
having suffered some form of loss or injury but still undefeated or discouraged
① From the poem 'Invictus' by William Henley

blue blood *see* **blue**

fresh/new blood
new members of any group of people, who are expected to add liveliness to it

in cold blood
deliberately and unemotionally
① From the medieval belief that emotion raised the temperature of the blood

like getting blood out of a stone
(usually of obtaining something) very difficult

make someone's blood boil
to make someone very angry
① From the medieval belief that certain emotions raised or lowered the temperature of the blood

make someone's blood run cold
to frighten or horrify them

sweat blood *see* **sweat**

blot

blot one's copybook
to do something that spoils one's previously good record or damages one's reputation
① From children getting ink blots on the book in which they are learning to write

blow

a blow-by-blow account
a very detailed description
① From a boxing commentary

blow one's brains out *see* **brain**

blow hot and cold on something or **someone**
to support and oppose an idea, person, etc unpredictably
Ⓛ From Aesop's fable of the centaur who believed that, because a man could both warm his hands and cool his food by blowing on them, he must be blowing hot and cold from the same mouth

blow it
slang to lose one's chance of success through one's own fault
• *They were offered the contract but they blew it*

blow someone's mind
to cause them to experience great mental excitement
Ⓛ Originally a drug term referring to the effect of certain drugs on the mind

blow over
to pass and become forgotten
Ⓛ Literally, of storm-clouds, to pass over without causing a storm

blow one's own trumpet *see* **trumpet**

blow the gaff *see* **gaff**

blow the lid off *see* **lid**

blow the whistle on *see* **whistle**

blow one's top *see* **top**

see which way/how the wind blows *see* **wind**[1]

strike a blow for something
to do something definite and noticeable to help (a cause, aim, etc)

blue

as blue as the sky
of a clear, bright blue
• *Her eyes were as blue as the sky*

blue blood
aristocratic ancestry
Ⓛ In Spanish *sangre azul*; the term describes Spanish aristocrats of pure, unmixed Germanic ancestry, under whose fair skins the blue veins showed very clearly

a blue-eyed boy
derogatory someone who is a favourite

the blues
informal low spirits; depression

a bluestocking
derogatory a highly-educated woman; a woman who is interested in serious, intellectual subjects
Ⓛ From a group of 18c London ladies who held philosophical evening-parties which at least one guest attended informally dressed in blue worsted stockings

a bolt from the blue *see* **bolt**

the boys in blue
informal the police
Ⓛ From the colour of police uniforms

feel blue
informal to feel miserable or depressed

in a blue funk *see* **funk**

into the blue
into the unknown
Ⓛ As if into the sky

make the air turn blue
informal to swear strongly and at some length

once in a blue moon
very seldom
Ⓛ The moon very occasionally appears to be tinged with blue

out of the blue
without warning
Ⓛ From lightning which strikes out of a clear sky

scream/yell blue murder
informal to make a great deal of noise and protest
Ⓛ Possibly connected with the French oath *morbleu* — 'blue death'

true blue
unchangingly faithful and loyal
• *You can rely on Michael — he's true blue*

until one is blue in the face
having made as much effort as possible
• *I told him not to play there until I was blue in the face*
Ⓛ Lack of oxygen makes one blue in the face and great effort, such as shouting, uses up oxygen

bluff

call someone's bluff
to demand that someone proves the genuineness of a claim, threat, or promise they have made

• *We did not really believe he would sue us, so we called his bluff and published the story*
Ⓞ From the game of poker

board

above board
open and honourable; not secret
Ⓞ From card-games, where anything that takes place under the table is likely to be against the rules

across the board
informal applying in all cases
Ⓞ Originally US, from horse-racing: a technical term for betting on the same horse to win, to be placed or to be fourth

go by the board
to be abandoned or thrown aside
Ⓞ A nautical term meaning 'to vanish overboard' — *board* = 'the ship's side'

as stiff as a board
extremely stiff, rigid
• *It was so cold that the clothes on the line were as stiff as a board*

sweep the board
to win everything
Ⓞ From card-games, where all the money to be won is placed on the 'board'

take something on board
informal
1 to receive and accept something, such as suggestions, new ideas, etc
2 to take something in mentally, to begin to realize something
Ⓞ From shipping

boat

burn one's boats
to do something which makes it impossible for one to return to one's former position, way of life, etc
Ⓞ A practice by which generals leading an invasion stiffened the resolve of their troops

in the same boat
informal in the same, usually difficult, position or circumstances

miss the boat *see* **miss**

rock the boat
informal to do something which endangers a pleasant or satisfactory situation etc in which one shares

Bob

Bob's your uncle
informal a catch phrase, meaning everything is fine
• *You just have to put the dish in the oven and Bob's your uncle — a delicious meal*
Ⓞ Origin uncertain

body

keep body and soul together
often facetious to remain alive — especially not to die of hunger

over my dead body *see* **dead**

bog

bogged down
prevented from making progress
Ⓞ A military term, literally meaning hindered in movement by mud etc

boil

boil down to
informal to mean in effect
• *His speech was a long one, but it boiled down to a warning that we would all have to work harder for less money*

come to the boil
to arrive at a critical state
Ⓞ Literally, to arrive at boiling-point

bolt

a bolt from the blue
a sudden, unexpected happening
Ⓞ Literally, a flash of lightning out of a cloudless sky

a bolthole
a place into which a person can escape
Ⓞ Literally, an exit-hole from a warren through which rabbits can escape from a predator

bolt upright
absolutely upright
Ⓞ Literally, 'as upright as a bolt', where *bolt* = arrow

have shot one's bolt
to be unable to do more than one has done
Ⓞ The image is of an archer with only one arrow or 'bolt' who is defenceless once he has fired it

make a bolt for it
to attempt to run away suddenly

the nuts and bolts *see* **nut**

bomb

a bombshell
a piece of startling and often very bad news

go like a bomb
informal
1 to move very fast
2 to sell extremely well; to be very successful

make a bomb
slang to make or earn a great deal of money

bone

as dry as a bone
completely dry

a bag of bones *see* **bag**

the bare bones
the essential facts of a subject

bone idle
informal very lazy

a bone of contention
formal a cause of argument or quarrelling
Ⓛ From the fact that dogs will fight over a bone

feel something in one's bones
to know it by instinct, without having any proof

have a bone to pick with someone
to have something to disagree, or argue, about with them
Ⓛ Probably from the fact that two dogs are unlikely to pick at the same bone without fighting

make no bones about
to have no hesitation about stating or doing something openly
Ⓛ An older version, *to find no bones in*, suggests that the reference was originally to bones in soup etc

close to/near the bone
informal
1 of a speech etc, referring too closely to something which should not be mentioned
• *I don't think he realized how near the bone some of his remarks were*
2 rather indecent
• *Some of his jokes were a bit near the bone*

never make old bones
not to live to old age

to the bone
1 thoroughly and completely
• *I was chilled to the bone*
2 to the minimum
• *I've cut my expenses to the bone*

work one's fingers to the bone *see* **finger**

bonnet

have a bee in one's bonnet *see* **bee**

boo

he etc **couldn't/wouldn't say boo to a goose** *see* **goose**

book

be in someone's good, bad/black books
to be in or out of favour with them

book of words
informal directions for use

a bookworm
informal: sometimes derogatory a person who reads a lot

bring someone to book
formal to make them explain, or suffer for, their behaviour

by the book
strictly according to the rules

a closed book
rather formal a subject which one knows nothing about or does not understand

cook the books *see* **cook**

get one's books
slang to be dismissed from one's job

in my etc **book**
in my opinion

an open book
something which can be understood easily or whose meaning etc is easily seen

read someone like a book
to understand completely their character, reasons for acting as they do, etc

suit someone's book
to be pleasing or favourable to them

take a leaf out of someone's book *see* **leaf**

throw the book at someone
to reprimand or punish them severely, especially for breaking rules

boot[1]

bet one's boots
informal used as an expression of certainty
• *You can bet your boots that they'll be late*

as tough as old boots
very tough or (figurative) strong, especially in health

the boot is on the other foot
the very opposite of what used to be the case, or of what is thought to be the case, is true
• *You're wrong if you think I borrowed money from Jane — in fact, the boot is on the other foot: she borrowed from me*

get the boot
slang to be dismissed, usually from one's job

give someone the boot
slang to dismiss them, usually from their job

lick someone's boots
to flatter them and do everything they want

put the boot in
slang to attack someone viciously and unfairly
Ⓞ Literally, 'to kick someone viciously'

boot[2]

to boot
formal in addition; also
• *She is beautiful, and wealthy to boot*

born

to be born with a silver spoon in one's mouth *see* **silver**

in all my born days
informal in my life
• *I never saw such a thing in all my born days!*

not born yesterday *see* **yesterday**

not to know one is born *see* **know**

to the manner born *see* **manner**

bosom

bosom friend
informal a close friend

bottle

a bottleneck
a place where progress slows down or stops, especially a narrow part of a road which becomes very crowded with traffic

bottle out
slang to lose one's nerve and withdraw from something requiring courage *see* **lose one's bottle**, below

bottle up
to prevent (eg one's feelings) from becoming known or obvious
• *You mustn't bottle up your anger — tell me what's annoying you*

crack a bottle *see* **crack**

hit the bottle
derogatory slang to begin to drink too much alcohol

lose one's bottle
slang to lose one's courage

on the bottle
slang in the habit of drinking too much alcohol

bottom

at bottom
rather formal in reality

be at the bottom of
to be the cause of (usually something bad)

bet one's bottom dollar
informal to bet everything one has (usually used in an expression of certainty about something)
Ⓞ Originally US

bottom drawer *see* **drawer**

the bottom line

1 the final outcome or result of something

2 the most important or basic point of something
Ⓞ From an accounting term for the last

line of a profit and loss account which shows whether a profit or loss has been made

bottoms up
a traditional toast wishing someone good luck
Ⓞ A reference to the fact that the bottom of the glass is raised as it is emptied

from the bottom of one's heart *see* **heart**

get to the bottom of
to discover the explanation, the real facts (of a mystery etc)

hit rock bottom *see* **rock**

bottomless

bottomless pit
facetious
1 hell
2 a seemingly insatiable appetite

bound

out of bounds
outside the permitted area or limits

bow[1]

bowed down with something
formal worried or troubled by having to deal with something difficult etc
• *He was bowed down with the responsibility of governing the country*

bow out
to leave or cease to take part in a situation, project etc

take a bow
to accept and show that one appreciates applause or recognition
Ⓞ Literally, to appear on stage at the end of a theatrical performance to acknowledge applause

bow[2]

draw the long bow
formal to make statements which go beyond the truth
• *When he told us he had captured three bank-robbers single-handed, I felt he was drawing the long bow*
Ⓞ Origin obscure

have more than one string to one's bow
to have at least one alternative (to an opportunity, course of action etc) already planned or available
Ⓞ An archer carries a spare bowstring in case one breaks

bow[3]

a shot across the bows *see* **shot**

bowl

bowl over
to cause to be overcome by emotion, especially gratitude, admiration or grief
• *She was bowled over by her colleagues' generosity*

Box

Box and Cox
two people who never meet and are never in the same place at the same time
• *The nightwatchman and the caretaker here are Box and Cox — when one arrives the other goes home*
Ⓞ From a 19c farce in which two men thus named rent the same room by night and by day respectively

boy

a blue-eyed boy *see* **blue**

the boy/girl next door
just an ordinary boy/girl

the boys in blue *see* **blue**

a whipping-boy *see* **whip**

brain

blow one's brains out
to kill oneself by shooting oneself in the head

someone's brainchild
a favourite theory, invention, etc thought up by a particular person

the brain drain
the loss of experts to another country usually in search of better salaries, etc

a brainstorm
a sudden mental disturbance
Ⓞ Originally a technical medical description for an attack of certain types of mental illness

brainwash someone
to force a person to obey, conform, confess etc by putting great psychological pressure on them

a brainwave
a sudden good idea

have something on the brain
to be unable to forget about it or to think about anything else

pick someone's brains
to ask them questions in order to get ideas, information, etc which one can use oneself

rack one's brains
to exert one's mind greatly in trying to think of something
Ⓣ From the old instrument of torture called *the rack*

branch

root and branch *see* **root**

brass

as bold as brass
derogatory very bold and usually impertinent

get down to brass tacks
informal to deal with basic principles or matters
Ⓣ Originally US

have the brass neck to do something
informal derogatory to be sufficiently shameless and impudent to do something unacceptable
Ⓣ Both *brass* and *neck* are dialect words for 'impudence'

the top brass
often derogatory people of the highest rank in the army, a business etc

brave

as brave as a lion
extremely courageous

brave new world
a desirable or perfect future society
Ⓣ From Shakespeare's *The Tempest* V.1 — also the title of a novel by Aldous Huxley (1932)

put on a brave front/face
to pretend that things are going well and that one is perfectly happy

bread

the best/greatest thing since sliced bread
often ironic a person or thing that is greatly liked or admired
• *He thinks that he's the greatest thing since sliced bread*
Ⓣ Sliced bread was considered a great invention since it was so convenient

one's bread and butter
a way of earning one's living, as opposed to what one does for enjoyment

bread-and-butter letter
a letter sent to thank a host or hostess for some form of hospitality

bread and circuses
events of popular appeal, mass entertainment to amuse the population of a country
Ⓣ A translation of 'panem et circenses' used by the Roman poet Juvenal in his Satires, to indicate that all the crowds wanted to keep them quiet was something to eat and some kind of amusement

a breadwinner
a person who earns money to keep a family

cast one's bread upon the waters
to spend time, effort or money, especially in the cause of others, without expecting any immediate benefit to oneself
Ⓣ From the Book of Ecclesiastes — 'Cast thy bread upon the waters: for thou shalt find it after many days'

daily bread
the food or amount of money necessary to keep someone alive
Ⓣ A reference to a passage in the Lord's Prayer in Christianity

know which side one's bread is buttered on
to know how one should act for one's own advantage

like one's bread buttered on both sides
to want to live etc in great comfort or luxury

on the breadline
informal with barely enough money to live on
Ⓣ Originally US — breadlines were queues of destitute people waiting for free food from soup-kitchens, especially those run by the government

take the bread from someone's mouth
to deprive them of an income or of a means of survival

break

break a butterfly on a wheel *see* **butterfly**

break a leg *see* **leg**

break cover *see* **cover**

break one's duck *see* **duck**

break even *see* **even**

break someone's heart *see* **heart**

break in
to make (shoes etc) less stiff by using them
Ⓛ A technical term for the process of training a young horse to carry a rider etc

break it to someone *see* **break the news**

break new/fresh ground *see* **ground**

break of day
literary dawn

break ranks *see* **rank**

break the back of *see* **back**

break the bank *see* **bank**

break the ice *see* **ice**

break the mould *see* **mould**

break one's neck *see* **neck**

break the news *see* **news**

break the record *see* **record**

break one's word *see* **word**

make a breakthrough
to solve, after much effort, a difficult problem, especially one of a scientific nature, that will open the way to further developments

breast

beat one's breast
to show great distress or anger

make a clean breast of something *see* **clean**

breath

a breath of fresh air
someone or something that is refreshing and new
• *The new young members are a breath of fresh air in the club*

catch one's breath
to stop breathing for an instant (often from fear, amazement etc or due to physical discomfort)

get one's breath back
to regain the ability to breathe properly (eg after exercise)

hold one's breath
to stop breathing (often because of anxiety)

in the same breath
at the same time

out of breath
breathless (through running etc)

save one's breath
not to bother to say anything
• *Save your breath — she won't listen to any advice*

take someone's breath away
to make someone breathless (with astonishment, delight etc)

under one's breath
in a whisper

waste one's breath
to say something which is not heeded
• *I don't know why I bother to talk to you — I'm just wasting my breath*

breathe

breathe again
to be relieved of a great worry etc
• *Breathe again — the police have gone!*

breathe one's last *see* **last**[1]

breathing

breathing down someone's neck
1 close behind them
2 extremely impatient
• *He's breathing down my neck for this letter I'm typing*

a breathing-space
a short time in which one can have a rest

brevity

brevity is the soul of wit
a proverb, meaning that the cleverest and most effective statements are made in relatively few words

brick

a brick short of a load
informal mentally not all there, mentally defective

bang one's head against a brick wall *see* **head**

drop a brick *see* **drop**

in with the bricks
informal having been in a place, organization etc, since the beginning
Ⓞ As if built into a building as bricks are

like a ton of bricks
immediately and heavily

try to make bricks without straw
to try to do a piece of work without the materials, tools etc necessary for it
Ⓞ A Biblical reference, to Exodus 5

bridge

cross a bridge when one comes to it
not to bother about a problem that is going to arise in the future until it actually affects one

water under the bridge *see* **water**

brief

hold no brief for
formal not to have any reason to support or speak in favour of
Ⓞ A legal term — 'to be employed to conduct a particular case in court'

in brief
formal in a few words
• *In brief, we have been successful*

bright

as bright as a button *see* **button**

bright and early
early; in good time

bright-eyed and bushy-tailed
a catch phrase, meaning lively and enthusiastic
Ⓞ A reference to the squirrel which has small bright eyes and a bushy tail

a bright spark
a very lively, cheerful person

bright young things
a name given to the young and fashionable social set in the 1920s and 1930s

look on the bright side
to be hopeful and consider the best features of something

bring

bring back/down to earth *see* **earth**

bring home to *see* **home**

bring something into line *see* **line**

bring into play *see* **play**

bring on the dancing girls *see* **dancing**

bring someone round
1 to bring them back from unconsciousness
2 to persuade them
• *We'll bring him round to the idea*

bring the house down *see* **house**

bring someone to
to bring them back to consciousness

bring something to a head *see* **head**

bring to light *see* **light**

bring someone up short *see* **short**

bring up the rear *see* **rear**

brine

the briny
informal the sea

bristle

bristle with
formal to be full of
• *They walked through streets bristling with tourists*

Bristol

shipshape and Bristol-fashion *see* **shipshape**

broad

be broad-minded
to be ready to allow others to think or act as they choose without criticizing them

broad in the beam *see* **beam**

have broad shoulders *see* **shoulder**

in broad daylight
during the day

broke

go for broke
informal to make an all-out bid or effort
Ⓛ From risking all one's money on a gamble

broken

broken-hearted
overcome by grief

broken home
the home of children whose parents are divorced or live apart

a broken reed
informal, derogatory a person who is too weak or unreliable to be depended on (to help, join in an activity etc)

broom

a new broom *see* **new**

broth

too many cooks spoil the broth *see* **cook**

brother

am I my brother's keeper?
I am not responsible for the actions of others

Big Brother *see* **big**

brow

knit one's brows *see* **knit**

the sweat of one's brow *see* **sweat**

brown

as brown as a berry *see* **berry**

browned off
informal
1 bored
- *I feel really browned off in this wet weather*

2 annoyed
- *I'm browned off with his behaviour*

brown-nosing
slang excessive flattery, sycophantic behaviour to someone in authority
- *He is said to have got his promotion from his brown-nosing of the boss*

Ⓛ From the act of kissing someone's backside

in a brown study
formal deep in thought
Ⓛ A very old phrase apparently derived from an obsolete meaning of *brown* — 'gloomy'

brownie

brownie points
credit or recognition for doing something good or for doing the right thing
- *You'll get a few brownie points from his wife if you are nice to her mother*

Ⓛ Originally US — perhaps connected with the Brownie Guides, the junior division of the Guides, or with a points system operating on the US railroads, called after the inventor of the system, and perhaps relating to brown-nosing (q.v.)

brush

as daft as a brush
informal extremely foolish, having no common sense

be tarred with the same brush *see* **tar**

brush something aside
to pay no attention to something

brush up on something
informal to refresh one's knowledge of a subject

brush-off

give or **get the brush-off**
informal to reject or be rejected abruptly

buck

the buck stops here
the final responsibility rests here
Ⓛ For origin see next entry

pass the buck
informal to pass on responsibility to someone else
- *Whenever he is blamed for anything, he tries to pass the buck*

Ⓛ In the game of poker the *buck* is a token object which is passed to the person who wins a jackpot, to remind him that when it is his turn to deal the next hand he must start another jackpot

bucket

come down in buckets
informal to be raining heavily

a drop in the bucket *see* **drop**

kick the bucket
slang to die
① This phrase is recorded in the 18c and may be connected with the wooden frame — called a *bucket* in East Anglia — from which a newly-killed pig was hung

weep buckets
informal to weep a great deal

Buckley

Buckley's chance
no chance at all, the slightest of chances
① Originally Australian — perhaps from William *Buckley*, a convict who escaped from a penal settlement in 1803 and lived for thirty-two years among the Aboriginals, perhaps from a pun on the Melbourne business firm, *Buckley* and Nunn

bud

nip something in the bud *see* **nip**

buff

in the buff
informal, usually facetious naked
① *Buff* is whitish-yellow leather with the grain removed, once used for military equipment and a similar colour to human skin

bug

get the bug
informal to be taken with a great enthusiasm for
- *He's got the travel/acting bug*

Buggins

Buggins' turn
one's turn to be promoted etc according to some mechanical system, not on merit

build

build castles in the air *see* **castle**

build on sand *see* **sand**

bull

like a bull in a china shop
informal a person who acts in a very clumsy or tactless way

like a red rag to a bull *see* **red**

take the bull by the horns
to tackle a difficulty boldly

bullet

bite (on) the bullet
to accept something unpleasant but unavoidable as bravely as possible
① From the practice among army doctors etc of giving a patient a soft lead bullet to bite on while setting bones, cleaning wounds etc

get the bullet
informal to be dismissed

give someone the bullet
informal to dismiss them

bull's-eye

hit the bull's-eye/score a bull's-eye
to make a remark, do something etc which is very apt, appropriate, true or relevant
① Literally, to hit the exact centre section of the dartboard in a game of darts

bully

bully for you
slang; often facetious good for you etc; that's nice for you etc
- *'The boss is allowing Anne time off to have her hair done.' 'Bully for her! What about the rest of us?'*

bum

a bum steer
slang a false, misleading or worthless piece of information, set of instructions etc
① Literally, in America, a *bum steer* was originally a poor or worthless young bullock

give someone the bum's rush
slang to get rid of them, or force them to leave a place, a job etc, very quickly
① Originally US, presumably from throwing tramps — bums — out of bars etc

bump

bump into someone
informal to meet them by accident

bump someone off
slang to kill them
① Originally US

bump up
informal to raise prices; to increase the size of

bun

have a bun in the oven
facetious to be pregnant

bunch

a bunch of fives *see* **five**

bundle

a bundle of nerves *see* **nerve**

go a bundle on
slang to like or be enthusiastic about
Ⓛ An American expression literally meaning 'to bet a lot of money on'

bunk

do a bunk
slang to go away in a hurry, especially in order to escape from something

burden

the burden of proof
the responsibility for proving something, especially a point in a court of law
• *The burden of proof rests with you*
Ⓛ A translation of the Latin legal term *onus probandi*

burn

burn one's boats *see* **boat**

burn one's fingers *see* **finger**

a burning question
a question of interest to, and eagerly discussed by, many people

burn the candle at both ends *see* **candle**

burn the midnight oil *see* **midnight**

a burnt offering
facetious a meal, or part of a meal, which has been burnt
Ⓛ Literally, a Jewish animal sacrifice, mentioned frequently in the Bible

get one's fingers burnt *see* **finger**

have money to burn *see* **money**

burst

be bursting at the seams
informal to be very full or crowded
Ⓛ From the seams of a garment which is too tight

burst a blood vessel
informal to become extremely angry

Burton

gone for a Burton
slang dead, ruined etc
Ⓛ 2nd World War RAF slang — a euphemistic phrase apparently meaning literally 'gone for a drink', *Burton* = 'Burton ale'

bus

like the back end of a bus
informal, derogatory very unattractive
• *He is quite good-looking, but his wife has a face like the back end of a bus*

miss the bus *see* **miss**

bush

beat about the bush
to approach a subject in an indirect way, without coming to the point
Ⓛ *Beating the bush* is an operation carried out while hunting birds

the bush telegraph
often facetious the fast spreading of information, usually by word of mouth
Ⓛ An Australian phrase

bushel

hide one's light under a bushel *see* **light**[1]

business

the business end of something
informal the end or part of something that actually does the work
• *He prised open the tin with the business end of a screwdriver*

funny business *see* **funny**

have no business to do something
informal to have no right to do or be doing it

like nobody's business *see* **nobody**

make it one's business to do something
to be interested or concerned enough to make sure that one does something
• *I make it my business to check that every advertisement our magazine prints is genuine*

mean business
informal to intend to do something serious and businesslike; not to be joking

mind one's own business
not polite to attend to one's own affairs, not interfering in other people's

monkey business *see* **monkey**

busman

a busman's holiday
a holiday spent doing something similar to what one does in one's job
Ⓞ Reputedly derived from the story of a certain horse-bus driver who spent his days off travelling back and forward in a bus driven by one of his friends

busy

as busy as a bee
extremely busy or active
Ⓞ Bees are traditionally very industrious

butter

butterfingers
informal a name given to a person who often drops, or is likely to drop, things that they are carrying

butter someone up
informal to flatter them, usually in order to gain a favour

know which side one's bread is buttered on, like one's bread buttered on both sides *see* **bread**

look as if butter wouldn't melt in one's mouth
to appear very innocent, honest, respectable etc, usually implying that the speaker believes one is not these things

butterfly

break a butterfly on a wheel
to use methods that are much more severe than is necessary to accomplish the task in which one is engaged
Ⓞ From the wheel as an instrument of torture to which people were tied

have butterflies in one's stomach
to feel a fluttering sensation in one's insides as a result of nervousness

button

as bright as a button
usually only of children or animals: appearing to be very intelligent and alert

buttoned up
slang successfully arranged; safely in one's possession

buttonhole

buttonhole someone
informal to catch their attention and hold them in conversation
Ⓞ The word was originally *buttonholed* — 'to catch and hold by the button'

buy

buy someone off
informal to bribe them

I'll buy that
slang I'll accept that explanation although it seems rather surprising

buzz

a buzz-word
informal an impressive-sounding but often nearly meaningless word used as part of the jargon of a particular subject, etc

by

by and by
after a short time
Ⓞ Like *presently*, this phrase originally meant 'at once'

by and large
mostly; considering everything together
Ⓞ A nautical expression, meaning 'both sailing into the wind' — *by* — 'and with the wind' — *large*

by the by(e)/by the way
incidentally
Ⓞ *By the bye* means literally 'by the way of a secondary route/subject'

bygone

let bygones be bygones
to forgive and forget past injuries, quarrels etc

C

cackle

cut the cackle
slang to stop talking about things and start acting

cage

rattle someone's cage
to upset or agitate them
Ⓞ From visitors to zoos rattling the cages of the animals to get them to react

cahoots

in cahoots
derogatory, slang joined together in a secret partnership, especially to do something wrong or dishonest
Ⓞ Originally US — *cahoot* = partnership, from the French *cahute* = cabin

Cain

raise Cain *see* **raise**

cake

cakes and ale
enjoyable, carefree activity
• *Being a public relations officer is not all cakes and ale*

have one's cake and eat it
to enjoy the advantages of two alternative courses of action etc when it is, or ought to be, impossible to do both at once

let them eat cake
a flippant, unsympathetic remark used of people in poverty or trouble
Ⓞ Marie Antoinette is reputed to have said this of French peasants who were starving from lack of bread to eat

the icing on the cake *see* **icing**

like hot cakes *see* **hot**

a piece of cake
informal something very easy
• *Winning the race was a piece of cake*

a slice of the cake *see* **slice**

calf

calf love
love felt by someone young and innocent

kill the fatted calf *see* **fat**

call

call a halt *see* **halt**

call a spade a spade *see* **spade**

call someone's bluff *see* **bluff**

call something into question *see* **question**

call it a day *see* **day**

call it quits *see* **quit**

call something off
to cancel something
• *The party's been called off*

call someone names *see* **name**

the call of nature *see* **nature**

call the shots *see* **shot**

call the tune *see* **tune**

call someone to account *see* **account**

a close call *see* **close**[1]

don't call us, we'll call you
informal, usually facetious
1 a catch phrase used to discourage someone from contacting one
2 a catch phrase used to indicate to someone that he or she has no talent at whatever he or she is doing
Ⓞ Originally used by US film or entertainment producers when auditioning people for parts

calm

as calm as a millpond *see* **millpond**

camel

the straw that breaks the camel's back *see* **the last straw,** at **last**[1]

can

a can of worms
informal an extremely complicated and problematic situation
ⓘ From the fact that worms would wriggle out of a can and get everywhere

carry the can
slang to take the blame
ⓘ Originally naval slang

in the can
slang accomplished, agreed, certain
• *He feels sure that the job is in the can after the interview*
ⓘ A reference to a completed cinema film that is stored in large metal containers

candle

burn the candle at both ends
to waste or use up something in two ways at once, especially to work hard during the day from early morning and also stay up late at night studying or enjoying oneself

the game is not worth the candle
the project is too difficult, troublesome etc for the advantages it would bring
ⓘ A literal translation of the French phrase *le jeu n'en vaut la chandelle*, referring to a gambling session in which the amount of money at stake is not sufficient to pay for the candle used up during play

not fit to hold a candle to
not good enough to be compared with
ⓘ Literally, not good enough even to hold a light so that someone else may see to do a job

cannon

cannon fodder
ordinary people or workers who are considered to be dispensable, taking the view that there are plenty more where they came from
ⓘ Originally used to describe ordinary soldiers who were considered by their commanders to be expendable

canoe

paddle one's own canoe
to control one's own affairs without help or control from anyone else
ⓘ An American idiom of the early 19c

cap

cap in hand
humbly
• *Their son has left home but he'll come back cap in hand when his money runs out*

a feather in one's cap *see* **feather**

if the cap fits
from the saying **if the cap fits, wear it**, which means that if you think what has been said applies to you, then you should certainly take notice of it

put on one's thinking cap *see* **think**

set one's cap at
to deliberately try to attract a member of the opposite sex
• *She set her cap at her boss as soon as she arrived here*
ⓘ Possibly a mis-translation from a French nautical expression — *mettre le cap à* — meaning to head towards

to cap it all
to surpass what has gone before, to make things even worse
• *We were late leaving and to cap it all the car broke down*

capital

make capital out of something
to use a situation, event etc for one's own advantage

card

get one's cards
informal to be dismissed (especially from one's job)

have/keep a card up one's sleeve
to have prepared but not revealed an argument, plan of action etc to be used as a separate tactic if necessary
ⓘ From cheating at cards

a house of cards *see* **house**

on the cards
informal likely
• *A February general election is very much on the cards*
ⓘ From trying to forecast future events using a pack of cards

play one's cards close to one's chest
to plan or carry out a course of action etc without letting anyone know what one intends to do

play one's cards right
to take the fullest possible advantage of one's chances of success

put one's cards on the table
to reveal honestly what one's aims are and how one intends to achieve them

stack the cards against someone
to make it very difficult for them to succeed
• *I will do my best to help you, but I'm afraid the cards are stacked against us*

carpet

on the carpet/mat
informal summoned before someone in authority for a reprimand
• *You'll be on the carpet for that!*
ⓘ From the piece of carpet in front of a desk where someone stands while being reprimanded

(the) red-carpet treatment *see* **red**

sweep something under the carpet
to try to put something unpleasant out of one's mind, or to hide it from the attention of others
ⓘ From a simple but unsatisfactory method of making a floor look clean

carrot

carrot and stick
a method of persuasion involving both reward and punishment, sometimes used alternately

hold out a carrot
to encourage someone to do something by promising a reward
ⓘ A reference to holding a carrot in front of a donkey to make it reach out for the carrot and so walk faster

carry

carry all before one
to be very successful

carry something off
to deal with a difficult situation, something awkward one is obliged to do etc successfully

carry on
1 *informal* to behave badly
• *The children always carry on when the teacher's out of the classroom*
2 *informal derogatory* to have a love-affair with
• *She's been carrying on with the boss for years*

carry the can *see* **can**

carry the day
formal to gain victory
ⓘ Originally a military phrase

carry a/the torch for *see* **torch**

carry weight
to have influence
• *His opinion carries a lot of weight around here*

get carried away
to be so affected by an emotion as to be unable to be sensible or to control one's actions

cart

put the cart before the horse
to do, plan or say things in the wrong order

carte blanche

be given carte blanche
formal to be allowed complete freedom to act as one thinks best
ⓘ Literally 'to be given a blank card'

case

a case in point
rather formal a relevant example
ⓘ The phrase *in point* meaning 'relevant' was once in general use

a case of the tail wagging the dog
a situation in which the person who should be in control is actually being controlled or in which an unimportant or subordinate issue is allowed to dictate the progress of the central issue

case the joint *see* **joint**

cash

cash cow
informal derogatory a regular source of income that requires little or no effort

cash in on something
informal to make money or other types of profit by taking advantage of a situation etc
• *He is the sort of person who cashes in on other people's misfortunes*

hard cash *see* **hard**

Cassandra

Cassandra
a person whose gloomy predictions about future events is not believed
Ⓘ Cassandra in Greek legend was the daughter of Priam, King of Troy. She had the gift of prophecy but was destined never to be believed — she predicted the fall of Troy

cast

cast a cloud over something *see* **cloud**

cast one's bread upon the waters *see* **bread**

cast in the same mould *see* **mould**

cast pearls before swine *see* **pearl**

the die is cast *see* **die**[2]

castle

build castles in the air
to have dreams and plans which are very unlikely to come true
• *I used to build castles in the air about travelling round the world*

cat

bell the cat
formal to take the leading part in a dangerous plan of action, especially if this is intended to benefit the group to which one belongs
Ⓘ From the folk-tale of the mice who decided that it would be of great benefit to them if the cat had a bell put round its neck so that they could hear it coming — however none of them would volunteer to do this

a cat may look at a king
there is no reason why someone humble may not look at someone important, usually said to someone who has accused someone else of staring at them

the cat's pyjamas/whiskers
slang anything very good
• *He thinks he's the cat's pyjamas since he got promotion*

curiosity killed the cat *see* **curiosity**

enough to make a cat laugh
often ironical something very funny or ridiculous

fight like Kilkenny cats *see* **Kilkenny**

grin like a Cheshire cat *see* **Cheshire**

has the cat got your tongue?
a remark addressed to someone who is not making any comment or reply in a situation which demands one

let the cat out of the bag
to let a secret become known unintentionally *see* **a pig in a poke,** at **pig**

like a cat on hot bricks/on a hot tin roof
very nervous and unable to keep still

like a scalded cat
extremely rapidly and suddenly
• *She leapt from her seat like a scalded cat when the phone rang*

like something the cat has brought in
informal derogatory untidy, soaking wet, or otherwise unpleasant to look at

like the cat that swallowed the canary/cream
extremely pleased with oneself, full of self-satisfaction

not to have a cat in hell's chance *see* **hell**

play cat-and-mouse with someone
to amuse oneself by treating someone who is in one's power in such a way that they do not know what one is planning to do with them

put the cat among the pigeons
to cause a disturbance, especially suddenly

rain cats and dogs
to rain very hard

room to swing a cat
the smallest amount of space necessary to live in, do something in etc
• *Her kitchen is tiny — there's hardly room to swing a cat*

see which way the cat jumps
to wait and see what is going to happen before making a definite decision or statement about one's own position

there's more than one way to kill/skin a cat
there is more than one way of getting something done or of bringing something about

when the cat's away (the mice will play)
a proverb, meaning that people can be expected to take advantage of the extra freedom of action they enjoy when their boss etc is not there

catch

catch one's breath *see* **breath**

catch one's death (of cold) *see* **death**

catch someone's eye *see* **eye**

catch someone in the act *see* **act**

catch it
to be punished or scolded
• *You'll catch it if your mother finds out you broke that cup*

catch someone napping *see* **napping**

catch someone on the hop *see* **hop**

catch someone red-handed *see* **red**

catch sight of *see* **sight**

catch the sun *see* **sun**

Catch 22
an absurd situation in which one can never win, being constantly balked by a clause, rule, etc which itself can change to block any change in one's course of action
Ⓛ The title of a novel by J Heller (1961)

catch someone with his pants down *see* **pants**

you won't catch me etc **doing that**
I certainly will not do that

caught

(be caught) with one's pants/trousers down *see* **pants**

cause

a lost cause *see* **lost**

cavalry

the cavalry are coming
help is at hand in a difficult or dangerous situation
Ⓛ A reference to the fact that the arrival of mounted soldiers was a great relief to those fighting a battle

caviare

caviare to the general
formal something too sophisticated to be liked or understood by most people
Ⓛ A quotation from Shakespeare — *Hamlet* II, ii

ceiling

go through/hit the ceiling
informal to become suddenly very angry

Cerberus

a sop to Cerberus
something given to someone to persuade them not to make trouble or be obstructive
Ⓛ A reference to Cerberus, the three-headed dog in classical mythology, who guarded the entrance to the underworld. The sibyl who conducted Aeneas to the underworld threw a cake seasoned with poppies and honey to send him to sleep

ceremony

stand on ceremony
to behave in a very formal manner

certain

in a certain condition
old pregnant

of a certain age
no longer young

chalk

as different as chalk from cheese
very different

chalk and talk
the formal traditional method of teaching that uses oral instruction and a blackboard

chalk something up to experience
to try not to regret that something unfortunate etc has happened but to try to make sure such a thing does not happen again

not by a long chalk
informal by no means
Ⓛ From the use of chalk lines to mark scores in a game

champing

champing at the bit *see* **bit[2]**

chance

chance one's arm
informal to do something risky; to take a risk

fancy one's chances
informal to rate one's chances of success extremely highly and usually very arrogantly

fat chance *see* **fat**

a fighting chance *see* **fighting**

not to have a cat in hell's chance, not to have a snowball's chance in hell *see* **hell**

not to have the ghost of a chance *see* **ghost**

on the off-chance *see* **off**

a sporting chance *see* **sporting**

with an eye to the main chance
thinking about one's own chances of getting profit out of something
• *He became a millionaire by making every decision with an eye to the main chance*
Ⓘ *The main chance* was the highest scoring throw in the dice game of hazard

change

change colour *see* **colour**

change hands *see* **hand**

change horses in midstream *see* **horse**

change one's mind *see* **mind**

the change of life
the menopause

change the subject *see* **subject**

change one's tune *see* **tune**

chop and change *see* **chop**

have a change of heart *see* **heart**

ring the changes
to use, do etc a small number of things in a variety of ways
• *I only have three shirts and two ties, but I ring the changes with them*
Ⓘ Literally to ring a small number of church bells one after the other in every order possible

chapter

chapter and verse
1 a detailed source for an opinion etc
• *He wanted us to give him chapter and verse for our belief that his department spends too much*
2 *informal* quoting word for word
• *She repeated what you said in your lecture, chapter and verse*
Ⓘ From the method of referring to texts from the Bible

a chapter of accidents
a whole series of misfortunes
Ⓘ The present meaning apparently stems from a play on words — *the chapter of accidents* was originally a term for 'everything that is to happen in the future'

charity

as cold as charity
very cold
Ⓘ *Charity* = money given to the poor etc without feeling for the particular individuals involved

charity begins at home
a proverb, meaning that one should look after oneself and one's relatives first before considering others

charm

work like a charm
to be extremely effective, sometimes unexpectedly so

lead a charmed life
to continually escape from harm, danger or misfortune without ill effect
Ⓘ It is as though a magic spell has been cast on someone as a protection against harm

chase

chase after rainbows *see* **rainbow**

chase the dragon *see* **dragon**

a wild-goose chase *see* **wild**

chattering

the chattering classes *see* **class**

cheap

cheap jack
informal derogatory cheap and of poor quality

ⓘ From 'cheap Jack', a travelling hawker who professed to give substantial bargains

cheek

cheek by jowl
side by side or close together

turn the other cheek
to accept injury, criticism, etc without defending oneself
ⓘ A biblical reference to the story of Jesus exhorting his followers — 'Unto him that smiteth thee on the one cheek offer also the other one' (Luke 6:29)

cheer

the cup that cheers *see* **cup**

cheese

a big cheese
informal a very important or influential person

cheesed off
slang bored or depressed

cheese-paring
derogatory meanness

hard cheese
informal bad luck, misfortune; a phrase usually used by someone who does not care in the least about the misfortune and may even be glad of it
• *It is just hard cheese if he arrived late for the interview*

say cheese
a humorous instruction sometimes given by a photographer to the person being photographed in order to get them to smile
ⓘ The pronounciation of 'cheese', especially in an exaggerated way, involves the same mouth action as a smile

cherry

have two bites at the cherry
to have a second chance to do something which one has failed to do or complete before
ⓘ From the fact that one is not normally expected to take more than one bite to eat a cherry

Cheshire

grin like a Cheshire cat
slightly derogatory to smile very broadly
ⓘ From the grinning cat in Lewis Carroll's *Alice's Adventures in Wonderland*

chest

get something off one's chest
informal to tell someone else about something that is worrying or upsetting one

chestnut

an old chestnut
an old joke, often no longer funny; a cliché

pull the chestnuts out of the fire
to take control and rescue someone from a difficult situation

chew

bite off more than one can chew *see* **bite**

chew the cud *see* **cud**

chew the fat *see* **fat**

chicken

the chicken and the egg/which came first, the chicken or the egg?
it is difficult or impossible to tell which of two closely related situations, problems etc occurred first and caused the other

chickenfeed
derogatory something, usually a sum of money, very small and unimportant

chickens come home to roost *see* **roost**

count one's chickens before they are hatched
to make plans which depend on something which is still uncertain

no spring chicken
informal derogatory no longer young

chief

all chiefs and no Indians
a saying used to criticize an organization, etc for having too many people in charge, or too many people who are trying to be in charge, and too few people engaged in the actual work of the organization
ⓘ A reference to the American Indians who had a chief in charge of each tribe

the big white chief
informal the most important person in an organization, often a domineering person

child

child's play
informal something very easy
• *Climbing that hill is child's play to the experienced mountaineer*

love child *see* **love**

the child is father of the man
a proverb, meaning that the character and nature of an adult is conditioned by influences experienced in childhood
⊕ A line from the poem 'My Heart Leaps Up' by William Wordsworth (1770–1850)

with child
arch or literary pregnant

childhood

someone's second childhood *see* **second**

chill

chilled to the marrow *see* **marrow**

chin

keep one's chin up
informal not to be overcome by fear, worry etc in a difficult situation

take something/it on the chin
to accept something upsetting, discouraging etc with courage or dignity
⊕ From receiving a punch on the jaw without falling to the ground

chink

a chink in someone's armour
a subject etc which provides a successful way of attacking or making an impression on someone who is otherwise not easy to attack etc

chip

cash in one's chips
slang to die
⊕ A gambler cashes in his or her chips, ie exchanges the tokens for money, at the end of a gambling session

a chip off the old block
informal someone who is very like one of his parents in personality

chips with everything
a catch phrase indicating someone's lack of taste or sophistication, applied, for example, to unadventurous British tourists abroad who refuse to try the local cuisine

have a chip on one's shoulder
to have rather an aggressive manner, as if always expecting to be insulted, ill-treated etc
⊕ 19c US — a reference to a man who carries a piece of wood balanced on his shoulder in the hope that someone will give him an excuse for a fight by knocking it off

have had one's chips
slang to have had all the chances of success that one is likely to be given and to have failed
⊕ A reference to gambling tokens

when the chips are down
informal at a critical moment; at a point when the important decision must be made
⊕ A gambling idiom — literally 'when the bet has been placed'

choice

Hobson's choice *see* **Hobson**

choose

there is nothing to choose between *see* **nothing**

chop

chop and change
to keep altering something

get the chop
slang to be discontinued or got rid of, usually suddenly

chord

strike a chord with someone
rather formal to cause someone to remember something
• *Her name strikes a chord*

touch a chord
to cause emotion or sympathy in someone

circle

come full circle
to return to the original position, situation etc
Ⓘ From the medieval image of the wheel of fortune, constantly turning, on which men rose and fell

go round in circles
to keep going over the same information or ideas without coming to a conclusion
Ⓘ A reference to someone who is lost and keeps coming back to the starting-point

run circles round someone
to defeat them decisively
Ⓘ A reference to a runner who is so good that he or she can supposedly move in circles and still beat an opponent who is running in a straight line

run round in circles
informal to be very active or busy without achieving anything

a vicious circle *see* **vicious**

claim

stake a claim *see* **stake**

clanger

drop a clanger *see* **drop**

clap

clap eyes on *see* **eye**

clapper

like the clappers
informal very fast indeed

class

in a class of its/his/her etc **own**
so good as to be without equal, excellent

the chattering classes
derogatory people who make a habit of discussing or analyzing topical issues to an excessive degree, simply talking for the sake of talking

clay

have feet of clay *see* **feet**

clean

as clean as a whistle *see* **whistle**

a clean slate
a fresh start
Ⓘ From the former use of slates to write on in schools

wipe the slate clean
to forget or disregard past mistakes, crimes, quarrels, etc and make a new start
Ⓘ See above

cleanliness is next to godliness
a proverb advocating the virtues of hygiene and neatness

come clean
informal to tell the truth about something, often something about which one has previously lied

give someone a clean bill of health
to declare that someone is fit and healthy

his etc **hands are clean** *see* **hand**

keep one's nose clean *see* **nose**

make a clean break
to end a relationship completely and finally

make a clean breast of something
to confess or admit to something, often something one has previously denied

make a clean sweep
to get rid of everything unnecessary or unwanted

Mr Clean
informal, often ironical a person who, on the surface at least, seems trustworthy and free from corruption

pick something or **somewhere clean**
to remove absolutely everything possible from something or somewhere
• *When she died her relatives picked her house clean*
Ⓘ From picking a bone clean to remove all the meat

show a clean pair of heels
to escape by running

squeaky clean
informal totally blameless or innocent
Ⓘ From the fact that very clean surfaces sometimes squeak when wiped

take someone to the cleaners
slang to cause someone to lose or spend all or a great deal of their money

clear

as clear as crystal *see* **crystal**

as clear as mud *see* **mud**

clear someone's name *see* **name**

clear off
informal to go away or leave

clear the air *see* **air**

in the clear
informal having been freed from suspicion, difficulty or debt

steer clear of someone or **something** *see* **steer**

the coast is clear *see* **coast**

cleft

in a cleft stick
not able to decide which of two possible courses of action to take, neither of them being ideal

climb

climb down
informal to accept defeat; to take back what one has said

climb the wall *see* **wall**

cling

a clinging vine
someone who is very dependent on someone else

clip

clip someone's wings *see* **wings**

cloak

cloak-and-dagger
involving or concerning a great deal of plotting and scheming
⏱ The name of a type of 17c Spanish comedy — from the normal dress of the class of character depicted — the current meaning arising from the kind of plot characteristic of the French version of the genre

clock

against the clock
trying to overcome a shortage of time

put back the clock
to return to the conditions etc of an earlier time in history
• *The union spokesman claimed that the management's decision had put back the clock thirty years in terms of working conditions*

round the clock
the whole day and the whole night

clockwork

as regular as clockwork
perfectly regular(ly)

like clockwork
very smoothly and without faults or problems

close[1]

at close quarters *see* **quarter**

a close call/shave
a narrow often lucky escape

sail close to the wind *see* **wind[1]**

too close for comfort
close or imminent enough to give cause for concern, panic or fear

close[2]

behind closed doors
in private

a closed book *see* **book**

close one's eyes to *see* **eye**

close ranks *see* **rank**

cloth

cut one's coat to suit/according to one's cloth *see* **coat**

cloud

cast a cloud over something
to spoil or reduce the joy or happiness of an occasion

cloud cuckoo land
derogatory an imaginary country where everything is perfect, usually implying a lack of understanding of reality

every cloud has a silver lining
a proverb, meaning that there are always compensations for every apparent difficulty or unpleasantness

have one's head in the clouds *see* **head**

on cloud nine
very happy
⏱ Originally US

under a cloud
under suspicion; in trouble or disgrace

clover

in clover
informal in great comfort and contentment

club

in the club
facetious informal pregnant

join the club!
informal you are in the same unfortunate situation that we are in
• *If he doesn't like you, join the club! He doesn't like us either*

clue

be clued up on something
slang to be well-informed or knowledgeable about something

not to have a clue
informal to be ignorant about something; not to have any knowledge about something

clutch

clutch at straws *see* **straw**

coach

drive a coach and horses through
to show the weak points of an argument etc and so make it ineffective
Ⓞ A reference to the fact that the defects or holes in the argument are so large that a coach and horses could be driven through them

coal

haul someone over the coals
informal to reprimand or scold someone very severely

heap coals (of fire) on someone's head
to make someone sorry for what they have done by being very kind and forgiving to them
Ⓞ A Biblical reference, to Proverbs 25:21–22, repeated in Romans 12:20

take/carry coals to Newcastle
to take something to a place where there is already a great deal of it
Ⓞ For over 150 years Newcastle was the centre which supplied most of the coal in England

coast

the coast is clear
there is no difficulty or danger (especially one already specified) in the way
• *Apparently a military term — 'there are no enemy forces near the coast', an important factor in a successful invasion*

coat

cut one's coat to suit/according to one's cloth
to make sure that one's aims etc are suitable to the circumstances

hang on someone's coat-tails
to achieve one's position as a result of the promotion of a person to whom one has attached oneself and not by one's own merit

turn one's coat
formal to change from one side, especially in politics, to the other
Ⓞ The image is of having a coat which is a different colour inside out

cobbler

the cobbler should stick to his last
a proverb, meaning that people should do what they are qualified to do and should leave other jobs to those who are qualified to do them

cock

a cock-and-bull story
an absurd, unbelievable and mostly untrue story
Ⓞ Origin unknown

cock a snook at someone
to express defiance or contempt towards someone, originally by means of a rude gesture

cock of the walk
the most important person in a group
Ⓞ *Walk* was the name for the pen in which fighting-cocks were bred and kept

go off at half-cock
not to be successful because of lack of preparation
Ⓞ At *half-cock*, the firing mechanism of a matchlock gun was raised, but not far enough to engage the trigger. If the gun then fired of its own accord, the shot would obviously be wasted

it beats cock-fighting
informal a saying used when something is either remarkable or superior in some way

cockle

warm the cockles of one's heart
to make one feel very warm, happy and comfortable

coffin

a nail in someone's coffin *see* **nail**

coin

coin it in
slang to make a great deal of money

pay someone (back) in his etc **own coin**
to punish them for treating one badly by treating them in the same way

to coin a phrase
1 to use a new phrase or expression
2 to repeat a cliché
• *To coin a phrase, everything in the garden's lovely*

the other side of the coin
the contrary or contrasting aspect of a situation, argument etc
• *She has a more highly paid job but the other side of the coin is that she works much longer hours*

cold

as cold as charity *see* **charity**

cold comfort
rather formal no consolation at all

a cold sweat *see* **sweat**

come in from the cold
to be allowed once again to be involved in some activity from which one was previously excluded

cold turkey
slang a sudden withdrawal from drug-taking, also extended to an abrupt cessation of other habits or activities
Ⓘ Origin uncertain

get cold feet
informal to lose courage and abandon a plan etc

give someone the cold shoulder
informal to show that one is unwilling to be friendly with them especially by deliberately ignoring them
Ⓘ Apparently a Scottish expression introduced to standard English by Sir Walter Scott

in cold blood *see* **blood**

in cold storage *see* **storage**

in the cold light of day *see* **light[1]**

knock someone cold *see* **knock**

leave someone cold
informal to fail to impress them

leave someone out in the cold
to neglect or ignore them

make someone's blood run cold *see* **blood**

throw cold water on/over
to discourage; to lessen enthusiasm for

collar

to have one's collar felt
slang to be arrested or apprehended by the police

colour

change colour
to become very pale or very red in the face because of emotion such as fear, anger etc

a horse of a different colour *see* **horse**

lend colour to something
to make it appear more likely, believable or reasonable

local colour *see* **local**

nail one's colours to the mast
formal to commit oneself to an opinion or course of action in a way that makes it impossible to change one's mind
Ⓘ A naval idiom — lowering a ship's flag was the traditional signal of surrender, and nailed colours obviously cannot be lowered

off-colour
informal not feeling very well

show oneself in one's true colours
to show or express one's real (and usually unattractive) character, opinion etc
Ⓘ From the former use of coloured ribbons and badges to show allegiance to a person or party

with flying colours
with ease and great success

Ⓘ A naval phrase — *colours* = flags

column

the agony column *see* **agony**

come

come a cropper *see* **cropper**

come back/down to earth *see* **earth**

come clean *see* **clean**

come hell or high water *see* **hell**

come in for something
to receive or be the target for abuse, criticism etc

come in from the cold *see* **cold**

come in handy *see* **handy**

come into one's own *see* **own**

come into play *see* **play**

come of age *see* **age**

come off it!
informal don't be ridiculous (especially in trying to persuade someone of something they do not believe)

come out
informal to declare one's homosexuality

come out in the wash *see* **wash**

come (out) into the open *see* **open**

come out of the closet
informal to declare one's homosexuality
Ⓘ In American English a closet is a cupboard or wardrobe

come to grief *see* **grief**

come to grips with *see* **grip**

come to light *see* **light[1]**

come to nothing *see* **nothing**

come to rest *see* **rest**

come to one's senses *see* **sense**

come to that/if it comes to that
if you want to take absolutely all the facts into consideration
• *I'm not one of her admirers — come to that, I don't even like her much*

come to the point *see* **point**

have it coming to one
informal to deserve the bad luck, punishment etc that one is going to get
• *Don't feel sorry for him — he had it coming/he's got it coming to him*

comfort

cold comfort *see* **cold**

one's creature comforts *see* **creature**

too close for comfort *see* **close[1]**

commission

out of commission
informal not in a usable, working condition
Ⓘ A naval phrase — a warship *in commission* is under the command of an officer and ready to put to sea. It would be *out of commission* if laid up or under repair

common

common-or-garden
derogatory ordinary; not unusual in any way
Ⓘ From the *common or garden variety*, a frequent description of the least exotic form of a plant

the common touch *see* **touch**

company

keep company (with)
old to be friendly with, especially as a boy- or girlfriend
• *They have kept company for more than two years*

keep someone company
to go, stay etc with them

compare

beyond compare
very formal so great, good etc as to have no rival

compliment

a back-handed/left-handed compliment
a remark etc that is intended to be or seems like a compliment, but in fact is not
• *He said he liked me a lot better than the last time he met me, which I thought was rather a back-handed compliment*

the compliments of the season
formal a greeting especially appropriate to a certain time of year, especially Christmas

con

the pros and cons *see* **pro**

concrete

a/the concrete jungle
informal derogatory modern cities when considered to be unattractive, dangerous or primitive places to live

confidence

a confidence trick
the trick of swindling someone out of money by first gaining their trust or confidence

take someone into one's confidence
to tell one's private thoughts, plans, secrets etc to them

a vote of confidence *see* **vote**

conjure

a name to conjure with *see* **name**

conscience

in all conscience
being fair and reasonable
• *In all conscience, I can't bring myself to do it*

contention

a bone of contention *see* **bone**

contradiction

a contradiction in terms
a statement, idea etc which contains a contradiction

conversation

a conversation piece
something which is so unusual in some way as always to cause a discussion and often kept deliberately for that purpose
Ⓒ In art, a *conversation piece* is an informal painting of a group of people. The modern meaning may have arisen from a misunderstanding or from a joke

converted

preach to the converted
to speak enthusiastically about something, recommend a course of action etc, to a person or persons who already agree with one

cook

cook someone's goose *see* **goose**

cook the books
to make false records, especially accounts, in order to hide the evidence of illegal or immoral behaviour

too many cooks spoil the broth
a proverb, meaning that a project is likely to be hindered rather than helped if too many people are involved in organizing it

what's cooking?
informal what is planned or about to happen?

cookie

that's the way the cookie crumbles
informal a catch phrase, meaning that's what the situation is; that's just what one would expect to happen
Ⓒ Originally US

cool

as cool as a cucumber *see* **cucumber**

cool, calm and collected
extremely calm, in complete control of oneself

cool one's heels *see* **heel**

keep, lose one's cool
slang not to, to become angry, over-excited or confused

play it cool
informal to deal with a situation, problem etc in a calm way

cop

cop it
slang to be punished

not much cop
derogatory slang not very good, desirable or useful
• *He turned out to be not much cop as an actor*

copy

a carbon copy
someone or something that is very similar to someone or something else
Ⓒ From carbon paper used to make copies of typed or written material

copybook

blot one's copybook *see* **blot**

corn

tread on someone's corns
to hurt their feelings

corner

cut corners
to use less money, effort, time etc when doing something than was thought necessary, often giving a poorer result

fight one's corner
to defend strongly one's own position, argument, etc
Ⓞ From boxing

from all corners of the world/earth
from a wide range of places in the world

a tight corner *see* **tight**

just around/round the corner
close at hand
• *Summer is just around the corner*

turn the corner
to get past the worst part of a difficulty or danger

correct

stand corrected *see* **stand**

corridor

the corridors of power
formal the higher levels of government administration
Ⓞ A phrase invented by C P Snow, in *Homecomings* (1956)

cost

at all costs
no matter what the cost or outcome may be
• *We must at all costs avoid being seen*

cost the earth *see* **earth**

count the cost
to take stock of the problems, risks, losses, etc involved in or caused by something

cost a packet *see* **packet**

not cost a penny *see* **penny**

to someone's cost
in a way that causes someone disadvantage, discomfort etc
• *The new boss appears very friendly, but I have found out to my cost that he is not*

couch

a couch potato *see* **potato**

cough

cough up
slang to pay what one owes

counsel

keep one's (own) counsel
formal to keep something secret

count

count one's chickens before they are hatched *see* **chicken**

count the cost *see* **cost**

out for the count
exhausted, deeply asleep or unconscious
Ⓞ Literally, in boxing, to be knocked unconscious and counted out

stand up and be counted *see* **stand**

counter

under the counter
used of giving or receiving, especially buying and selling, secretly or illegally; not in the official manner

country

country cousin
derogatory a person who lives in the country and is regarded as unsophisticated by town-dwellers

go to the country
to find out the opinion of the electorate on a political question by holding a general election

courage

Dutch courage *see* **Dutch**

have the courage of one's convictions
rather formal to be brave enough to act according to one's opinions

pluck up the courage/screw up one's courage to do something
to finally become brave enough to do it

course

(there are) horses for courses *see* **horse**

par for the course *see* **par**

run/take its course
to continue on to what is considered to be the usual or natural conclusion
• *His bout of flu ran its course*

stay the course *see* **stay**

court

be laughed out of court *see* **laugh**

have a friend at court *see* **friend**

pay court to someone
old to try to win their affection or love

rule something out of court
to refuse to allow it to be considered or to take place
• *The staff asked for an extra day's holiday but management ruled it out of court*
Ⓞ Of legal origin — when a matter is ruled out of court it is not allowed by the law court to be taken into consideration in the decision of a case

Coventry

send someone to Coventry
not to allow them to associate with others; to refuse to speak to them, usually because of something they have done
Ⓞ The most likely explanation for this phrase is that it is from an incident during the English Civil War when groups of Royalists captured in Birmingham were sent for safe-keeping to the Parliamentary stronghold of Coventry

cover

break cover
to appear suddenly from a hiding-place
Ⓞ A hunting term

cover up for someone
to try to prevent their dishonest, illegal etc deeds from being discovered, by concealing the truth, lying etc

cow

a sacred cow *see* **sacred**

till the cows come home
for a very long time

crack

at the crack of dawn
very early in the morning

crack a bottle
open a bottle of an alcoholic drink etc

crack a joke
to tell a funny story; to make a funny remark

crack down on
informal to take strong action against

crack the whip *see* **whip**

a fair crack of the whip
a fair and sufficient period of importance, dominance etc
• *Each of the three speakers was given a fair crack of the whip*

get cracking
informal to get moving quickly; to get busy

a hard nut to crack *see* **nut**

have a crack (at)
informal to have a try at; to make an attempt to

not all it's etc **cracked up to be**
slang not as good as it is said to be

paper over the cracks *see* **paper**

take a sledgehammer to crack a nut *see* **nut**

cradle

the hand that rocks the cradle *see* **hand**

cramp

cramp someone's style *see* **style**

crazy

crazy like a fox *see* **fox**

creature

one's creature comforts
often facetious things (food, alcohol, warmth etc) contributing to one's physical pleasure
Ⓞ A 17c phrase

credibility

credibility gap
the difference between what is officially claimed to be the case and what is actually the case; the phrase is often used in connection with political statements

credit

be a credit to someone or **something/do someone** or **something credit**
formal to bring honour or respect to someone or something
• *Your son is a credit to you; Your honesty does you credit*

creek

up the creek
slang in serious difficulties
ⓘ 2nd World War slang

creep

give someone the creeps
informal to make someone feel fear and disgust

make someone's flesh creep *see* **flesh**

cricket

as lively as a cricket
very lively

not cricket
fig unfair or unsporting

crocodile

crocodile tears
pretended tears of grief
ⓘ The crocodile was once reputed to weep bitterly, either to attract the attention of potential victims (Hakluyt's *Voyages*, 1600) or while eating them (Mandeville's *Travels*, 1400)

crop

crop up
informal to happen or appear unexpectedly

cropper

come a cropper
informal to meet misfortune
ⓘ A hunting phrase for 'take a serious fall', probably from *neck and crop* = completely

cross

at cross purposes
(of two or more people) misunderstanding one another because of talking or thinking about different things
• *I think we've been talking at cross purposes*

cross a bridge when one comes to it *see* **bridge**

cross one's fingers *see* **finger**

cross someone's mind *see* **mind**

cross my heart *see* **heart**

cross swords *see* **sword**

cross the Rubicon *see* **Rubicon**

dot one's i's and cross one's t's *see* **dot**

have a cross to bear
to have to endure a heavy responsibility or misfortune of some kind
ⓘ From the fact that people who had been condemned to crucifixion had to carry their own crosses to the scene of execution

have one's wires crossed *see* **wire**

crow

as the crow flies
measured in a straight line, not following the route one would have to take on the ground

eat crow
informal to have to admit with humility that one has been wrong

crowd

far from the madding crowd
in a quiet or secluded place
ⓘ From 'Elegy Written in a Country Churchyard' (1750) by Thomas Gray

crunch

when the crunch comes/when it comes to the crunch
when the actual moment of testing or trial arrives

crush

have a crush on
informal usually of a young girl or boy, to have a great sexual liking for someone; to be in love with someone

cry

cry one's eyes out *see* **eye**

cry for the moon *see* **moon**

cry off
informal to cancel an engagement or agreement
• *After promising to come to the party, she cried off at the last minute*

cry over spilt milk *see* **spill**

cry wolf *see* **wolf**

a far cry from
a long way from; something quite different from
• *This job is a far cry from the last one I had*
◷ Apparently from a Gaelic saying introduced to standard English by being quoted in Sir Walter Scott's *Rob Roy*

in full cry
enthusiastically pursuing something
• *The woman rushed into the sale in full cry after the bargains*
◷ Literally used of hunting dogs

a shoulder to cry on *see* **shoulder**

crying

be crying out for something
to be in urgent and obvious need of something

a crying need
something urgently requiring notice or attention
• *There is a crying need for more hospitals*

a crying shame
a very great shame

for crying out loud
slang an expression of frustration, anger, impatience etc
• *Oh, for crying out loud! That's the third time I've phoned the office and no-one has answered*

crystal

as clear as crystal
very clear; very easy to understand

a crystal ball
something which helps one to see into the future
• *How should I know what is going to happen? Do you think I have a crystal ball?*

cuckoo

cloud cuckoo land *see* **cloud**

cucumber

as cool as a cucumber
very calm and not at all upset or worried

cud

chew the cud
fig to think deeply
◷ Literally of cows etc, to bring food from the first stomach back into the mouth and chew it again

cudgel

take up the cudgels on behalf of/for someone or **something**
to defend a person, cause etc vigorously

cue

take one's cue from someone
to copy the way someone is reacting to a situation etc
◷ Literally, in the theatre, to use the words of another actor as a signal to speak, move etc

cuff

off the cuff
without planning; unprepared
◷ Probably from the reputed habit of speech-makers of scribbling brief headings on the celluloid cuffs of their evening-shirts

culture

culture vulture
derogatory someone who is more than normally interested in painting, music, drama etc

cup

the cup that cheers
a cup of tea

someone's cup of tea
informal: usually in negative the sort of thing they like or prefer
• *Classical music isn't really my cup of tea*

in one's cups
old or facetious under the influence of alcohol

there's many a slip 'twixt cup and lip *see* **slip**

cupboard

cupboard love
attachment to a person because of the material things, food, etc which they can provide

a skeleton in the cupboard *see* **skeleton**

curiosity

curiosity killed the cat
a proverb, meaning that showing too much interest in other people's affairs can be dangerous or harmful to one

curl

make someone's hair curl *see* **hair**

curry

curry favour with someone
to seek a favour from them by flattery
Ⓛ Originally *curry favel*, from the Old French *estriller fauvel*. *Fauvel* — 'chestnut horse' — was the name of a centaur in a romance, and as centaurs traditionally symbolized the subhuman, it is possible that 'grooming Fauvel' was a metaphor for 'making oneself the servant of an unworthy creature'

curtain

be curtains for someone
informal to be the end or death of them
• *It was nearly curtains for him when the runaway car mounted the pavement*
Ⓛ A theatrical idiom

curtain lecture
a private scolding, especially one given by a wife to her husband
Ⓛ A reference to the fact that in former times beds used to have curtains around them to conserve heat

a curtain raiser
a first subject for discussion, first action etc, which is not the most important one planned, but which is useful to get things started or to show how things are likely to continue

the Iron Curtain *see* **iron**

ring down the curtain on something
formal to end a project etc
Ⓛ A theatrical image, from the bell used as a signal to lower the curtain at the end of a performance

cut

a cut above someone or **something**
obviously better than them or it

cut a long story short *see* **story**

cut and dried
often derogatory fixed and definite
• *His views on this are very cut and dried*
Ⓛ Originally describing one form — as opposed to fresh — in which herbs were sold

cut and thrust
formal fierce competition
• *She enjoys the cut and thrust of big business*
Ⓛ From sword-fighting

cut back on something
to reduce it considerably

cut both ways
informal to affect both parts of a question, have advantages to both people involved, have both good and bad points etc

cut one's coat to suit/according to one's cloth *see* **coat**

cut corners *see* **corner**

cut someone dead *see* **dead**

cut someone down to size *see* **size**

cut it fine *see* **fine**

cut it out
impolite; informal to stop doing something wrong
• *He kept interrupting me until I told him to cut it out*

cut no ice *see* **ice**

cut off one's nose to spite one's face *see* **nose**

cut one's own throat *see* **throat**

cut one's teeth on *see* **teeth**

cut someone off at the pass *see* **pass**

cut someone off without a shilling *see* **shilling**

cut the cackle *see* **cackle**

cut someone to the quick *see* **quick**

cut up
slang very upset

cut up rough *see* **rough**

not cut out for something
not naturally suited to or able for it

the cutting edge *see* **edge**

cylinder

firing on all cylinders
informal working at full strength or perfectly
Ⓛ Literally used of an internal-combustion engine, for instance of a car

D

dab

a dab hand at something
informal an expert at something

daddy

the daddy of them all
informal facetious the most extreme example (especially bad or astonishing) of anything
• *I've had hangovers before, but this one's the daddy of them all*

a sugar daddy *see* **sugar**

daft

as daft as a brush *see* **brush**

dagger

at daggers drawn
formal ready to start fighting or quarrelling at any minute

cloak-and-dagger *see* **cloak**

look daggers at someone
to look at them in a hostile manner

daily

daily bread *see* **bread**

the daily grind
one's daily routine

daily dozen *see* **dozen**

daisy

as fresh as a daisy
very bright, active and untired

be pushing up the daisies
slang to be dead

damage

what's the damage?
informal facetious what is the total cost?
• *'What's the damage?' he asked the waiter*

damn

damn all
informal nothing at all

damn someone or **something with faint praise**
to condemn them or it indirectly by not praising enthusiastically enough
① A quotation from Alexander Pope's *Epistle to Dr Arbuthnot*

not to give a damn
informal not to care in the least
• *I'm sorry, but I don't give a damn for his opinion!*

not worth a damn
informal completely worthless

damnedest

do one's damnedest
informal to do one's very best

Damocles

the sword of Damocles *see* **sword**

damp

a damp squib
something which is expected to be exciting, effective etc but which completely fails to be so

damper

put a damper on something
to lessen the enjoyment, hope, etc of something

dance

dance attendance on someone
to wait near them ready to carry out their wishes

dance to a different tune *see* **tune**

lead someone a (merry) dance
to keep them constantly involved in a series of problems and irritations

dancing

bring on the dancing girls
a catch phrase used to suggest that people are bored and in need of entertainment to relieve the boredom

dander

get one's dander up
informal to (cause one to) become angry or hostile
• *By this time he had got his dander up and was becoming angry; Rudeness always gets his dander up*
① Originally northern dialect and US

dandy

fine and dandy *see* **fine**

Darby

a Darby and Joan
a devoted elderly married couple
① From a poem by Henry Woodfall in the *Gentleman's Magazine*, 1735

dark

a dark horse
a person about whose abilities etc little is known
① 19c racing slang

a leap in the dark
an action the consequences of which are unknown, an action taken without forethought

in the dark
in a state of ignorance or unawareness especially of particular facts

keep it dark
informal to keep something a secret

a shot in the dark *see* **shot**

darken

not to darken someone's door
not to dare to visit their house

dash

cut a dash
to have an impressive (usually smart or fashionable) appearance

date

out of date
1 old-fashioned
2 no longer able to be legally used; no longer valid

to date
formal up to the present time

up to date
1 completed etc up to the present time
• *I try to keep my correspondence up to date*
2 modern and in touch with the latest ideas and fashion

daunt

nothing daunted
formal; often facetious not at all discouraged; not frightened or made less enthusiastic etc
• *She was an old lady but, nothing daunted, she hit her attacker over the head with her umbrella*

Davy Jones

Davy Jones's locker
usually facetious the bottom of the sea
① For obscure reasons, 18c seamen gave the name Davy Jones to the ruler of the evil spirits of the sea

dawn

at the crack of dawn *see* **crack**

dawn on someone
to become suddenly clear to them

day

all in a/the day's work *see* **work**

as happy as the day is long
very happy, especially in how one is spending one's time

at the end of the day
when everything has been considered and final decisions are being made

call it a day
informal to bring something to an end; to stop (eg working)
① This phrase originally meant 'to reckon what one has already done to be a full day's work', and thus by inference 'to stop work early'

carry the day *see* **carry**

day in, day out
every day without exception

daylight robbery *see* **robbery**

his etc **days are numbered**
he is about to die, to be dismissed from his job etc

D-day
a day on which something important is due to take place or begin
Ⓞ D is short for 'day' and is used simply for emphasis — the original *D-day* was June 6, 1944, the day on which the Allies began their landings in Northern France with a view to pushing back the German forces

halcyon days
a time that is remembered as being happy and peaceful
Ⓞ A reference to an ancient belief that the kingfisher — halcyon is the Greek name for a kingfisher — laid its eggs in the sea during a fourteen-day period of calm weather

have a field day *see* **field**

have had one's day
informal to be past the most successful etc period of one's life
Ⓞ Probably from the saying **every dog has his day**, which means that everyone can expect to enjoy a period of success at some time

have seen better days *see* **better**

in this day and age
at the present advanced period of time

live from day to day
to think only about the present without making any plans for the future

make someone's day
to make them very happy

name the day
rather facetious to announce a date for something, especially the date on which one is to be married

not to be someone's day
to be a day on which they are not able to be successful, or on which things go wrong for them
Ⓞ As **have had one's day** above

one of these days
informal at some time in the near future

one of those days
informal a day on which everything goes wrong

the order of the day *see* **order**

the other day
not long ago

save the day
to prevent something from going wrong, from failing etc

see daylight
1 to approach the end of a long task
2 to understand suddenly

some day
at some time in the future

that will be the day
informal that is very unlikely
• *'Perhaps your husband will buy you flowers for your birthday.' 'That'll be the day!'*
Ⓞ Originally Australian, possibly from German *der Tag* — 'the day (of victory)' — a favourite catch phrase of the German forces during the 1st World War, much parodied by Allied troops

those were the days
the time we are talking about was a good one

to this day
even now; up to the present time

win the day
to be successful
• *Common sense will win the day*
Ⓞ A military phrase — literally, 'to win the battle'

dead

as dead as a/the dodo *see* **dodo**

as dead as a doornail *see* **doornail**

cut someone dead
to ignore them completely, especially by acting as if one has not seen them

dead beat
informal exhausted or very tired

dead but it, he etc**, won't lie down**
informal a catch phrase indicating that someone or something has been defeated or destroyed completely, but will not accept the fact and goes on making futile gestures

a dead cert
informal something absolutely certain
Ⓞ Originally a racing term for a horse that is considered certain to win

a dead duck
informal a project, person etc unlikely to continue or to survive

a dead end
a situation etc from which it is impossible to progress
◷ Literally, a road closed off at one end

dead from the neck up *see* **neck**

a dead loss
informal something completely useless or unprofitable

(the) dead of night
the middle of the night

dead on one's feet
informal utterly exhausted

a dead ringer for someone *see* **ringer**

Dead Sea fruit *see* **fruit**

dead set on something
determined or very anxious to obtain it
• *My wife is dead set on that house; I'm dead set on going to America*

the dead spit of *see* **spit**

dead to the world
fast asleep
◷ Probably from the use of this phrase in a religious context to describe the situation of a person who had entered a convent or monastery

drop dead! *see* **drop**

enough to waken the dead
extremely and unpleasantly loud

flog a dead horse *see* **horse**

let the dead bury the dead
a proverb indicating that the past with all its problems, sadnesses, etc is best forgotten
• *I know you quarrelled with him years ago but it's time to let the dead bury the dead*

over my dead body
an expression showing that one is strongly opposed to a certain proposal, plan etc
• *That woman will be invited to our party over my dead body!*

step into dead men's shoes
to take over the job, position etc of someone who has died, or of someone who has left in unfortunate circumstances

I etc **would not be seen dead with, in** etc
I have a very strong dislike of a person, an article of clothing etc
• *I would not be seen dead in the hat my mother-in-law was wearing*

stop dead *see* **stop**

deaf

fall on deaf ears *see* **ear**

turn a deaf ear to something *see* **ear**

deal

big deal!
an ironic expression indicating that one is not very impressed by something one has just been told

a raw deal *see* **raw**

a square deal *see* **square**

dear

a Dear John letter *see* **letter**

dear knows
I do not know at all

for dear life
extremely fast, hard, busily etc
• *As the exam drew to an end, many of the students were still scribbling for dear life*

death

at death's door
on the point of dying
◷ From the version of Psalm 107:18 in the Church of England Prayer Book — 'Their soul abhorred all manner of meat; and they were even hard at death's door'

be in at the death
to be present during the final stages of a course of events, especially a hunt of some kind
◷ A hunting term

catch one's death (of cold)
informal to get a very bad cold

death by a thousand cuts
a downfall that is brought about not by one attacking blow, incident, etc but by a series of them

deathless prose
ironical unforgettable writing, writing that is so bad that it is eminently forgettable

a death-trap
a place, building etc in which one is in danger of being killed or harmed

dice with death *see* **dice**

die a natural death *see* **die[1]**

die the death
informal to be unsuccessful, to fail utterly
Ⓛ The phrase originally referred to a performer getting a poor reception from an audience

flog something to death
to talk or think about a subject so much that it is no longer interesting

hang/hold on like grim death *see* **grim**

the kiss of death *see* **kiss**

like death warmed up
often facetious in a very poor state, especially appearing ill, exhausted etc
• *He always looks like death warmed up first thing in the morning*

as pale as death
extremely pale of complexion, especially from illness or fear

put the fear of death into *see* **fear**

sick to death of something *see* **sick**

sign one's own death warrant
to be the cause of one's own misfortune or downfall

deck

clear the decks
to tidy up, especially to remove everything unnecessary in preparation for starting an important task
Ⓛ Originally an operation to prepare a warship for battle

hit the deck
slang to fall down
Ⓛ Deck in American English means the ground or the floor

deep

be thrown in at the deep end
to have to start an activity, job etc with little experience or by doing something quite difficult
Ⓛ From the 'deep end' of a swimming pool

go off the deep end
to express strong feelings in a very strong, often angry, manner

in deep water
in difficulties or trouble

degree

give someone the third degree
informal; often facetious to question someone very intensely, using very severe methods
Ⓛ From an interrogation method involving bullying and ill-treatment once used by the American police

to the nth degree *see* **n**

delicate

in a delicate condition
old euphemism pregnant

deliver

deliver the goods *see* **goods**

den

a den of thieves *see* **thief**

dent

make a dent in something
to lessen by a considerable amount
• *The repairs to the house certainly made a dent in our savings*

depart

the departed
euphemism a person who is or people who are dead

a new departure
a change of purpose or method in doing something

depth

in depth
deeply and thoroughly
• *I have studied the subject in depth*

out of one's depth
in a situation with which one cannot deal
Ⓛ Literally, in water deeper than one can stand up in

plumb the depths
to reach the lowest level of misfortune, depression, etc

desert

desert a sinking ship
to leave an organization etc which is in some kind of difficulty so that one will escape the consequences of its downfall. A longer version of the phrase is **like rats deserting a sinking ship**

get one's just deserts *see* **just**

design

have designs on something
to be trying to get (usually something belonging to someone else)

desire

leave a lot to be desired
rather facetious not to be very good or satisfactory
• *Her cooking leaves a lot to be desired*

devil

between the devil and the deep blue sea
faced with a choice between two risky or undesirable courses of action etc

the devil of a job
informal something that is extremely difficult to do
• *We had the devil of a job to change the wheel*

the devil to pay
serious trouble
• *There will be the devil to pay when your mother sees this mess!*
① From legendary bargains made with the devil, in which the bargainer usually agreed to give the devil his soul at a later date in payment for immediate worldly success etc

devil take the hindmost
a short form of the phrase **every man for himself and devil take the hindmost**, meaning that everyone acts or should act only to benefit himself without thinking about what is happening to other people

give the devil his due
to be fair to someone one dislikes or disapproves of

needs must when the devil rides *see* **need**

play the devil's advocate
to put forward objections to a plan, arguments against something etc in order to test the arguments for it
① The devil's advocate — *advocatus diaboli* — was the man given the role of opposing the canonization of a saint in the medieval Church, 'putting the devil's point of view' and thus ensuring that the evidence for canonization was sound

talk of the devil
here comes the very person we have just been speaking about
① From the saying *talk of the devil and see his horns,* which originally expressed the superstition that talking about evil gave it power to appear, happen etc

diamond

a rough diamond
a person who is probably basically good and valuable, but who looks unattractive and/or behaves in a rude, uncivilized manner

dice

dice with death
often facetious to do something very risky and dangerous

load the dice against someone
to take away any chance they have of succeeding at something
• *The dice were loaded against him and he had to give in*
① From a method of cheating in gambling games by using dice with a weight inside, tending to make them show the same score every time

no dice
slang an expression used to indicate lack of success
• *I tried to get him to help us, but no dice*

die[1]

die a natural death
to fade away or die out of its own accord without any form of intervention

die hard
to struggle hard against death or to take a long time to disappear etc
• *Old customs die hard*

die in harness *see* **harness**

die the death *see* **death**

die with one's boots on
informal to die while one is still working

never say die
a saying, meaning that one should never give up and admit that one has been defeated

die[2]

the die is cast
a step has been taken which makes the future inevitable
Ⓘ In Latin *jacta alea est*, traditionally Julius Caesar's comment on crossing the River Rubicon into Italy with his army in 49BC, thus effectively declaring war on the Roman administration

difference

sink our, your etc **differences** *see* **sink**

split the difference
to settle an argument by agreeing that each side should give up half of the thing, especially an amount of money, that is being argued about

different

different as chalk from cheese *see* **chalk**

dance to a different tune
to act in a completely different way, especially when one is forced to do so

a different kettle of fish *see* **kettle**

different strokes for different folks
not everyone is the same and everyone has individual tastes
Ⓘ Originally Black American

dig

dig in
informal to make an energetic start on something, especially eating a meal

dig in one's heels *see* **heel**

dig one's own grave *see* **grave**

dig the dirt on someone *see* **dirt**

dignity

beneath someone's dignity
not fitting to what they think their position in the world is; too lowly or ordinary an action for them to do
• *Now she is the manager, she thinks it is beneath her dignity to answer the telephone*

stand on one's dignity
rather formal to be ready to take offence very easily

dilemma

on the horns of a dilemma
in a position where it is necessary to choose between two undesirable courses of action etc
Ⓘ In medieval rhetoric a *dilemma* was a way of arguing which consisted of proving that one of two statements must be true, both being damaging to one's opponent's case. It was likened to a two-horned animal. In choosing which of the two statements he preferred to admit as the truth, the opponent was pictured as having to throw himself on to one or other of the 'horns'

dim

take a dim view of
informal to disapprove of

dime

a dime a dozen *see* **dozen**

dine

dine out on
informal to be socially successful because one possesses eg interesting information
• *It was such a good story, even if untrue, that he dined out on it for years*

dip

dip into
to look briefly at a book or to study a subject in a casual manner

a lucky dip *see* **luck**

dirt

dig the dirt on someone
slang to search around for and reveal unsavoury or scandalous incidents in their life

dirt cheap
informal very cheap

dish the dirt on someone
slang to spread scandalous or spiteful stories about them

dirty

dirty one's hands *see* **hand**

dirty old man
an elderly or middle-aged man, traditionally clad in a raincoat, who shows an unhealthy sexual interest in young people

dirty word
1 a four-letter word, a swear-word
2 something that is disapproved of or is not acceptable

dirty work at the crossroads
foul play, underhand dealings
Ⓞ The origin is uncertain but it has been suggested that it is connected with the old custom of burying at a crossroads people, such as outlaws or suicides, who were not eligible for a churchyard burial

do someone's dirty work
to do an unpleasant task or morally wrong action on behalf of someone else

do the dirty on
slang to play an unpleasant, mean trick on

wash one's dirty linen in public *see* **linen**

discord

an apple of discord *see* **apple**

discretion

discretion is the better part of valour
a proverb, meaning that it is wise not to take unnecessary risks

disease

the British/English disease
extreme militancy in industrial relations, especially the frequent application of strike action

dish

dish the dirt on someone *see* **dirt**

dishwater

as dull as dishwater
same as **as dull as ditchwater** *see* **ditchwater**

distance

come, be within striking distance *see* **striking**

go the distance
to complete something, to go on until the end of something
Ⓞ Perhaps a reference to a racehorse who finishes the course

keep one's distance
not to be too friendly; not to come too close

ditchwater

as dull as ditchwater
very boring or uninteresting

divide

divide and rule
to win or achieve a position of control by getting one's opponents to quarrel amongst themselves

do

I etc **could do with/could be doing with something**
it would be better if I had or did it
• *I could do with a cup of coffee; This house could be doing with a coat of paint*

do someone a good turn *see* **turn**

do away with someone or **something**
informal
1 to get rid of it, especially to abolish it officially
2 to kill someone, especially secretly

do someone down
Brit informal to cheat or overcome them in some way

do someone in
very informal to kill them

do justice (to) *see* **justice**

do one's nut *see* **nut**

don't do anything I wouldn't do
informal a catch phrase used humorously to someone to whom one is saying goodbye

do or die
to succeed or to die, ruin oneself etc in trying to succeed

do someone out of something
informal to prevent them from getting it, especially by using dishonest methods
• *He feels he has been done out of a day's holiday*

do someone over
slang to give them a severe beating

do someone proud *see* **proud**

do the honours *see* **honour**

do the trick *see* **trick**

do one's (own) thing *see* **thing**

do time *see* **time**

do something up
to repair, redecorate etc it in order to put it into a better condition than before

fair do's *see* **fair**

doctor

what the doctor ordered
the very thing that is needed
• *At this moment a cup of tea is just what the doctor ordered*

dodo

as dead as a/the dodo
completely dead or no longer fashionable, useful, popular etc
ⓘ From a flightless bird discovered on the island of Mauritius in the early 17c and extinct by 1700

dog

be top dog *see* **top**

a case of the tail wagging the dog *see* **case**

dog eat dog
(of) a situation in which one has to compete ruthlessly in order to survive or be successful
• *He is not ambitious and hates the dog-eat-dog business world*

a dog in the manger
someone who tries to prevent another person from having or doing something which he himself does not want, cannot do etc
ⓘ The image is of a dog which lies in the hay-rack of a cow-shed, thus preventing the cattle from eating the hay

dog Latin *see* **Latin**

a dogsbody
someone who is given odd jobs, especially unpleasant ones, to do

a dog's breakfast/dinner
informal an untidy mess
• *What a dog's breakfast you've made of your homework!*

every dog has his day *see* **have had one's day,** at **day**

go to the dogs
informal to be ruined, especially to ruin oneself

help a lame dog over the stile
to give assistance to someone who is in difficulties

in the doghouse
informal in disgrace
ⓘ The image is of someone banished from the house and forced to take shelter in an outdoor kennel

lead a dog's life
to lead an unhappy life, especially because one is ruled by a person who makes one unhappy

let sleeping dogs lie
a proverb, meaning that one should not try to reform or improve people etc who might cause trouble but are not doing so at present

let the dog see the rabbit
a phrase used to get people to stand back and let one get a better view of something

why keep a dog and bark yourself?
why employ someone to do something and then do it yourself?
• *I see no reason to employ a gardener and then cut the lawn. Why keep a dog and bark yourself?*

doggo

lie doggo
informal to remain in hiding without giving any sign of one's presence; not to do anything that would draw attention to oneself

doing

nothing doing! *see* **nothing**

take some doing
to be very difficult
• *He's more untidy than you are, and that takes some doing!*

dollar

bet one's bottom dollar *see* **bottom**

done

done for
informal ruined or about to be killed etc without there being any hope of rescue or recovery

done to a turn *see* **turn**

have done with *see* **have**

(not) the done thing
(not) acceptable behaviour

Don Juan
a womanizer
Ⓛ A reference to a fourteenth-century Spanish lover and libertine

donkey
donkey's ages/years
informal a very long time
• *I haven't seen him in donkey's ages*
Ⓛ From a pun on 'donkey's ears' — which are very long

donkey work
the hard, unrewarding part of any task

talk the hind leg off a donkey
derogatory to talk a great deal and for a long time

don't
don't call us, we'll call you *see* **call**

don't do anything I wouldn't do *see* **do**

doom
a prophet of doom
a person who always believes that the worst will happen and tells everyone so

door
at death's door *see* **death**

behind closed doors *see* **close**[2]

have a foot in the door *see* **foot**

keep the wolf from the door *see* **wolf**

lay something at someone's door
to blame it on them, to hold them responsible for it

not to darken someone's door *see* **darken**

open the door to something
to allow the possibility of something
• *The initial discussion opened the door to formal talks*

out of doors
outside; not in a house etc

show someone the door
to make them leave the house

when one door closes
a remark used to indicate that one should not get downhearted when one is unsuccessful at something as other opportunities are likely to present themselves
Ⓛ A shortened version of **when one door closes another opens**

doornail
dead as a doornail
completely without life
• *He was dead as a doornail by the time the police got there; The phone is as dead as a doornail*

doorstep
on someone's doorstep
very close to where they live

dose
a dose of someone's own medicine *see* **medicine**

go through something like a dose of salts
informal to finish it very quickly
Ⓛ From the use of Epsom salts as a purgative

dot
dot one's i's and cross one's t's
to take great care over details

from/since the year dot
for a very long time
Ⓛ The year dot implies 'a year too long ago to be specified'

on the dot (of)
exactly at a given time
• *The train left at nine o'clock on the dot; The train left on the dot of nine o'clock*
Ⓛ From the dots marking the minutes on a clock face

double
at the double
very quickly
Ⓛ A military term — literally, at twice the normal marching pace

do a double take
to look at or think about someone or something a second time since one has not seen or understood properly the first time

double back
to turn and go back the way one came

double Dutch *see* **Dutch**

see double *see* **see**

doubting

a doubting Thomas
a person who will not believe something without strong proof
Ⓛ In the Bible, Thomas was the apostle who refused to believe that Jesus had risen from the dead until he had touched him

dovecote

flutter the dovecotes
to cause upset or confusion

down

be, go down with
to be or become ill with
• *The children all went down with measles one after the other*

down-and-out
derogatory (a person) having no money, no means of earning a living, and no hope of ever doing so

down-at-heel
shabby, untidy and not well looked after or well-dressed
Ⓛ Literally, of shoes, having worn-down heels

down in the dumps *see* **dumps**

down in the mouth *see* **mouth**

down on one's luck *see* **luck**

down the drain *see* **drain**

down the hatch! *see* **hatch**

down the tube
same as **down the drain** *see* **drain**

down-to-earth
practical and not concerned with theories, ideals or possibilities

down tools
informal to stop working

down under
often facetious in or to Australia or New Zealand

fall down on *see* **fall**

get down to
to begin working seriously at or on

have a down on
informal to be very hostile or opposed to

play something down *see* **play**

sell someone down the river *see* **river**

suit someone down to the ground *see* **ground**

talk down to someone *see* **talk**

downhill

go downhill
to become worse and worse

dozen

a baker's dozen *see* **baker**

daily dozen
physical exercises done every day, usually every morning

a dime a dozen
extremely readily available and cheap
Ⓛ Dime is American English for ten cents

(talk) nineteen to the dozen *see* **nineteen**

drag

drag one's feet on/over something
to deliberately take a long time over doing it

dragon

chase the dragon
slang to smoke heroin, especially when it is heated on a piece of aluminium foil and the fumes inhaled through a tube
Ⓛ Origin uncertain

drain

down the drain
derogatory informal completely wasted
• *We had to scrap everything and start again — 6 months' work down the drain*

draught

feel the draught
to be unpleasantly aware of difficult conditions, especially lack of money

draw

the days/nights are drawing in
the days are getting quickly shorter and the nights longer, as happens in early autumn

draw a blank *see* **blank**

draw a veil over *see* **veil**

draw in one's horns *see* **horn**

draw the line *see* **line**

draw the teeth of *see* **teeth**

long drawn out
going on for a long time

drawer
someone's bottom drawer
bed-linen, table-linen etc which a girl is given or collects for use in her own house when she gets married

out of the top drawer
often facetious from the upper social classes

drawing-board
back to the drawing-board
I will have to start again from the very beginning and make new plans (said when a project has failed, been rejected etc)
Ⓛ From the fact that many projects begin with a design sketch

dream
go like a dream
to progress etc very well
• *My new car goes like a dream; It was a complicated operation, moving office, but it went like a dream*

dress
dressed to kill
informal dressed in one's best clothes, especially in clothes designed to attract attention

a dressing-down
informal a scolding

drib
dribs and drabs
informal very small quantities

drift
catch/get the drift of something
informal to understand the general meaning or subject of what is being said etc

drink
be meat and drink to *see* **meat**

drink something in
to take something in rapidly or eagerly
• *The audience were fascinated, drinking in his every word*

drink like a fish *see* **fish**

drink to someone's health *see* **health**

drink someone under the table *see* **table**

dripping
a dripping roast
something which continues to provide profit for a long time and without a great deal of effort

drive
as pure as the driven snow
facetious completely pure

drive a hard bargain *see* **bargain**

drive something home
to try to make it completely understood or accepted
• *The manager drove home the need for everyone to try to save the firm's money*

drive someone up the wall *see* **wall**

driving
be driving at
informal to be trying to say or suggest

drop
at the drop of a hat
immediately and needing only the slightest reason or excuse

drop a brick/clanger
to mention a subject or communicate a piece of information to a person or persons to whom one should not have mentioned it, especially to do so in such a way that the mistake cannot be covered up

drop someone a line *see* **line**

drop by
informal to visit someone casually and without being invited

drop dead
an angry interjection used to someone to get him or her to go away, stop talking etc

drop in
informal to arrive informally to visit someone

a drop in the bucket/ocean
a tiny part of the quantity which is needed
Ⓛ A Biblical reference, to Isaiah 40:15

drop into someone's lap *see* **lap**[1]

drop like flies *see* **fly**

drop off
informal to fall asleep

a drop of the hard stuff *see* **hard**

drop out
to withdraw, especially from a course at university etc or from the normal life of society
• *There are only two of us going to the theatre now Mary has dropped out; She's dropped out of college*

let something drop
to allow it to become known as if by accident

name dropping *see* **name**

the penny drops *see* **penny**

you could hear a pin drop *see* **pin**

drown

drown one's sorrows
to take an alcoholic drink in order to forget a disappointment etc

like a drowned rat *see* **rat**

drug

a drug on the market
a commodity for which there is little or no demand and of which there is therefore an oversupply

drum

beat the drum for something or **someone**
to try to attract public notice to it or them
🕔 From the former use of a drum to attract attention to a person making an announcement in a public place etc

drum someone out
to send someone away in disgrace, especially publicly
• *He was drummed out of his bridge club for cheating*
🕔 From the military use of drums to emphasize the dismissal of an officer from his regiment for misconduct etc

drunk

as drunk as a lord *see* **lord**

punch-drunk *see* **punch**

roaring drunk *see* **roaring**

dry

as dry as a bone *see* **bone**

dry someone out
informal to cure an alcoholic

a dry run
an attempt at carrying out a procedure, especially if complicated or requiring very careful timing etc, made beforehand in order to practise

dry up
informal (of a speaker) to forget what to say, eg in a play

go dry
informal (of a place) to cease to have any shops, public houses etc that sell alcohol

high and dry *see* **high**

home and dry *see* **home**

duck

be like water off a duck's back *see* **water**

break one's duck
to have one's first success, especially in playing a game
🕔 A cricketing term — no score in cricket is called a *duck*, from *duck egg*, a reference to the shape of the figure 0

a dead duck *see* **dead**

duck and dive
informal to use various forms of evasive action in order to avoid being found out

duck soup
informal something extremely easy
🕔 Originally US — origin uncertain

a lame duck
sometimes derogatory a helpless or inefficient person

like a dying duck
derogatory behaving in a weak, pathetic and sad manner

a sitting duck *see* **sitting**

duckling

an ugly duckling *see* **ugly**

dull

as dull as ditchwater *see* **ditchwater**

dump

(down) in the dumps
in a state of depression or low spirits

dust

bite the dust
informal; often facetious to cease to exist; to be unsuccessful
Ⓞ A phrase, meaning simply 'to die', much used in 19c adventure stories and 20c Westerns

not to see someone for dust
not to see them again because they have gone away rapidly and suddenly
Ⓞ A reference to the dust thrown up by horses or vehicles when they are moving very fast

shake the dust of somewhere from one's feet
to leave somewhere for good, usually with pleasure

throw dust in someone's eyes
to attempt to deceive someone
Ⓞ From a method of temporarily blinding an enemy

Dutch

double Dutch
informal nonsense
- *I couldn't understand what he was saying — it was double Dutch to me*

a Dutch auction
a kind of auction at which the auctioneer begins by asking for a high price and then reduces it until someone offers to pay the price he is asking

Dutch courage
artificial courage gained by drinking alcohol
Ⓞ Either from a belief that the Dutch were heavy drinkers or from the fact that gin was introduced into England by the Dutch followers of William III

Dutch treat
a social occasion, such as a meal in a restaurant, in which each of the people involved pay equal shares
Ⓞ See **go Dutch** below

go Dutch
informal to pay each for oneself at a restaurant, cinema etc
Ⓞ An American phrase, from a kind of party — a *Dutch lunch* — to which all the guests are expected to contribute food

like a Dutch uncle
in a scolding manner
Ⓞ Supposedly from the Dutch reputation for severe family discipline

Dutchman

I'm a Dutchman!
a catch phrase used to emphasize the fact that one does not believe something
- *If that's her husband I'm a Dutchman*

dye

dyed-in-the-wool
derogatory of firmly fixed opinions
- *He's a dyed-in-the-wool Tory*

Ⓞ Once a technical term for yarn dyed before being spun, implying that a person's attitudes etc were acquired very young — in figurative use by the 16c

dying

be dying for something
informal to want something very much, to long for something

like a dying duck *see* **duck**

E

eager

eager beaver *see* **beaver**

eagle

legal eagle *see* **legal**

under the eagle eye of someone *see* **eye**

ear

about someone's ears
all around someone, used of something falling on top of someone or attacking someone
• *The house is so dilapidated it is likely to fall about our ears at any moment*

be all ears
informal to listen with keen attention

bend someone's ear *see* **bend**

be wet behind the ears *see* **wet**

my etc **ears are burning**
someone elsewhere is talking about me
• *Your ears should have been burning this morning — the manager was singing your praises to the rest of us*
◷ The belief that one's ears grow hot when someone is talking about one is mentioned by the Roman writer Pliny

fall on deaf ears
not to be listened to

a flea in one's ear *see* **flea**

give someone a thick ear *see* **thick**

give one's ears for something/to do something
informal to wish so much for something/to do something that one would go to any lengths to achieve it

go in one ear and out the other
of advice, instructions etc: not to make any lasting impression

have someone's ear
formal to be sure that they will pay attention to what you say and will do what you ask etc

have/keep one's ear to the ground
to pay attention to, and keep oneself well informed about, all that is happening around one
◷ From a reputed Red Indian tracking technique

lend an ear
usually facetious to listen

pin back one's ears
informal to listen carefully

play something by ear
to play a piece of music without using printed music

play it by ear
informal to do what a situation requires as and when it is required, without making a fixed plan beforehand
◷ From previous idiom

prick up one's ears *see* **prick**

set someone by the ears
to cause trouble between or among two or more people
• *They got on well enough together until the question of promotion set them all by the ears*

turn a deaf ear to something
to deliberately ignore or refuse to take any notice of it

up to one's ears (in)
deeply involved in

walls have ears *see* **wall**

you can't make a silk purse out of a sow's ear *see* **silk**

early

an early bird
informal a person who gains advantage by acting more promptly than others
◷ From the proverb **the early bird**

catches the worm, meaning that those who act most promptly are the ones most likely to be successful in obtaining what they want

it's early days
it is too soon to know, have results etc

earth

bring, come back/down to earth
to (cause to) start being aware of the practical details of life after a period of dreaming, great happiness etc

cost, pay the earth
informal to cost, pay a great deal of money

go to earth
rather formal to disappear into a hiding-place
Ⓘ A hunting term used of a fox which escapes into its hole

like nothing on earth
informal extremely ill, ugly, untidy etc, usually an exaggeration
• *You look like nothing on earth in that dress; If I drink too much wine, I feel like nothing on earth the next morning*

move heaven and earth *see* **heaven**

on earth
a phrase added to a question for emphasis
• *What on earth are you doing?; Why on earth did you do that?*

pay the earth *see* **cost the earth,** above

run someone or **something to earth**
to find someone or something after a long search
Ⓘ A hunting term — 'to chase or hunt a fox into its hole'

the salt of the earth *see* **salt**

earthly

not to have an earthly
informal **1** to have not the slightest chance of success
2 to have no knowledge or information about
Ⓘ A contraction of *not to have an earthly hope* — originally a religious reference — and thus by analogy *not to have an earthly idea*

easy

as easy as falling off a log *see* **log**

as easy as pie *see* **pie**

easier said than done
more difficult to do than it sounds

easy come, easy go
a saying, referring to something, money etc, which someone gets without much effort and which they are therefore quite happy to lose, spend etc in a casual manner

easy meat *see* **meat**

easy on the eye
informal pleasant to look at
Ⓘ Originally US

go easy on someone or **something**
informal **1** not to make things difficult for someone
2 not to use too much of something

take it easy
1 not to work etc hard or energetically; to avoid using much effort
2 *usually in imperative* not to get upset, angry etc

eat

eat one's heart out *see* **heart**

eat humble pie *see* **humble**

eat like a bird *see* **bird**

eat like a horse *see* **horse**

eat someone out of house and home *see* **house**

eat one's words *see* **word**

I'll eat my hat *see* **hat**

what's eating you?
informal what is bothering you?

ebb

at a low ebb
in a poor or depressed state
Ⓘ Literally, of the tide, 'very far out'

economical

be economical with the truth *see* **truth**

edge

edge someone out
to remove or get rid of them gradually

have the edge on/over someone
to have an advantage over them
Ⓞ Originally US

on edge
uneasy, nervous or irritable

set someone's teeth on edge *see* **teeth**

take the edge off something
to reduce the strength, keenness, effect etc of something

the cutting edge
the forefront of new developments, as in the fields of science and technology
Ⓞ The cutting edge of a knife or sword is at the front in a cutting or attacking process

edgeways

get a word in edgeways *see* **word**

egg

as sure as eggs is eggs
absolutely certain, with no room for doubt
Ⓞ The origin is uncertain although it has been suggested that it is based on the mathematical statement '*x* is *x*'

a bad egg
informal a completely worthless person

egg someone on
informal to urge them on to do something
Ⓞ From the Old Norse verb *eggja* = to urge on — no connection with the noun *egg*

have egg on one's face
informal to be left looking foolish

lay an egg
informal
1 to make a mistake, usually rather an embarrassing one
2 of a theatrical performance, to fail, to flop
Ⓞ Formerly to get a duck's egg in cricket was to score 0 and so to fail to score

like the curate's egg
inconsistent or patchy, satisfactory in some ways but not in others. The phrase is sometimes extended to **good in parts — like the curate's egg**
Ⓞ From a story in the magazine *Punch* (1845) about a timid curate who was asked by a senior member of the church if his breakfast egg was all right. Too nervous to offend his host and say outright that it was bad, he replied that it was 'good in parts'

a nest-egg *see* **nest**

put all one's eggs in one basket
to depend entirely on the success of one scheme, plan etc

take eggs for money
to be put off with mere promises of payment rather than actually being paid

teach one's grandmother to suck eggs
to try to show someone more experienced than oneself how to do something they can already do
• *I've been organizing fêtes for years — don't teach your grandmother to suck eggs!*

tread on eggs
to be in a situation in which one has to proceed very cautiously and often tactfully
Ⓞ Eggs are extremely fragile

eight

a figure of eight
a pattern, movement etc in the shape of the figure 8

one over the eight
slang one drink too many

the eighth wonder of the world *see* **wonder**

elbow

elbow-grease
informal facetious hard work; energy

elbow-room
space enough for moving or doing something

give someone the elbow
informal to dismiss them, to get rid of them

more power to his elbow *see* **power**

out at elbow
formal ragged; shabby; worn out

El Dorado

El Dorado
a place where it is easy to make money, often only in theory, or in the imagination
Ⓞ This name — in Spanish 'the gilded one' — was given to a legendary 16c South American chieftain and later to his fabulously wealthy kingdom, which was believed to exist somewhere in the jungles of South and Central America

element

in one's element
in the surroundings that are most natural or pleasing to one
Ⓞ Literally, referring to the four 'elements' of medieval science — fire, earth, air and water — to one of which every creature was believed to belong by nature

elementary

elementary, my dear Watson
a catch phrase used to indicate that something, particularly some kind of problem or piece of deduction, is very simple
Ⓞ A reference to Dr Watson, assistant to the famous fictional detective, Sherlock Holmes, although it is not an actual quotation from any of the books

elephant

elephants never forget
a phrase used to indicate that someone is going to remember something, often something bad, such as an insult, an act of wrongdoing etc, for a very long time. An alternative form of the same theme is **have a memory like an elephant**
Ⓞ There is in fact no evidence to suggest that elephants have particularly good memories

a white elephant
something which is useless and a nuisance or which causes much trouble while doing little good
• *That enormous wardrobe your mother gave us has been nothing but a white elephant*
Ⓞ In Thailand, where white elephants were traditionally treated like royalty, the king was reputed to bestow one on courtiers with whom he was displeased, because the cost of its upkeep was likely to ruin them

eleventh

at the eleventh hour
at the last possible moment; only just in time
Ⓞ A Biblical reference, to the parable of the labourers in the vineyard — Matthew 20

the eleventh commandment
facetious thou shalt not be found out
Ⓞ Based on the Ten Commandments given by God to Moses on Mount Sinai, as described in the Old Testament Book of Exodus

eloquent

an eloquent silence *see* **silence**

emperor

a case of the emperor's new clothes
a situation in which people are deceived into thinking that something is the case when in fact it is not, largely because other people have also been deceived in this way and no one has the courage to point out the error
Ⓞ From the story (1835) by Hans Christian Andersen, in which tailors deceive an emperor into ordering a magnificent new suit which is supposedly not visible to unworthy people. In fact the suit is non-existent and the emperor is naked but neither he nor any of his people wish to be thought unworthy. Finally a young boy tells the truth

empty

empty vessels make most noise
a proverb, meaning that it is usually the most foolish people, and those whose views are least valuable, who are the most concerned to make their opinions known
Ⓞ Quoted by Shakespeare, *Henry V* IV, iv, but certainly older

end

a dead end *see* **dead**

at a loose end *see* **loose**

at the end of one's tether
emotionally exhausted because of worry, anger etc; having no more patience

ⓘ From a grazing animal which can only go a certain distance from the peg to which it is tethered

at the end of the day *see* **day**

at one's wits' end *see* **wit**

be the end of
not usually used seriously to cause the death of
• *That child will be the end of me!*

come to a sticky end *see* **sticky**

the end justifies the means
a proverb, meaning that if the result of an action is good, it doesn't matter whether the action itself was morally right or not

the end of the road/line
the point beyond which one can no longer continue or survive

end up
informal to end or finish in a certain way; to do something in the end
• *He said he would not go, but he ended up by going; He refused to believe her, but he ended up apologizing*

get (hold of) the wrong end of the stick *see* **stick**

keep one's end up
informal to perform one's part in something equally as well as all the others who are involved
ⓘ A cricketing term — 'not to lose one's wicket'

make (both) ends meet
to live within one's income; not to get into debt
ⓘ The French version of this phrase, *faire joindre les deux bouts de l'année*, suggests that the 'ends' are the start and finish of one's yearly income

no end (of)
very informal very much
• *I feel no end of a fool; I liked it no end*

enemy

the enemy at the door/gate
a person, event, etc that is a threat or an increasing threat

be one's own worst enemy
to be personally responsible, by reason of one's own deeds, shortcomings etc., for any misfortune that happens to one

the enemy within
an internal, rather than an external, threat, a person who is acting against the interests of the group of which he or she is a member

how goes the enemy?
what time is it?
ⓘ Popularized by appearing in Dickens's *Nicholas Nickleby*, but in fact coined by Frederic Reynolds in his play *The Dramatist* (1789)

public enemy number one
a person who is considered extremely undesirable to a particular group of people
ⓘ A term first applied to an American outlaw, John Dillinger (1903–34) by the then Attorney General, Homer Cummings

enfant

an enfant terrible
a child or young person, or a person, organization etc with new, unconventional ideas, who embarrasses older or more conventional people, organizations etc by the things he says and the attitudes he expresses
ⓘ *Les enfants terribles* was the title of a series of prints by the 19c French caricaturist Paul Gavarni

English

English as she is spoke
facetious a form of ungrammatical or unidiomatic English of the kind that might be spoken by foreigners or very uneducated people
ⓘ From the title of a Portuguese/English phrasebook edited by A W Tuer (1838–1910) and noted for its inept handling of English phraseology

enough

enough is as good as a feast *see* **feast**

enough said!
a phrase indicating that no more detail or amplification is necessary, as everyone already has a clear idea of the situation. A humorous version of this is **nuff said!**

enough to waken the dead *see* **dead**

give someone enough rope *see* **rope**

enter

enter the lists *see* **lists**

envy

be the envy of someone
to be envied by them

equal

all things being equal *see* **thing**

err

err on the side of (a quality etc)
to be guilty of a fault, or what might be seen as a fault, in order to avoid an opposite and greater fault
• *It is better to err on the side of leniency when punishing a child*

errand

a fool's errand
a useless journey

run errands
to do jobs for someone

error

trial and error *see* **trial**

essence

of the essence
formal of the greatest importance

establishment

the Establishment
Brit the people, as a group, who hold important positions in a country, society or community

eternal

the Eternal City
Rome

the eternal triangle
an emotional situation involving two women and a man or two men and a woman
Ⓛ Coined by a book reviewer in the *Daily Chronicle* in 1907

hope springs eternal *see* **hope**

even

be, keep on an even keel *see* **keel**

break even
to make neither profit nor loss

even money
a situation in which either of two possibilities is equally likely

get even with someone
informal to be revenged on them

have an even chance
to be equally likely to be successful or unsuccessful
Ⓛ A gambling term

event

be wise after the event *see* **wise**

in the event
in the end; as it happens/happened/may happen
• *In the event I did not need to go to hospital*
Ⓛ From an otherwise obsolete meaning of *event* = result

every

every man jack *see* **jack**

every now and then/again *see* **now**

every other *see* **other**

every minute counts *see* **minute**

every Tom, Dick, and/or Harry *see* **Tom**

everything

everything in the garden is lovely *see* **garden**

everything in its place and a place for everything
a proverb used to advocate the virtues of tidiness and neatness, the implication being that if everything is in the place where one would expect it to be then it is easier to find. This is a alternative version of **a place for everything and everything in its place**

evidence

turn King's/Queen's evidence
of an accomplice in a crime: to give evidence against his partner(s) with the result that his own sentence is less severe
Ⓛ *Evidence* here means 'witness(es)'

evil

the evil eye *see* **eye**

put off the evil hour
to postpone something unpleasant

ewe

a ewe lamb
usually facetious a person, project etc which is one's dearest possession
Ⓞ A Biblical reference, to the man in II Samuel 12:3 who 'had nothing save one little ewe lamb ...'

example

make an example of someone
to punish them as a warning to others

set someone an example
to act in such a good way that others will copy one's behaviour

exception

the exception proves the rule
a proverb, meaning that the fact that an exception has to be made for a particular example of something proves that there is a general rule
• *I know that what I have said does not apply to Brian, but I think in his case the exception proves the rule*
Ⓞ A legal maxim — in full *the exception proves the rule in cases not excepted*

excuse

excuse my French *see* **French**

exhibition

make an exhibition of oneself
derogatory to behave foolishly in public

expecting

be expecting
informal euphemism to be pregnant

expense

at the expense of someone or **something**
causing harm, embarrassment etc to them or it
• *She pursued her ambitions at the expense of her marriage*

explore

explore every avenue
to investigate every conceivable area that may be related to the matter in question

eye

all my eye
slang simply not true

the apple of someone's eye *see* **apple**

catch someone's eye
to make them notice one

clap/lay/set eyes on someone or **something**
informal to see them or it, especially for the first time

close one's eyes to something
to ignore something, especially something blameworthy

cry one's eyes out
informal to weep bitterly

easy on the eye *see* **easy**

the evil eye
the supposed power of causing harm by a look
• *Nothing is going right for me — I think he put the evil eye on me*

eyeball to eyeball
informal in direct confrontation, for the purpose of frank and firm discussion

an eye for an eye
a punishment exactly the same as the offence committed
Ⓞ A Biblical reference, to Exodus 21:23, often considered to sum up the stern moral code of the Old Testament

an eye-opener
informal something which reveals an unexpected fact etc

an eyesore
informal something, especially a building, that is ugly to look at

have to have eyes in the back of one's head
to be in a situation that requires one to be very observant and alert

in a twinkling of an eye *see* **twinkling**

in one's mind's eye
in one's imagination
Probably from Shakespeare — *Hamlet* I, ii, 'I see my father ... in my mind's eye, Horatio' — although the image had been used before

keep an eye on someone or **something**
1 to watch them or it closely
2 to look after them or it

keep one's beady eye on someone or **something**
informal, usually facetious to keep them or it under close observation

keep a weather eye (open) *see* **weather**

keep one's eyes peeled/skinned
to watch carefully for something

make eyes at someone
to look at them with sexual interest or admiration

the naked eye
the eye unassisted by spectacles, a telescope, a microscope etc

not to be able to take one's eyes off someone or **something**
not to be able to stop watching them or it

one in the eye (for)
informal a direct rejection or refusal for
• *The men's decision to accept the pay offer was one in the eye for the militants who had wanted them to strike*

open someone's eyes to something
to make them see or understand something of which they were not previously aware

a private eye *see* **private**

pull the wool over someone's eyes *see* **wool**

see eye to eye
usually in negative to be in agreement
• *We've never seen eye to eye about this matter*
Ⓘ From an interpretation of an obscure phrase in the Bible — Isaiah 52:8 — which the New English Bible retranslates as 'see with their own eyes'

see with half an eye
to see without difficulty

a sight for sore eyes *see* **sight**

a smack in the eye *see* **smack**

there's more to something than meets the eye
it is more complicated, or better, than it appears

turn a blind eye to something
to pretend not to see or notice it

under the eagle eye of someone
under the keen observation of someone
Ⓘ Eagles are thought to have keen vision

up to one's eyes in something
deeply involved in it

with an eye to something
with something as an aim

with an eye to the main chance *see* **chance**

with one's eyes open
with full awareness of what one is doing

eyelid

not to bat an eyelid
to appear to feel no surprise, distress etc

F

face

at face value
as being as valuable etc as it appears
• *You must take this offer at face value*
Ⓞ Literally, as being worth the value printed on the face of a coin, bank-note, stamp etc

be staring someone in the face
informal to be very obvious or easy for them to see

cut off one's nose to spite one's face *see* **nose**

face someone down
to assert one's superiority over them merely by looking stern
• *He was always able to face down people who interrupted him when he was making a speech*

his etc **face fell**
he looked suddenly disappointed

the face that launched a thousand ships
often ironical a person of extraordinary beauty
Ⓞ A reference to Christopher Marlowe's description of Helen of Troy, the cause of the Trojan War, in his play *Doctor Faustus* (1588) — 'Was this the face that launched a thousand ships and burnt the topless towers of Ilium?'

face the music *see* **music**

face to face
both or all people concerned actually being present
• *They finally met face to face to discuss the problem*

face up to something
to meet or accept it boldly

fly in the face of something
to oppose or defy it; to treat it with contempt
Ⓞ Originally used of a dog attacking a person

grind the face(s) of someone
to govern them cruelly, by imposing harsh taxation etc
Ⓞ A Biblical reference, to Isaiah 3:15

have a face like a fiddle *see* **fiddle**

have a long face
to look unhappy or disapproving

in the face of something
in spite of having to deal with it
• *She succeeded in the face of great difficulties*
Ⓞ Literally, this phrase originally meant 'in the presence of'

laugh on the other side of one's face *see* **laugh**

let's face it
if one is to be honest
• *Let's face it, none of us like him much*

lose face
to suffer a loss of respect or reputation
Ⓞ This phrase, and **save face** *below*, were first used by English-speaking residents in China. **Lose face** is a translation of the Chinese *tiu lien*

make/pull a face
to twist one's face into strange expressions
• *That child is making faces at me*

on the face of it
as it appears at first glance, usually deceptively

put a good face on it
to give the appearance of being satisfied etc with something when actually one is not

save one's/someone's face
to prevent oneself/someone else from appearing stupid or wrong *see* **lose face,** *above*

set one's face against something
to oppose it very determinedly
◷ A Hebrew idiom from the Bible, Leviticus 20:3

show one's face
usually in negative to be sufficiently confident or unashamed to be able to go to a particular place
• *I'll never be able to show my face in there again*

a slap in the face *see* **slap**

to someone's face
while someone is present
• *You wouldn't be brave enough to say that to his face!*

facelift

give something a facelift
to carry out improvements intended to make something, eg a building, look better
◷ From *facelifting*, an operating to raise the skin of the lower face, and thus eliminate wrinkles

fact

the facts of life *see* **life**

the hard facts *see* **hard**

fag

a/the fag-end
informal the very end of something
• *He only heard the fag-end of the conversation*
◷ Originally a term for the last section of a piece of cloth, often woven with odd remnants of yarn

fail

words fail me *see* **word**

faint

faint heart never won fair lady
a proverb, meaning that it is necessary to be bold to achieve what one desires

not to have the faintest
informal not to know at all
◷ A contraction of **not to have the faintest idea**

fair

a fair crack of the whip *see* **crack**

all the fun of the fair *see* **fun**

all is fair in love and war
a saying indicating that in certain situations, especially those involving a spirit of competition, any tactic or strategy is permissible

bid fair to *see* **bid**

by fair means or foul
in any possible way, just or unjust

fair and square
straight or directly
• *He hit him fair and square on the chin*

fair do's/fair's fair
informal an expression appealing for, or agreeing to, fair play, complete honesty etc
• *Come on, fair do's — I babysat for you; now it's your turn to babysit for me; Fair's fair — it's your turn to do the washing-up*

fair game
something which it is quite reasonable and permissible to attack, laugh at etc
◷ A hunting term

fair play
honest treatment; an absence of cheating, biased actions etc

the fair sex
usually facetious women

in a fair way to
likely to succeed in
• *He's in a fair way to becoming a millionaire*

play fair *see* **play**

fairweather

fairweather friends
people who are only friendly to one so long as everything is going well for one

faith

in (all) good faith
sincerely

fall

fall about
informal to collapse with laughter
• *When I told them the joke they fell about laughing*

fall back on something or **someone**
informal to use it or them, or to go to it or them for help, after everything else has been tried

fall behind with something
to become late in (regular payment, letter-writing etc)

fall between two stools *see* **stool**

fall by the wayside *see* **wayside**

fall down on something
informal to fail in it

fall flat
informal especially of jokes etc, to fail completely or to have no effect

fall for something or **someone**
informal
1 to be deceived by something
2 to fall in love with someone

fall foul of *see* **foul**

fall from grace *see* **grace**

fall in
to join a group of people doing something
Ⓘ Literally, of soldiers, to take places in ranks

fall into place *see* **place**

fall in with someone or **something**
1 to join with someone for company
2 to agree with a plan, idea etc

fall off
to become smaller in number or amount

fall off a lorry *see* **lorry**

fall on something
to begin to do something with something, especially to eat it, very eagerly or vigorously
Ⓘ Literally, to attack

fall on deaf ears *see* **ear**

fall on one's feet *see* **feet**

fall out
to quarrel

fall over oneself
informal to be very busy and put oneself to a great deal of trouble to do something

fall short
often with **of**, to be not enough or not good enough etc

fall through
of plans etc, to fail or come to nothing

fall to
old to begin enthusiastically, especially eating

pride goes before a fall *see* **pride**

riding for a fall *see* **riding**

false

a false alarm
a warning of something which does not in fact happen

false pretences
acts or behaviour intended to deceive people
• *He got the money by/on/under false pretences*
Ⓘ A legal term

a false start
a beginning in some activity which is unsuccessful and so has to be repeated
Ⓘ Literally, a start to a race that has to be repeated, eg because one of the runners has left the starting-point before the correct signal has been given

a false step
a mistake

sail under false colours
to pretend to be different in character, attitudes, beliefs, status, etc, than is actually the case
Ⓘ A reference to a ship flying a flag other than its own, as pirate ships sometimes did

familiarity

familiarity breeds contempt
a proverb, meaning that one ceases to be fully aware of and to appreciate the qualities, beauty, goodness, danger etc, of something one knows very well

family

a family tree
a plan showing a person's ancestors and sometimes his descendants

in the family way
euphemism pregnant

run in the family
to be a feature found in many members of a particular family

famous

famous last words *see* **last[1]**

fancy

fancy one's chances *see* **chance**

fancy oneself
informal to think of oneself as being, or as likely to be, good, especially at a particular thing
• *She always fancied herself as an actress*

fancy free
not in love with anyone
Ⓞ Probably from Shakespeare, *A Midsummer Night's Dream* II, i

someone's fancy man/woman
derogatory slang someone's male/female lover

a little of what you fancy *see* **little**

take a fancy to someone or **something**
to become fond of them or it, often suddenly or unexpectedly

take someone's fancy
to be liked or wanted by them

tickle someone's fancy *see* **tickle**

Fanny

sweet Fanny Adams
slang absolutely nothing at all
Ⓞ Originally servicemen's slang

far

far and away
by a very great amount

far be it from me
usually ironic I have no right or desire to do something
• *Far be it from me to tell you how to do your job, but isn't that a silly thing to do?*

a far cry from *see* **cry**

far from the madding crowd *see* **crowd**

go far
to be extremely successful
• *The teachers all said that he would go far*

go too far
to do or say something that goes beyond the limits of what is acceptable or allowed

so far, so good
the operation has been successful up to now

fashion

after a fashion
in a way, but not very well
• *He can speak French after a fashion*

fast

the fast lane
a high-pressure, competitive way of life
Ⓞ A reference to the fastest lane of a motorway which is used to overtake other vehicles

play fast and loose
informal to do what one likes with; to act irresponsibly with
Ⓞ From the name of an old trick in which one player made loops in a piece of string which the other player tried to secure by thrusting a stick through them — however this was never possible because of the way the loops were constructed

pull a fast one on someone
informal to deceive them
Ⓞ Literally, to bowl a fast ball in cricket

stand fast *see* **stand**

fat

chew the fat
slang to have a chat or discussion

fat chance
informal not at all likely

the fat is in the fire
trouble can be expected

a fat lot of
slang not much
• *It's a fat lot of use coming round to see me when I'm out at work!*

kill the fatted calf
to have a great celebration to welcome someone, especially someone whom one has not seen for a long time
Ⓞ A Biblical reference, to the parable of the Prodigal Son, Luke 15

live off the fat of the land
often derogatory to live in a very luxurious manner
Ⓞ A Biblical reference, to Genesis 45:18

until the fat lady sings
until the very end
• *We won't know the result of the match until the fat lady sings*
Ⓞ A reference to opera

fate

a fate worse than death
informal: often facetious a dreadful happening
Ⓒ Originally coined as a euphemism for seduction or rape

seal someone's fate
to ensure that something, usually something unpleasant, happens to them in the future
• *He sealed his fate when he had a quarrel with the boss — he got the sack*

tempt fate
to act in such a way that seems likely to bring misfortune or disaster on oneself

father

the father and mother of
a very extreme, especially bad, example of
• *There'll be the father and mother of a row if your wife sees you like that!*

be gathered to one's fathers
arch or facetious to die
Ⓒ A Hebrew idiom from the Bible, Judges 2:10

be old enough to be someone's father *see* **old**

the child is the father of the man *see* **child**

like father, like son
a saying, meaning that someone is like his father in some way

fault

find fault with someone
to criticize or scold them, especially unreasonably, for something they have done

to a fault
formal excessively; to too great an extent

favour

curry favour with *see* **curry**

feast

feast or famine, feast or fast
a saying describing a situation in which there is sometimes an overabundance and sometimes a shortage or lack

enough is as good as a feast
a proverb, meaning that as long as people have the basic requirements to live their daily lives, then they do not require any more

fear

no fear
informal not likely; often a refusal to agree or comply

put the fear of death/God into someone
informal to terrify them

strike fear into someone *see* **strike**

there is not much fear of something
it is not likely that it will happen

feather

as light as a feather
extremely light in weight or texture

a feather in one's cap
something one can be proud of

feather one's (own) nest
derogatory to gain money for oneself or to make oneself rich while serving others in a position of trust

fine feathers make fine birds
a proverb, meaning that people often appear attractive etc because they are expensively dressed

make the feathers fly
to attack suddenly with great effect
Ⓒ A reference to an animal attacking poultry

ruffle someone's feathers
to upset, distress or annoy someone slightly

show the white feather
to show signs of cowardice
Ⓒ A white feather in the tail was a sign of inferior breeding in a fighting-cock

you could have knocked me down with a feather
informal I was astonished

featherbed

featherbed someone
to make things easy for them
• *He was featherbedded in his early life by his father's immense wealth*

fed

fed up/fed to the back teeth
informal tired; bored and annoyed

feel

feel at home *see* **home**

feel free (to)
you may do what you wish
• *Feel free to ask if you need any help*

feel in one's bones *see* **bone**

feel small *see* **small**

feel the draught *see* **draught**

feel the pinch *see* **pinch**

get the feel of something
informal to become accustomed to it

feet

be/sit at someone's feet
to admire them greatly and be greatly influenced by them

be rushed off one's feet
to be extremely busy

drag one's feet
to deliberately delay or take a long time to do something

fall/land on one's feet
to have some unexpected good luck, especially after or because of something bad or unpleasant

find one's feet
to become able to cope with a new situation

get cold feet *see* **cold**

have feet of clay
to have a weakness which was previously unsuspected

have both feet/have (both) one's feet on the ground
to act always with good sense

have two left feet *see* **left**

the patter of tiny feet *see* **patter**

put one's feet up
to take a rest by lying down or sitting with one's feet supported on something

sit at someone's feet *see* **be at someone's feet**

stand on one's own (two) feet
to manage one's own affairs without help

sweep someone off his etc **feet**
to affect them with strong emotion or enthusiasm
• *She was swept off her feet by a dark, handsome stranger*

fell

at one fell swoop *see* **swoop**

fence

mend fences
to put things right after a dispute or disagreement
Ⓘ From neighbours mending broken fences that might give rise to disagreement

rush one's fences
to act in too much of a hurry, without enough care
Ⓘ A horse-riding idiom

sit on the fence
to appear to remain neutral and not take sides in a dispute etc
Ⓘ An early 19c US idiom, implying that one is undecided on which side of the fence to come down

fetch

fetch and carry
to go back and forward getting things which are needed

fetch up
informal to come finally to a halt in a particular place
• *She got on an express train by mistake and fetched up in Manchester*
Ⓘ A nautical term

fettle

in fine/good fettle
extremely healthy

fiddle

fiddle while Rome burns
to occupy oneself with trivial things when there are extremely important things that require one's attention
Ⓘ A reference to a legend of ancient Rome according to which the Emperor Nero played his lyre while watching the burning of Rome from a tower

fit as a fiddle
extremely fit

have a face like a fiddle
not to look cheerful or happy

on the fiddle
derogatory slang making money dishonestly
• *He's always on the fiddle*

play second fiddle to someone *see* **second**

field

have a field day
usually facetious to spend time in great activity or with great success
Ⓞ A *field day* was literally a military review, or a series of large-scale field exercises for the army

fresh fields and pastures new *see* **fresh**

fifth

a fifth-columnist
one of a group of people in a town, country etc who try to help the people with whom that town or country is at war
Ⓞ In 1936, during the Spanish Civil War, General Mola encircled Madrid with four columns of troops. He claimed, however, that he could count on the help of *la quinta columna* — 'the fifth column' — within the city

a fifth wheel *see* **wheel**

fig

not to give a fig for something
old not to care about it at all

fight

fight a losing battle
to struggle against something with little or no chance of success

fight it out
to argue until a decisive end is reached

fight like Kilkenny cats *see* **Kilkenny**

fight shy of something
to avoid it
Ⓞ Apparently a term from prize-fighting

put up a good fight
to fight or compete well or bravely

fighting

a fighting chance
a chance of success if a great effort is made

fighting fit
in very good physical condition

live like fighting-cocks
to have the best of food and drink
Ⓞ Fighting-cocks were very carefully looked after and well fed

figment

a figment of one's imagination
formal something one has imagined and which has no reality

figure

a figure of eight *see* **eight**

that figures
slang this is what I would expect
• *He has gone away? That figures — he always disappears without warning*
Ⓞ Originally US

file

in Indian/single file
moving along singly, one behind the other
Ⓞ From the usual method of travel of Native Americans

the rank and file *see* **rank**

fill

fill in (for someone)
informal to do someone's job temporarily

fill someone in
informal to give them all the necessary information

fill out
to become rounder or fatter

find

find fault with someone *see* **fault**

find one's feet *see* **feet**

find it in one's heart *see* **heart**

find one's/its (own) level *see* **level**

finder

finders keepers
informal a saying, especially used by children, meaning that a person who finds something is entitled to keep it

fine

cut it fine
informal to allow barely enough time, money etc for something that must be done
• *If you want to catch the noon train, you're cutting it a bit fine*

fine and dandy
informal absolutely fine

fine feathers make fine birds *see* **feather**

fine words butter no parsnips *see* **word**

go through something with a fine-tooth(ed) comb
to search, or look at something very carefully
Ⓘ From the standard method of finding and removing lice and fleas

not to put too fine a point on it
to speak bluntly and honestly

finger

be all fingers and thumbs, my etc **fingers are all thumbs**
informal to be, I am, very awkward and clumsy for the moment in handling or holding things

cross one's fingers
to hope for good luck
Ⓘ From an old superstition

get one's fingers burnt/burn one's fingers
to suffer because one has interfered, taken part in buying and selling of shares etc

get/pull one's/the finger out
rather vulgar to begin working, doing one's job thoroughly or efficiently etc
Ⓘ RAF slang

have a finger in the pie/in every pie
informal, often derogatory
1 to have an interest or share in a plan, business etc or in several plans, businesses etc
2 to be involved in everything that happens

have something at one's fingertips
to know all the details of a subject thoroughly

have green fingers *see* **green**

keep one's finger on the pulse *see* **pulse**

let something slip through one's fingers
to lose an advantage etc which one had the chance of getting for oneself

the moving finger
a phrase used to comment on the inexorability of fate or on the impossibility of undoing the past
Ⓘ From the phrase **the moving finger writes and having writ moves on,** a quotation from Edward Fitzgerald's translation of the *Rubaiyat of Omar Khayyam* (1879)

not to lift a finger
informal to do nothing
• *She did not lift a finger to prevent his arrest*

point the finger at someone
to call attention to them by blaming them for something

put one's finger on something
to point it out or describe it exactly; to identify it

to one's fingertips
completely or perfectly
• *She is an artist to her fingertips*

twist someone round one's little finger
to make someone act exactly as one wants

work one's fingers to the bone
to work extremely hard
Ⓘ Literally, to wear the flesh off one's fingers by working

finishing

the finishing touches
the final details which complete a work of art etc

fire

add fuel to the fire *see* **fuel**

the fat is in the fire *see* **fat**

fire away
informal to begin doing something; to go ahead

a firebrand
a person who causes political or social trouble or excitement
Ⓘ Literally, 'a piece of burning wood'

firing on all cylinders *see* **cylinder**

hang fire
to delay or to be delayed
Ⓘ A term applied to flintlock guns in which, because of the firing mechanism, there was sometimes a delay between the pulling of the trigger and the gun firing

have several irons in the fire *see* **iron**

like a house on fire *see* **house**

open fire on someone or **something**
to begin shooting at them or it

out of the frying-pan into the fire *see* **frying-pan**

play with fire
to do something dangerous or risky

there's no smoke without fire *see* **smoke**

under fire
being criticized or blamed
Ⓒ Literally, being shot at

first

at first hand
obtained etc directly

first and foremost
formal first of all; before anything else

(in) the first flush of *see* **flush**

first refusal *see* **refusal**

first thing
before doing anything else

get to/make first base *see* **base**

in the first place *see* **place**

not to know the first thing about something
informal to know nothing about it

of the first magnitude
of the highest quality
Ⓒ A reference to the method of categorizing stars according to magnitude or brightness

of the first water
formal of the highest quality
Ⓒ A technical term for a completely colourless diamond; in the 18c diamonds were graded into three 'waters'. The idiom may derive originally from Arabic

fish

a big fish
slang an important or leading person
Ⓒ From the saying **a big fish in a small pond**

drink like a fish
derogatory to drink too much alcohol

fish in troubled waters
derogatory to take advantage of a disturbance, difficulties, problems etc to obtain benefits for oneself

have other fish to fry
to have something else to do or to attend to and therefore unable to devote all one's attention to the subject being discussed

like a fish out of water
in an uncomfortable or unaccustomed situation; ill at ease

make fish of one and flesh of another
formal to treat one thing unfairly as being different from another

neither fish nor flesh nor good red herring
neither one thing nor another

a pretty kettle of fish *see* **kettle**

smell/be a bit fishy
to give grounds for suspicion
Ⓒ Fish that is not fresh smells strongly

a queer fish
informal derogatory a person with odd habits, or a person whose personality one does not understand

there's plenty more fish in the sea
a saying, used when an opportunity of some sort has been lost, meaning that more opportunities of the same kind can be expected to arise

fist

hand over fist *see* **hand**

fit

by fits and starts
irregularly; often stopping and starting again

fit as a fiddle *see* **fiddle**

fit like a glove *see* **glove**

have/throw a fit
informal to behave wildly because of extreme feelings, especially of anger, fear or reluctance, usually an exaggeration

see/think fit
usually with **to** to consider that some action is right, suitable etc
• *I won't tell you what to do — you may do as you see fit (to do)*

five

a bunch of fives
old slang a clenched fist when used to strike someone etc

fix

fix on something
informal to decide or choose it

fix someone up with something
informal to provide it for them

flag

a flag of convenience
a foreign flag under which ships are registered in order to avoid taxes etc at home

hang/put out the flags
to celebrate something or mark something as being a special occasion
Ⓛ Flags are hung out on certain celebratory occasions

show the flag
to appear at a gathering etc in order to make sure that the firm, country etc to which one belongs is not forgotten by others; to be loyal and supportive

flagpole

run it up the flagpole
to put forward an idea or plan in order to gauge reactions to it

flake

flake out
informal to collapse from tiredness or illness

flame

fan the flames
to make an angry or difficult situation worse

an old flame *see* **old**

shoot down in flames *see* **shoot**

flash

a flash in the pan
a sudden brief success which is not likely to happen again
Ⓛ In a flintlock gun the spark from the flint ignited a pinch of gunpowder in the priming pan, from which the flash travelled to the main charge in the barrel. If this then failed to go off, only 'a flash in the pan' resulted

flat

fall flat *see* **fall**

flat out
informal as fast, energetically etc as possible
• *He ran flat out down the road; She worked flat out to get it finished*

in a flat spin
slang in a state of confused excitement
Ⓛ An aviation term, probably from the 1st World War. A plane descending in circles while remaining nearly horizontal — 'flat' — quickly went out of control

that's flat
I am telling you definitely

flavour

flavour of the month
a person or thing that is particularly liked by someone at the moment
Ⓛ From the practice of some ice cream firms of specializing in a particular flavour in a particular month

flea

a flea in one's ear
often facetious a sharp scolding

a flea market
informal a shop etc selling second-hand goods, originally especially clothes
Ⓛ From the famous *Marché aux Puces* in Paris

a flea-pit
derogatory a public building, especially a cinema or theatre, of an inferior kind, which is or appears to be infested with fleas etc

flesh

flesh and blood
1 someone's relations; family
• *She is my own flesh and blood*
2 human nature
• *It is more than flesh and blood can tolerate*

the flesh-pots
luxurious living
Ⓛ A Biblical reference, to Exodus 16:3

get/have one's pound of flesh *see* **pound**

in the flesh
in person, in real life, not in a photograph or painting

make fish of one and flesh of another *see* **fish**

make someone's flesh creep
to cause them to feel as if horrible creatures are crawling all over them; to horrify them

neither fish nor flesh nor good red herring *see* **fish**

the spirit is willing but the flesh is weak *see* **spirit**

a thorn in someone's flesh *see* **thorn**

flier

a high-flier *see* **high**

flight

a flight of fancy
usually facetious an example of rather too free a use of the imagination

top-flight
formal of the highest class

fling

have a final fling
to enjoy a last period of gaiety or extravagance before a change in one's circumstances etc

flip

flip one's lid *see* **lid**

flog

flog a dead horse *see* **horse**

flog something to death *see* **death**

flood

before the Flood
facetious a very long time ago
• *Some of her ideas date from before the Flood*
Ⓞ A reference to the Great Flood in the Bible, Genesis 7:9

floor

hold the floor
to be the dominant person at a meeting, party etc because one talks a great deal
Ⓞ *The floor* here is the main area of a Parliamentary chamber, where the delegates sit

take the floor
rather formal
1 to rise to speak to a group of people
2 to begin to dance

wipe the floor with someone
to defeat them completely

flotsam

flotsam and jetsam
1 odds and ends of little use or value that remain
2 vagrants
Ⓞ *Flotsam* refers to goods lost by shipwreck and found floating in the sea, while *jetsam* refers to things that are thrown overboard and washed to shore

flower

the flower of
formal the best of

flush

a busted flush
slang something that has to be abandoned as a failure
Ⓞ Literally, in poker, a sequence of cards which the player is unable to complete in time to win the hand

(in) the first flush of something
in the early stages of something when a person is feeling fresh, strong, enthusiastic etc

flutter

flutter the dovecotes *see* **dovecote**

fly

drop like flies
to collapse rapidly in quick succession

fly a kite *see* **kite**

fly-by-night
derogatory not able to be trusted, especially used of someone who is likely to disappear without notice

fly in the face of *see* **face**

a fly in the ointment
something that spoils something or makes something less perfect, less valuable etc
Ⓞ Possibly a Biblical reference, to Ecclesiastes 10:1, 'Dead flies cause ... ointment ... to send forth a stinking savour'

fly off the handle *see* **handle**

fly the coop
informal to leave home
Ⓛ A coop is where hens and chickens are kept

let (something) fly (at someone or **something)**
to throw, shoot or send out (something) violently; to strike at or speak sharply to (someone)
• *He aimed carefully and let fly an arrow at the target; She let fly at him for being late*

pigs might fly *see* **pig**

there are no flies on someone
informal there is no lack of intelligence and cunning in them

time flies *see* **time**

I etc **would like to be a fly on the wall**
I would like to be present at a meeting, conversation etc without being seen so that I could see and hear what happens without taking part

he etc **wouldn't hurt a fly**
he is very gentle

flying

be flying high
to be going through a period of great success or power

a flying visit
a very short, often unexpected, visit

get off to a flying start
to have a very successful beginning
Ⓛ Literally, a flying start is a beginning to a race where all the competitors are already moving

send someone or **something flying**
informal to hit or knock someone or something so that they fall down or fall backward

with flying colours *see* **colour**

foam

foam at the mouth
informal to be extremely angry

foggiest

not to have the foggiest (idea)
informal to have no knowledge or ideas about something

follow

follow in someone's footsteps *see* **footstep**

follow one's nose *see* **nose**

follow suit
formal to do just as someone else has done
Ⓛ Literally, in card games, 'to play a card of the same suit as the one played by the last player'

food

food for thought
something which should be considered carefully
• *My conversation with the priest gave me a great deal of food for thought*

fool

a fool and his money are soon parted
a proverb emphasizing the folly of spending money too lavishly

a fool's errand *see* **errand**

a fool's paradise
a happy state caused by something which is deceptive or not to be trusted

fools rush in where angels fear to tread
a proverb, meaning that people with little knowledge, experience or tact often try to tackle difficult or sensitive situations which a more experienced or sensitive person would avoid

make a fool of someone
to make them appear ridiculous or stupid

make a fool of oneself
to act in such a way that people consider one ridiculous or stupid

more fool you *see* **more**

nobody's fool
a sensible person
• *He thinks she's taken in by his lies, but she's nobody's fool*

play the fool
not informal to act in a foolish manner, especially with the intention of amusing other people

suffer fools gladly *see* **suffer**

foot

the boot is on the other foot *see* **boot**[1]

get off on the wrong foot
to make a bad beginning
• *She got off on the wrong foot by being late for her interview*
Ⓣ A reference to marching out of step

have a foot in the door
to have completed the first stage towards achieving a usually difficult aim

have one foot in the grave
facetious informal to be not far from death, especially because of being old, usually an exaggeration

not to put a foot wrong
not to make a mistake of any kind

put one's best foot forward
to make the best attempt possible

put one's foot down
not formal to be firm about something

put one's foot in it
informal to do or say something stupid

set foot in (somewhere)
to arrive at or on (somewhere)

footstep

follow in someone's footsteps
to do the same as someone has done before one

forbidden

forbidden fruit *see* **fruit**

force

force someone's hand *see* **hand**

from force of habit *see* **habit**

fore

to the fore
formal in the front; easily seen; prominent
• *He has recently come to the fore in local politics*
Ⓣ Originally a Scots/Irish expression

forewarned is forearmed
a proverb emphasizing that advance knowledge or information about something enables one to prepare for it adequately

fork

fork (something) out
informal to pay, usually unwillingly; to hand over (usually money)
• *I'll have to fork out the cost of the meal*

speak with a forked tongue
facetious to tell lies; to attempt to deceive others
Ⓣ An idiom reputedly used by Native Americans

form

be good, bad form
formal according to or not according to custom
• *It's bad form to laugh at a funeral*

be in/on good form
not formal to be in a good mood

fort

hold the fort
to take temporary charge (of a job, task etc)
Ⓣ A military image from a once-popular Moody & Sankey hymn

forty

forty winks
informal a short sleep

forward

look forward to something
to wait with pleasure for something which is going to happen

foul

fall foul of someone or **something**
formal to get into a position where someone or something is hostile to or angry with one
Ⓣ A nautical term used of a ship which becomes entangled with another ship

foul one's nest *see* **nest**

foul play
formal a criminal act, especially involving murder
Ⓣ A long-established legal term

four

on all fours
informal on hands and knees

fox

crazy like a fox
informal considered to be mad or very foolish but actually very clever in a cunning way
① The fox is traditionally associated with cunning

free

as free as a bird *see* **bird**

a free-for-all
usually derogatory an argument, discussion etc in which everybody is allowed to express their opinions without control

free, gratis and for nothing
informal a phrase meaning absolutely free, without payment being necessary
① All three elements of the expression mean 'free'

a free hand
freedom to do whatever one likes

make free with someone or **something**
1 *derogatory often facetious* to behave in too friendly and informal a way towards someone
2 to eat or drink large quantities of (usually something which belongs to someone else)

make so free as to
rather formal to be bold enough to

no such thing as a free lunch
a proverb that indicates that one should always be suspicious of being offered something for which one does not appear to have to do anything

scot-free *see* **scot**

with a free hand
generously or liberally

French

excuse/pardon my French
informal excuse my swearing

take French leave
to be absent or on holiday, especially from work or military duty, without permission
① From the 18c French custom of leaving a party without saying goodbye to the host or hostess

fresh

as fresh as a daisy *see* **daisy**

fresh blood *see* **blood**

fresh fields and pastures new
new places or new activities
① A misquotation from *Lycidas* by John Milton — 'fresh woods and pastures new'

Freud

a Freudian slip
a mistake, especially the use of the wrong word etc while speaking, that is supposed to indicate an unconscious thought
① From the theories of the psychologist Sigmund Freud

Friday

a Man Friday *see* **man**

friend

fairweather friends *see* **fairweather**

a friend in need is a friend indeed
a proverb, meaning that someone who helps out when one is in trouble is really worthy of the name friend

have a friend at court
formal to have a friend in a position where his influence is likely to be useful to one

friendship

platonic friendship *see* **platonic**

frighten

frighten someone out of his etc **wits** *see* **wit**

fro

to and fro *see* **to**

frog

have a frog in one's throat
to be hoarse

front

the front of the house
in a theatre, all the activities such as selling tickets and programmes which involve dealing directly with the audience

fruit

bear fruit *see* **bear**[1]

forbidden fruit
a source of illicit pleasure
① From the biblical story of Adam and

Eve in which Eve caused Adam and herself to be expelled from the Garden of Eden because she ate the forbidden fruit of the tree of Knowledge

Dead Sea fruit
something that is expected to be of great value or worth but turns out not to be so
Ⓞ A reference to the apple of Sodon, which was thought to have grown on trees on the shores of the Dead Sea and which was beautiful in appearance but became like ashes when touched or tasted

fry

have other fish to fry *see* **fish**

small fry
derogatory unimportant people or things

frying-pan

out of the frying-pan into the fire
a saying, meaning that someone has got out of a difficult or dangerous situation only to find themselves in a worse one

fuel

add fuel to the fire
to make an angry person angrier, an argument more heated etc

full

at full blast *see* **blast**

at full pelt *see* **pelt**

at full stretch *see* **stretch**

at full tilt *see* **tilt**

be full of oneself
derogatory informal to have a good opinion of oneself; to be conceited

come full circle *see* **circle**

come to a full stop *see* **stop**

full steam ahead *see* **steam**

full up
completely filled

in full
formal completely
• *Write your name in full; He paid his bill in full*

in full cry *see* **cry**

in full swing *see* **swing**

to the full
as much as possible; completely
• *She enjoys life to the full*

fullness

in the fullness of time
formal or literary when the proper time has arrived; eventually
Ⓞ An idiom from the Bible, Galatians 4:4

fun

all the fun of the fair
often facetious all the amusements etc suitable to the occasion

fun and games
1 a lively time, an enjoyable time
2 *ironical* trouble
• *There will be fun and games when he sees the damage to his car*

like fun
1 *slang facetious* very quickly, hard or strongly
• *We were all working like fun to get it finished*
2 not at all
• *'I think you should go.' 'Like fun I will.'*

make fun of someone
to laugh at them usually unkindly

poke fun at someone *see* **poke**

funeral

that's my etc **funeral**
often in negative that is something for me in particular to worry about

funk

in a blue funk
slang in a state of terror or extreme fear
Ⓞ Apparently originally Oxford University slang

funny

funny business
informal tricks or deceptions etc
• *The hijackers told the pilot that if he tried any funny business they would shoot him*
Ⓞ Originally theatrical slang for comic action performed by a clown etc

funny money
money which is either counterfeit or has come from a doubtful source

funny ha-ha
'funny' meaning 'amusing' as opposed to **funny peculiar**

funny peculiar
'funny' meaning 'queer' or 'odd' as opposed to **funny ha-ha**

fur

the fur was flying
a fight or serious argument was taking place
ⓘ From fights between animals

furniture

be part of the furniture
to be taken no notice of as if one were just part of the usual background
• *The boss treats his secretary as though she is part of the furniture*

furrow

plough a lonely furrow
to have to work alone or to have to get on with one's life alone
ⓘ From ploughing furrows in a field where crops are to be grown

fury

like fury
informal with great effort, enthusiasm etc

fuss

make a fuss
informal to complain

make a fuss of someone
informal to pay a lot of attention to them

G

gab

the gift of the gab
informal derogatory the ability to speak fluently and articulately

gaff

blow the gaff
slang to tell something secret to someone

gain

gain ground *see* **ground**

gain time *see* **time**

nothing ventured, nothing gained *see* **nothing**

gallery

play to the gallery
to try to become popular by doing, saying etc what would appeal to the less educated, less sophisticated section of the population, a group etc
Ⓛ A theatrical expression. The cheapest seats in a theatre are in the gallery

game

fair game *see* **fair**

the game is not worth the candle *see* **candle**

the game is up
the plan or trick has failed or has been found out

game, set and match to someone
someone has won a decisive victory of some kind
Ⓛ A reference to the system of scoring in lawn tennis

give the game away *see* **give**

a mug's game *see* **mug**

the name of the game *see* **name**

play a losing game *see* **losing**

play the game
to act fairly and honestly

two can play at that game
a phrase used to someone who has just done something offensive, deceptive, dishonest, etc to the speaker indicating that he or she will use such tactics in return

gap

the credibility gap *see* **credibility**

the generation gap *see* **generation**

garbage

garbage in, garbage out
a catch phrase indicating that the quality of what one gets out of anything is dependent on the quality of what one puts in to it
Ⓛ Originally applied to computer systems

garden

bear garden *see* **bear[2]**

everything in the garden is lovely
a phrase indicating that things are going very well and everything is absolutely fine

lead someone up the garden path
to mislead them or cause them to take a wrong decision, direction etc in a very gradual and not an obvious manner

gasp

at one's last gasp
just about to collapse, die, give up etc
Ⓛ A Biblical reference, to II Maccabees 2:32 in the Apocrypha

gauntlet

run the gauntlet (of)
to suffer or be exposed to criticism, blame, danger etc (of)
Ⓛ *Running the 'gatlopp'* was a Swedish military punishment in which the culprit

had to run between two lines of men with whips who struck him as he passed. The phrase came into English during the Thirty Years War, about 1640, and *gatlopp* was soon replaced by a word more familiar to English speakers

throw down the gauntlet
to make a challenge
• *He threw down the gauntlet by calling his opponent a liar*
⌚ From the traditional method of challenging an opponent to fight a duel

gay

a gay Lothario *see* **Lothario**

generation

the generation gap
the difference in attitudes, lifestyles, etc that exists between one generation and the next and which tends to give rise to lack of understanding and criticism

gentle

the gentle sex
often facetious women

gentleman

a gentleman's agreement
an unwritten agreement that is assumed to be binding, since both parties are regarded as being people of honour who will keep their word

get

get away from it all
informal to go away somewhere, or have a holiday somewhere, where one does not need to think about one's job, one's family, one's problems etc

get off with someone
slang to form a close, often sexual, relationship with them, eg at a dance, party

get set *see* **set**

tell someone where to get off/where he etc **gets off**
Brit informal to tell them that their bad, arrogant etc behaviour will not be tolerated

getting

be getting on for
informal to be close to a particular age, time etc

ghost

give up the ghost
formal or facetious to die, cease to work etc
⌚ An idiom from the Bible, Acts 7:23

not to have the ghost of a chance
informal to have no chance of success at all

gift

the gift of the gab *see* **gab**

a Greek gift *see* **Greek**

look a gift horse in the mouth
to criticize something which has been given to one
⌚ Looking at a horse's teeth is the standard way of telling its age, and thus its value

gild

gild the lily *see* **lily**

gilt

take the gilt off the gingerbread
to spoil the attractiveness of a plan, situation etc
⌚ Up to the middle of the 19c, gingerbread was often sold baked in fancy shapes and decorated with gold leaf

give

give something a miss *see* **miss**

give and take
a willingness to grant or allow a person etc something in return for being granted something oneself
• *There must be some give and take in discussions between trade unions and management*

give someone a piece of one's mind *see* **mind**

give as good as one gets *see* **good**

give something away
to cause or allow information, one's plans etc to become known, usually accidentally

give someone hell *see* **hell**

give someone his head *see* **head**

give in
to stop fighting etc and admit that one has been defeated

give it a whirl *see* **whirl**

give or take something
informal adding or taking away something within certain limits
• *I weigh sixty-five kilos, give or take a kilo (= I weigh between sixty-four and sixty-six kilos)*

give out
informal to come to an end or be used up
• *At this point my patience/money gave out*

give someone pause *see* **pause**

give rise to *see* **rise**

give the game/show away
informal to let a secret, trick etc become known, usually accidentally

give someone the glad eye *see* **glad**

give someone the works *see* **works**

give up something
to stop doing something, seeing, eating or using something, or trying to do something

give up the ghost *see* **ghost**

give vent to *see* **vent**

what gives?
slang what is happening?; what is the matter?

glad

give someone the glad eye
informal to look at someone as though one is romantically or sexually interested in him or her

glad rags
facetious informal one's best clothes, worn for special occasions
Ⓣ Originally US, c.1900

glass

people who live in glass houses shouldn't throw stones
a proverb used to warn people that it is unwise to criticize others etc if one is in a position where one could be criticized (especially for the same thing) oneself
Ⓣ This proverb dates back to the 14c

glory

Old Glory
the Stars and Stripes, the national flag of the United States of America
Ⓣ The name is said to have been coined in 1831 by William Driver of Salem, Mass.

glove

be hand in glove *see* **hand**

fit like a glove
to fit perfectly

the gloves are off
informal the serious fighting or argument is about to begin
Ⓣ The reference is probably to boxing gloves

handle someone or **something with kid gloves** *see* **kid**

glutton

a glutton for punishment
not derogatory someone who seems eager to continue to do something difficult, unpleasant or unrewarding

gnash

gnash one's teeth *see* **teeth**

gnome

the gnomes of Zurich
the big international bankers
Ⓣ Traditionally, gnomes were considered to be guardians of the earth's treasures

go

at one go
all at the same time

be going on
informal to be near or close to a time, age etc
• *He must be going on (for) eighty*

from the word go
from the very beginning

give someone or **something the go-by**
slang to ignore someone in an unfriendly way; to ignore something or not to deal with it

go against the grain *see* **grain**

go back on something
to fail to carry out a promise etc to do something
• *I never go back on my word*

go for someone or **something**
informal
1 to attack a person, animal etc physically or in words

2 to be attracted by a person, thing etc

go for nothing *see* **nothing**

go great guns *see* **gun**

go in for something
to take part in it or to do it as a hobby, job, subject for study, habit etc

go native *see* **native**

go off *see* **off**

go places *see* **place**

go short *see* **short**

go slow *see* **slow**

go steady *see* **steady**

go the whole hog *see* **hog**

go through with something
to do or finish doing something which is difficult, unpleasant or disapproved of

go to someone's head *see* **head**

go to pot *see* **pot**

go to the wall *see* **wall**

go to town *see* **town**

go to work *see* **work**

go wrong *see* **wrong**

have a go
informal to make an attempt
• *I'm not sure that I can do it, but I'll certainly have a go*

it goes without saying (that)
it is obvious and doesn't need to be stated (that)

make a go of something
informal to make a success of something

no go
informal unsuccessful; useless; not getting approval or agreement
• *I asked if he would agree to our plans, but it's no go, I'm afraid*

on the go
very busy or active

goal

score an own goal
to incur criticism or disadvantage by one's own mistaken decision or judgement
Ⓛ From association football

goalpost

move the goalposts
to change the rules or conditions after a project of some kind is under way, especially in order to prevent someone else from achieving success
Ⓛ In many ballgames, such as football, players try to score goals by hitting the ball between two posts

goat

act the goat
informal to behave intentionally in a silly way; to play the fool

get someone's goat
informal to annoy or irritate them
Ⓛ Early 20c US, of obscure origin

separate the sheep from the goats *see* **sheep**

god, God

an act of God *see* **act**

God rest his soul *see* **rest**

the gods
informal the top balcony in a theatre
Ⓛ From the position of the top balcony directly under the ceiling, which was often painted with clouds

God's (own) country
especially US the country, or part of the country, to which one belongs

in the lap of the gods *see* **lap**

the mills of God grind slowly but they grind exceeding small *see* **mill**

put the fear of God into *see* **fear**

there but for the grace of God go I
a phrase indicating that something unpleasant that has happened to someone else could easily have happened to oneself had one not been more fortunate

think one is God's gift to something or **someone**
derogatory informal to have a very high opinion of one's ability to do something or of one's attractiveness to someone
• *He thinks he is God's gift to tennis/women*

a tin god *see* **tin**

gold

as good as gold
used especially of children very well-behaved

the crock/pot of gold at the end of the rainbow
wealth or good fortune that one can never achieve although one may dream of it
Ⓛ From a legend

a gold-digger
derogatory slang a woman who is friendly towards men merely for the sake of the presents they give her

a gold-mine
informal a source of wealth or profit

like gold dust
extremely scarce or rare, often because of being so much in demand
• *Tickets for the football final are like gold dust*

worth its/one's weight in gold *see* **weight**

golden

a/the golden age
literary
1 an imaginary time in the past of great happiness
2 any time of great achievement, especially in art, literature etc

a golden boy, a golden girl
a young man or woman of great talent who is expected to become famous in his career

golden egg/goose *see* **goose**

a golden handshake
a large amount of money given to a person who is leaving a job, especially to one who is forced to leave it

a golden opportunity
a very good or favourable chance

the golden rule
the rule which is the most important for a particular person, in carrying out a particular purpose etc
Ⓛ Originally the golden rule was specifically that one should do to others as one would wish them to do to oneself

silence is golden *see* **silence**

good

all in good time *see* **time**

all to the good *see* **to the good,** *below*

as good as
almost; virtually
• *He as good as called me a thief; The job's as good as done*

as good as gold *see* **gold**

be as good as one's word
to keep one's promises; to do what one has promised to do

be in someone's good books *see* **book**

be on to a good thing
informal to be in a situation, job etc which is particularly good, pleasant, desirable, rewarding etc

be up to no good
informal to be doing, or to be about to do, something wrong or illegal

do a power of good *see* **power**

for good and all
informal for ever; permanently

for good measure *see* **measure**

give as good as one gets
in an argument, fight etc, to be as successful as one's opponent; to do as much harm as one's opponent does; to give as good arguments or replies as one's opponent does

(a) good-for-nothing
derogatory someone who is useless and lazy

good in parts
not consistently good, satisfactory in some ways, but not in others
Ⓛ From the story of the curate's egg, *see* **curate**

a good job *see* **job**

good riddance to *see* **riddance**

good show! *see* **show**

have a good mind to *see* **mind**

have a good thing going
slang to have arranged a particularly pleasant or profitable position, relationship etc

have seen good service *see* **service**

in good hands *see* **hand**

in good heart *see* **heart**

in good nick *see* **nick**

in good time *see* **time**

in good voice *see* **voice**

in good working/running order *see* **order**

in someone's own good time *see* **time**

make good
informal to be successful

make good time *see* **time**

make good use of *see* **use**

one good turn deserves another *see* **turn**

no news is good news *see* **news**

put in/say a good word *see* **word**

take something in good part *see* **part**

throw good money after bad *see* **money**

to good purpose *see* **purpose**

to the good
1 also **all to the good**, to someone's benefit
• *'That's all to the good — we need all the help we can get!'*
2 richer; with gain or profit of a certain amount
• *After buying and selling some of these paintings, we finished up £100 to the good*

you can't keep a good man down *see* **man**

goodness

goodness knows
I do not know at all
Ⓛ A euphemism for *God knows*

to goodness
a phrase used for emphasis
• *I wish to goodness you'd make up your mind!; Surely to goodness you know how old your father is!*

goods

(deliver) the goods
slang to do what one has promised to do, what one is expected to do, or what is required etc
Ⓛ Originally US

goods and chattels
facetious informal all movable property
Ⓛ An old legal term

goose

cook someone's goose
informal to ruin completely their chances of success etc

kill the goose that lays the golden eggs
to destroy something, sometimes referred to as a **golden goose**, which is a source of profit to oneself, usually in the false hope of making more profit by doing so
Ⓛ From a fable by Aesop, in which the owner of the goose killed it to get immediate hold of the many golden eggs he believed were inside it, only to discover that there were none

he etc **can't/couldn't/wouldn't say boo to a goose**
he is very timid

what's sauce for the goose is sauce for the gander *see* **sauce**

a wild-goose chase *see* **wild**

gooseberry

play gooseberry
informal to be with two other people, usually people who are in love, who wish that one was not there
Ⓛ Apparently originally Devonshire dialect for 'act as a chaperone', but the derivation is obscure

Gordian

cut the Gordian knot *see* **knot**

gory

the gory details
the unpleasant details connected with something
• *He told us all the gory details of his divorce*
Ⓛ *Gore* means blood and the phrase was applied literally to death or injury

gospel

take something as gospel
to regard it as completely truthful or reliable

grab

how does that grab you?
slang what do you think of that?

up for grabs
slang ready to be taken, bought etc

grace

fall from grace
to lose one's privileged and favoured position
Ⓞ A religious term

a saving grace
a good quality that makes someone or something less bad than he, it etc would otherwise have been

with a bad, good grace
in a bad-tempered and rude or pleasant and good-tempered manner

grade

make the grade
informal to do as well as necessary in an examination, job etc
Ⓞ Originally a US railroading phrase, used of a locomotive which succeeded in climbing a steep section of track

grain

go against the grain
to be against a person's wishes, feelings, natural inclinations etc
• *It goes against the grain for me to tell lies*
Ⓞ A woodworking expression; it is easier to cut or plane wood with the grain than against, ie across it

take something with a grain of salt *see* **salt**

grandmother

teach one's grandmother to suck eggs *see* **egg**

grant

take something or **someone for granted**
1 to assume that something is true, will happen etc without checking
• *I just took it for granted that you had been told about this*
2 to treat someone, something, casually, without giving him or it much thought
• *People take electricity for granted until their supply is cut off*

grape

sour grapes
saying or pretending that something is not worth having because one cannot obtain it
Ⓞ From Aesop's fable of the fox who, having failed to reach a bunch of grapes growing above his head, went away saying, 'I see they are sour'

grapevine

the grapevine
informal an informal means of passing news, rumours etc from person to person eg in an office
• *This isn't official but I did hear through the grapevine that he is leaving*

grasp

grasp the nettle *see* **nettle**

grass

the grass is always greener on the other side of the fence
a proverb, meaning that one always tends to feel that others are in a better or more favourable position than oneself, or that one would be in a better position if circumstances were different
Ⓞ From the habit of cows etc of grazing through the fence separating them from the next field

the grass roots
the ordinary people in an association, trade union, country etc as opposed to those who take decisions
• *There is some dissatisfaction at the grass roots about our union's policies*

a grass widow
a woman whose husband is temporarily not living with her
Ⓞ Originally 'an unmarried woman who has borne a child', possibly from the fact that many illicit sexual encounters took place out of doors

let the grass grow under one's feet
to delay or waste time

put someone out to grass
to cause them to retire as no longer useful
Ⓞ Literally, to turn a horse permanently out into a field at the end of its working life

a snake in the grass *see* **snake**

grasshopper

knee-high to a grasshopper *see* **knee**

grave

dig one's own grave
to bring about one's own downfall or misfortune

from the cradle to the grave
one's whole life through

have one foot in the grave *see* **foot**

turn in one's grave
informal of someone who is dead, to be disturbed in one's rest by displeasing events in the world of living people, not intended literally

gravy

the gravy train
slang a position in which one has much more chance than other people of obtaining advantages for oneself
Ⓛ From the slang meaning of *gravy*, easy gain or profit

grease

grease someone's palm *see* **palm**

great

go great guns *see* **gun**

greater love hath no man *see* **love**

great minds think alike *see* **mind**

the great unwashed *see* **unwashed**

Greek

the Greek calends
never
Ⓛ The *calends* was the first day of the Roman month, but was not a part of the Greek calendar — the phrase was coined by the Emperor Augustus

a Greek gift
a dangerous gift
Ⓛ From the story of the Trojan horse, told in Virgil's *Aeneid* ii, which was apparently a gift from the Greeks but which was actually a trick leading to the fall of Troy

it's (all) Greek to me
informal I don't understand
Ⓛ A quotation from Shakespeare, *Julius Caesar* I, ii

when Greek meets Greek
when people of similar ability or calibre meet or are competing against each other

green

be green
to be without training or experience; to be easily fooled

green about the gills
informal looking ill as though one were about to be sick
Ⓛ From the greenish complexion some people have when they are feeling sick

a green belt
open land surrounding a town or city

the green-eyed monster
jealousy
• *I'm afraid Susan's in the grip of the green-eyed monster, and that's why she's so unpleasant to her sister*
Ⓛ A quotation from Shakespeare, *Othello* III, iii

the green light
informal permission to begin doing something

the green stuff
informal paper money, banknotes
Ⓛ In the US banknotes are green

have green fingers, (*US*) a green thumb
informal to be skilled at gardening

not to be as green as one is cabbage-looking
informal not to be as stupid or as easily fooled as people might think

grey

a grey area
a part of a subject etc where it is difficult to distinguish between one category etc and another

a grey eminence
a person, etc who is very influential but remains in the background
Ⓛ From the French *Eminence Grise* — 'the cardinal in grey' — the nickname given to Cardinal Richelieu's secretary and adviser, Père Joseph, who was a Capuchin friar and wore a grey habit

grey matter
informal brain, powers of thought or reasoning

men in grey suits
formally dressed men who often have positions in the Establishment but who are not at all memorable

grief

come to grief
to be unsuccessful, suffer some bad luck etc

grim

the grim reaper
death
Ⓘ From the personification of death as an old man carrying a scythe as though going to reap

hang/hold on like grim death
informal to take a very firm hold of something in difficult circumstances

grin

grin and bear it
informal to put up with something unpleasant without complaining

grin like a Cheshire cat *see* **Cheshire**

grind

grind the face(s) of (someone) *see* **face**

grind to a halt *see* **halt**

have an axe to grind *see* **axe**

grindstone

back to the grindstone
informal facetious back to work

keep (some)one's nose to the grindstone
to (force someone to) work hard, without stopping

grip

get a grip (on oneself)
to stop being foolish, afraid etc

get/come to grips with something
to deal with a problem, difficulty etc

in the grip of someone or **something**
in the control or power of
• *He seemed to be in the grip of some deep emotion*

lose one's grip
to lose control or understanding of something

grist

grist to the mill
something which brings profit or advantage
Ⓘ *Grist* = 'corn for grinding' ie something to keep the mill profitably operating

grit

grit one's teeth *see* **teeth**

ground

break new/fresh ground
to deal with a new subject for the first time
Ⓘ Literally, to plough up land which has not previously been cultivated

cover the ground of something
to deal with something adequately or thoroughly
• *The teacher is trying to cover the ground of the new syllabus before the exams*

cut the ground from under someone's feet
to cause their actions, plans, etc to be ineffective or to prevent them from acting at all, often by acting before they can do so

gain ground
to become more generally accepted or influential

get something off the ground
to get a project etc started
Ⓘ A phrase from aviation

give ground
to be forced to move away from a strong position
Ⓘ A military idiom

ground rules
the basic rules or principles that have to be observed in any system, enterprise, organization etc

have both feet on the ground *see* **feet**

have/keep one's ear to the ground *see* **ear**

hit the ground running
to take advantage of an opportunity as soon as possible, to take immediate action
Ⓘ Originally US and of uncertain origin. One theory is that the phrase refers to members of the armed forces who are

dropped by parachutes or from helicopters into a combat zone

hold/stand one's ground
to refuse to give in or make concessions
Ⓞ A military idiom

let someone in on the ground floor
to take someone into a business etc on the same terms as the people who started it

lose ground
to lose one's advantage; to lose one's good, strong or leading position
Ⓞ A military idiom

on one's own ground
dealing with a situation etc which one knows and understands

run someone or **something to ground**
to hunt out or track down them or it
• *She finally ran to ground the book she wanted in a second-hand bookshop*
Ⓞ A hunting term

shift one's ground
to change one's opinions, arguments etc
Ⓞ A military idiom — 'to alter the position in which one has drawn up one's army'

stand one's ground *see* **hold one's ground,** *above*

suit someone down to the ground
to suit someone completely or perfectly

thin on the ground *see* **thin**

grove

the groves of academe
often facetious or derogatory university or college life, higher education
Ⓞ A reference to the Grove of Academicus, an olive grove outside Athens which adjoined Plato's house and where he met his students

grow

grow on someone
informal to become gradually liked by them

grow out of something
to stop doing, liking etc it as one grows older

Grub

Grub Street
of writings, of very poor quality
Ⓞ From a street in London, now renamed Milton Street, and once the home of many inferior writers

Grundy

Mrs Grundy
a narrow-minded person who constantly criticizes the behaviour of others
Ⓞ From *Mrs Grundy* in the play *Speed the Plough* by Thomas Morton (1798)

guard

catch someone off guard
to do something to them or cause them to do something when they are surprised or not prepared to prevent it
Ⓞ A fencing/boxing term

guess

anybody's guess
informal something that no-one can be certain about

guess what?
an interjection used to introduce a piece of usually surprising news
• *Guess what? She's not coming after all!*

your guess is as good as mine
informal I have no idea

guest

be my guest
informal: only in the imperative please do the thing you are wanting to do

guiding

guiding light *see* **light**

guinea-pig

a guinea-pig
sometimes derogatory a person used as the subject of an experiment

gullet

stick in someone's gullet
same as **stick in one's throat** at **throat**

gum

gum up the works
informal to cause a machine, a system of working etc to break down

up a gum tree
informal in a very difficult or hopeless position
ⓘ From the usual place of refuge of a hunted opossum

gun

the big guns
informal the important people in any group, organization etc

go great guns
informal to be doing well; to be moving steadily towards one's goal
ⓘ A term — in the form **blow great guns** — originally used of a high wind making a sound like cannon fire

jump the gun
informal to start before the proper time
ⓘ Literally, to make a false start in a race

spike someone's guns
to spoil an opponent's plans by making it impossible to carry them out
ⓘ A military term: captured enemy guns which could not be moved were made useless by driving a metal spike into the touch-hole

stick to one's guns
to hold to one's position in an argument

with both guns blazing
in a fierce, aggressive mood
ⓘ From cowboy fights in Western films

gunning

be gunning for someone
informal to try to attack or criticize them

gut

bust a gut
slang to make the greatest possible effort

hate someone's guts
slang to dislike them very strongly

gutful

have had a gutful of something
slang to have had as much of it as one can take or tolerate

gutter

the gutter press
derogatory such newspapers as give a great deal of space to scandal and gossip

H

habit

from force of habit
because one is used to doing something

hackle

make someone's hackles rise
to make them angry
Ⓞ From the long feathers — *hackles* — on the necks of certain birds, including fighting-cocks, which are raised when the bird is angry

hail

hail-fellow-well-met
having a friendly manner, often in rather a superficial way, towards everyone

hair

get in someone's hair
informal to annoy them

hair of the dog
informal facetious an alcoholic drink taken in the morning by someone who has drunk too much the night before
Ⓞ From the phrase **a hair of the dog that bit you**, formerly a recipe recommended as a cure for rabies

hair-raising
terrifying

have someone by the short hairs
to have complete power over them

keep one's hair on
informal to remain calm and not become angry
• *Keep your hair on — I'm working as fast as I can*

let one's hair down
informal to behave in a free and relaxed manner

make someone's hair curl/stand on end
to horrify or terrify a person

not to turn a hair
to remain calm

split hairs
to make small unnecessary distinctions; to worry about unimportant details

tear one's hair
informal to show great irritation or despair

wear a hair shirt
to be penitent for some act of wrongdoing
Ⓞ Shirts made of horsehair and course wool were formerly worn as an act of penance

halcyon

halcyon days *see* **day**

hale

hale and hearty
extremely healthy
Ⓞ Hale means healthy

half

at half mast *see* **mast**

be half the battle *see* **battle**

someone's better half
informal someone's wife or husband

by half
informal to too great an extent
• *He's too clever by half*

do things by halves
informal; usually in negative to do things in an incomplete, careless etc way
• *He never does things by halves — his parties are always very lavish affairs*

go halves with someone
informal to share the cost of something with them

go off at half-cock *see* **cock**

half a loaf is better than no bread *see* **loaf**

half-baked
slang stupid

have half a mind to *see* **mind**

meet someone halfway
to reach an agreement with someone by meeting some of his demands in return for his meeting some of one's own

not half
slang very much so
• *'Are you enjoying yourself?' 'Not half!'*

not to know the half of it
to be extremely poorly informed about something, to know only about a small part of a problem, situation, etc

see with half an eye *see* **eye**

halt

call a halt to something
to stop it; to put an end to it

grind to a halt
to gradually come to a complete standstill

ham

ham-fisted
informal derogatory clumsy
Ⓛ Literally, having hands which are the size of hams and are therefore clumsy

hammer

come under the hammer
to be sold at an auction
Ⓛ A reference to the hammer with which an auctioneer indicates that a sale has been made

go/be at it hammer and tongs
to fight or argue violently
Ⓛ The reference is to a blacksmith holding a piece of heated iron in his tongs and striking it repeatedly with his hammer

hammer away at something
informal to keep working on a problem etc

hammer something home
to make great efforts to make a person realize or understand something
• *We'll have to hammer home to them the problems we face with this project*

hammering

give someone a hammering
slang to beat them severely

hand

at first hand *see* **first**

at/to hand
formal available; able to be used; ready for use when needed

at second hand *see* **second**

be hand in glove with someone
to be very closely associated with them, usually in a bad sense, for a bad purpose
Ⓛ The idiom was originally **hand and glove** — ie as close as can be imagined

bite the hand that feeds one
to be ungrateful to someone who has helped one
Ⓛ A quotation from an essay by Edmund Burke

change hands
to pass into different ownership

close/near at hand
near

a dab hand at *see* **dab**

dirty one's hands
to become involved in something dishonest or illegal

force someone's hand
to force them to do something either which they do not want to do or sooner than they want to do it
Ⓛ A French idiom, from card-playing

a free hand *see* **free**

get one's hands on someone or **something**
informal
1 to catch someone who has usually done something bad
2 to get or obtain the use of something

give/lend a (helping) hand
to help or assist someone

go hand in hand (with)
to be found always in close connection (with)
Ⓛ Literally, of two or more people, to walk with one person holding the hand of another

a golden handshake *see* **golden**

hand something down
to pass on a precious object, a belief, a

tradition etc from one generation to the next

hand over fist
informal in large amounts; very quickly
• *He's making money hand over fist in that shop*
ⓘ Originally a nautical term expressing steady and rapid progress, such as can be achieved by hauling on a line with one hand after another

his etc **hands are clean**
he etc is not guilty of a crime or misdeed

his etc **hands are tied**
he is unable to act as he would wish because of something which prevents him

hands off!
informal do not touch or take something

the hand that rocks the cradle
a mother, a woman, usually found in contexts emphasizing the importance of women in society, the phrase being a shortened version of **the hand that rocks the cradle rules the world**
ⓘ *The Hand That Rules The World* is a poem by US poet William Ross Wallace (died 1881)

someone has only one pair of hands
one person can only do a certain amount of work, there being a physical limitation on this

have a hand in something
formal to be one of the people who have caused, done etc something

have someone eating out of one's hand
to have them behaving very submissively towards one and doing as one says
ⓘ From a tame animal taking food from a person's hand

have something handed to one on a plate *see* **plate**

have one's hands full
informal to be very busy

have/get the upper hand *see* **upper**

have the whip hand *see* **whip**

have time on one's hands *see* **time**

high-handed *see* **high**

in good hands
receiving care and attention

in hand
1 not used etc; remaining
2 being dealt with; being done etc
• *These two football teams have won the same number of points but one of them has a game in hand* (= has played one game less than the other)
ⓘ Originally used of a horse which responds easily to the rider or to the driver's hand on the reins

keep one's hand in
informal to remain good or skilful at doing something by doing it occasionally
ⓘ **Have one's hand in** was an idiom, dating from the Middle Ages, for 'to be in practice'

lay one's hands on someone or **something**
informal
1 to reach or find something one is looking for
2 to catch someone who has usually done something bad

the left hand does not know what the right hand is doing
said of an organization, group etc where one department or part seems to be acting without regard to the rest, thus causing difficulties; also used of a person, some of whose actions seem at variance with others and possibly contrary to the person's interests

lend a hand *see* **give a hand,** *above*

live (from) hand to mouth
to be able to get only what one needs at present, without having anything extra to save up
ⓘ The implication is that whatever money comes into one's hand is immediately used to feed oneself

many hands make light work
a proverb, meaning that a job becomes much easier if there are a number of people to help to do it

near at hand *see* **close at hand,** *above*

an old hand *see* **old**

on hand
near; present; ready for use etc
• *We always keep some candles on hand in case there's a power failure; You'd better be on hand in case you are needed*

(left) on one's hands
informal left over; remaining; not sold etc
• *We were left with a lot of rubbish on our hands at the end of the sale*

out of hand
1 unable to be controlled
• *The angry crowd was getting out of hand*
2 quickly; without thinking, waiting etc
• *The soldiers shot the bandits out of hand* (= without a trial)

not to do a hand's turn
derogatory not to do any work, not to do anything to help, usually said as a criticism of someone who is not doing his or her fair share of the work

play into someone's hands
to do exactly what an opponent or enemy wants one to do
Ⓞ Literally, in card games, to play so as to benefit another player

put one's hand in one's pocket *see* **pocket**

show one's hand
to allow one's plans or intentions to become known
Ⓞ From card games

a show of hands *see* **show**

take someone in hand
to look after, discipline or train someone
Ⓞ As **in hand** above

take one's life in one's hands *see* **life**

take something off someone's hands
to relieve them of it, to remove the responsibility of ownership of it from them

throw in one's hand
to abandon a plan, course of action etc
Ⓞ From the method of resigning in card-games

try one's hand at something
informal to see if one can do it

turn one's hand to something
to have the ability to do a job etc

wash one's hands of someone or **something**
to say that one is no longer willing to be involved in a project etc or to be responsible for a project, a person etc
Ⓞ A Biblical allusion, to the action of Pontius Pilate (Matthew 27:24) symbolizing his dissociation from the wish of the people to crucify Jesus

win hands down
informal to win very easily
Ⓞ A racing term, referring to a jockey who relaxes his hold on the reins because he sees he is winning easily

with one's bare hands
using one's hands only, not tools or weapons

you have (got) to hand it to someone
you must give them the praise or admiration which they deserve
Ⓞ Originally US

handle

a handle to one's name
informal a title

fly off the handle
informal to lose one's temper
Ⓞ Originally US — the allusion is to an axehead which flies off the handle while one is using it

handle someone or **something with kid gloves** *see* **kid**

handsaw

know a hawk from a handsaw *see* **hawk**

handsome

handsome is as handsome does
a proverb indicating that good looks are all very well but they have their limitations and more is required of people

handy

come in handy
informal to be useful
Ⓞ This phrase, and others with **come in**, originally applied to fruit and vegetables etc coming in to season just when they are most needed

hang

I'll etc **be hanged if I'll do something**
old informal I am determined not to do it
Ⓞ A euphemism for **I'll be damned if ...**

get the hang of something
informal to learn, or begin to understand, how to do it
Ⓞ An American expression, originally meaning 'to become accustomed to and learn the use of tools etc'

hang about/around
informal
1 to stand around doing nothing
• *I don't like to see all these youths hanging about street corners*
2 to be close to a person frequently
• *I don't want you hanging about my daughter*
3 to wait
• *Hang about! I think we're being offered a cup of coffee*

hang by a thread *see* **thread**

hang fire *see* **fire**

hang one's head *see* **head**

hang on
informal to wait

hang on like grim death *see* **grim**

hang on someone's words *see* **word**

hang out
slang to live or spend one's time

hang out the flags *see* **flag**

hang together
to agree or be consistent
• *His statements just do not hang together — he must be lying*

hang up
to put the receiver back after a telephone conversation

hang up one's hat *see* **hat**

hung up (on)
slang obsessed (with)

a peg on which to hang something *see* **peg**

thereby hangs a tale *see* **tale**

hanging

a hanging matter
informal a serious question, offence etc
Ⓞ Literally, a crime punishable by death

happy

as happy as a lark *see* **lark**

as happy as a pig in muck *see* **pig**

as happy as a sand-boy *see* **sand**

happy event
euphemism usually facetious a birth

happy-go-lucky
not worrying abut what might happen

happy hunting-ground
informal a place where one often goes, especially to obtain something or to make money
Ⓞ From the name of the Native Americans' Paradise

a happy medium
a sensible middle course between two extreme positions

trigger-happy *see* **trigger**

hard

as hard as nails *see* **nail**

be hard on someone
1 to punish or criticize them severely
• *Don't be too hard on the boy — he's too young to know that he was doing wrong*
2 to be unfair to them
• *I know we can't make exceptions to our rules, but it's a bit hard on those who did nothing wrong*

be hard put to it to do something
to have difficulty in doing it

a hard act to follow *see* **act**

hard-and-fast
of rules, that can never be changed or ignored
Ⓞ A nautical phrase, describing a ship which has run aground

hard-bitten
informal of people, tough; toughened by experience; stubborn
Ⓞ Originally a term applied to dogs, meaning 'biting hard'

hard-boiled
informal unfeeling and not influenced by emotion
Ⓞ Originally US

a hard case
informal a person who is difficult to deal with or reform

hard cash
informal coins and banknotes, as opposed to cheques

hard cheese *see* **cheese**

a hard core
a part of something which is very difficult to change, especially the most loyal or stubborn members of a group etc

hard done by
informal unfairly treated

the hard facts
facts that cannot be denied

hard-headed
clever; practical; not influenced by emotion

hard lines
informal bad luck
Ⓞ Apparently a nautical idiom, probably referring to ropes stiffened by ice

a hard-luck story
often derogatory the story of a person's bad luck and suffering, usually intended to gain sympathy for the person concerned

a hard nut to crack *see* **nut**

hard of hearing
euphemism rather deaf

hard on someone's heels
close behind them

hard-pressed
in difficulties
• *We will be hard-pressed to find the money to pay the staff this week*

(a drop of) the hard stuff
facetious informal some alcoholic drink, usually spirits and especially whisky

a hard time (of it)
trouble, unpleasantness, difficulty, worry etc
• *The audience gave the speaker a hard time of it at the meeting; The speaker had a hard time of it trying to make himself heard*

hard up
informal not having much (especially money)
• *I'm a bit hard up at the moment; You must be hard up for boyfriends if you are going out with him*
Ⓞ Probably originally nautical slang — meaning literally 'aground'

play hard to get *see* **play**

the school of hard knocks *see* **school**

take a hard line
to take strong action on something, or hold firmly to decisions, policies etc that have been made
• *The government is taking a hard line over its new pay policy*

hare

run with the hare and hunt with the hounds
to try to be on both sides of an argument etc at once

start a hare
to introduce a subject of conversation, problem etc which is not important to the main issues being considered
Ⓞ Literally, to cause a hare to leave its hiding-place, something likely to distract hounds engaged in, for example, a fox-hunt

hark

hark back (to)
formal to refer to something that has been said or done earlier
Ⓞ A hunting term — **hark back** is a command to hounds and their handlers to double back and try to pick up a lost scent

harm

out of harm's way
in a safe place

harness

die in harness
to die while one is still working and not retired
Ⓞ Horses are harnessed when they are working

harp

harp on something
informal to keep on talking or to talk too much about it
Ⓞ A reference to the old idiom **harp on one string** — ie to become boring on a subject

hash

make a hash of something
informal to spoil it completely; to do it badly

settle someone's hash
slang to deal with them in such a way that they cease to be a nuisance, or are unable to do what they intended to do
ⓘ Apparently a cooking term of obscure implication

haste

the more haste/hurry the less speed
a proverb, meaning that by hurrying too much one makes more mistakes etc

hat

at the drop of a hat *see* **drop**

a bad hat
a bad and worthless person

hang up one's hat
to move into a house, office etc for a long stay

hats off to (a particular person)
informal everyone should admire and praise (a person)
• *Hats off to Mrs Smith for the best meal I've had in years!*

a hat trick
1 in cricket, the putting out of three batsmen by three balls in a row
2 in football, three goals scored by one player in a match
3 any action done successfully three times in a row
ⓘ The cricketing meaning is the original one; it is claimed that the feat described entitled a bowler to a new hat from his club

I'll eat my hat
informal I shall be amazed; used to express a strong belief that a proposition or eventuality is unlikely

keep something under one's hat
informal to keep something secret

knock someone or **something into a cocked hat**
informal to damage or ruin them or it; to surpass completely

old hat
informal something very old-fashioned

pass/send round the hat for someone
to ask for or collect money on their behalf
ⓘ From a traditional method of making impromptu collections of money

take one's hat off to someone
informal to admire them for doing something

talk through one's hat
informal to talk nonsense

throw one's hat into the ring
to make a challenge
ⓘ From a method of making a challenge to prize-fighters at a showground etc

wear another hat/several hats
to speak or act as the holder of a different official position, several official positions

hatch

batten down the hatches
to prepare for trouble, a quarrel etc
ⓘ From preparations for a storm on a ship at sea

hatches, matches and dispatches
facetious informal the announcement of births, marriages and deaths in the newspapers

hatchet

bury the hatchet
to agree to end hostilities and be friends again
ⓘ A reference to a Native American custom of burying their tomahawks when peace was declared

hatter

as mad as a hatter
utterly crazy; completely insane
ⓘ Hatmaking used to involve treating fur with nitrate of mercury, prolonged exposure to which could result in a nervous illness interpreted in those days as a symptom of insanity

haul

haul someone over the coals *see* **coal**

a long haul
informal a long or tiring job etc

have

have a go *see* **go**

have done with something
to stop or put an end to it

have had it
informal to be dead, ruined etc

have it coming to one *see* **come**

have it in for someone
informal to dislike them and therefore be unpleasant to or try to cause trouble for them

have it in one etc
to have the courage or ability to do something

have it off with someone
slang to have sexual intercourse with them; to have an affair with them

have it out with someone
to argue with them in order to put an end to some disagreement

have someone on
Brit informal to try to make them believe something which is not true
• *You're having me on — that's not really true, is it?*

have something on
informal to be busy

have someone up
Brit informal to make a person appear in court to answer some charge
• *He was had up for drunken driving*

have what it takes
informal to have the qualities or ability that one needs to do something

let someone have it
informal to attack them suddenly and vigorously with words or blows

havoc

play havoc with something
to cause a lot of damage to it; to ruin it

hawk

hawks and doves
respectively those who are for and those who are against military or aggressive action
Ⓞ Hawks are birds of prey and so attackers, while the dove is traditionally a symbol of peace

know a hawk from a handsaw
to be able to judge between things fairly well
Ⓞ A Shakespearian quotation, *Hamlet* II, ii

watch someone like a hawk
to watch them very carefully and alertly

hay

hit the hay
facetious informal to go to bed
Ⓞ Originally US

like looking for a needle in a haystack
see **needle**

make hay (while the sun shines)
to make use of an opportunity while it is available to one
Ⓞ From the fact that haymaking is only possible in fine weather

haywire

go haywire
informal to stop working properly; to go crazy
Ⓞ Originally US, probably from the use of **haywire** to describe an inefficient and makeshift organization — ie one in which the equipment was held together with pieces of wire etc

head

above someone's head
informal too difficult for them to understand

bang one's head against a brick wall
to try in vain to make someone understand something, agree with one's point of view etc

be head and shoulders above someone
to be far better, much more talented, etc than them
Ⓞ A reference to someone who is very tall in comparison with other people

bite/snap someone's head off
to answer them sharply and angrily

bring something to a head, come to a head
to cause something to come to a state of climax or crisis when urgent action is needed

bury one's head in the sand
to avoid trying to deal with a problem, danger etc by ignoring it or deliberately knowing nothing about it
Ⓞ From the old belief that the ostrich reacted to danger by burying its head in the sand, thinking that being unable to see, it could not be seen

by a short head *see* **short**

get a head start *see* **start**

get something into someone's head
informal to make them recognize that something is true, necessary etc
• *I can't get it into his head that he will never be an artist*

give someone his etc **head**
to allow them to do what they want with regard to something
Ⓞ Literally, **to give a horse its head** means to slacken one's hold on the reins

go to someone's head
of praise, success etc, to make them arrogant, foolish, careless etc
Ⓞ Literally (of alcoholic drinks) to make someone slightly drunk, from the way in which alcohol in the body appears to behave

hang one's head
to look ashamed or embarrassed

have a head for something
to be good at dealing with it

have a (good) head on one's shoulders
to be calm, clever and sensible

have a roof over one's head *see* **roof**

have one's head in the clouds
to be dreaming and not attending to what is going on

have one's head screwed on the right way
informal to have a sensible or practical nature

head over heels
completely
• *He fell head over heels in love*
Ⓞ Literally, 'turning a complete somersault'

heads will roll
slightly facetious someone will get into very serious trouble
Ⓞ From the use of the guillotine to execute criminals

hold a pistol to someone's head *see* **pistol**

hold one's head up
not to feel ashamed, guilty etc

keep one's head
to remain calm and sensible, eg in a crisis or sudden difficulty

keep one's head above water
informal to get or earn enough money, profits etc to remain out of debt

knock something on the head
informal to destroy or put an end to a plan etc
Ⓞ From a method of slaughtering animals

laugh one's head off
to laugh extremely heartily

lose one's head
to become angry or excited, or to act foolishly, eg in a crisis or sudden difficulty, or when someone does something wrong etc

need something like someone needs a hole in the head *see* **hole**

need one's head examined
informal to be foolish, stupid or slightly insane

not (quite) right in the head *see* **right**

not to be able to make head nor tail of something
informal to be unable to understand it

off/out of one's head
informal mad

off the top of one's head
informal without much thought; without making sure that what is said etc is correct

on your etc **own head be it**
you will bear the responsibility for any harm caused by your actions or wishes

(be/go) over someone's head
1 (in a way which is) too difficult for them to understand
• *What he said was/went over the heads of the children in the audience*
2 when others (seem to) have a better right to it
• *He was promoted over the heads of three people who were senior to him*

a price on someone's head *see* **price**

put one's head on the block/in a noose
to put oneself into a position where one could easily be harmed

put our etc **heads together**
informal to discuss a plan, problem etc among ourselves

rear its ugly head
informal (used of something unpleasant or unwelcome) to appear or happen

soft in the head
informal stupid or unintelligent

take/get it into one's head
1 to come to believe, usually wrongly, that something is true etc
• *He's taken it into his head that everybody hates him*
2 to decide to do something, usually implying that it is foolish
• *He's taken it into his head to have a cold shower every morning*

talk one's head off *see* **talk**

talk through a hole in one's head *see* **hole**

talk through the back of one's head *see* **back**

turn someone's head
to make them conceited etc with constant praise

two heads are better than one
a proverb, meaning that two people working together are more likely to be able to find a solution to a problem etc than one person alone

headline

hit the headlines
informal to attract a great deal of attention and interest from the newspapers, television etc

headway

make headway
to go forward; to make progress
Ⓣ A nautical idiom — **headway** is a contraction of **ahead-way**, ie 'progress forwards'

health

drink to someone's health
to drink a toast to them, wishing them good health, often using the words 'Your health!'

heap

heap coals (of fire) on someone's head *see* **coal**

knock/strike someone all of a heap
informal to astonish them usually so completely that they are not able to do or say anything
Ⓣ This phrase first appears in a play by Sheridan

hear

hear tell of someone or **something**
old to hear of or about them or it

I etc **will, would not hear of (something)**
I will or would not allow (someone to do something)
• *He would not hear of her walking home, and insisted on calling a taxi*

heart

after someone's own heart
of people, of exactly the type someone likes
• *You're a man after my own heart*
Ⓣ A Biblical reference, to I Samuel 13:14

at heart
formal really; basically
• *She appears rather stern but she is at heart a very kind person*

break someone's heart
to cause them great sorrow

by heart
so that one has (a poem, a set of facts etc) accurately and completely in one's memory

cross my etc **heart**
informal said especially by children to emphasize the truth of what is being said, sometimes appointed by movement of the hand making an X over the heart

do someone's heart good
old to give them a feeling of pleasure
Ⓣ Probably derived from Shakespeare, *A Midsummer Night's Dream* I, ii

eat one's heart out
to make oneself ill by being unhappy, by longing for something one cannot have etc

faint heart never won fair lady *see* **faint**

find it in one's heart to do something
formal to manage or persuade oneself to do it
• *Can you find it in your heart to forgive me?*

from the bottom of one's heart
very much; very sincerely
• *She thanked him from the bottom of her heart for all his help*

give someone heart failure
informal to give them a very bad shock

have a change of heart
to change a decision etc, usually to a better, kinder one

have a heart!
informal show some pity or kindness

have a heart of gold
to be a very kind, generous, worthy person

have something at heart
formal to have or feel a kind concern for or interest in it

have one's heart in one's boots
to be very depressed or lacking in hope

have one's heart in one's mouth
to be extremely worried and anxious

have one's heart in the right place
to be basically kind, generous etc even though not always appearing to be so

have one's heart set on something *see* **set one's heart on something,** *below*

heart and soul
completely; with all one's attention and energy
• *She devoted herself heart and soul to working for the church*

my etc **heart goes out to someone**
I feel pity, sympathy etc for them

my etc **heart is not in something**
I am not really eager or enthusiastic to do it

my etc **heart sinks**
I feel depressed and lose hope, cheerfulness etc

a heart-throb
facetious slang someone (especially a singer, actor etc) who is very attractive to (young) people of the opposite sex

a heart-to-heart
informal an open and sincere talk, usually in private

heart-warming
causing a person to feel pleasure

in good heart
rather formal
1 in a good, healthy condition
2 in good spirits and full of courage

in one's heart of hearts
in one's deepest and most hidden thoughts and feelings

lose heart
to become discouraged
Ⓘ Moral courage was once thought to be created in the heart

my heart bleeds for you etc
ironic I am very sympathetic towards you, implying that one is not at all sympathetic because one does not feel that the other person is in a particularly bad position

not to have the heart to do something
not to want or be unkind enough to do something unpleasant

pour one's heart out
to reveal all one's personal feelings and problems

put new heart into someone
to make them once again more cheerful and hopeful
Ⓘ As **lose heart** above

set one's heart on something/have one's heart set on something
to want it very much

sick at heart
rather literary very sorrowful and unhappy

take heart
formal to become encouraged or more confident
Ⓘ As **lose heart** above

take something to heart
1 to be made very sad or upset by something
2 to pay great attention to something

to one's heart's content
as much as one wants

warm the cockles of the heart *see* **cockle**

wear one's heart on one's sleeve
to show one's feelings openly
Ⓘ Probably a Shakespearian quotation, *Othello* I, i

with a heavy heart *see* **heavy**

with all one's heart
very willingly or sincerely
• *I hope with all my heart that you will be happy*

heartache
a feeling of great sadness, eg as caused by the loss of, or the failure to get, a person's love

heartfelt
formal sincere

heartstring
tug at the heartstrings
to appeal to one's feelings, especially of pity
ⓘ In medieval anatomy, the heartstrings were thought of as nerves or sinews which braced and supported the heart

heat
if you can't stand the heat, get out of the kitchen
if you do not like, or cannot cope with, the situation, then you should leave it rather than stay and complain about it
ⓘ A saying attributed to Harry S Truman, a US president, when he was announcing (1952) that he would not be standing for president again

in/on heat
of female animals, sexually aroused in the breeding season

in the heat of the moment
while influenced by the excitement or emotion caused by something

take the heat out of something
to make a quarrel, a difficult situation etc, less emotional and disturbing

turn on the heat
slang to put pressure on someone by treating them cruelly or very severely

heather
set the heather on fire
to cause a great deal of general interest and excitement

heatwave
a heatwave
a period of very hot weather

heave
heave in sight
to come into sight; to appear
ⓘ A nautical idiom

give someone the (old) heave-ho
slang to tell them to leave; to get rid of them
ⓘ Originally US

heaven
for heaven's sake
an expression used to show anger, surprise etc

heaven knows
1 I don't know at all
2 certainly
• *Heaven knows, I ought to have seen that I couldn't trust him*

(good) heavens
interjection an expression of surprise, dismay etc

the heavens opened
facetious there was a sudden downpour of rain

in (the) seventh heaven
extremely happy
ⓘ From the mystical Jewish cabbala, a system of belief which held that there were seven heavens in ascending order of excellence. Muslims have a similar belief

manna from heaven *see* **manna**

move heaven and earth
to do everything that one possibly can

stink to high heaven
informal to have a very strong and unpleasant smell

thank heavens
an expression used to show that a person is glad something or someone is all right, satisfactory etc
• *Thank heavens he isn't coming!*

heavy
heavy going
informal (something) causing difficulty in doing, understanding or making progress
• *I found his book very heavy going*
ⓘ Literally 'damp, sticky ground', especially when there is to be hunting or racing on it

heavy-handed
not showing good judgement or good taste; made in too dramatic, shocking, lengthy, emphatic etc a way

lie heavy on *see* **lie**

make heavy weather of something
informal to find great difficulty in doing something which should usually be easy to do
① A nautical idiom used of a ship — 'to handle badly in difficult conditions'

with a heavy heart
literary with a feeling of sadness

hedge

hedge one's bets *see* **bet**

look as if one had been dragged through a hedge backwards
derogatory informal to be extremely untidy

heel

an Achilles' heel
a person's vulnerable or weak point
① From the legendary Greek hero, whose mother, a sea-nymph, dipped him in the River Styx as a baby to make him invulnerable. Only his heel, by which she was holding him, remained unprotected, and he was finally killed by an arrow in the heel

bring someone to heel
to make them obey and behave as one wishes

dig in one's heels
informal to refuse to do, allow etc something

down-at-heel *see* **down**

hard on someone's heels *see* **hard**

head over heels *see* **head**

kick/cool one's heels
informal to be kept waiting for some time
• *Although I arrived on time for the meeting, I was left kicking my heels for half an hour*

set someone by the heels
old to put them in prison

show a clean pair of heels *see* **clean**

take to one's heels
informal to run away

turn on one's heel
to turn round or away suddenly, usually with the intention of moving in the opposite direction

hell

all hell breaks loose
there is sudden and complete, unpleasant, confusion, uproar etc
① A quotation from Milton's *Paradise Lost*

come hell or high water
whatever difficulties have to be overcome

for the hell of it
informal for no particular reason; just for fun

from hell
a phrase indicating that the person or thing mentioned is the very worst possible
• *The landlady from hell has raised the rent again*

give someone hell
informal to treat them very severely, especially to scold them severely

hell has no fury like a woman scorned
one should beware of a woman who has been rejected by a lover or husband because she will be very angry and will be seeking revenge
① An adaptation of the closing lines of 'The Mourning Bride' (1697) by William Congreve — 'Heaven has no rage, like love to hatred turned, nor Hell a fury like a woman scorned'

hell for leather
very fast
① Possibly from **all of a lather** and certainly applied originally only to riding on horseback

not to have a cat in hell's chance/a snowball's chance in hell
informal not to have any chance at all

play (merry) hell with
informal to harm or damage

raise hell *see* **raise**

there will be hell to pay
some form of serious trouble or punishment is bound to arise
• *There will be hell to pay when he sees the damage to his car*

the way/road to hell is paved with good intentions
a proverb indicating that many people end up performing wrong or bad actions although they originally started out planning to act in a good, virtuous, generous etc way

until hell freezes over
never
• *He will not forgive you until hell freezes over*

what the hell!
informal what does it matter; I don't care

hellbent
hellbent on something
informal determined to do it

helm
at the helm
in charge or in control
Ⓘ Literally, 'steering the ship'

help
help oneself (to something)
informal facetious
1 to give oneself or take (food etc)
2 to steal (something)

helping
give/lend a helping hand *see* **hand**

helpmeet
a helpmeet
a partner who helps one, especially a wife or husband
Ⓘ A Biblical reference, from a misinterpretation of Genesis 2:18 'an help meet for him', ie 'a suitable help for him'

hen
like a hen on a hot griddle
very nervous and excited

henpecked
informal of a man, ruled by his wife
Ⓘ From the fact that hens do in fact peck feathers out of the plumage of cocks

here
here's to someone or **something**
used as a toast to the health, success etc of them or it

here, there, and everywhere
all over the place, a phrase used to indicate the widespread nature of something

here today, gone tomorrow
a phrase emphasizing the fleeting or ephemeral nature of something

neither here nor there
not important
• *His opinion of us is neither here nor there*

hereafter
the hereafter
formal life after death

hero
unsung heroes *see* **unsung**

herring
(packed) like herring in a barrel
very closely packed

neither fish nor flesh nor good red herring *see* **fish**

a red herring *see* **red**

hide
hide one's light under a bushel *see* **light**

neither hide nor hair of someone or **something**
no trace at all of them or it

tan someone's hide
to beat them
Ⓘ The reference is to leather-making

hiding
on a hiding to nothing
slang in a situation where one cannot win, no matter what one does
Ⓘ Reputed to be a boxing idiom

high
for the high jump
slang about to be punished etc because one has done something wrong
• *If the boss finds out that you broke that machine, you'll be for the high jump*
Ⓘ Originally army slang

have high hopes
to be extremely hopeful or optimistic about one's chances of success

high and dry
in a difficult position, without the means to continue normally

• *Her husband has left her high and dry without any money*
Ⓘ A nautical idiom, for a boat stranded on a beach etc

(hunt) high and low
informal to search everywhere

high and mighty
derogatory informal thinking, or behaving, as if one thinks that one is very important

high as a kite
slang very happy, excited or drunk, or very much under the influence of drugs

high-falutin, high-faluting
informal very, usually too, showy or grand
Ⓘ 19c US, probably an elaboration of **high-flown**

a high-flier
a person who is ambitious or who has natural characteristics which will cause him or her to be successful

high-handed
derogatory
1 of people, acting without thought or consideration for others
2 of actions etc, done without thought or consideration for others

a high spot
an especially good part or section of something *see* **hit the high spots,** *below*

hit the high spots
informal to reach a high level

it is etc **high time**
informal something ought to be or have been done etc by this time
• *It's high time someone told him what they think of him*

on one's high horse
difficult to argue with etc, eg because one is determined to show that one is very important or that one has not been shown enough respect etc
Ⓘ A **high horse** was the charger of a mounted knight, and riding one was a sign of superior rank

riding high *see* **riding**

run high
of feelings, tempers etc, to be excited, angry etc
Ⓘ Literally used of the sea, when there is a strong current and a high tide, or high waves

highbrow

a highbrow
1 a person who is interested in intellectual pursuits such as classical music, great literature etc
2 of things such as classical music, great literature etc

hightail

hightail it
informal to hurry away
Ⓘ Originally US, from the raised tail of a fleeing animal

hill

as old as the hills
very old

over the hill
informal past one's best; too old

hilt

be up to the hilt in something
to the utmost, to the maximum
• *The house is mortgaged up to the hilt*

hindmost

devil take the hindmost *see* **devil**

hint

take a/the hint
informal to understand what a person is hinting at, and do what the person wants

hip

have someone on the hip
to gain an advantage over them
Ⓘ From wrestling

hit

be a hit with someone
informal to be extremely popular with them

hit a bad patch *see* **patch**

hit a man when he is down *see* **man**

hit-and-run
1 of a driver, causing injury to a person and driving away without stopping or reporting the accident
2 of an accident, caused by such a driver

① Originally a term for a tactic in baseball, with no connection in meaning to its present use

hit it off
informal to become friendly
• *We hit it off as soon as we met; I hit it off with him*

hit (up)on something
informal to find an answer etc by chance

hit-or-miss
without any system or planning; careless

hit the deck *see* **deck**

hit the ceiling *see* **ceiling**

hit the ground running *see* **ground**

hit the hay *see* **hay**

hit the headlines *see* **headline**

hit the jackpot *see* **jackpot**

hit the mark *see* **mark**

hit the nail on the head *see* **nail**

hit the roof *see* **roof**

hit the spot *see* **spot**

make a hit with someone
informal to make oneself liked or approved of by them

a smash hit *see* **smash**

hitch

hitch one's wagon to a star *see* **wagon**

hive

hive something off
informal: often derogatory
1 to give some work, part of a job etc to some other person, firm etc
• *If we can't meet the schedule, we can hive off some of the work to another firm*
2 to make part of an organization independent
• *We can hive off part of the company and make it a separate firm*

Hobson

Hobson's choice
the choice between taking what one is offered and getting nothing at all
① Reputedly from a 17c Cambridge livery-stable keeper, who only offered customers the hire of the horse nearest the door

hog

go the whole hog
informal to do something completely
① Probably from the fact that *hog* was once a slang word for a shilling

hoist

hoist with one's own petard *see* **petard**

hold

get hold of someone or **something**
informal
1 to manage to speak to someone
2 to get, buy or obtain something

have hold over someone
to have power or influence over them

hold (the line)
of a person who is making a telephone call, to wait while the person one is calling comes to the telephone, finishes what he is doing etc

hold something against someone
to dislike, have a bad opinion of etc, a person etc, because one knows that that person has done something bad, wrong etc

hold a pistol to someone's head *see* **pistol**

hold (a job) down
to keep or be allowed to stay in (a job)

hold forth
usually derogatory to talk or give one's opinions, often loudly, at great length and forcefully or dogmatically
• *The prime minister held forth for hours on the success of his government*
① Originally meaning 'to preach' — a Biblical reference to Philippians 2:16, 'holding forth the word of life'

hold good
to be true or valid; to apply

hold one's head up *see* **head**

hold it!
informal stop or wait

hold off
informal of weather conditions, to stay away

hold on like grim death *see* **grim**

hold out on someone
informal to keep back money, information etc from them

hold one's own *see* **own**

hold one's peace *see* **peace**

hold sway *see* **sway**

hold the floor *see* **floor**

hold the fort *see* **fort**

hold someone to something
to make them keep a promise, follow a decision etc

hold one's tongue *see* **tongue**

hold someone to ransom *see* **ransom**

hold water *see* **water**

hold your horses *see* **horse**

no holds barred
no restrictions on what is fair, allowed etc
Ⓞ From wrestling, where certain holds are sometimes not allowed to be used in a match

not hold with something
to disapprove of it

hole

be in a hole
informal to be in an extremely difficult situation
• *We are in a bit of a financial hole*

burn a hole in someone's pocket *see* **pocket**

hole-and-corner
carried out in a secretive manner, suggesting dishonesty

make a hole in something
informal to use a large part of it

need something like someone needs a hole in the head
informal a phrase used to emphasize how undesirable or how unwelcome something is
• *The farmers need hot weather just now like they need a hole in the head*

pick holes in something
informal to criticize or find faults in an argument, theory etc

talk through a hole in one's head
informal to talk absolute nonsense, to talk about something about which one knows nothing

holy

holier-than-thou
derogatory behaving towards other people in a way which shows one thinks one is better, especially more holy and virtuous, than they are
Ⓞ A Biblical reference, to Isaiah 65:5 '... come not near to me, for I am holier than thou'

the holy of holies
facetious a very special place right inside a building etc
Ⓞ A literal translation of the Hebrew name of the inner sanctuary in the Jewish Temple, where the Ark of the Covenant was kept

a holy terror
informal
1 a person who is feared
2 a badly-behaved child

home

bring something home to someone
to prove something to someone in a way which makes it impossible not to believe it

do one's homework
informal to prepare for a meeting etc by making sure one knows all the relevant figures, facts etc

drive something home *see* **drive**

feel at home
to feel as relaxed as one does in one's own home or in a place or situation one knows well

home and dry
having succeeded in what one wanted to do etc
Ⓞ Probably from cross-country running

a home from home
informal a place where one feels as relaxed, happy etc as when one is at home

home is where the heart is
a proverb indicating that, wherever one is actually living, one's true home is where the person or people whom one loves are

home, James, and don't spare the horses
a catch phrase used as an instruction to a driver to set off and get to the destination with all possible speed

ⓘ From an instruction given to a coachman by his employer

a home truth
a plain statement of something which is unpleasant but true, about a person, his behaviour etc, said directly to the person

make oneself at home
to make oneself as comfortable, or to behave in as relaxed a way, as one would at home

nothing to write home about
informal not very exciting, important etc

romp home *see* **romp**

Homer

even Homer nods
even the wisest and greatest among us occasionally makes a mistake
ⓘ *Homer* was a famous Greek epic poet of the eighth century BC

honest

honest Injun
facetious truthfully
• *I didn't break the plate, honest Injun!*
ⓘ Originally an American children's phrase, possibly from an assurance of reliability once demanded from Native Americans by white settlers

make an honest woman of (someone)
facetious to marry (a woman, originally one with whom one has already had sexual relations)

honesty

honesty is the best policy
a proverb advocating the virtues of telling the truth, the implication being that if one is not honest one might very well be found out

honour

do the honours
formal or facetious to do what is expected of a person who has guests, especially serve food etc to them

honourable

honourable mention *see* **mention**

hook

by hook or by crook
informal by some means or another; in any way possible
ⓘ Origin obscure

hook, line and sinker
informal completely; in all details
• *He fell for the story hook, line and sinker*
ⓘ A fishing idiom, from a fish which swallows not only the hook but the entire end section of the line

off the hook
slang free from some difficulty or problem
ⓘ From fishing

sling one's hook
slang to go away, found as an angry instruction to someone whom one wants rid of

hoop

jump through hoops
to go to excessive lengths to please or gain favour with someone
ⓘ From the actions of animals which are trained to jump through hoops in circuses

put someone through the hoop
to cause them to suffer something unpleasant
ⓘ Probably from circus performers

hoot

not to give/care a hoot/two hoots (in hell)
informal not to care in the least

hop

catch someone on the hop
informal to do something to them when they are not prepared

hop it
Brit slang to go away

keep someone on the hop
to keep them busy, active, alert etc

hope

great white hope
informal, often ironical someone or something that people hope will bring victory or success to a group or organization
ⓘ Originally a reference to a white boxer in the US attempting to defeat a black boxer, black boxers often being the champions

have high hopes *see* **high**

hope against hope
to continue hoping that something will not happen etc, when there is no reason or no longer any reason for this hope
① A Biblical allusion, to Romans 4:18

hope springs eternal
people tend to go on hoping, no matter how gloomy the prospects appear
① The phrase is a shortened version of **hope springs eternal in the human breast**, a quotation from Alexander Pope's *An Essay on Criticism* (1711)

not to have a hope (in hell) of (something)
informal to be certainly not going to do, be, have etc (something)

pin one's hopes on *see* **pin**

raise someone's hopes
to give them good reason to believe that something will (not) happen, has (not) happened etc

while there's life there's hope *see* **life**

hopping

hopping mad
informal very angry

horn

draw in one's horns
to behave in a quieter manner, especially to spend less money
① The reference is to a snail

horn in on something
derogatory informal to join in an activity etc without being wanted or invited

lock horns with someone
to quarrel or engage in an argument with them
① A reference to horned animals, such as stags, using their horns when fighting each other

on the horns of a dilemma *see* **dilemma**

hornet

stir up a hornet's nest
to do something which causes a great deal of anger and resentment

horse

back the wrong horse
to give one's support to the person who proves unsuccessful in a contest of some kind
① A reference to putting a bet on a horse that loses a race

change horses in midstream
to alter one's views, plans etc in the middle of a project
① Apparently an image either coined or popularized by Abraham Lincoln

a dark horse *see* **dark**

eat like a horse
to eat a great deal

flog a dead horse
to try to make people interested in a subject which everyone has already fully discussed, which is no longer interesting etc

hold your horses
wait a moment; don't go so fast
① From driving a carriage

a horse laugh
a loud, harsh laugh

a horse of a different colour
something or someone of a completely different kind

horse sense
plain good sense

(there are) horses for courses
certain people are better suited to do certain jobs, especially certain particular tasks
① An allusion to the theory that certain racehorses are most likely to win on certain racecourses and that this factor should influence the races they are entered for, the odds offered by bookmakers etc

the iron horse *see* **iron**

lock the stable door after the horse has bolted *see* **stable**

look a gift horse in the mouth *see* **gift**

on one's high horse *see* **high**

put the cart before the horse *see* **cart**

straight from the horse's mouth
from a well-informed and reliable source
① Possibly originally used for 'infallible' tips in horse-racing

wild horses would not do something etc *see* **wild**

a willing horse
someone who is willing to work, to help people etc
⌚ An allusion to a saying which exists in several forms, eg **a willing horse never wants work**, all of which mean that if one member of a group etc is prepared to do all the work, the others will give him or her all the work to do

you can take a horse to (the) water but you can't make it drink
a proverb, meaning that one cannot actually force someone else to perform an action, only encourage him or her to do it

horseplay
rough and noisy play

hot
blow hot and cold *see* **blow**

hot air
informal boastful words, promises that will not be kept etc

hot-blooded
1 passionate; having strong sexual feelings
2 easily made angry; excitable
⌚ From the medieval belief that emotion raised the temperature of the blood

a hot line
informal a line of quick communication between two, usually important, people etc for use in emergencies

hot on something
informal fond of it; interested in and enthusiastic about it

hot stuff
slang
1 a person etc of a high quality, ability etc
2 a person who has or arouses strong sexual passions

a hot potato *see* **potato**

hot under the collar
cross and/or embarrassed

like a cat on hot bricks *see* **cat**

in hot water
informal in trouble

in the hot seat
informal in an uncomfortable or difficult position
⌚ Originally US slang for 'in the electric chair'

like hot cakes
informal (of selling, disappearing etc) very quickly

make it hot for someone
to make things unpleasant or impossible for them

piping hot *see* **piping**

red hot *see* **red**

hotbed
a hotbed of something
a place where something unpleasant grows or increases rapidly
⌚ Literally, a **hotbed** is a heated bed of soil in a greenhouse etc for forcing plants

hotfoot
informal in a great hurry
• *He arrived hotfoot from the meeting*

hothead
a hothead
a person who is easily made angry or who is inclined to act suddenly and without sufficient thought for the consequences

hour
after hours
after the end of a working day or after the time during which a shop etc is normally open

at all hours
informal at irregular times, especially late at night
• *He comes home at all hours*

at the eleventh hour *see* **eleventh**

in someone's hour of need
formal or facetious at a time when they are in need of help

the rush hour *see* **rush**

the small hours *see* **small**

house
as safe as houses
completely safe

bring the house down
to produce great applause or laughter
Ⓞ A theatrical phrase

eat someone out of house and home
to be so expensive to feed and keep that the person who is paying cannot afford it

a house of cards
completely insubstantial or without sound foundation
Ⓞ From building a 'house' by balancing playing cards on each other, a structure which is very liable to collapse

keep open house
to be prepared to entertain anyone who arrives

like a house on fire
informal
1 very well
2 very quickly

on the house
paid for by the provider
Ⓞ Originally US and applied only to drinks paid for by the landlord of a public house

put one's house in order
to make sure that all one's affairs are in order

household

a household name/word
a person or thing that is extremely well known

houseproud

rather derogatory very concerned about the appearance of one's house

how

and how
slang yes indeed; very much so
• *'That was a terrific party last night.' 'And how!'*
Ⓞ Originally US

any old how *see* **any**

how about?
informal
1 I would like to suggest
• *'Where shall we go tonight?' 'How about the cinema?'*
2 what is he etc going to do?; what does he etc think?
• *I rather like that picture. How about you?*

how come?
informal for what reason?
Ⓞ Originally US

hue

a hue and cry
a loud protest
Ⓞ An Anglo-Norman legal term, *hu et cri*, for the customary summons to the public to join the hunt for the perpetrator of a crime. *Hue* may originally have meant 'noise', including the sound of trumpets etc, as opposed to *cry*, 'shouting'

huff

in a/the huff
informal derogatory being or becoming silent because one is angry, displeased etc

hum

hum and haw
to make sounds which express doubt, uncertainty etc

make things hum
to cause everything to work quickly and smoothly

human

the milk of human kindness *see* **milk**

humble

eat humble pie
to humble oneself, eg by admitting a mistake
Ⓞ **Humble pie** was a dish made from the offal or *umble* of deer and eaten by estate servants as opposed to estate owners

hump

be over the hump
to have passed a crisis or difficulty

hunt

(hunt) high and low *see* **high**

run with the hare and hunt with the hounds *see* **hare**

hunting

a happy hunting-ground *see* **happy**

hurry

the more hurry the less speed *see* **haste**

hush

hush-hush

informal secret

⌚ 1st World War military slang for an especially important secret military or naval project, specifically for the development of tanks

hush money

slang money which is paid to a person to persuade him not to make certain facts known to someone else

hush something up

informal to prevent it becoming known to the general public

Hyde *see* Jekyll

I

ice

break the ice
to overcome the first shyness etc in a new situation

cut no ice
to have no effect
• *That sort of flattery cuts no ice with me*
Ⓣ Originally 19c US

just/only the tip of the iceberg
only a small, visible, part of a very much larger hidden problem, state of affairs etc
Ⓣ From the fact that an estimated 90% of an iceberg is hidden underwater

on ice
put aside for use, attention etc at a later date
Ⓣ From a method of preserving perishable food

(skating) on thin ice
in a risky or dangerous position

icing

the icing on the cake
a desirable but not necessary addition

if

if anything can go wrong it will *see* **wrong**

if the cap fits *see* **cap**

ifs and buts
informal excuses
• *The boss was tired of all her ifs and buts every time he wanted something done*

ill

go ill with someone or **something**
to end in danger or misfortune for them or it

ill-gotten gains
formal or facetious money got in a bad or unlawful way

it's an ill wind (that blows nobody any good)
a proverb, meaning that almost every unfortunate etc happening benefits someone in some way, used to indicate that the speaker recognizes that some good has come of an apparent misfortune

take it ill
formal to be offended (that)

illusion

be under an/the illusion (that)
to have a false impression or belief (about something)

I'm

I'm all right, Jack *see* **Jack**

image

the spitting image *see* **spitting**

imagination

a figment of one's imagination *see* **figment**

immemorial

from time immemorial
from a time beyond anyone's memory or written records; for a very long time
Ⓣ In legal phraseology, *immemorial* means 'before the beginning of legal memory', ie before the accession of Richard I in 1157

impression

be under the impression that
to have the (often wrong) feeling or idea that (something is the case)

in

fall in *see* **fall**

in for something
informal likely to experience it (usually something bad)

in for it
informal about to experience trouble; likely to be punished

in on something
informal knowing it; having a share in it
• *I'm in on the secret*

the ins and outs
informal the complex details of a plan etc

(well) in with someone
informal very friendly with them

there is etc **nothing in it**
1 there is no truth, no importance or no difficulty in the matter
2 there is no important difference between two or more things, scores etc
• *As the swimmers reached the last hundred metres of the race, there was nothing in it between first and second*

inch

come within an inch of something/doing something
to come very close to it/doing it

every inch
completely; entirely; in every way
• *He is every inch a gentleman*

give him etc **an inch (and he'll take an ell/a yard/a mile)**
a saying, meaning that it is unwise to make any concession at all to a person because they will take advantage of the concession to obtain even more

inch by inch
very gradually and often cautiously

include

include me out
informal an emphatic way of saying that one does not want any part in something

Indian

an Indian summer
a time of fine, still weather in autumn
Ⓛ From a feature of the N American climate, probably named simply because when it was first observed the country was inhabited by Native Americans

in Indian file *see* **file**

influence

under the influence
informal affected by alcohol, drunk

innings

have a good innings
Brit to live for a reasonable length of time, or to enjoy a reasonably long period of success or power
Ⓛ A cricketing term

inside

know something inside out *see* **know**

instance

in the first instance
formal as the first step in an action
• *If you want to join the club, you should apply to the secretary in the first instance*
Ⓛ A legal term: *instance* here means 'a legal process in a court of law', and *the second instance* would be an appeal

insult

add insult to injury
to behave badly towards someone whom one has already harmed in another way
Ⓛ A quotation from Edward Moore's play *The Foundling* (1748)

intent

to all intents (and purposes)
formal almost exactly; in all important ways
• *There are slight differences between the two plans, but to all intents and purposes they are the same*
Ⓛ A legal term

interest

in one's etc **(own) (best) interest(s)**
bringing, or in order to bring, advantage, benefit, help etc to oneself
• *It would be in our interest to help him, as he may be able to help us in the future*

in the interest(s) of something
formal in order to get, achieve, increase etc something
• *The political march was banned in the interests of public safety*

a vested interest *see* **vested**

with interest
to an even greater extent than

something has been done etc to someone

• *She vowed to repay the insult with interest*

interesting

in an interesting condition
old euphemism pregnant

iron

have several, too many etc **irons in the fire**
to be involved in, or doing, several etc things at the same time
Ⓛ The reference is to blacksmith's work. It is only possible to work successfully at the correct temperature, and, while it is useful to have some spare pieces heating in case of failure, it is unproductive to heat too many at once

the Iron Curtain
the barrier, considered to exist between Communist countries and other countries and preventing free communication and trading
Ⓛ The idiom dates from c.1920, but was made popular by Winston Churchill's use of it in a speech in 1946. It may derive ultimately from the use of an iron curtain as a fire precaution in theatres

the iron hand/fist in the velvet glove
a strong or ruthless type of government etc which is hidden by a surface appearance of softness and courtesy

the iron horse
old the railway

iron something out
to solve a problem, to smooth out a difficulty

rule someone with a rod of iron
to control a person or persons very severely and sternly
Ⓛ An apparent Biblical reference, to Psalm 2

strike while the iron is hot
to act etc while the situation is favourable
Ⓛ An idiom from blacksmith's work

issue

make an issue of something
to make it the subject of an argument

the point at issue
formal the question that is being discussed

take issue with someone
formal to disagree with them

it

it'll be all right on the night *see* **night**

it takes two to tango *see* **two**

itching

be itching to do something
informal to be very eager to do it

have an itching palm
to be very greedy for money
Ⓛ An old superstition held that an itching palm meant that one was about to receive money

ivory

an ivory tower
derogatory a way of living in which one is protected from all the difficult and unpleasant features of life
Ⓛ A phrase — *la tour d'ivoire* — coined in 1837 by the French poet Charles Augustin Sainte-Beuve

J

Jack

all work and no play makes Jack a dull boy *see* **work**

before you can say Jack Robinson
very quickly
⏲ Origin unknown

I'm all right, Jack
a catch phrase indicating that as long as someone's own life is happy and comfortable he or she has no intention of worrying about other people
⏲ A shortened version of **pull up the ladder, Jack, I'm all right**, which is nautical in origin

jack

every man jack
informal everybody
• *Every man jack of us must help*
⏲ Probably from the prevalence of *Jack* as a Christian name

a jack-of-all-trades
sometimes derogatory someone who can and does work at a number of different jobs, usually doing none of them particularly well

jackpot

hit the jackpot
informal to win or obtain a lot of money or success
⏲ The jackpot is a pool of money in poker which continues to accumulate without being won until someone is able to begin the betting with a pair of jacks or better

jam

(there will be) jam tomorrow
a saying, indicating that the speaker believes that benefits, prosperity, happiness etc which are promised will never in fact come
• *For years politicians have persuaded the people of this country to put up with hardships by promising them jam tomorrow*
⏲ From Lewis Carroll's *Alice Through the Looking-Glass*, in which the Red Queen offers Alice a job with 'Twopence a week, and jam every other day ... jam tomorrow, and jam yesterday — but never jam today'

money for jam *see* **money**

want jam on it
facetious derogatory to be dissatisfied with an already favourable state of affairs

jaw

his etc **jaw dropped**
he etc was extremely surprised
⏲ Sometimes one's mouth falls open if one is very surprised

jazz

and all that jazz
slang and so on, and other things of a similar nature
• *If we want to play tennis there, we'll have to have white shorts and all that jazz*
⏲ US in origin

Jekyll

a Jekyll and Hyde
a person with two sides to his personality, often one good and one bad
⏲ From the hero of Robert Louis Stevenson's novel *Doctor Jekyll and Mr Hyde* (1886)

jet

the jet set
often derogatory very wealthy people who enjoy a life of frequent travel by jet and expensive holidays

jetsam

flotsam and jetsam *see* **flotsam**

jewel

the jewel in the crown
the most valuable or the most important part of something
• *The jewel in the city's crown is the cathedral*

jib

the cut of someone's jib
the general appearance and nature of someone
Ⓘ Originally referred to the condition of the jib or foresail of a ship

Job

have the patience of Job *see* **patience**

a Job's comforter
a person who intends to comfort someone in distress but who in fact makes things worse
• *My mother is a real Job's comforter when I'm ill — she comes to see me and tells me how ill I look and how much worse I'm going to feel before I'm better*
Ⓘ From the three friends of Job in the Bible

job

the devil of a job *see* **devil**

give something up as a bad job
informal to decide that it is not worth doing, or impossible to do, and so stop doing it

a good job
informal a lucky or satisfactory state of affairs
• *It's a good job that she can't hear what you're saying*

have a job
informal to have difficulty doing something, to do something, with something

a job lot
a mixed collection, eg of goods, especially if of poor quality

jobs for the boys
informal a catch phrase originally applied mainly to political situations, but later applied more generally, indicating that people are getting jobs because they are friends or relatives of the people in charge, rather than on the grounds of merit

just the job
informal entirely suitable; exactly what is needed

make the best of a bad job *see* **best**

on the job
working

a put-up job *see* **put**

jockey

jockey for position
to try to push one's way into a favourable position
Ⓘ A *jockey* was originally a horse-trader, a profession generally regarded as characterized by deviousness, if not outright dishonesty

Joe

Joe Public/Joe Bloggs
informal an ordinary member of the public, an average person

join

join the club *see* **club**

joint

case the joint
slang to survey a place with a view to committing a burglary there

put someone's nose out of joint *see* **nose**

joke

beyond a joke
past the limit of being humorous

crack a joke *see* **crack**

it's no joke
informal it is a serious or worrying matter

joking apart/aside
let us stop joking and talk seriously

a practical joke *see* **practical**

a standing joke *see* **standing**

jolly

jolly someone along
informal to keep them in a good temper in order to gain their goodwill or co-operation
Ⓘ Originally US

the Jolly Roger
the black flag with a white skull and crossbones reputed to be flown by pirate ships
Ⓘ It appears that Roger was thought of as being the name of the person whose skull appears on the flag — *jolly* is ironic. Another, early 18c, name was *Old Roger*

Jones

keep up with the Joneses
to make sure that one remains equal socially with one's neighbours by doing the same things, buying the same type of car, television etc
Ⓘ From the title of a comic strip by Arthur R Momand which appeared in the New York *Globe* from 1913 until the early 1940s

jowl

cheek by jowl *see* **cheek**

joy

be someone's pride and joy *see* **pride**

no joy
slang no luck, news, information etc

wish someone joy of something *see* **wish**

not to get any joy out of someone or **something**
to be unsuccessful in achieving an aim
• *She was hoping to get some compensation for damages but she did not get any joy out of the insurance company*

Judas

a Judas
a person who is disloyal, a traitor
Ⓘ A biblical reference to Judas Iscariot who betrayed Jesus Christ

judge

as sober as a judge
1 extremely serious
2 not at all drunk

judgement

sit in judgement on someone
to take upon oneself the responsibility of criticizing others

juice

stew in one's own juice
informal to suffer as a result of one's own stupidity etc

jump

for the high jump *see* **high**

jump down someone's throat *see* **throat**

jump on the bandwagon *see* **bandwagon**

jump out of one's skin *see* **skin**

jump the gun *see* **gun**

jump the queue *see* **queue**

jump through hoops *see* **hoop**

jump to it
informal to hurry up

jumping

a jumping-off place/point
a place from which to start

jungle

blackboard jungle *see* **black**

concrete jungle *see* **concrete**

the law of the jungle *see* **law**

just

get one's just deserts
to suffer the fate or results etc which one deserves, especially if bad

just one of those things *see* **thing**

just so
1 very neat and ordered
2 precisely; exactly
• *'We can't expect any results until Friday.' 'Just so.'*

just the job *see* **job**

justice

do someone or **something justice/do justice to someone** or **something**
facetious
1 to treat someone fairly or properly
2 to fulfil the highest possibilities of someone; to get the best results from someone or something
3 to show someone or something fully or fairly
• *The portrait is good, but doesn't do justice to her beauty*

poetic justice *see* **poetic**

K

keel

be, keep on an even keel
to be, keep or remain in a calm and untroubled state
• *He kept the business on an even keel in spite of the many changes in staff*
Ⓣ A nautical idiom

keel over
informal to fall over, usually suddenly or unexpectedly

keen

as keen as mustard *see* **mustard**

keep

for keeps
informal permanently

keep an eye on *see* **eye**

keep an open mind *see* **open**

keep at arm's length *see* **arm**

keep at it
informal to go on doing something, especially to continue to work at something until one succeeds or finishes

keep company (with) *see* **company**

keep one's cool *see* **cool**

keep one's (own) counsel *see* **counsel**

keep one's distance *see* **distance**

keep one's end up *see* **end**

keep one's hair on *see* **hair**

keep one's hand in *see* **hand**

keep one's head *see* **head**

keep one's head above water *see* **head**

keep in mind *see* **mind**

keep in with someone
informal to remain friendly with them, usually for a special reason

keep it up
informal to carry on doing something at the same speed or as well as one is doing it at present
Ⓣ Probably from the game of shuttlecock, the main aim of which was to keep the shuttlecock in the air. The idiom was originally applied to prolonged drinking parties etc

keep one's nose clean *see* **nose**

keep on at someone
informal to urge them constantly to do something

keep pace with *see* **pace**

keep someone posted *see* **post**

keep someone right *see* **right**

keep one's shirt on *see* **shirt**

keep sight of *see* **sight**

keep tabs on *see* **tab**

keep one's temper *see* **temper**

keep the peace *see* **peace**

keep the wolf from the door *see* **wolf**

keep time *see* **time**

keep oneself etc **to oneself**
informal to tell others very little about oneself, and not to be very friendly or sociable

keep something to oneself
not to tell anyone something

keep track of someone or **something** *see* **track**

keep something under one's hat *see* **hat**

keep something under wraps *see* **wrap**

keep up appearances *see* **appearance**

keep up with the Joneses *see* **Jones**

keep one's word *see* **word**

keeping

in keeping with
formal suited to
• *He has moved to a house more in keeping with his position as an MP*

ken

beyond one's ken
outside the extent of one's knowledge or understanding
⊙ *Ken*, in the 17–18c, meant 'range of sight'

kettle

the pot calling the kettle black *see* **pot**

a pretty kettle of fish
informal a mess or awkward situation
⊙ Origin obscure

key

(all) keyed up
informal excited; tense
⊙ A musical idiom — *key up* means 'to tune to a higher pitch'

kibosh

put the kibosh on something
to prevent it from being fulfilled or being successful
• *The wet weather put the kibosh on our picnic plans*
⊙ It has been suggested that kibosh is Yiddish in derivation but the origin of the phrase is uncertain

kick

for a kick-off
slang in the first place or to start an argument or complaint etc
⊙ From the first kick of the match in football

for kicks
slang in order to get a thrill; for fun

kick the bucket *see* **bucket**

kick oneself
informal to be annoyed with oneself because one has been stupid or has made a mistake etc

kick one's heels *see* **heel**

kid

handle someone or **something with kid gloves**
to deal with a person or situation in a delicate and tactful manner

kid's stuff
slang something very easy and undemanding

Kilkenny

fight like Kilkenny cats
to fight or quarrel extremely fiercely
⊙ A reference to a story about two cats in the town of Kilkenny who were tied together by their tails and fought until only their tails were left

Kilroy

Kilroy was here
a common piece of graffiti written on the walls of public places. As the fashion for graffiti has increased various other names are frequently substituted for Kilroy
⊙ The origin is uncertain and is the subject of conjecture, one theory being that it was a phrase chalked on the shipyard equipment and material which he had inspected by an inspector in Quincy, Massachusetts

kill

be in at the kill
to be present at the most exciting or advantageous moment
⊙ A hunting term

curiosity killed the cat *see* **curiosity**

dressed to kill *see* **dress**

kill the fatted calf *see* **fat**

kill the goose that lays the golden eggs *see* **goose**

kill time *see* **time**

kill two birds with one stone *see* **bird**

killing

make a killing
informal to make a great deal of money, a large profit etc
⊙ Originally a racing term meaning 'to win a great deal of money'

kin

one's next of kin
legal one's nearest relative(s)

kind

in kind
formal in the same way or with the same treatment

• *He spoke rudely to her and she replied in kind*

nothing of the kind
not at all what is/was expected, supposed etc
• *I thought he would be helpful, but he was nothing of the kind — he was positively rude*

of a kind
derogatory scarcely deserving the name
• *We received hospitality of a kind at their house but we had to have a meal at a restaurant on the way home*

two of a kind *see* **two**

king

a king's ransom *see* **ransom**

take the king's shilling
hist to join the army
Ⓞ From the method of joining, which was by accepting a shilling from the recruiting officer as an advance on wages

turn King's evidence *see* **evidence**

kingdom

go/be sent etc **to kingdom come**
usually facetious to die, to be killed
Ⓞ From the phrase 'thy kingdom come' in the Lord's Prayer

till kingdom come
for a very long time
Ⓞ As previous entry

kiss

have kissed the Blarney stone
informal to be very eloquent and persuasive
Ⓞ Legend has it that whoever can climb the high wall of Blarney Castle, near Cork in Ireland and kiss a stone set high in the wall will acquire the gift of eloquence

kiss and tell
to betray a close secret, specifically to have a secret love affair and then make it public
Ⓞ A journalistic phrase used to describe the actions of someone who has an affair with someone well-known and then sells the story of the affair to a newspaper. The phrase is in fact much older than this, occurring in *Burlesque* (1675) by Charles Cotton — 'And if he must kiss and tell, I'll kick him headlong into hell'

kiss something goodbye
slang a phrase indicating that one will not see something again, usually because it has been stolen or lent to someone who will not return it

the kiss of death
usually facetious something especially if apparently helpful, which causes ruin, death etc
• *A recommendation from him would be the kiss of death — he is very unpopular*
Ⓞ A Biblical reference, to the kiss by means of which Judas betrayed Jesus — Matthew 26; Mark 14

kite

fly a kite
informal to start a rumour about a new project etc in order to find out whether or not people would support it if it was really put into operation
Ⓞ From the use of kites to discover the direction and strength of the wind

high as a kite *see* **high**

kitten

as weak as a kitten
very weak

have kittens
informal to be very nervous, upset or angry
• *She didn't get home until 2 am and her mother was having kittens wondering where she was*

knee

bring someone to his etc **knees**
to make someone humble; to make someone realize that they have been defeated

knee-high to a grasshopper
facetious very small
Ⓞ Originally US

knickers

get one's knickers in a twist
impolite informal to become worried or excited

knife

have one's knife in someone
informal to be continually hostile or unfair towards them

the night of the long knives
a surprise purge in which people are rapidly removed from their jobs unexpectedly at the instigation of their leader or colleagues
① A translation of *Die Nacht der langer Messer*, used to describe the night (June 29, 1934) of the liquidation of stormtroopers who had helped Hitler to power but who were proving to be an obstruction to his dealings with the German army

knight

a knight in shining armour
a person who comes to someone's rescue, especially when the situation is not looking hopeful
① A reference to the armour-clad knights of medieval legend who rescued maidens in distress

knit

knit one's brows
formal to draw together or wrinkle the brows; to frown

knock

knock someone all of a heap *see* **heap**

knock around/about
1 to move about in a casual manner without a definite destination or purpose
• *He spent six months knocking around Europe seeing the sights and living as cheaply as possible*
2 to be present without doing anything in particular
• *Three youths were knocking around outside the cinema when the incident occurred*

knock something back
informal to eat or drink something, especially quickly and/or in large quantities
• *He knocked back three pints of beer in the space of ten minutes*

knock someone cold
informal to make them unconscious by a blow

knock someone for six *see* **six**

knock someone or **something into a cocked hat** *see* **hat**

knock something into shape *see* **shape**

knock it off!
slang stop it!

knock off
1 *informal* to stop working
2 *slang* to steal something

knock something on the head *see* **head**

knock spots off *see* **spot**

knock the living daylights out of someone *see* **living**

knock the stuffing out of *see* **stuffing**

you could have knocked me down with a feather *see* **feather**

knot

at a rate of knots
very quickly
① A nautical idiom

cut the Gordian knot
to solve a problem or overcome a difficulty by a vigorous or drastic method
• *He hated moving the lawn and so he cut the Gordian knot by digging up all the grass and putting down concrete*
① A reference to a Greek legend, in which anyone who was able to untie a knot in a rope belonging to King Gordius, King of Phrygia, would automatically become ruler of all Asia. The task was accomplished by Alexander the Great who severed the knot by cutting through it with his sword

get knotted
slang a scornful expression of annoyance, refusal to do what one is asked, disbelief etc

tie oneself/someone (up) in knots
to get oneself, someone else into a confused or difficult situation

know

before one knows where one is
very quickly and especially before one has time to understand a problem, situation etc fully

for all I etc **know**
because I do not know anything about the subject, usually implying either that one ought to have been informed or that one has no interest

• *For all I know she might be dead — I haven't heard from her for years*

in the know
informal having information possessed by a small group of people and not by those outside it

know a hawk from a handsaw *see* **hawk**

know all the answers *see* **answer**

know a thing or two *see* **thing**

know something backwards/inside out
to know extremely well or perfectly

know better
to be too wise or well-taught to do something
• *We should have known better than to trust them*

know someone by sight *see* **sight**

know-how
informal the practical knowledge and skill to deal with something

know one's onions *see* **onion**

know one's place *see* **place**

know the ropes *see* **rope**

know the score *see* **score**

know what's what *see* **what**

know where one stands *see* **stand**

know which side one's bread is buttered (on) *see* **bread**

not to know one is born
derogatory to lead a very trouble-free, protected life

not to know one's own mind *see* **mind**

what do you know?
informal: especially US an expression of surprise
• *What do you know? I thought that man over there died last year*

I wouldn't know
informal I am not in a position to know

you never know
it is possible that

knowing

there's no knowing
it is impossible to know

knowledge

come to someone's knowledge
to be discovered by someone

to one's knowledge
rather formal according to what one has been told, knows etc
• *'Has Henry been invited?' 'Not to my knowledge'*

knuckle

knuckle down to something
to start working seriously at it

knuckle under
informal to give in to someone else

near the knuckle
informal rather too indecent

L

labour

a labour of love
a job etc which one does for one's own satisfaction or pleasure or for that of someone whom one loves and for which one is usually not paid

lady

a ladies' man
a man who likes the company of women

a lady-killer
informal: usually derogatory a man who is said to be very popular with women

laid

laid up
informal unwell, confined to bed because of illness or accident

lamb

as well be hanged for a sheep as a lamb *see* **sheep**

a ewe lamb *see* **ewe**

like a lamb to the slaughter
quietly and without arguing or complaining, used of someone going into danger or difficulty, about to be punished etc
Ⓞ A Biblical reference, to Isaiah 53:7

two shakes of a lamb's tail *see* **shake**

lame

help a lame dog over the stile *see* **dog**

a lame duck *see* **duck**

lamp

smell of the lamp
usually derogatory of books etc, to show signs that the writer has done a lot of research for or revision of his book
• *His best novels were written quickly — anything he spent a lot of time over tended to smell of the lamp*

land

in the land of the living
informal alive

a land of milk and honey
an area which is very fertile
Ⓞ A Biblical quotation, from Exodus 3:8, describing the Promised Land of the Israelites

the Land of Nod *see* **Nod**

land on one's feet *see* **feet**

land up
informal to finish or come eventually to be (in a certain, usually the wrong, place or a certain, usually bad, condition)
• *If you go on like that, you'll land up in jail*
Ⓞ A nautical idiom

land someone with something
informal to give or pass a job, an object etc which is unpleasant or unwanted to someone else

the lie of the land *see* **lie[2]**

a no-man's land *see* **man**

the promised land
a place or situation of ultimate happiness or success
Ⓞ A Biblical reference to Genesis 12:7, in which God promises the land of Canaan to Abraham, Isaac and Jacob and their descendants. Later the name referred to the Holy Land

see how the land lies
to look at the conditions, state of affairs etc which exist before taking an action or making a decision
Ⓞ A nautical idiom, literally implying 'to see where exactly one is'

spy out the land *see* **spy**

landslide

a landslide victory
a victory in an election by a very large majority of votes

language

bad language
informal swearing

speak the same language as someone
to have a good mutual understanding with them, having similar tastes and thoughts

strong language *see* **strong**

lap[1]

drop into someone's lap
to achieve or acquire something without any effort on someone's part

in the lap of luxury
in very luxurious conditions

in the lap of the gods
of a situation, left to chance, so that it is impossible to affect what happens or even to know what will happen
Ⓞ A Greek idiom found frequently in Homer

lap[2]

lap it up
informal to accept or believe something readily and eagerly
Ⓞ From a thirsty animal lapping up water, etc

large

as large as life *see* **life**

loom large *see* **loom**

lark

as happy as a lark
very happy

get up with the lark
to rise early in the morning

Larry

as happy as Larry
extremely happy, totally carefree
Ⓞ Origin uncertain

lash

lash out
informal to spend money in large quantities

lash out at someone or **something**
to attack someone or something either physically or verbally

last[1]

as a/in the last resort *see* **resort**

at one's last gasp *see* **gasp**

at (long) last
in the end, especially after a long delay

breathe one's last
literary euphemism to die

famous last words
a saying used to indicate that the person who has just said something will live to regret them or be proved wrong

a last-ditch effort
a final, and often rather desperate, attempt to do something
Ⓞ A reference to soldiers defending a crucial military position

the last of the Mohicans
the last one of a group or set that is left after the rest have gone or been used
Ⓞ The title of a novel by James Fenimore Cooper (1836)

last but not least
a saying used to introduce the name of the last person or thing on a list to indicate that the order given is not necessarily an order of merit

the last of the big spenders
informal, ironic a saying used to describe someone who is mean and does not like parting with money

the last person
someone who is very unlikely, unwilling etc to do something; someone that it is dangerous, unsuitable etc to do something tc
• *She's the last person you would suspect of such a thing*

last resting-place *see* **resting**

the last straw
a fact, happening etc which, when added to all other facts or happenings, makes a situation finally impossible to bear
Ⓞ An allusion to the saying **it is the last straw that breaks the camel's back,** which means than when one trivial

annoyance, worry etc is added to another there comes a point when the addition of yet one more causes a disaster

the last word
informal
1 the final remark in an argument
• *She must always have the last word!*
2 the final decision
• *The last word on the project rests with the manager*
3 something very fashionable or up to date
• *Her hat was the last word in elegance*

on one's last legs
very near to falling down or collapsing with exhaustion, old age etc

see, hear the last of someone or **something**
to see or hear of them or it for the last time

last[2]

the cobbler should stick to his last *see* **cobbler**

latch

latch on to someone or **something**
1 to join oneself to a person, group etc
2 to come to understand an idea etc

latchkey

a latchkey child
a child who frequently comes home to an empty house, and therefore carries a key to the door with him or her

late

better late than never
a saying, meaning that it is better that something should happen, occur etc rather later than one would have wished than not at all

late in the day
when a project, activity has been going on for some time, especially if it is considered to be too late to make proposed changes, decisions etc

lather

in a lather
informal very excited or upset
ⓘ Literally applies to horses

Latin

dog Latin
very incorrect Latin as compared to Classical Latin

laugh

be laughed out of court
to cause so much amusement or scorn, usually by what one says, is asking etc that one's complaint, case etc is not fully considered

have the last laugh
to succeed or to be proved right, after suffering a great deal of scorn, disbelief etc
ⓘ An allusion to the saying **he who laughs last laughs longest**, ie 'the final victory is the most complete one'

a horse laugh *see* **horse**

laugh all the way to the bank
to be delighted at having made a great deal of money

laugh and the world laughs with you, weep and you weep alone
a proverb indicating that when a person is cheerful other people are willing to associate with them and to share in their happiness but people tend to avoid a person who is sad or miserable

laugh one's head off *see* **head**

laugh like a drain
informal to laugh heartily and loudly
ⓘ The laughter is likened to the noise of water gurgling as it goes down a drain

laugh something off
to treat injuries, problems etc as unimportant

laugh on the other side of one's face
to be made to feel disappointment or sorrow (by implication, deservedly) after seeming to be lucky or successful

laugh up one's sleeve *see* **sleeve**

laughing

be laughing
to be about to be in a good position, with no further worries, problems etc

kill oneself laughing
to laugh extremely heartily so that one can hardly stop

a laughing-stock
someone who is laughed at

no laughing matter
a very serious matter

laurel

look to one's laurels
to be careful not to lose a position or reputation because of better performances etc by others
Ⓘ From the laurel wreath with which the Greeks crowned poets, winners at the Pythian games etc

rest on one's laurels
to keep a position or reputation because of past successes without actually doing anything more
Ⓘ As previous entry

law

the (long) arm of the law *see* **arm**

be a law unto oneself
not to obey rules or orders
Ⓘ A Biblical reference, to Romans 2:3

have the law on someone
informal: usually used as a threat to make sure that legal action is taken against someone who is breaking the law

the law
informal the police

the law of the jungle
the rules for succeeding or surviving in a difficult or dangerous situation by the use of force etc
Ⓘ A phrase coined by Rudyard Kipling

lay down the law
to state something in a way that indicates that one expects one's opinion and orders to be accepted without argument

the letter of the law *see* **letter**

take the law into one's own hands
to obtain justice in a way not involving the law, the police etc

an unwritten law
a rule or regulation that is not official but is observed by custom or tradition

lay

lay about one
to strike blows in all directions

lay down one's arms *see* **arm**

lay down the law *see* **law**

lay one's hands on *see* **hand**

lay into someone
to attack them strongly, especially to beat them thoroughly

lay it on the line *see* **line**

lay it on thick *see* **thick**

lay it on with a trowel *see* **trowel**

lay someone low *see* **low**

lay off
1 to dismiss employees temporarily
2 *informal* to stop doing something
• *I told him to lay off following me or he'd be sorry!*

lay something on the line *see* **line**

lay oneself open to something *see* **open**

lay someone to rest *see* **rest**

lay waste *see* **waste**

lead[1]

lead a charmed life *see* **charm**

lead someone a (merry) dance *see* **dance**

lead someone by the nose *see* **nose**

lead someone on
to deceive them by causing them to have false hopes

lead the way
to go first, especially to show the way
• *Our country has led the way in the field of electronics for years*

lead someone up the garden path *see* **garden**

lead up to something
to prepare (to do something, for something to happen etc) by steps or stages
• *He talked for a long time and seemed to be leading up to something*

lead[2]

swing the lead
slang to neglect one's work, usually inventing excuses to hide the fact; to try to make others believe something that is not true, in order to hide one's own mistakes, inefficiency etc
Ⓘ Originally naval slang

leading

a leading light
sometimes facetious a very important and influential person in a certain field
Ⓛ Literally a nautical term for a light used with other marks as a guide to the entrance of a harbour, a channel etc

a leading question
a question asked in such a way as to suggest the answer the questioner wants to hear
Ⓛ A legal term

leaf

take a leaf out of someone's book
to use them as an example

turn over a new leaf
to begin a new and better way of behaving, working etc
Ⓛ Literally, to start writing on a fresh page of a notebook etc

league

be top/bottom of the league
to be best/worst in a particular area of activity, quality etc
Ⓛ From the grouping of clubs in soccer etc

in league with someone
having joined together with a person, organization etc, usually for a bad purpose

not in the same league as someone
not as able, as important, as good etc as them

leak

leak out
to come to be known by the public

lean

lean on someone
slang to use slight force to persuade them to do something etc

leap

by leaps and bounds
extremely rapidly and successfully

a leap in the dark
an action, decision etc whose results cannot be foreseen

learn

learn the hard way
to gain knowledge of something only by a process involving difficulties or unpleasant experiences

learning

a little learning is a dangerous thing *see* **little**

lease

give someone or **something a new lease of life**
to cause them or it to have a longer period of active life, usefulness etc than they would otherwise have had

least

least said, soonest mended
a proverb, meaning that the less one says in a difficult situation, the less one is likely to offend or hurt someone

to say the least
not to exaggerate in any way
• *When I admitted I'd forgotten our date, she was rather annoyed, to say the least*

leave

leave someone alone
not to disturb, upset or tease them

leave someone in the lurch *see* **lurch**

leave no stone unturned *see* **stone**

leave of absence
permission to be away from one's duty etc, or the time that one is permitted to be away

leave someone to one's own devices
to leave them to do as they wish or please rather than to give them something specific to do

leave/let well alone *see* **let**

take French leave *see* **French**

take it or leave it *see* **take**

take leave of one's senses *see* **sense**

leeway

make up leeway
to recover from a setback, disadvantage etc which has caused one to fall behind others, a schedule etc
Ⓛ A nautical idiom — **leeway** is the unwanted progress sideways made by a sailing ship in response to the sideways pressure of the wind — as opposed to **headway**, 'progress forwards'

left

the left hand does not know what the right hand is doing *see* **hand**

have two left feet
informal to be clumsy or awkward, eg in dancing

left, right and centre
informal in large quantities
• *We won't make much money if we hand out free tickets left, right and centre*

leg

break a leg
a traditional theatrical greeting of good luck said before a performance because it is thought to be back luck to wish someone good luck directly

get one's sea legs *see* **sea**

give someone a leg up
informal to help them to achieve something
① Literally, to support someone's leg and foot to help them to climb up on to something

not to have a leg to stand on
informal to have no way of excusing one's behaviour, justifying one's requests etc

on one's last legs *see* **last**

pull someone's leg
informal to try as a joke to make them believe something which is not true

shake a leg
informal
1 to hurry up
2 to dance

stretch one's legs *see* **stretch**

legal

legal eagle
informal a lawyer or barrister

legend

a legend in one's own lifetime
someone who achieves great fame in his or her own lifetime. A humorous version of this is **a legend in one's own lunchtime** which indicates that the fame of a person has been short-lived

legion

their name is legion
rather formal there are a very great many of them
• *I don't know how many people have written complaining, but their name is legion*
① A Biblical reference, to Mark 5:9

lemon

the answer is a lemon
one is given an unsatisfactory answer or no answer at all
① US, of obscure origin

lend

lend a hand *see* **hand**

lend an ear *see* **ear**

lend itself to (something)
to be suitable for or adapt easily to
• *This room lends itself to formal occasions*

length

at length
1 in detail; taking a long time
2 *formal* at last

go to any lengths
to do anything, no matter how extreme, dishonest, wicked etc to get what one wants

the length and breadth of somewhere
the whole of somewhere, from or in all parts of somewhere

leopard

a leopard never changes its spots
a saying indicating that the basic character or nature of a person is very unlikely to change

let

let alone someone or **something**
not to mention someone etc; without taking someone etc into consideration

let someone down
to disappoint or fail to help them when necessary etc

let fly *see* **fly**

let oneself go
1 to act without attempting to restrain oneself
2 to lose interest in and cease to take trouble over one's appearance, the way one lives etc

let go of something
to stop holding it

let one's hair down *see* **hair**

let someone have it *see* **have**

let someone in for something
to cause them to be involved in something unpleasant or difficult
• *When I agreed to do the job, I didn't know what I was letting myself in for, or I would have refused*

let someone in on something
informal to share a secret etc with them

let off steam *see* **steam**

let on
1 to pretend, or allow something untrue to be believed
• *I let on that I had never heard of him*
2 to reveal or show
• *I didn't let on that I knew him*

let something slide *see* **slide**

let something slip *see* **slip**

let the dead bury the dead *see* **dead**

let them eat cake *see* **cake**

let the grass grow under one's feet *see* **grass**

let/leave well alone
to allow things to remain as they are, in order not to make them worse

to let
available to be rented

letter

a Dear John letter
a letter or note sent by a wife, fiancée or girlfriend to let the recipient know that her relationship with him is at an end
Ⓞ The phrase originated in the armed services during World War II when such letters were common because of the pressures imposed by the long periods of enforced separation

the letter of the law
an interpretation of the law which follows exactly what it says as opposed to what the writer actually meant
Ⓞ A Biblical reference, to II Corinthians 3:6

a red-letter day *see* **red**

to the letter
exactly; following every detail
• *He followed his father's instructions to the letter*

level

do one's level best *see* **best**

find one's/it's (own) level
to find the place, rank etc to which one/it naturally belongs
Ⓞ Originally used of two connected bodies of liquid, meaning 'to arrive at a common level'

level-headed
calm and having good sense

level pegging
informal (of two or more people etc) doing equally well, having equal scores etc
• *The two teams at the top of the football league are level pegging at the moment*
Ⓞ Probably from scoring by means of pegs and numbered holes

on the level
slang fair; honest
• *Is his offer on the level?*
Ⓞ Originally US, probably from the idea that *level*, like *straight* and *square*, implies rightness

liar

a liar needs a good memory
if people are going to tell lies they require to have good memories so that they can make their lies consistent

liberty

at liberty to do something
free, permitted etc to do it

Liberty Hall
facetious a place where one can do whatever one wishes

take liberties with someone or **something**
to treat them or it with too much freedom, without enough respect or in an indecent manner

take the liberty of doing something
formal to do something without permission

lick

a lick and a promise
informal a short and not very thorough wash or clean

lick someone or **something into shape**
informal to put something into a more perfect form or make someone more efficient

lick one's lips *see* **lip**

lid

blow the lid off something
slang to expose a scandal etc

flip one's lid
slang to go crazy, to become very angry

put the (tin) lid on something
slang to add the final unpleasant detail to something very unsatisfactory etc

lie[1]

give the lie to something
formal to show a statement etc to be false
⏀ Literally, this phrase means 'to call someone a liar'

lie in one's teeth
informal to lie very obviously and shamelessly

a white lie *see* **white**

lie[2]

lie heavy on someone
to be a worry or a burden to them

lie in wait for someone or **something**
to be waiting to catch or attack them or it

lie low *see* **low**

the lie of the land
the details of any particular situation
⏀ A nautical idiom — literally 'the direction and characteristics of the coastline'

see how the land lies *see* **land**

take something lying down
usually in negative to accept or suffer something without arguing, complaining or trying to avoid it

life

as large as life
in person; actually
⏀ Literally 'life-size', used of a painting, sculpture etc

the facts of life
the facts relating to sex and reproduction

for dear life *see* **dear**

for the life of me
informal even if it was necessary in order to save my life (usually with exaggeration)
• *I couldn't for the life of me remember his name!*

have the time of one's life *see* **time**

lead a charmed life *see* **charm**

the life and soul of the party
a person who is very active, enthusiastic, amusing etc at a party

life begins at forty
a proverb indicating that, contrary to what used to be assumed, there is a great deal to look forward to in middle age

life is just a bowl of cherries
often ironic everything is just fine
• *My washing-machine has broken down and the car won't start — isn't life just a bowl of cherries?*
⏀ The title of a song popularized by the US singer Ethel Merman (1931)

the life of Riley
slang an easy, troublefree life
⏀ Origin obscure

a matter of life and death *see* **matter**

not on your life!
informal certainly not!

see life
not formal: often facetious to find out how other people live, especially if they live strangely or not respectably

take one's life in one's hands
often facetious
to take the risk of being killed or attacked etc

to the life
exactly like
• *When he put on that uniform, he was Napoleon to the life*

while there's life there's hope
a saying, meaning that one should not despair of a situation while it is still possible for it to improve

lift

not to lift a finger *see* **finger**

thumb a lift *see* **thumb**

light[1]

according to one's lights
formal following one's own standards
• *He was a good father according to his lights, but very strict*
ⓘ Apparently a translation of a French idiom — *lights* in French means 'mental ability'

bring to light
to reveal or cause to be noticed

come to light
to be revealed or discovered

go out like a light
informal to fall quickly and deeply asleep

guiding light
someone or something that acts as a good example or source of inspiration
ⓘ From a torch or other light which shows the way in the dark

hide one's light under a bushel
to hide, or try not to attract attention to, one's talent or ability
ⓘ A Biblical allusion, to Matthew 5:15 — 'Neither do men light a candle, and put it under a bushel, but on a candlestick ... let your light so shine before men that they may see your good works'

in the cold light of day
when a plan etc is considered in a practical manner, not in an atmosphere of emotion

in the light of something
formal taking into consideration information acquired etc

a leading light *see* **leading**

a/the light at the end of the tunnel
a cheerful or optimistic situation or solution that emerges after a long period of depression or trouble
ⓘ A reference to a railway tunnel

light-fingered
likely to steal

make light of something
to treat it as unimportant

many hands make light work *see* **hand**

see the light
often facetious
1 often **see the light of day**, to be discovered, produced etc
2 to be converted to someone else's point of view etc
• *That was one of our projects which never saw the light of day at all*

shed/throw light on something
to make a reason, subject etc clearer

light[2]

as light as a feather *see* **feather**

lightning

as quick as lightning
very quickly

lightning never strikes in the same place twice
a saying, meaning that an unusual accident, mishap etc is very unlikely to be repeated exactly

like (greased/a streak of) lightning
very quickly

like

the likes of
informal people such as

likely

a likely story!
informal I don't believe you, him etc

not likely!
informal certainly not!

lily

gild the lily
to add unnecessary decoration, exaggeration etc to something
ⓘ An adaptation of a quotation from Shakespeare, *King John* IV, ii — 'To gild refined gold, to paint the lily ... Is wasteful and ridiculous excess'

lily-livered
literary cowardly
ⓘ Probably a direct quotation from Shakespeare, *Macbeth* V, iii, from the old scientific belief that the liver of a coward contained no blood

limb

out on a limb
having ideas or opinions not

shared by others; in a dangerous or disadvantageous position
① The reference is to being isolated on a branch of a tree out of contact with the main trunk

limbo

in limbo
formal forgotten, neglected or cast aside
① A Latin term — 'on the border' — for the region in the borderland of Hell held by orthodox Catholic theology to be inhabited by the souls of the unbaptized and the righteous who lived before Christ

limelight

in the limelight
in a situation or position where one attracts a great deal of attention from the public
① From a type of brilliant light formerly used for spotlights in theatres

limit

the limit
informal only just able to be tolerated
• *That firm is the limit! This is the sixth time they have sent us faulty goods!*

off limits
beyond what is allowed

the sky's the limit *see* **sky**

within limits
to a reasonable degree
• *They can have as much time off as they need — within limits*

line

all along the line
not formal at every point in a process etc
① A military idiom

be in someone's line (of country)
to be the kind of thing they understand, like, can deal with etc

bring something into line
to make it agree with, the same as etc, a number of other things

draw the line
to fix a limit especially for what one is prepared to do

drop someone a line
informal to write them a brief letter or note

hard lines *see* **hard**

in line for something
likely to get or to be given something

hold the line *see* **hold**

a hot line *see* **hot**

in, out of line with something
formal in or out of agreement or harmony with

lay it on the line
informal to speak frankly in order to make a subject, especially one's orders, opinions, conditions etc, quite clear
① Originally US

lay something on the line
informal to risk losing (money, one's job etc)
① Originally US

the line of least resistance
a course of action etc that will cause the least trouble, argument or difficulty
① A technical term from engineering

line one's pockets *see* **pocket**

on the lines of something
in a particular manner or direction, similar to something else

read between the lines
to understand something from a situation, statement etc which is not actually stated
① From a method of sending secret messages by writing in invisible ink between the lines of another message

shoot a line
slang to exaggerate, especially in order to boast about oneself
① Originally US

step out of line
to behave in a way different from what is usual or accepted
① A military image, of lines of soldiers

take a hard line *see* **hard**

toe the line *see* **toe**

linen

wash one's dirty linen in public
to have a discussion or argument in public, in a manner which attracts attention etc, about private problems, scandals etc

lion

a lion-hunter
derogatory a person who tries to become friendly with famous people, invites them to parties etc
Ⓞ The use of the word *lion* to mean 'celebrity' is from the phrase **to see the lions** — 'to see all the noteworthy attractions of a place', celebrities being ironically included — which itself derives from the custom of including a visit to see the lions, kept until the 1830s in the Tower of London, as an essential part of sightseeing in the city

the lion's share
the largest share
Ⓞ In the wild, the lion does in fact get the first and largest share of meat killed by the lionesses in his pride

put one's head in the lion's mouth
to place oneself in a dangerous position
Ⓞ From a celebrated circus trick

throw someone to the lions
to put someone else in a position where they will be attacked, usually to protect oneself
Ⓞ From the Roman entertainment in which prisoners were attacked and killed by wild animals

lip

bite one's lip
to try to restrain one's anger or laughter

keep a stiff upper lip
to appear very determined and unaffected by emotion

lick one's lips
informal to look forward to something with pleasure, especially because one expects to benefit from it

my etc **lips are sealed**
often facetious I am unable to reveal something secret

pay lip-service to something
formal to pretend to agree with and approve of an idea, way of thinking etc without really doing so

there's many a slip 'twixt cup and lip *see* **slip**

list

enter the lists
rather formal to join in a contest or argument
Ⓞ Literally, 'to take part in a tournament', the *lists* being the arena used for jousting

listen

listen in
often with **on** to listen intentionally to a telephone conversation, to a message intended for someone else etc

listen to reason *see* **reason**

little

a little learning is a dangerous thing
a proverb indicating that it is sometimes worse to know a little about something than nothing at all since one tends to assume that one knows more than one actually does. The proverb is more commonly found as **a little knowledge is a dangerous thing**
Ⓞ The original form is from Alexander Pope's *An Essay on Criticism* (1711)

a little of what you fancy
a small amount, or an amount within reason, of something which you like
Ⓞ The full version is **a little of what you fancy does you good**. It is a reference to a song popularized by Marie Lloyd (1870–1922)

little pitchers have big ears *see* **pitcher**

make little of something
1 to treat something as unimportant, not serious etc
2 not to be able to understand much of something

live[1]

live and let live
to tolerate other people's actions and expect them to tolerate one's own
Ⓞ Apparently from a Dutch proverb

live a lie
to live a way of life which is based on some form of deception

live by one's wits *see* **wit**

live something down
to continue living in a normal way until a wrong action, mistake etc is forgotten
• *It took her a long time to live down the scandal caused by her arrest*

live from hand to mouth *see* **hand**

live in sin *see* **sin**

live it up
slang to live in a rather too active and expensive manner

live like fighting-cocks *see* **fighting**

live like a lord *see* **lord**

live on borrowed time *see* **time**

live up to someone or **something**
to behave as well etc as someone or in a manner worthy of something

live up to one's reputation *see* **reputation**

live[2]

a live wire
informal a person who is full of energy and enthusiasm
Ⓘ Literally, a wire with an electric current running through it

lively

as lively as a cricket *see* **cricket**

living

beat/knock the living daylights out of someone
to beat them severely

load

get a load of
slang, usually derogatory listen to, look at or pay attention to

a loaded question
a question intended to lead someone into saying, admitting or agreeing to something which he is unwilling to do
Ⓘ The reference is to 'loaded' dice, which are weighted so as to have a tendency always to show the same score, and thus to make it possible to cheat

a load off one's mind
relief from something which has been worrying one

loaf

half a loaf is better than no bread
a proverb, meaning that one should not be ungrateful for what one achieves, is given etc, even if it is not all that one wanted, because it is better than nothing

use one's loaf
informal to use one's brain, to act in a sensible way etc

local

local colour
details in a story etc which are characteristic of the time or place in which it is set

lock

lock horns with someone *see* **horn**

lock, stock and barrel
completely or with all the various parts included
Ⓘ From the three main components of a gun

lock the stable door after the horse has bolted *see* **stable**

under lock and key
in a place which is locked

log

as easy as falling off a log
informal very easy

sleep like a log
informal to sleep very well

loggerheads

at loggerheads
rather formal quarrelling
• *We have been at loggerheads with the neighbours for years*
Ⓘ A **loggerhead** was a long iron bar with a ball at the end used, when heated, for melting buckets of tar and pitch. It was probably an obvious weapon among shipwrights etc

loins

gird up one's loins
arch or facetious to prepare for energetic action
Ⓘ A Biblical phrase, from the fact that the Hebrews wore loose, flowing robes which were impractical for working or travelling in unless they were fastened up with a girdle

lone

a lone wolf
a person who prefers to be by himself, without companions

long

be, get etc **long in the tooth** *see* **tooth**

draw the long bow *see* **bow²**

go a long way to(wards) *see* **way**

have a long face *see* **face**

in the long run
in the end; considering something over a period of time

the long and the short of it
informal the story etc told in a few words

the long arm of the law *see* **arm**

a long haul *see* **haul**

a long shot *see* **shot**

long time no see
informal a greeting used to someone whom one has not met for a considerable time

long-winded
derogatory of a speaker or his speech, tiresomely long

not long for this world
euphemism about to die

the night of the long knives *see* **knife**

look

by the look(s) of someone or **something**
judging from the appearance of someone or something it seems likely or probable that

have a look of
informal to look like; to resemble

look after someone or **something**
to attend to or take care of them or it

look before you leap
a saying, stressing the importance of considering the possible consequences of one's actions before one acts
🕔 From Aesop's fable in which the fox, who is unable to get out of a well into which he has fallen, persuades the goat to leap into the well and let the fox stand on his back in order to get out

look daggers at someone *see* **dagger**

look down one's nose at *see* **nose**

look down on someone or **something**
to think of them or it as being inferior

look forward to *see* **forward**

look in on someone
informal to visit briefly and without invitation

look sharp *see* **sharp**

look small *see* **small**

look smart *see* **smart**

look snappy *see* **snappy**

look the other way *see* **way**

look the part *see* **part**

look to one's laurels *see* **laurels**

look up
1 to improve or become better
• *Things have been looking up lately and most of my worries have disappeared*
2 to pay a visit to a person
• *I hadn't seen them for months so I thought it was time I looked them up*

look up to someone
to respect their conduct, opinions etc

not much to look at
informal plain or unattractive

not to get/have a look-in
informal not to have any attention paid to one

loom

loom large
to be a very important influence, possibility etc, especially if likely to cause a problem or danger
🕔 Originally a nautical term for the sudden appearing of a shadowy shape

loop

loop the loop
of aeroplanes etc, to move in a complete vertical loop or circle

loose

at a loose end
informal with nothing to do

have a screw loose *see* **screw**

on the loose
informal enjoying a time of freedom

Lord

Lord knows who, what etc
I do not know who, what etc, and I don't believe anyone else does
• *Lord knows how much trouble this is going to cause us*

lord

as drunk as a lord
informal very drunk

live like a lord
to live in a very rich and luxurious manner

one's lord and master
facetious one's husband

lord it over someone
informal to act like a lord, or like a master, towards them

lorry

fall off a lorry
slang to be acquired by dubious or dishonest means
• *He did not buy that bike in a shop — it fell off a lorry*

lose

lose one's cool *see* **cool**

lose face *see* **face**

lose one's grip *see* **grip**

lose ground *see* **ground**

lose one's head *see* **head**

lose heart *see* **heart**

lose one's marbles *see* **marble**

lose one's nerve *see* **nerve**

lose oneself in something
to have all one's attention taken up by it

lose out
to suffer loss or be at a disadvantage

lose one's rag *see* **rag**

lose one's reason *see* **reason**

lose sight of *see* **sight**

lose sleep *see* **sleep**

lose one's temper *see* **temper**

lose the thread *see* **thread**

lose the toss *see* **toss**

lose touch *see* **touch**

lose track of someone or **something** *see* **track**

lose one's voice *see* **voice**

lose one's way *see* **way**

losing

play a losing game
to attempt to do something, carry on an argument etc in which it is obvious that one is not going to succeed

loss

cut one's losses
to decide not to spend any more time, money etc on something unprofitable on which one has already wasted time, money etc

a dead loss *see* **dead**

lost

a lost cause
an aim, ideal etc that cannot be achieved

lost on someone
informal wasted, or having no effect, on them

lost to something
formal no longer, or not, feeling in a certain way etc
• *She was lost to all sense of shame*

get lost
informal a rude way of saying 'go away!'

Lothario

a gay Lothario
a man who has had love affairs with many women, a womanizer
Ⓞ A reference to a character in *The Fair Penitent* (1703), a play by Nicholas Rowe

love

calf love *see* **calf**

for the love of Mike
informal an expression of exasperation or surprise
Ⓞ Originally an Irishism

greater love hath no man
now usually facetious a saying used to indicate a great sacrifice as a demonstration of friendship
Ⓞ Originally it was used for acts of supreme sacrifice, such as laying down one's life for one's friend, but nowadays it is used of much more trivial situations

love is blind
a person who is very much in love with someone is unable to see any faults in him or her

love child
a child born to two people who have had a love affair but who are not married, an illegitimate child

love nest
a place, usually a secret one, where people carry on a love affair, usually an illicit one

not for love or money
informal not in any way at all
- *We couldn't get a taxi for love or money*

there's no love lost between them
they dislike one another
Ⓞ This phrase originally meant exactly the opposite — the shift in meaning is unexplained

lovely

lovely weather for ducks *see* **weather**

low

be low on something
informal not to have much or enough of it

(hunt) high and low *see* **high**

keep a low profile *see* **profile**

lay someone low
of an illness, to affect someone
- *I was laid low by pneumonia just before my exams*

lie low
to stay quiet or hidden

the low-down
slang, especially US information, especially confidential and/or damaging, about a person, organization or activity

luck

down on one's luck
formal or literary experiencing misfortune

a hard-luck story *see* **hard**

the luck of the draw
chance, good luck
Ⓞ From drawing a card at random from a pack of playing-cards

push one's luck
informal to risk complete failure by trying to gain too much when one has already been reasonably successful

take pot-luck *see* **pot**

tough luck *see* **tough**

try one's luck at something
to try to do something at which one may or may not be successful
Ⓞ *Try* here means 'test'

worse luck!
informal most unfortunately

lucky

a lucky dip
a situation in which one has to accept whatever is given to one, happens etc without being able to make a choice
Ⓞ Literally, a fairground sideshow etc in which one chooses a parcel at random in a tub full of bran

strike (it) lucky
to have good luck in a particular matter
Ⓞ An idiom from the gold- and silver-mining camps of the 1850s and 60s

thank one's lucky stars
informal to be grateful for one's good luck

third time lucky *see* **third**

lull

lull someone into a false sense of security
to lead them to believe that everything is going well, in order to attack when they are not expecting it

lumber

be/get lumbered with someone or **something**
informal to be given an unpleasant, unwanted responsibility or task

lump

if you don't like it, you can lump it
informal whether you like the situation or not, you'll have to endure it

lunatic

the lunatic fringe
derogatory the more extreme or ridiculous members of a group

lunch

out to lunch

slang insane, extremely foolish

lurch

leave someone in the lurch

informal to leave them in a difficult situation and without help

① A *lurch* is a position at the end of certain games (such as cribbage) in which the loser has lost by an enormous margin, or in some games scores no points at all

lute

a rift in the lute *see* **rift**

luxury

in the lap of luxury *see* **lap**

M

mackerel

a sprat to catch a mackerel *see* **sprat**

mad

as mad as a March hare *see* **March**

far from the madding crowd *see* **crowd**

hopping mad *see* **hopping**

like mad
informal wildly, desperately, very quickly etc
• *We lit the fuse and ran like mad*

as mad as a hatter *see* **hatter**

midsummer madness *see* **midsummer**

there is method in his etc **madness** *see* **method**

made

be made for someone or **something**
informal to be ideally suitable for them or it

made to measure *see* **measure**

Mahomet

if the mountain will not come to Mohamed/Mahomet, then Mohamed/Mahomet must go to the mountain *see* **mountain**

magic

wave a magic wand
to do something that produces a desired result rapidly and often unexpectedly, as if by magic

work like magic
to be extremely effective

magnitude

of the first magnitude *see* **first**

maid

an old maid *see* **old**

maiden

a maiden lady
formal a middle-aged or elderly unmarried woman

a maiden speech
especially Brit a Member of Parliament's first speech

a maiden voyage
a ship's first voyage

main

in the main
formal mostly
• *In the main, I find this composer's music pleasant to listen to*

with an eye to the main chance *see* **chance**

with might and main *see* **might**

mainbrace

splice the mainbrace *see* **splice**

majority

the silent majority *see* **silent**

make

be the making of someone
to be the thing or person that ensures the success or improvement of someone
• *Two years in the navy will probably be the making of him!*

have the makings of something
formal to have the clear ability for becoming something
• *Your son has the makings of an excellent engineer*

in the making
formal being made or formed at this very moment

make a clean break *see* **clean**

make a day, night of it
to spend a whole day, night enjoying oneself in some way

make a dent in something *see* **dent**

make a face *see* **face**

make a fool of *see* **fool**

make a go of *see* **go**

make a meal of *see* **meal**

make a name for oneself *see* **name**

make a night of it *see* **make a day of it**

make a pass at *see* **pass**

make a play for *see* **play**

make a point of *see* **point**

make as if to do something
formal to behave as if one were about to do something
• *He made as if to hit me, but he was only pretending*

make a stand *see* **stand**

make believe *see* **believe**

make do with something
to use something as a poor quality or temporary alternative to the real thing

make eyes at *see* **eye**

make good *see* **good**

make hay while the sun shines *see* **hay**

make heavy weather of something *see* **heavy**

make it
informal to be successful; to achieve one's purpose

make it up
informal to become friends again after a quarrel

make light of *see* **light**

make one's mark *see* **mark**

make merry *see* **merry**

make much of *see* **much**

make-or-break
involving the important test that brings final success or failure to a person, a project etc

make one's peace with *see* **peace**

make one's point *see* **point**

make the best of it/a bad job *see* **best**

make the grade *see* **grade**

make the most of *see* **most**

make tracks *see* **track**

make up for something
to supply a reward, substitute etc for disappointment, damage, loss of money or time etc

make up one's mind *see* **mind**

make up to someone
informal to try to gain the favour or love of someone by flattery etc

make one's way *see* **way**

make waves *see* **wave**

make way *see* **way**

go to meet one's maker
to die

on the make
slang trying to make a profit often unfairly large or illegal

man

be a marked man *see* **mark**

be one's own man
to be independent, not relying on, or controlled by, anyone else

the child is father of the man *see* **child**

dirty old man *see* **dirty**

every man jack *see* **jack**

hit a man when he is down
to attack someone who is already suffering under a misfortune, disappointment, setback etc
ⓘ From a prohibited action in prizefighting

a man-about-town
a man who lives and acts fashionably and in a sophisticated way

man and boy
all a person's life
• *He worked on the farm man and boy*

man cannot live by bread alone
if life is to be worth living people need more than just the bare necessities; they also need spiritual and intellectual stimulation
ⓘ A Biblical reference, to Deuteronomy 8:3

a Man Friday
a general servant or employee who does all kinds of jobs
Ⓛ From the native who acts as Robinson Crusoe's servant — 'my man Friday' — in Daniel Defoe's book of 1719

a man for all seasons *see* **season**

the man in the street
the ordinary, typical, average man

a man of his word
someone who is known to keep promises

a man of many parts
a person who has a wide range of talents

a man of straw
1 an imaginary enemy
2 a person who is regarded as not being of much worth or substance

the man of the moment
the person who is dealing with, or is best able to deal with, the present situation, especially political

a man of the world
sometimes facetious a sophisticated man who is not likely to be shocked or surprised by most things

a man's gotta do what a man's gotta do
facetious a saying indicating that people have to carry out those tasks for which they are responsible
Ⓛ A catchphrase common in Western films

man to man
as one man to another; openly or frankly

a marked man *see* **marked**

a no-man's land
an area which lies between two subjects, areas of interest etc and is usually not governed by any rules or conventions
Ⓛ Originally the name of a piece of wasteland on the north side of medieval London where executions were carried out; later applied to the wasteland between the German and Allied trenches in the 1st World War

odd man out *see* **odd**

a right-hand man *see* **right**

see a man about a dog
a phrase used when someone does not wish to reveal where or why he or she is going

the man on the Clapham omnibus
same as **the man in the street** *above*
Ⓛ First used by Lord Bowen (1903) when hearing a case of negligence in court

take one's medicine like a man *see* **medicine**

to a man
rather formal every one, without exception

you can't keep a good man down
a person who is determined or ambitious enough will succeed, no matter what obstructions there may be in the way

manger

a dog in the manger *see* **dog**

manna

manna from heaven
something good which comes to one unexpectedly or by chance, especially as a help or comfort in difficulty
Ⓛ A Biblical reference, to Exodus 16:15

manner

in a manner of speaking
a certain way; to a certain extent
• *I suppose, in a manner of speaking, you could call me an engineer*

manners maketh man
a saying advocating the virtues of politeness and courtesy and indicating that a person is judged by his or her good manners or by the lack of these

to the manner born
facetious as if accustomed since birth to a particular occupation, role etc
• *He speaks in public as if to the manner born*
Ⓛ A Shakespearian quotation, from *Hamlet* I, iv

many

many hands make light work *see* **hand**

many happy returns *see* **return**

map

put (a place) on the map
informal to cause a place to be important

marble

as cold as marble
1 extremely cold to the touch
2 of a person, extremely unfeeling or unsympathetic

have marbles in one's mouth
informal to speak in a manner that supposedly resembles the way that members of the upper classes or aristocracy speak

lose one's marbles
slang to lose one's mind, to become insane or extremely foolish

march

get one's marching orders
informal to be dismissed from a job etc
Ⓞ A military term

steal a march on someone
to gain an advantage, especially in time, over someone, especially in a secretive manner
• *We stole a march on our rivals by issuing our new formula shampoo two weeks before they launched theirs*
Ⓞ A military term, meaning to move an army unexpectedly while the enemy is resting

March

as mad as a March hare
insane, crazy, extremely eccentric
Ⓞ Hares tend to leap around wildly during their breeding season in March

mare

a mare's nest
a supposed discovery of something which turns out to be imaginary

marine

tell that to the marines
informal I do not believe you
Ⓞ Originally continuing '— the sailors won't believe it', this phrase derives from the seaman's contempt for the marine's ignorance of the sea

mark

be a marked man
to be in danger because enemies are trying to harm one
Ⓞ *Marked* here means 'watched'

to be close/near to the mark
to be very nearly absolutely correct or accurate
• *She was close to the mark when she called him a thief — he operates just on the right side of the law*

beside/off/wide of the mark
formal off the target or subject

be up to the mark
to reach the required or normal standard
Ⓞ Probably from the use of a mark to represent a standard height or length for measuring goods etc against

get off the/one's mark
to begin an undertaking etc, especially quickly, without wasting any time
Ⓞ From track athletics

hit the mark
to be right, to be accurate
Ⓞ A reference to hitting the target in archery

make one's mark
to make a permanent or strong impression
• *He is beginning to make his mark as an actor*

mark something down, up
to bring down or increase the price of an article for sale in a shop

mark time *see* **time**

overstep the mark
to go beyond what are accepted as the permitted limits

quick off the mark
acting promptly
• *She was very quick off the mark, calling a meeting at 8 in the morning*
Ⓞ Literally, starting quickly in a race

a soft mark *see* **soft**

market

be in the market for something
informal wishing to buy something

be on the market
to be for sale

drive one's pigs to market *see* **pig**

a drug on the market *see* **drug**

price something/oneself out of the market *see* **price**

marrow

chilled/frozen to the marrow
extremely cold
Ⓞ The reference is to the marrow in the centre of one's bones

mass

in the mass
considered as a whole, not separately
• *In the mass the population is bigoted and unsympathetic*

the masses
derogatory the ordinary people, especially of the working class

mast

at half mast
facetious of socks, trousers etc falling down
Ⓞ Literally used of a flag flown half-way up a mast or flagpole, often signalling a death

before the mast
old as an ordinary sailor, not as an officer or in a position of responsibility
Ⓞ From the position of the crew's quarters in a ship

nail one's colours to the mast *see* **colour**

master

an old master *see* **old**

a past master *see* **past**

serve two masters
to support two principles, schools of thought, etc which are completely different and which are often opposed to each other
• *He would like to serve two masters and be on the management committee as well as on the trade union executive*

mat

on the mat *see* **on the carpet** *at* **carpet**

match

be a match for someone
to be as good at something or as successful as someone, especially to be able to resist successfully a strong personality etc

meet one's match
1 to have to deal with someone who is able successfully to resist one
2 to meet or have to compete with someone who is as good at something as, or better than, one is oneself

material

raw material *see* **raw**

matter

as a matter of course
as something that one expects automatically to happen, be done etc

be the matter
often with **with** to be the/a trouble, difficulty or thing that is wrong
• *Is anything the matter? What's the matter with you? He would not tell me what the matter was*

a case of mind over matter *see* **mind**

for that matter
used eg when referring to some alternative or additional possibility; as far as that is concerned

grey matter *see* **grey**

a matter of
1 used in giving quantity, time etc approximately
• *This job will only take a matter of minutes*
2 used in saying what is involved or necessary
• *It's a matter of asking her to do it*

a matter of life and death
a matter of great importance

a matter of opinion
a matter that is open to argument or disagreement

no laughing matter *see* **laugh**

not to mince matters *see* **mince**

May

a case of May and December
a marriage or relationship between a young person and a much older person

meal

make a meal of something
informal to take more than the necessary

amount of time or trouble over something or make something seem more complicated than it really is

a meal ticket
a person, organization, etc who is regarded as a continuous provider of support or help without receiving anything in return for this
• *She regards her husband just as a meal ticket for life*

mealy-mouthed
derogatory not frank or sincere in what one says

a square meal *see* **square**

means

by all means
rather formal yes, of course
• *If you want to use the telephone, by all means do*

by fair means *see* **fair**

by no means
formal
1 also **not by any means,** not at all
• *I'm by no means certain to win; He's not the best person for the job by any means*
2 definitely not
• *'Is this better?' 'By no means!'*

live beyond one's means
to spend more money than one earns, to lead an extravagant lifestyle

live within one's means
to live within the limits of what one earns and so not to have to borrow money

ways and means *see* **way**

measure

for good measure
as something extra or above the minimum necessary
Ⓛ Literally 'in order not to give short weight to a customer'

get/have someone's measure/the measure of someone
formal to form an idea or judgement of someone

measure one's length
informal to stumble and fall

made to measure
of clothing, made to fit the measurements of a particular person

measure up something
to reach a certain required standard

short measure
less than the correct or stated amount

meat

be meat and drink to someone
to be very important in someone's life

easy meat
slang a person who is easily taken advantage of

one man's meat is another man's poison
a saying, meaning that something liked by one person may well be disliked intensely by another
Ⓛ A Latin proverb from Lucretius, *De Rerum Natura*

Mecca

a/the Mecca
a place which is very important to a particular group of people, and which they feel they have to visit
Ⓛ From the town in Arabia which is the birthplace of Mohammed, to which all Muslims try to make at least one pilgrimage

medicine

a dose/taste of someone's own medicine
something unpleasant done to a person who is in the habit of doing the same kind of thing to other people

take one's medicine like a man
to accept bravely or boldly the punishment or unpleasant consequences that one deserves

medium

a happy medium *see* **happy**

meet

meet someone halfway *see* **half**

meet one's match *see* **match**

meet one's Waterloo *see* **Waterloo**

there's more to something than meets the eye *see* **eye**

melt

be in the melting pot
to be in the process of changing and

forming something new
⌚ The image is of melting down and recasting metal

memory

have a memory like an elephant *see* **elephants never forget,** *at* **elephant**

have a memory like a sieve
to have an extremely poor memory
⌚ A sieve is a kitchen utensil with a great many small holes through which liquids or very fine solids can pass

a liar needs a good memory *see* **liar**

take a trip down memory lane
to think back on the past, usually the pleasurable past

within living memory
such as can be remembered by people who are currently still alive

men

dead men
informal empty bottles, especially those formerly containing alcoholic drinks

men in grey suits *see* **grey**

separate the men from the boys
to show a distinction between those who are brave, talented, experienced, etc and those who are not
• *The final climb to the summit will separate the men from the boys*

step into dead men's shoes *see* **dead**

mend

be on the mend
informal to be getting better

least said, soonest mended *see* **least**

mend fences *see* **fence**

mend one's ways *see* **way**

mention

honourable mention
an award in a competition etc which does not entitle one to one of the prizes

not to mention
often facetious a phrase used to emphasize something important or to excuse oneself for mentioning something relatively unimportant.
• *It's far too late for you to go out and play football, not to mention the fact that it's raining*

mercy

an angel of mercy *see* **angel**

at the mercy of something or **someone**
wholly in the power of or liable to be harmed by something or someone

be thankful for small mercies
to appreciate the small benefits, advantages etc which are assisting one in a generally difficult situation

leave someone to someone's tender mercies *see* **tender**

merry

lead someone a merry dance *see* **dance**

make merry
to enjoy oneself, usually in a party of some kind

a merry-go-round
an activity in which one seems to be busy without making any progress
⌚ From the fairground amusement

play merry hell with *see* **hell**

the more the merrier *see* **more**

mess

a mess of pottage
something one has received in exchange for something more valuable, a reference to the saying **to sell one's birthright for a mess of pottage**
⌚ From the heading to Genesis 25 in the Geneva Bible — 'Esau selleth his birthright for a mess of pottage'

message

get the message
slang to understand
• *I kept hinting to Simon that it was time he went home, but he didn't seem to get the message*

message received!
a phrase indicating that someone has understood the situation and got the point. A short form of **message received and understood**
⌚ From the standard reply given in response to a radio message in the military services in World War II

method

there is method in his etc **madness**
although he seems to be doing things in the wrong way, he is in fact following a logical plan
① A reference to a Shakespearian quotation from *Hamlet*, II ii — 'Though this be madness, yet there is method in it'

mettle

put someone on his etc **mettle**
formal to rouse or stimulate someone to his best efforts

mickey

a Mickey Finn
slang a drugged drink
① Origin obscure

take the mick(ey) out of someone
informal to make fun of or ridicule someone or something

Midas

the Midas touch
formal the ability to make money easily
① From a king of Phrygia in Greek legend whose touch turned everything to gold

middle

be in the middle of doing something
to be busily occupied with something or doing something

knock someone into the middle of next week
slang to strike someone extremely hard

middle-of-the-road
midway between extremes; moderate

midnight

burn the midnight oil
to work or study until late at night
① Apparently a not uncommon literary image in the 17c

midstream

change horses in midstream *see* **horse**

halt/stop/pause etc **in midstream**
formal to pause while doing something busily, especially talking
• *He stopped speaking in midstream when the door opened*

midsummer

midsummer madness
rather old silly behaviour occurring during the hot weather of midsummer
① From the old belief that hot weather caused insanity

might

high and mighty *see* **high**

with might and main
literary with all the strength and power that one has
① An Anglo-Saxon phrase — the two words were almost synonymous in Old English, meaning 'power' and 'strength'

Mike

for the love of Mike *see* **love**

mile

give him etc **an inch and he'll take a mile** *see* **inch**

a milestone
a very important event
① Literally, a stone set at the side of the road to show the distance from a given town

a miss is as good as a mile *see* **miss**

run a mile
informal to go to great lengths to avoid someone or something
• *She runs a mile if someone mentions extra work*

stand/stick out a mile
informal to be very obvious
• *The fact that he was very nervous stuck out a mile*

talk a mile a minute
informal to talk rapidly and continuously

milk

cry over spilt milk *see* **spill**

a land of milk and honey *see* **land**

milk and water
derogatory something very weak and usually lacking in liveliness or interest

mother's milk *see* **mother**

the milk of human kindness
often facetious natural kindness and pity towards other people
① A Shakespearian quotation, from *Macbeth* I, v

mill

grist to the mill *see* **grist**

a millstone round someone's neck
something that is a heavy burden or responsibility to someone, and prevents easy progress

put someone through/go through the mill
to put someone through, or to go through, a series of difficult tests or troublesome experiences
◷ The reference is to corn which goes through the grinding process in the mill and emerges in a refined form as flour at the other side

run-of-the-mill
not special or unusual
◷ Originally an American term for ungraded sawn timber as produced by a sawmill

the mills of God grind slowly but they grind exceeding small
due punishment or reward may appear to be slow in coming to someone but it will certainly come — often shortened to **the mills of God**

million

one in a million
informal something or especially someone that is very special or very good in some way

millpond

as calm as a millpond
very calm
◷ Probably suggested by the contrast between the still water in a millpond and the often fast-flowing stream which supplies it

mince

make mincemeat of someone
informal to defeat or destroy someone completely, or punish them severely
◷ From the original meaning of *mincemeat* — 'finely chopped meat'

not to mince matters/one's words
formal to be entirely frank and open, not trying to make one's words have less effect than they should
◷ The only surviving use of *mince* meaning 'to soften or diminish in strength'

mind

bear/keep in mind
to remember or take into consideration

be/go out of one's mind
informal to be, become mad

blow one's/someone's mind
slang to amaze or excite one/someone greatly
◷ From drug users' slang describing the effect on the mind of hallucinogenic drugs

bring to mind
to cause one to remember or think of

a case of mind over matter
a situation in which a person uses or should use reasoning abilities, strength of mind, determination, etc to solve a physical problem
• *Doctors told him he would never work again but he now does. It was a real case of mind over matter*

change one's mind
to alter one's intention or opinion about something

cross someone's mind
to enter someone's mind for a moment only

give someone a piece of one's mind
informal to scold or blame someone angrily

great minds think alike
often facetious a saying, meaning that clever people tend to have the same ideas and opinions, and usually said when one discovers that someone else shares yours

have a good mind to do something
informal to feel very much inclined to do something

have a mind of one's own
to be able to think for oneself, not accepting other people's opinions without question

have a one-track mind *see* **one**

have half a mind to do something
to feel slightly inclined to do something

in one's mind's eye *see* **eye**

in one's right mind
usually in a negative context sane

① An idiom which probably came into widespread use as a quotation from the Bible, Mark 5:15

in two minds
undecided

keep an open mind *see* **open**

keep in mind *see* **bear in mind**

keep one's mind on something
to give all one's attention to something

a load off one's mind *see* **load**

make up one's mind
to decide

the mind boggles
slang I am extremely surprised or incredulous

mind one's own business *see* **business**

mind one's p's and q's *see* **p**

mind the store *see* **store**

mind you
but a fact, opinion etc has also to be taken into consideration along with what I have just said

not to know one's own mind
not to know what one really thinks, wants to do etc

out of sight, out of mind *see* **sight**

peace of mind *see* **peace**

presence of mind *see* **presence**

put someone in mind of something
to remind someone of something

put/set someone's mind at rest
to free someone from anxiety or worry

put one's mind to something
to concentrate one's thoughts on doing something, solving a problem etc

slip one's mind
to be usually temporarily forgotten

small things please small minds *see* **small**

speak one's mind
to say frankly what one means or thinks

take someone's mind off something
to turn someone's attention from something; to prevent someone from thinking about something

to my mind
rather formal in my opinion
• *To my mind, you're better off working here than in most other places*

mine

a gold-mine *see* **gold**

a mine of information
a plentiful source of information

mint

in mint condition
used, but in extremely good condition
① Literally, in the unused condition of a newly-minted coin

minute

every minute counts
there is very little time to do what has to be done and it must be used as effectively as possible

not to have a minute/moment to call one's own
informal to be extremely busy working with little time for rest or leisure

there's one born every minute
informal there is always someone around who is easily deceived or taken in by other people

up to the minute
most modern, fashionable, or recent

miscarriage

a miscarriage of justice
formal a mistaken decision in a court of law etc

mischief

do someone/oneself a mischief
informal to hurt someone/oneself

make mischief
formal to cause trouble etc

misery

put someone out of his etc **misery**
to end a period of worry, suspense etc for someone by giving him information which he wants etc
① Originally a euphemism for killing a wounded and suffering man or animal

miss

give something a miss
informal to leave something out, not to go to something etc

ⓘ A term from billiards — **to give a miss** is to give away points intentionally, by missing the ball, in order to be able to put the cue-ball in a safe position

hit-or-miss *see* **hit**

a miss is as good as a mile
a saying, meaning that if one fails in something it makes no difference how close one came to succeeding
ⓘ The proverb originally was **an inch of a miss is as good as a mile**

miss the boat/bus
informal to be left behind, miss an opportunity etc

a near miss *see* **near**

never to miss a trick *see* **trick**

mission

mission accomplished
the relevant task has been completed
• *Mission accomplished! Can we go home now?*
ⓘ Originally a military term dating from World War II

mistake

and no mistake
informal without any doubt
• *Henry's mother is a fierce old woman and no mistake*

mix

a mixed bag
a very varied group or collection of objects, people etc
ⓘ A shooting term

a mixed blessing
something which has both advantages and disadvantages

mocker

put the mockers on something
slang to ruin or destroy a plan, enterprise etc, especially by bringing bad luck or ill fortune to it
ⓘ An Australian idiom

Mohammed

if the mountain will not go to Mohammed/Mahomet, then Mohammed/Mahomet must go to the mountain *see* **mountain**

Mohican

the last of the Mohicans *see* **last**

Molotov

Molotov cocktail
a home-made incendiary device
ⓘ Such devices were used by the Finnish people against Russian tanks during the Russian invasion of Finland, in the early part of World War II, the Soviet Minister for Foreign Affairs being V. M. Molotov

moment

have one's moments
informal to be good, admirable, clever etc at times only
• *The film was rather dull most of the time, but it had its moments*

the man of the moment *see* **man**

the moment of truth
formal or facetious a moment when one is suddenly forced to face a crisis, make an important decision etc
ⓘ From the Spanish *el momento de la verdad*, the moment at the climax of a bullfight when the matador kills the bull

not to have a moment to call one's own *see* **minute**

on the spur of the moment *see* **spur**

a weak moment *see* **weak**

money

ask to see the colour of someone's money
to ask for proof that they can pay for something that they are about to purchase from one

be in the money
informal to be wealthy
ⓘ Literally, to be among the prizewinners in a horse-race etc

even money *see* **even**

a fool and his money are soon parted *see* **fool**

for my money
informal in my opinion; if I were to choose
• *For my money, I'd rather have an amusing friend than an honest one*
ⓘ Literally implying that something is what one would choose to spend one's money on

funny money *see* **funny**

get one's money's worth
to get full value for one's money

have money to burn
to have enough money to be able to spend it in ways the speaker thinks are foolish

hush money *see* **hush**

money does not grow on trees
a saying emphasizing how difficult money is to obtain or earn, usually said to someone who seems not to appreciate this fact

money for jam/old rope
informal money very easily obtained
Ⓒ It has been suggested that *money for jam* refers to the enormous quantities of jam supplied to the army in World War I

money is no object *see* **object**

money is the root of all evil
a great many of the world's troubles are caused by money or by people's desire for it
Ⓒ A misquotation of a biblical reference — 'For the love of money is the root of all evil', in Timothy 6:10

money talks
a saying, meaning that rich people are important and have influence simply because they are rich

not for love or money *see* **love**

not made of money
informal not very wealthy

put one's money where one's mouth is
informal to supply money for a purpose which one has been saying one supports
Ⓒ Originally US

a (good) run for one's money *see* **run**

spend money like water/spend money like it was going out of fashion
derogatory to spend money very freely

throw good money after bad
derogatory to spend money in an unsuccessful attempt to get back money one has already lost

time is money *see* **time**

you pays your money and you takes your choice
informal in a situation where there is little difference between several possible courses of action, etc one might as well just trust to luck

monkey

make a monkey out of someone
informal to make them appear stupid or ridiculous

monkey business
informal mischievous or illegal happenings etc

not to give a monkey's
slang not to care in the least

month

flavour of the month *see* **flavour**

a month of Sundays
informal: usually in negative an extremely long time
• *You'll never finish that job in a month of Sundays*

moon

bay at the moon
to do something completely futile
Ⓒ From hounds baying — the expression occurs in Shakespeare's *Julius Caesar* IV, 3

cry for the moon
to want or ask for something which is impossible to get

once in a blue moon *see* **blue**

over the moon
very happy and excited

moonlight

do a moonlight (flit/flitting)
Brit slang to move away suddenly, especially at night usually to avoid people to whom one owes money

moral

moral support
encouragement, but not actual or physical help

more

more fool you
informal you are/were foolish

more or less
approximately or almost

• *They've more or less finished the job; The distance is ten kilometres, more or less*

more's the pity
it is to be regretted

the more the merrier
a saying, meaning that the more people or things there are, the better it will be

morning

the morning after the night before
a morning when one has a hangover from drinking too much the previous night

mortal

shuffle off this mortal coil
now usually facetious to die
① From Shakespeare, *Hamlet* III, i — 'When we have shuffled off this mortal coil'

most

at (the) most
taking the greatest estimate

for the most part *see* **part**

make the most of something
to take advantage of an opportunity etc to the greatest possible extent

mother

be old enough to be someone's mother *see* **old**

a mother's boy
a boy or man who depends too much on his mother, a weak and effeminate man

mother's milk
something that a person enjoys or needs very much

some mothers do 'ave 'em
informal a catch phrase indicating how foolish or incompetent some people are
① A popular catch phrase from about the 1920s revived in the 1970s in the title of a television comedy series

motion

go through the motions
informal to pretend, or make an unenthusiastic attempt, to do something

set the wheels in motion *see* **wheel**

motley

on with the motley!
1 a phrase indicating that something enjoyable should begin
2 something must be proceeded with, whatever obstacles there are
① A reference to 'vesti la giubba', the Clown's cry in Leoncavallo's opera I Pagliacci (1892)

mould

break the mould
to do away with traditional methods or systems and make a completely new start
• *The new leader said that it was time to break the mould of the country's economic policy*
① A reference to the breaking of the mould from which iron machinery was made, making it necessary to make a new mould

cast in the same mould as someone
very similar to them
① An idiom from iron-working

mountain

if the mountain will not come to Mohammed/Mahomet, then Mohammed/Mahomet must go to the mountain
a proverb indicating that people should make an effort to help themselves and not simply wait for circumstances to suit them or depend on other people acting in accordance with their wishes
① From a story about Mohammed in which he is asked to demonstrate his power by getting Mount Sofa to come to him. When this did not occur he is supposed to have said, 'If the hill will not come to Mahomet, Mahomet will go to the hill'

make a mountain out of a molehill
to exaggerate the importance of a problem etc

mouse

as quiet as a mouse
extremely quiet

as poor as a church mouse
very poor, in extreme poverty

mouth

be all mouth and trousers
informal to have a tendency to talk a great deal but to take very little action in connection with what one says

by word of mouth *see* **word**

down in the mouth
miserable or in low spirits

foam at the mouth *see* **foam**

have a big mouth
slang to be in the habit of talking too loudly or too much, or of saying things one shouldn't

leave a nasty taste in one's mouth *see* **nasty**

put one's money where one's mouth is *see* **money**

shoot one's mouth off
slang to talk in a careless, loud or boastful manner
Ⓘ Originally US

shut/stop someone's mouth
impolite to make them be quiet, especially about something secret

straight from the horse's mouth *see* **horse**

take the words out of someone's mouth *see* **word**

move

get a move on
informal to hurry or move quickly

move the goalposts *see* **goalpost**

move with the times *see* **time**

on the move
1 moving from place to place
2 advancing or making progress

moveable

a moveable feast
an event or occasion the date of which can be changed around
Ⓘ From ecclesiastical feasts, such as Easter, which do not fall on a fixed date

mover

movers and shakers
informal people with the energy and power to make changes or get things done

moving

the moving finger *see* **finger**

Mrs

Mrs Grundy *see* **Grundy**

much

be too much for someone
to overwhelm them; to be difficult etc for them

make much of someone or **something**
to make a fuss of someone or about something

much of a muchness
informal: usually derogatory of several things, not very different
Ⓘ First recorded in a play by Vanbrugh in *The Provok'd Husband* (1728), from *muchness* = size, greatness

not much of a
not a very good or great thing of a particular kind
• *That wasn't much of a lecture*

not think much of *see* **think**

not up to much
informal not very good

so much for something
derogatory that shows the poor quality of something
• *He arrived half an hour late — so much for his punctuality!*

too much
informal more than can be tolerated or accepted

without so much as
derogatory without even
• *He took my umbrella without so much as asking*

muck

make a muck of something
slang to make a mess of it

muck in (with someone)
slang to share eg accommodation, work etc (with them)
Ⓘ Originally army slang

muck-raking
derogatory the activity of searching for and making public scandalous information about a person or people
Ⓘ Originally from 'the Man with the

Muck-Rake' in Bunyan's *Pilgrim's Progress*, who was actually an image for greed — the change in meaning came about through the other connotations of *muck*

where there's muck there's brass
a proverb, meaning where there is dirt and ugliness in an area there is often much industry and wealth

mud

as clear as mud
informal not at all clear

here's mud in your eye!
rather old a drinking toast
① Originally used by soldiers fighting in the muddy battlefields of World War I

my etc **name is mud**
informal I am considered to have misbehaved; I am disapproved of
① *Mud* was an 18c slang term for a fool, and this phrase thus meant 'I am a fool' — but the other association of *mud* as something worthless has since altered the meaning

sling/throw mud at someone or **something**
to be insulting about someone or something; to call someone or something names

a stick-in-the-mud *see* **stick**

muddle

muddle through
informal to progress in spite of one's unsatisfactory methods and foolish mistakes

muddy

muddy the waters
to cause confusion or trouble in a situation that was previously clear

mug

a mug's game
slang something which only fools would do or be involved in

mule

as stubborn as a mule
very stubborn

multitude

cover a multitude of sins
often facetious to be able to be applied to, include or refer to a great number of different things
① A deliberately misapplied quotation from the Bible, I Peter 3:8 — 'Charity shall cover the multitude of sins'

mum

keep mum
informal to keep quiet, not to reveal something

mum's the word
rather old don't say anything about a particular subject
① A quotation from a play by the 18c playwright George Colman, manager of the Haymarket Theatre and the source of several common phrases

murder

get away with murder
informal to do something wrong, bad, daring, etc without ever suffering any form of punishment or disadvantage

scream/yell blue murder *see* **blue**

Murphy

Murphy's law *see* **wrong**

muscle

flex one's muscles
to test one's strength, ability, etc in a relatively unimportant situation in preparation for that demanded in a much more important or testing situation

museum

a museum piece
derogatory an old-fashioned or out-of-date person or thing that is past its or his best

music

be music to one's/someone's ears
to give one/someone pleasure
• *The news of his team's victory was music to his ears*

face the music
to confront the consequences of one's actions or mistakes
① Origin uncertain — perhaps a reference to an actor facing the orchestra at the same time as facing the audience which will judge the performance

musical

play musical chairs
to swap jobs, situations, etc in a rapid and confusing way
Ⓞ From a children's game in which the players walk to music around a row of chairs. When the music stops each player must find a chair but since there is always one more player than chairs the player without a chair is eliminated

mustard

as keen as mustard
very eager or enthusiastic
Ⓞ From *keen* = 'spicy'

cut the mustard
slang to be capable of achieving success in one's given task
Ⓞ Originally *US* of uncertain origin

muster

pass muster
to be regarded as good enough
Ⓞ A reference to the calling together of servicemen to make sure that their dress and equipment are in good condition

mutton

mutton dressed as lamb
an older person, usually a woman, who is dressed in clothes suitable for a much younger person
Ⓞ Mutton comes from an older sheep, lamb from a younger

mutual

a mutual admiration society
often derogatory shared feeling of respect and regard, either real or pretended, between two people

N

n

to the nth degree
to the greatest extent, amount etc that can be imagined
• *She will get everything organized in time — she is efficient to the nth degree!*

nail

a bed of nails *see* **bed**

as hard as nails
derogatory of a person, very unfeeling and lacking in pity, kindness etc, but able to bear a great deal of hardship or trouble

hit the nail on the head
to be absolutely accurate in one's description of something or someone, in an estimate of something etc

nail one's colours to the mast *see* **colour**

a nail in someone's coffin
something which leads to harm, destruction, ruin, etc

on the nail
informal immediately; exactly

tooth and nail *see* **tooth**

naked

the naked eye *see* **eye**

the naked truth *see* **truth**

name

call someone names
to insult them by applying rude names to them

clear someone's name
to prove that they did not commit a crime etc of which they have been accused

give someone or **something a bad name**
to cause harm to the reputation of someone or something

in name alone/only
only by title, not really in practice
• *They are married in name only, since they have been living apart for years*

in the name of someone
formal by the authority of someone

make a name for oneself
to become famous, get a (usually good) reputation etc

name-dropping
mentioning the names of important or well-known persons in a way that suggests that they are one's friends in order to impress people

my etc **name is mud** *see* **mud**

name names
to specify peoply by name, especially people who are either guilty of a crime or misdeed or who have been accused of wrongdoing

the name of the game
informal the thing that is important, central or essential about an activity etc

name the day *see* **day**

a name to conjure with
the name of someone or something very well-known, important or influential
• *His was a name to conjure with — he was one of the most famous football players ever*
◔ The suggestion is that such people have magical powers of the kind conjurers have

name your poison
slang what would you like to drink?

no names, no pack-drill
if no names are mentioned, no-one will get into trouble; usually said to explain that one is not going to mention any names, or to advise someone else not to

Ⓘ An army phrase, from a form of punishment which involved offenders marching up and down carrying full equipment

not to have a penny to one's name *see* **penny**

take someone's name in vain *see* **vain**

their name is legion *see* **legion**

to one's name
owned by one or in one's possession
• *He hasn't a penny to his name*

worthy of the name
that deserves to be so called

you name it, he etc **has, has done etc it**
informal he has, has done everything you can think of

napping

catch someone napping
informal to meet or find them when they are not prepared
Ⓘ Literally, to catch someone asleep

narrow

narrow-minded
derogatory unwilling to accept ideas different from one's own

a narrow squeak *see* **squeak**

(on) the straight and narrow (path) *see* **straight**

nasty

leave a nasty taste in one's mouth
to leave one with a bad or unpleasant impression

a nasty piece of work
derogatory informal a person whose character and/or behaviour is extremely unpleasant

something nasty in the woodshed
some kind of shameful secret, often of a sexual kind
Ⓘ Derived from an incident in Stella Gibbon's *Cold Comfort Farm* (1932)

native

go native
to live according to the customs, manners etc of a country other than one's own
Ⓘ Originally derogatory, used of white officials etc in Africa and India who chose to live with the native tribesmen and adopt their dress, religion etc

nature

the call of nature
facetious the need to go to the lavatory

in a state of nature
euphemism, usually facetious without any clothes on

in the nature of something
formal having the qualities of something
• *His words were in the nature of a threat*

nature abhors a vacuum
a saying indicating that any kind of empty space is usually soon filled

second nature *see* **second**

near

as near as dammit
informal very nearly
• *Our jumble sale raised £500, as near as dammit*

a near miss
something unpleasant that very nearly happened

near the bone *see* **bone**

near the knuckle *see* **knuckle**

a near thing
the act or state of just avoiding an accident, punishment etc

nowhere near *see* **nowhere**

one's nearest and dearest
one's immediate family

neat

as neat as a new pin *see* **pin**

necessity

make a virtue of necessity *see* **virtue**

necessity is the mother of invention
a proverb indicating that when people are faced with a very difficult and important problem they will usually call upon all their skill and resources to help them overcome it

neck

an albatross round one's neck an inescapable burden or piece of misfortune, sometimes one which reminds one of some misdeed committed in the past

Ⓞ A reference to Coleridge's "The Rime of the Ancient Mariner" (1798) in which a sailor gets a dead albatross slung round his neck as a punishment for shooting an albatross, an action that was considered to be unlucky and brought misfortune to the ship

be in something up to one's neck
very much and very seriously involved in something, especially something bad

break one's neck
informal to do something at great speed and often recklessly
• *You don't have to break your neck to finish that work tonight*

breathing down someone's neck *see* **breathing**

dead from the neck up
slang extremely stupid

get it in the neck
slang to be given the blame and be severely scolded or punished for something one has done etc

have the brass neck to *see* **brass**

a millstone round someone's neck *see* **mill**

neck and neck
(in a race) exactly equal
Ⓞ A term from horse-racing

this, that etc **neck of the woods**
informal a particular place or part of the country
Ⓞ Originally a term for a remote community in the woods of the early 19c American frontier

a pain in the neck *see* **pain**

risk one's neck
to do something that puts one's life, job etc in danger

save someone's neck
to help them to escape from danger, death, ruin, etc

stick one's neck out
informal to take a risk

talk through the back of one's neck *see* **back**

nectar

nectar of the gods
a delicious drink of some kind
Ⓞ In classical mythology nectar was the life-giving drink of the gods

need

a friend in need is a friend indeed *see* **friend**

in someone's hour of need *see* **hour**

need something like someone needs a hole in the head *see* **hole**

needs must (when the devil drives)
a proverb, meaning that if it is necessary to do something, act in a certain way etc, one has to do it even if it is disagreeable

needful

the needful
slang available money

needle

like looking for a needle in a haystack
(of a search) hopeless

a needle match
a match or competition in which the competitive spirit between the opponents is exceptionally keen and often very hostile

on pins and needles *see* **pin**

pins and needles *see* **pin**

neighbourhood

in the neighbourhood of
formal approximately
• *There must have been in the neighbourhood of five hundred people there*

nellie

not on your nellie!
slang certainly not
Ⓞ Reputedly from **not on your puff** = life via Cockney rhyming slang *not on your Nellie Duff*

nerve

a bag/bundle of nerves
a very excitable, anxious, easily frightened person

get on someone's nerves
informal to irritate them

have a nerve
informal to show rudeness and lack of respect in one's words or actions

lose one's nerve
to become frightened and lose the ability to continue with a course of action etc

nest

feather one's (own) nest *see* **feather**

foul one's nest
to cause harm or damage to one's own interests, family, home, etc

a mare's nest *see* **mare**

a nest-egg
informal something saved up for the future, usually money
Ⓛ Literally, a real or artificial egg placed in a nest to encourage hens etc to lay more there

nettle

grasp the nettle
to begin an unpleasant or difficult task in a firm, determined manner
Ⓛ From the fact that nettles are less likely to sting one if grasped firmly

never

never fear, (so-and-so) is here
facetious a saying indicating that the speaker is present or is at hand to help

never-never land
an imaginary place where conditions are too good ever to exist in real life
Ⓛ From the idealized setting of J M Barrie's play *Peter Pan* (1904), itself suggested by the fact that *never-never land* was a 19c name for North Queensland in Australia

never say die *see* **die**[1]

on the never-never
informal by hire purchase

new

as neat as a new pin *see* **pin**

be a new one on someone
informal facetious
be a situation etc that they have not previously heard of and often do not believe in

give someone or **something a new lease of life** *see* **lease**

new blood *see* **blood**

a new broom
person who has newly been given a job, responsibility etc and who is very enthusiastic about working hard, reforming the system etc
Ⓛ From the saying **a new broom sweeps clean**, a new broom being more efficient than an old one

the New World
North and South America

put new heart into *see* **heart**

put new wine in old bottles *see* **wine**

turn over a new leaf *see* **leaf**

news

be news to someone
to be a fact etc not previously known to them

break the news
to tell someone about something, usually something unpleasant, that has happened

no news is good news
a proverb, meaning that if one has had no information about a person, a project etc for some time, it means that all is well, as one would certainly have heard if something bad had happened

next

next (door) to
informal very nearly; virtually
• *His behaviour was next door to absolute rudeness*

next to nothing
informal almost nothing

one's next of kin *see* **kin**

nice

nice guys finish last
informal people have to be a bit ruthless and aggressive if they are to be successful
Ⓛ Associated with the US baseball coach, Leo Durocher, with reference to the New York Giants team (1948)

nice work if you can get it
informal a phrase indicating approval or

admiration of something done, obtained, etc

nick

in good/reasonable nick
Brit slang in good especially physical or working condition
① Origin obscure

in the nick of time
at the last possible moment; just in time
① A reference to measurements marked by notches in a stick etc

nigger

the nigger in the woodpile
a hidden factor, person etc that is causing trouble or having a bad effect on something (especially deliberately)
① A US expression, apparently originally attributing unexplained disappearances of food etc to the unseen presence of a runaway slave

night

it'll be all right on the night
a saying encouraging optimism in an undertaking, despite early difficulties
① Originally a theatrical idiom

make a night of it *see* **make**

the night of the long knives *see* **knife**

a night on the town
informal a night spent out celebrating or enjoying oneself at a bar, restaurant, club, etc

a night-owl
a person who is in the habit of staying up late at night

a one-night stand *see* **one**

turn night into day
to stay up all night or until early in the morning either enjoying oneself or working

nightcap

a nightcap
a drink often alcoholic taken just before going to bed at night
① Literally, a cap worn in bed at night

nine

dressed up to the nines
very carefully and strikingly dressed
① Origin obscure

a nine days' wonder
something that amazes and interests everyone for a short time and then is forgotten
① From an old saying, referred to by Chaucer, that 'there is no wonder so great that it lasts more than nine days', ie even the most amazing events are quickly forgotten

on cloud nine *see* **cloud**

nineteen

the nineteenth hole
the bar of the clubhouse of a golf course
① The standard golf-course has eighteen holes

(talk) nineteen to the dozen
informal to talk continually or for a long time

nip

nip and tuck
especially Amer same as **neck and neck**

nip something in the bud
to stop it as soon as it starts
① From the gardener's method of preventing a plant from flowering

nit

nit-picking
informal; derogatory the act of finding unimportant faults in something
① Originally US

nitty-gritty

get down to the nitty-gritty
to begin discussion etc of basic practical details
① Originally US, of unproved etymology, but presumably invented to combine an idea of small size *nit* with something basic and intractable *grit*

no

it's no joke *see* **joke**

no can do
slang I cannot do that, I cannot help you, etc
• *Will your bike be repaired by tomorrow? Sorry, no can do*

no end (of) *see* **end**

no go
informal unsuccessful; useless; not getting agreement or approval
• *I asked if he would agree to our plans, but it's no go, I'm afraid*

no holds barred *see* **hold**

a no-mans-land *see* **man**

no news is good news *see* **news**

no picnic *see* **picnic**

no rest for the wicked *see* **rest**

no spring chicken *see* **chicken**

no such thing *see* **thing**

no such thing as a free lunch *see* **free**

no sweat *see* **sweat**

no thanks to *see* **thank**

no time (at all) *see* **time**

no two ways about it *see* **way**

no way
slang certainly not; under no circumstances
• *She was looking for an invitation, but no way was I inviting her!*
⌚ Originally US

to no purpose *see* **purpose**

noble

the noble savage
a designation reflecting a belief that primitive people are less corrupt and more praiseworthy than civilized people
⌚ A quotation from Dryden, developed as a theory by the 18c French philosopher Rousseau

nobody

like nobody's business
informal very hard or energetically

nobody's fool *see* **fool**

Nod

the Land of Nod
old or facetious sleep
⌚ From a place mentioned in the Bible, Genesis 4:16, because of the association of nodding with falling asleep

nod

even Homer nods *see* **Homer**

a nod is as good as a wink to a blind horse
a hint is often all that is necessary to communicate one's thoughts or feelings

nod off
informal to fall asleep

on the nod
by general agreement, without actually taking a vote
• *The resolution was passed by the committee on the nod*

nodding

have a nodding acquaintance with someone or **something**
to know someone or something slightly
⌚ From the greeting once considered correct for a person one knew only slightly

noise

a big noise
slang a very important person
⌚ Originally US

empty vessels make most noise *see* **empty**

none

none of something
an expression used to tell a person not to do something or to stop doing something, usually something bad
• *(I'll have) none of your impertinence*

none other than
the very same person as

none the wiser *see* **wise**

none the worse *see* **worse**

none too
slightly facetious not very
• *He lent me a handkerchief which was none too clean*

nonsense

stuff and nonsense *see* **stuff**

nook

every nook and cranny
informal everywhere
⌚ *Nook* is a 'corner', *cranny* 'a crack'

noose

put one's head in a noose *see* **head**

nose

as plain as the nose on your face
extremely obvious

cut off one's nose to spite one's face
derogatory to proceed with an action which harms oneself rather than miss the opportunity which it offers of harming someone else

follow one's nose
not formal to go straight forward

get a bloody nose
to be defeated very thoroughly in a contest, argument, etc and so have one's pride damaged

have a nose for
to be good at discovering or investigating things
• *She has a nose for a bargain*
Ⓞ A reference to a dog used in hunting

keep one's nose clean
informal to keep out of trouble by not behaving badly or dishonestly

keep someone's nose to the grindstone *see* **grindstone**

lead someone by the nose
to make a person do whatever one wants
Ⓞ The reference is to a bull with a ring in its nose, forced to be docile and obedient

look down one's nose at someone
to think of and/or treat them with contempt

no skin off one's nose *see* **skin**

pay through the nose
slang to pay a lot for something

poke one's nose into
informal: derogatory to interfere with other people's business
Ⓞ The reference is to an animal such as a dog

powder one's nose
informal to go to the toilet

put someone's nose out of joint
to disconcert someone by one's presence or actions
• *Their three-year-old is very spoilt — the new baby will certainly put her nose out of joint*

rub someone's nose in it
to remind someone very often of something they have done wrong
Ⓞ From a frequently recommended method of house-training animals

see beyond/further than the end of one's nose
usually in negative to understand more than simply what is happening in the present; to see what future effect one's actions will have etc

thumb one's nose at *see* **thumb**

turn up one's nose at something
to treat it with contempt

under someone's (very) nose
1 right in front of someone; clearly to be seen by someone
2 while someone is there

with one's nose in the air
in a proud or disdainful manner

nosey

a nosey parker
derogatory informal someone who takes too much interest in other people and what they are doing
Ⓞ Origin unknown

not

not tonight, Josephine
a catch phrase used to indicate one's disinclination to take part in some activity
Ⓞ Originally referred to a man declining to have sexual intercourse with a partner; the phrase has been attributed to Napoleon Bonaparte with reference to the Empress Josephine

note

compare notes
to exchange details of experiences, opinions, etc

of note
formal famous, distinguished or important; worth mentioning

strike the right note
to say, do etc something suitable or pleasing to someone
Ⓞ A musical idiom

nothing

all for nothing
without any result or benefit; in vain

be/have nothing to do with someone
to be something which they should not be interested in

come to nothing
rather formal to fail

for nothing
free; without payment

go for nothing
to have no result; to be wasted
• *All his notes were destroyed in the fire — three years of research gone for nothing!*

have nothing on someone
informal
1 to be not good etc enough to compete with them
2 to have no evidence of their wrong or immoral behaviour

have nothing to do with someone or **something**
to avoid them or it completely

like nothing on earth *see* **earth**

make nothing of something
formal not to understand it

next to nothing *see* **next**

nothing but
just; only
• *You're nothing but a fool!; 'Does he drink whisky?' 'Nothing but!'*

nothing doing!
informal an expression used to show a strong or emphatic refusal

nothing if not
certainly; very
• *His life has been nothing if not exciting*

nothing of the kind *see* **kind**

nothing short of *see* **short**

nothing to write home about *see* **home**

nothing ventured, nothing gained
a saying, meaning that one cannot achieve anything without taking risks

stop at nothing *see* **stop**

sweet nothings *see* **sweet**

there is etc **nothing for it but (to do something)**
the only possible thing (to do) is (something)

there is etc **nothing to choose between (two or more people, things etc)**
there is hardly any difference of quality etc between (two or more people or things)

there is nothing to it
informal it is easy

think nothing of something
not to consider it difficult, unusual etc to do something

think nothing of it
it doesn't matter; it is not important

to say nothing of something
as well as something; and in addition
• *When her mother comes to stay, she brings all of her jewellery, to say nothing of her three fur coats*

notice

at short notice *see* **short**

sit up and take notice *see* **sit**

now

as of now
from this time on

every now and then/again
sometimes; occasionally

nowhere

get nowhere
informal to (cause someone to) make no progress; to get or produce no results
• *Flattering me will get you nowhere*

nowhere near
informal not nearly
• *We've nowhere near enough money to buy a car*

nude

in the nude
not wearing any clothes

nudge

nudge nudge, wink wink
a phrase indicating that there is some form of sexual innuendo in something that has just been said

nuff

nuff said *see* **enough said** *at* **enough**

number

back number *see* **back**

his etc **days are numbered** *see* **day**

get someone's number
slang to find out what kind of person they are
Ⓛ Origin unknown

in penny numbers *see* **penny**

look after number one
informal to take one's own interests into consideration before anything or anyone else

his etc **number is up**
informal he is about to die, to suffer something unpleasant etc
Ⓛ The reference is to numbers in a lottery, and to the display of winning — or in this case losing — numbers

number one
informal oneself

someone's opposite number *see* **opposite**

there's safety in numbers *see* **safety**

nurse

nurse a viper in one's bosom *see* **viper**

nursery

nursery slopes
the first easy stages of anything
Ⓛ From the easy hillsides on which beginners learn to ski

nut

be nuts about something or **someone**
informal to be very enthusiastic or keen about it or them, often to a ridiculous extent

do one's nut
slang to become violently angry

a hard nut to crack
a difficult problem

the nuts and bolts
the basic facts or important practical details about something

take a sledgehammer to crack a nut
to use unnecessary force or effort to cope with a slight problem or difficulty

nutshell

in a nutshell
expressed, described etc very briefly

nutty

be nuttier than a fruitcake
informal to be crazy, to be extremely eccentric

O

oar

chain someone to the oars
to make them work very hard all the time
Ⓞ Slaves in ancient times were chained to their positions in ships and forced to row

put/stick one's oar in
derogatory informal to interfere in what another person is saying, doing etc by offering opinions etc when they are not wanted
Ⓞ From an old expression **to have an oar in another man's boat** = to have an interest in someone else's affairs

rest on one's oars
to rest, especially after working very hard
Ⓞ From rowing

oats

get one's oats
slang to get sexual satisfaction

off one's oats
facetious not very well and therefore not eating much
Ⓞ Literally used of horses

sow one's wild oats *see* **wild**

object

money is no object
money is not considered important in the particular circumstances which apply
Ⓞ Originally **money is no object** actually meant 'I etc am not primarily trying to make money from this' — the present uses arose from misapplications of the phrase, which was much used in advertisements

occasion

rise to the occasion
to be able to do what is required in an emergency etc

ocean

a drop in the ocean *see* **drop**

odd

against all the odds
in spite of very great difficulties or problems

be at odds with someone
formal to be quarrelling, not in agreement etc with them, usually over a particular matter

make no odds
to be unimportant
Ⓞ In this phrase, and **what's the odds** below, *odds* simply means 'difference'

odd man out/odd one out
1 a person or thing that is different from others
2 a person or thing that is left over when teams, sets etc are made up
Ⓞ From a method of selection among an uneven number of people by tossing a coin etc

odds and ends
small objects etc of different kinds

odds and sods
informal a mixed collection of people or things considered unimportant

over the odds
more than expected, normal, necessary etc
Ⓞ From horse-racing — literally 'more money than one's winning bet actually entitles one to'

what's the odds?
it's not important; it doesn't matter; *see* **make no odds**, *above*

oddball

an oddball
informal a person who behaves in a strange way

Ⓞ Originally US

odour

in bad odour with someone
having a bad reputation with them; disapproved of by them

an odour of sanctity
derogatory, usually facetious an atmosphere of excessive holiness or goodness
Ⓞ From a French term for the sweet smell reputed to come from the dead bodies of saints, especially when exhumed some time after burial

off

badly, well off *see* **bad, well**

fall off *see* **fall**

get off to a good, bad start *see* **start**

get off to a running start *see* **start**

go off
of food, to become rotten or less good

go off someone or something
to begin to dislike someone or something once liked

have it off *see* **have**

off and on/on and off
informal sometimes; occasionally

off limits *see* **limit**

the off season
the period, at a hotel, holiday resort etc, when there are few visitors

off the cuff *see* **cuff**

off the peg *see* **peg**

off the hook *see* **hook**

off the rails *see* **rail**

off the record *see* **record**

off one's trolley *see* **trolley**

off the wall *see* **wall**

on the off-chance
because of a slight chance that something might be so, happen etc

put someone or **something off** *see* **put**

put someone off something *see* **put**

put someone off his etc **stroke** *see* **stroke**

office

through the (kind) offices of someone
very formal with the help of someone

offing

in the offing
informal about to happen, appear etc
Ⓞ A nautical term: the *offing* is the whole area of sea that can be seen from a particular point on shore

oil

burn the midnight oil *see* **midnight**

no oil painting
informal not very attractive to look at

oil the wheels
to make something easier to do or obtain
Ⓞ From the fact that wheels turn more easily when oil is applied to them

pour oil on troubled waters
to try to calm and soothe a person, a difficult situation etc
Ⓞ From an old method of calming the sea temporarily

strike oil
informal to be successful, find what one is looking for etc

ointment

a fly in the ointment *see* **fly**

old

any old how *see* **any**

be old enough to be someone's father/mother
a saying applied to a much older person who is having a relationship with a young person

be old enough to know better
to reach an age at which one can be expected to behave responsibly and have good judgement

as old as the hills *see* **hill**

money for old rope *see* **money**

an old boy/girl
a former pupil of a school

the Old Bill
informal the police, particularly the London Metropolitan Police
Ⓞ Origin uncertain — perhaps from the

fact that many policemen wore walrus moustaches after World War I and resembled a cartoon character called Old Bill

the old boy network
a group of people, usually upper-class, who are all closely connected and who share information and get jobs etc for one another
Ⓞ An allusion to the fact that the basic connection between such people is often that they were at school together

an old chestnut *see* **chestnut**

the old country
the country from which an immigrant or his parents, grandparents etc originally came

an old flame
informal a former girlfriend or boyfriend

the old guard
the older and less modern members of a group
Ⓞ From the title — *L'Ancienne Garde* — of the most experienced section of the Imperial Guard, the élite of Napoleon's army

an old hand
informal a person who is very experienced at doing something

an old maid
informal a woman who has never married

an old master
any great painter or painting of a period before the 19c, especially of the 15c and 16c

the old school
people whose ideas etc are the same as those which were important in the past
• *Her father is a member of the old school who believe in the importance of obedience to one's parents*

an old timer
slightly derogatory an old person, especially one who has been doing a particular job etc for a long time or did it a long time ago
Ⓞ Originally US

an old wives' tale *see* **tale**

put new wine in old bottles *see* **wine**

a ripe old age *see* **ripe**

olive

an olive branch
a sign of a wish for peace
Ⓞ A symbol for peace in the ancient world

omelette

you can't make an omelette without breaking eggs
a proverb, meaning it is often impossible to achieve a desirable aim without doing some kind of damage, hurting someone, etc in the process
Ⓞ A translation of a French proverb

on

be on to someone
to have discovered their trick, secret etc

fall on *see* **fall**

on and off *see* **off**

on with the motley *see* **motley**

once

give someone or **something the once-over**
to look at, study or examine someone or something quickly

once and for all
decisively; finally
Ⓞ Originally **once for all**

once in a while
occasionally

one

be at one with someone
formal to be in agreement with them

be one up on someone
informal to have an advantage over them

go back to square one *see* **square**

have a one-track mind
to think obsessively of one thing all the time

have only one pair of hands *see* **hands**

not be oneself
to look or feel different from usual, because of illness, anxiety etc

number one *see* **number**

one and all
everyone; all of a group

one by one
of a number of people, things etc, each one alone; one after the other

one for the road *see* **road**

one good turn deserves another *see* **turn**

a one-horse race
a competition etc in which one side or person is certain to win
Ⓛ Racing slang

one in a million *see* **million**

one in the eye *see* **eye**

a one-man show
an activity, planned operation etc in which one person appears to be doing everything and getting all the attention
Ⓛ A theatrical term

a one-night stand
a state of affairs, arrangement, relationship etc that lasts only for one evening or night
Ⓛ Literally, a single concert etc in one place performed by musicians etc on tour

one-off
informal something made, intended etc for one occasion only

(just) one of those things *see* **thing**

one over the eight *see* **eight**

one-sided
1 of a competition etc, with one person or side having a great advantage over the other
2 seeing, accepting or representing only one aspect of a subject

one step forwards, two backwards *see* **step**

the one that got away *see* **away**

one way and another *see* **way**

when one door closes *see* **door**

with one voice *see* **voice**

onion

know one's onions
to know one's job, the subject one studies etc well

only

only too
very
• *I'll be only too pleased to come*

open

bring something out into the open
to make it public
Ⓛ Literally, 'to bring something out from a hiding-place'

come (out) into the open
to make one's opinions known

in the open air
outside; not in a building

keep an open mind
to have a willingness to listen to or accept new ideas, other people's suggestions etc

keep open house
to be prepared to receive and give good etc to anyone who comes or is brought to one's house

keep one's options open *see* **option**

lay oneself open to something
to put oneself in a position where one is likely to receive blame, criticism, insults etc

open and shut
(of a case, problem etc) simple, obvious and/or easily decided

an open book *see* **book**

open someone's eyes to *see* **eye**

open fire *see* **fire**

open Pandora's box *see* **Pandora**

an open secret
something known to many people although supposed to be a secret

open sesame
an effective means of achieving a desired goal or achieving success
• *He thought that his relationship to the managing director was the open sesame to any job in the firm*
Ⓛ From the story *Ali Baba and the Forty Thieves*, in which Ali Baba uses the words 'Open sesame!' as a password to open the door of the robbers' treasure cave

open the door to something *see* **door**

with one's eyes open *see* **eye**

with open arms
in a very friendly way

operative

the operative word(s)
the most important word(s) in a phrase, document, statement etc
• *The operative words in that instruction are 'if possible'. If it isn't possible, we don't need to comply with it*
Ⓛ Literally a legal term for the actual words in a document which express the purpose of the document — eg 'devise and bequeath' in a will

opinion

a matter of opinion *see* **matter**

opposite

someone's opposite number
informal the person who does the same job etc as someone in another company, country etc

the Opposition
Brit the main political party which is opposed to the governing party

option

keep one's options open
to delay making a definite decision about what one will do etc for as long as possible

a soft option *see* **soft**

oracle

work the oracle
to produce the desired result
• *They had difficulty in finding a drug to cure her illness but the latest one seems to have worked the oracle*
Ⓛ A reference to the ancient oracle at Delphi in Greece

order

be in, take (holy) orders
formal to be, or become, a priest, minister etc

get one's marching orders *see* **marching**

in apple-pie order *see* **apple**

in (good) running/working order
(of a machine etc) working well or able to work well

in short order
immediately, rapidly

in working order *see* **in (good) running order** *above*

on order
having been ordered but not yet supplied

orders is orders
informal a saying indicating that someone has to do what they have been told to do, irrespective of what others think
Ⓛ Originally military slang

the order of the day
something necessary, normal, common or particularly fashionable at a certain time
• *Hats with feathers are the order of the day at fashionable weddings this year*
Ⓛ Originally the term for the list of items for discussion in Parliament on a particular day

out of order
1 not working properly
2 not correct according to what is regularly done, especially in meetings etc

the pecking order *see* **pecking**

put one's house in order *see* **house**

a tall order *see* **tall**

what the doctor ordered *see* **doctor**

ordinary

out of the ordinary
unusual

other

every other
using, involving etc one person or thing in a series, then leaving or not involving the next before going on to the next again

look the other way *see* **way**

or other
not known or not decided
• *He must have hidden it somewhere or other*

pass by on the other side *see* **side**

pull the other one!
informal an extension of **pull someone's leg** at **leg**, used to indicate that one thinks that someone is trying to make one believe something that is absolutely untrue or ridiculous

out

be, go out of one's mind *see* **mind**

be out of the swim of things *see* **swim**

be well out of *see* **well**

come out *see* **come**

fall out *see* **fall**

have it out with someone *see* **have**

like something out of the ark *see* **ark**

out and about
of a person who has been ill in bed, in hospital etc, well enough to go out, go to work etc

out-and-out
rather formal complete; very bad
- *He's an out-and-out liar*

out at elbow *see* **elbow**

out for something
informal wanting or intending to get it

out of commission *see* **commission**

out of one's depth *see* **depth**

out of hand *see* **hand**

out of it
informal not part of, or wanted in, a group, activity etc

out of mind *see* **out of sight, out of mind,** *under* **sight**

out of order *see* **order**

out of pocket *see* **pocket**

out of (all) proportion *see* **proportion**

out of sight *see* **sight**

out of sorts *see* **sort**

out of the ordinary *see* **ordinary**

out of touch *see* **touch**

out of turn *see* **turn**

out of work *see* **work**

out on a limb *see* **limb**

out the window *see* **window**

out to do something
informal determined to do it

out to lunch *see* **lunch**

out with it!
informal say what you want to say or have to say

take it out of someone *see* **take**

take it out on someone *see* **take**

outside

at the outside
informal at the most

outstay

outstay one's welcome *see* **welcome**

over

be all over someone
usually derogatory to make too much of a fuss of them; to be too friendly towards them

be over the hump *see* **hump**

fall over oneself *see* **fall**

over and above
formal in addition to

over and done with
finished; no longer important

over and over (again)
continually repeated

over my dead body *see* **dead**

over the hill *see* **hill**

over the odds *see* **odd**

over the top *see* **top**

overboard

go overboard about/for something
informal: often derogatory to be very enthusiastic, often too enthusiastic about it

overdo

overdo it
1 to work too hard
2 do something to excess

overstep

overstep the mark *see* **mark**

own

be one's own man *see* **man**

be one's own worst enemy *see* **enemy**

come into one's own
to have the chance to show one's good qualities, abilities, intelligence etc
- *She is very calm and efficient, and really comes into her own when everyone else is panicking during a crisis*

Ⓘ Literally, to take possession of something to which one has a right

do one's (own) thing *see* **thing**

get one's own back (on someone)
informal to revenge oneself (on them)

get/have one's own way *see* **way**

hold one's own
to be as successful in a fight, argument etc as one's opponent

in one's own right *see* **right**

not to have a minute to call one's own *see* **minute**

(all) on one's own
1 alone
2 with no-one else's help
Ⓘ The second meaning is the original

own up to something
to admit that one has done it

score an own goal *see* **goal**

oyster

the world is his etc **oyster**
he etc can go anywhere and do anything
Ⓘ A quotation from Shakespeare, *The Merry Wives of Windsor*, II ii

P

p

mind one's p's and q's
informal to be very careful
Ⓞ Perhaps originally a warning to a printer to be careful not to mix up the letters p and q

pace

at a snail's pace *see* **snail**

keep pace with someone or **something**
to maintain a position of knowledge, understanding, control, equality etc with regard to them or it
• *It is difficult to keep pace with scientific discoveries*
Ⓞ Literally, in a race, 'to go as fast as someone else'

put someone or **something through his** etc **paces**
to make someone or something show what they are capable of
Ⓞ From the standard method of assessing the quality of a horse by watching it move in all four gaits *paces*

set the pace for
to go forward at a particular speed which everyone else has to follow
Ⓞ From racing

show one's paces
to show what one can do
Ⓞ Literally used of horses; *see* **put someone** or **something through his paces** *above*

stay the pace
to maintain progress in any activity at the same rate as everyone else

pack

no names, no pack-drill *see* **name**

pack a punch *see* **punch**

pack it in
slang to stop doing whatever one is doing
Ⓞ From an earlier idiom **pack the game in**

packed like herring in a barrel *see* **herring**

packed like sardines *see* **sardine**

packed out
informal containing as many people as possible

pack up
slang to stop working or operating
Ⓞ World War I army slang, from packing up equipment on ceasing a particular operation etc

packet

cost a packet
informal to cost a great deal of money

packing

send someone packing
informal to send them away firmly and without politeness
Ⓞ From an old use of *pack* meaning 'to leave in a hurry'

paddle

paddle one's own canoe *see* **canoe**

pain

be at pains/take pains
formal to take great trouble and care to do something

for one's pains
formal or facetious as a (poor) reward for one's trouble and effort in doing something

on/under pain of something
formal or facetious at the risk of being given some kind of punishment

• *The employees were forbidden, on pain of instant dismissal, to tell anyone about the project*

a pain in the neck
derogatory informal a person who is constantly annoying
Ⓞ Originally such a person was said to *give one a pain in the neck*, for reasons which are obscure

paint

be as black as one is painted *see* **black**

paint something in glowing colours *see* **colour**

paint the town (red)
to go out and enjoy oneself in a noisy and expensive manner
Ⓞ Originally 19c US

painting

no oil painting *see* **oil**

pair

have only one pair of hands *see* **hand**

pair off
to join together with one person to make a pair

show a clean pair of heels *see* **clean**

pal

bosom pals
informal same as **bosom friend** at **bosom**

pale

as pale as death *see* **death**

beyond the pale
outside the normal limits of good behaviour, what is acceptable etc
Ⓞ *The Pale* was, especially in the 16c, the limited area of English government either around Calais or around Dublin, the people who lived outside it in the latter case being regarded as uncivilized barbarians

palm

bear the palm
to be victorious or successful in a contest, competition etc
Ⓞ In ancient Rome a branch of a palm tree was given to the winner of a contest or game

grease someone's palm
slang to give them money

have an itching palm *see* **itching**

have someone in the palm of one's hand
to have them in one's power or ready to act etc as one wishes

palm something or **someone off on someone**
informal to get rid of an undesirable thing or person by giving, selling it etc to someone else
Ⓞ From illusion and trickery performed by concealing objects in the palm of one's hand

pan

a flash in the pan *see* **flash**

out of the frying-pan into the fire *see* **frying-pan**

pancake

as flat as a pancake
extremely flat

Pandora

open Pandora's box
to uncover difficult and unsuspected problems
Ⓞ Pandora, in Greek legend the first mortal woman, had a box in which were sealed all the evils of the world. When she opened it they all escaped, only hope being left in the box

panic

press the panic button
to react in an overdramatic or hysterical way to a difficult situation
Ⓞ A reference to the button pressed by test pilots to bring about an emergency ejection

pants

(be caught) with one's pants/trousers down
informal to be revealed at an embarrassing moment, especially because one is shown to be completely unprepared to act, respond etc

bore the pants off someone
informal to bore them very much, to be very tedious to them

have ants in one's pants *see* **ant**

paper

on paper
in theory, but not in practice

paper over the cracks
informal to pretend that no mistake has been made or that there has been no argument
⌚ From the practice of hiding cracks in the wall of a house with wallpaper

paper tiger
someone or something that has the appearance of being very powerful or threatening but is in practice completely ineffective

par

below par/not up to par
informal
1 not up to the usual standard
• *Your work is not up to par this week*
2 not well
• *She had a cold and was feeling below par*

on a par with something
as good as it

par for the course
what might have been expected
⌚ From golf — literally, the number of strokes that would be made in a perfect round on that course

paradise

a fool's paradise *see* **fool**

pardon

beg someone's pardon
to say one is sorry usually for having offended someone else etc

pardon/excuse my French *see* **French**

parrot

parrot-fashion
informal without understanding the meaning of what one has learnt, is saying etc

sick as a parrot *see* **sick**

parsnip

fine words butter no parsnips *see* **word**

part

be part of the furniture *see* **furniture**

for my etc **part**
formal as far as I etc am concerned

for the most part
rather formal mainly or chiefly

good in parts *see* **good**

look the part
to have the appearance from the point of view of clothes, behaviour, etc of being a particular kind of person

a man of many parts *see* **man**

part and parcel
informal something which is naturally part of something

part company
1 to go in different directions
2 to leave each other or end a friendship, partnership etc

play a part
1 to be involved or concerned
2 to pretend to be what one is not

take something in good part
to accept it without being hurt or offended

take someone's part
to support them in an argument etc

take part in something
to be one of a group of people doing something; to take an active share in eg playing a game, performing a play, holding a discussion etc

parting

the parting of the ways
the point at which people must take different decisions, follow different courses of action etc
⌚ A Biblical reference, to Ezekiel 21:21

party

be party to something
to be involved in or know about it (often something secret or wrong)

the life and soul of the party *see* **life**

the party line
the ideas and opinions approved by the leaders of a particular group

someone's party piece
an act, song, joke, etc that they frequently perform in public

the party's over
informal a particularly happy, favourable, enjoyable etc time has come to an end

pass

cut someone off at the pass
to use preventive tactics
Ⓞ A reference to Western films in which a mountain pass was a convenient place at which to ambush someone

let something pass
to ignore something rather than take the trouble to argue about it

make a pass at someone
slang to try and make them sexually interested in one
Ⓞ A fencing term — 'to thrust at someone with a fencing foil' — the slang use is originally US

pass as/for something
to be mistaken for or accepted as something
• *Some man-made materials could pass as silk*

pass away
euphemism to die

pass by on the other side *see* **side**

pass something or **someone off as something** or **someone**
to pretend that something or someone is something or someone else

pass out
informal to faint
Ⓞ From a late 19c euphemism for 'to die' — probably as an abbreviation for **pass out of sight**, via World War I slang for 'to become unconscious through drink'

pass someone over
informal to ignore or overlook them

pass round the hat *see* **hat**

pass the buck *see* **buck**

pass something up
informal not to accept a chance, opportunity etc

a pretty pass *see* **pretty**

ships that pass in the night *see* **ship**

passing

in passing
rather formal while doing or talking about something else; without explaining fully what one means
• *He told her the story, and said in passing that he did not completely believe it*

past

past one's best/past it
informal less strong, good, efficient etc than one was, because one is getting older

a past master
usually slightly derogatory someone who is extremely skilful at an activity which requires skill
Ⓞ Literally, 'a person who has held the post of Master in a lodge of freemasons etc', but the phrase has been influenced by the expression *passed master* = 'a person who has qualified as a master'

I etc **would not put it past someone to (do something)**
derogatory informal I think they are perfectly capable of, especially immoral enough to (do something bad)

pasture

fresh fields and pastures new *see* **fresh**

put someone out to pasture
to end their employment, usually because of old age

pat

a pat on the back
informal a demonstration of approval or praise

patch

hit/strike a bad patch
informal to have a difficult time, meet unfavourable conditions etc

not to be a patch on something
informal to be not nearly as good as it
Ⓞ Perhaps deriving from **like a patch on** — 'obviously inferior to' — and originally US

patch something up
informal to settle a quarrel

path

beat a path to someone's door
to visit them very often or in very large numbers

cross someone's path
to be met or noticed casually or accidentally by someone

the primrose path
a pleasurable, easy way of life, especially when this is regarded as the way to ruin

patience

enough to try the patience of a saint
informal something extremely irritating or annoying

have the patience of Job
to be extremely patient
Ⓞ From the story of Job in the Bible

patter

the patter of tiny feet
often facetious
the presence of small children

pause

give someone pause
formal to make them hesitate for a moment
Ⓞ A Shakespearian quotation, from *Hamlet* III, i

pave

pave the way for something
to make it easy or possible for it to happen
• *The scientific discoveries of the eighteenth century paved the way for the Industrial Revolution in Britain*
Ⓞ From paving roads in order to make traffic faster and easier

pay

the devil to pay *see* **devil**

in someone's pay
informal: usually derogatory employed by, or given money by, someone, usually for a bad purpose

pay court to someone *see* **court**

pay someone in his own coin *see* **coin**

pay lip-service *see* **lip**

pay one's respects *see* **respect**

pay the earth *see* **earth**

pay the piper *see* **piper**

pay through the nose *see* **nose**

pay one's way *see* **way**

put paid to something
to prevent a person from doing something he planned or wanted to do
Ⓞ Apparently from the book-keeping habit of writing 'paid' against accounts etc finally settled in a ledger

rob Peter to pay Paul *see* **rob**

you pays your money and you takes your choice *see* **money**

pea

as (a)like as two peas (in a pod)
exactly alike

peace

hold one's peace
old or formal to remain silent

keep the peace
to prevent fighting, quarrelling etc
Ⓞ Literally a legal term for not creating a public disturbance

make one's peace with someone
to become freindly again with them, or especially to get them to be friendly again towards oneself, after a period of quarrelling etc

peace of mind
freedom from worry, distress etc

peacock

as proud as a peacock
very proud

pearl

cast pearls before swine
usually facetious to give or offer something valuable to people who are unable to appreciate it
Ⓞ A Biblical reference, to Matthew 7:6

pebble

there are plenty of pebbles left on the beach
same as **there's plenty more fish in the sea** at **fish**

pecker

keep one's pecker up
slang to remain cheerful and hopeful
Ⓞ Probably from *pecker* = beak

pecking

the pecking order
the order of importance in a group of people
• *I have very little influence on the firm's policy — I'm a long way down the pecking order*
Ⓞ A translation of a German word, *Hackordnung*, coined in the 1920s for a social system first noticed in domestic hens, whereby each bird in a group is allowed to peck the bird next below it in rank and has to submit to being pecked by the bird next above it

pedestal

put someone on a pedestal
derogatory to think of and treat them as being much better and more admirable than normal people
Ⓞ From the method of mounting public statues of heroes etc

peeping

a peeping Tom *see* **Tom**

peg

bring/take someone down a peg (or two)
informal to make a proud person more humble
Ⓞ The reference is to tuning musical instruments, and dates from the 16c

off the peg
of clothes, ready to wear

a peg on which to hang something
a topic or theme which gives someone an opportunity to express an idea, opinion, etc

peg out
informal to die
Ⓞ From the game of cribbage in which players move their pegs until they read a winning score, at which point they are said to 'peg out' and the game ends

a square peg in a round hole
a person who does not fit into a particular situation or environment and feels uncomfortable in it

pegging

level pegging *see* **level**

pelt

at full pelt
running as fast as possible

pendulum

the swing of the pendulum
change from one side to another, especially when this is regarded as being natural or unavoidable
• *According to the swing of the pendulum we are due for a change of government*

penny

in for a penny, in for a pound
a saying, meaning that once one has decided to take a risk, act in a particular way etc, one ought to do so boldly

in penny numbers
a very few, or a very little, at a time
Ⓞ From a method of selling encyclopedias etc in sections, formerly often at a penny a part

not cost a penny
not to cost anything at all

not have a penny to one's name
to have no money at all

the penny drops
informal I etc understand
• *He didn't grasp her meaning at first, but eventually the penny dropped*
Ⓞ The reference is to a coin taking a long time to operate the machinery of a slot machine

a penny for them
what are you thinking about?
Ⓞ In full, a **penny for your thoughts**, a saying recorded in the 16c

penny wise and pound foolish
saving small amounts of money in everyday matters while wasting large sums in other ways

a pretty penny *see* **pretty**

spend a penny
informal euphemism to urinate
Ⓞ From the former long-established price of admission to a cubicle in public lavatories

turn an honest penny
to earn some money honestly

turn up like a bad penny
of someone disliked or unwanted, to

reappear, especially frequently and/or unexpectedly

two a penny
derogatory very common; of little value
① Literally, sold in bulk at a halfpenny each

pennyworth
get one's pennyworth
to get full value for one's money, effort, etc

pep
a pep-talk
informal a talk intended to arouse enthusiasm, or to make people work harder, better etc

perch
fall off the perch
slang to die

knock someone off his/her perch
to make them more humble or less important
① A reference to a bird's perch

perfect
practice makes perfect *see* **practice**

perfection
the pink of perfection *see* **pink**

to perfection
formal so that something is perfect

peril
at one's peril
often facetious at one's own risk

period
a period piece
a person or thing eg a play, piece of furniture, painting that is very typical of the time when he or it was born or made, especially if interesting mainly because of this fact

perish
perish the thought
usually facetious I should not think or say such a terrible thing
① A quotation from Colley Cibber's 18c version of Shakespeare's *Richard III* V, v

person
be no respecter of persons *see* **respect**

in person
personally; one's self, not represented by someone else

the last person *see* **last**

perspective
in, out of perspective
with, without a correct or sensible understanding of something's true importance
① Literally, of an object in a painting etc, having, or not having, the correct size, shape or angle in relation to the rest of the picture

petard
be hoist with one's own petard
to be the victim of, or ruined by, one's own trick which one intended to ruin or harm someone else
• *The councillor who introduced parking restrictions to the town of Southwood was hoist with his own petard when he was himself fined for parking outside the Town Hall.*
① A Shakespearian quotation, *Hamlet* III, iv. A *petard* was a kind of bomb used by military engineers

Peter
the Peter principle
a theory which suggests that employees tend to be promoted to the level of their own incompetence
① The title of a book by Laurence Peter and Raymond Hill (1969)

petrel
a stormy petrel *see* **stormy**

philistine
a philistine
a person who does not take any interest in or appreciate the arts
① The Philistines were a fierce people who fought against the Israelites in biblical times. The word was used by eighteenth century German students about those not interested in education

phoenix
rise like a phoenix from the ashes *see* **ash**

phrase
to coin a phrase *see* **coin**

a turn of phrase *see* **turn**

phut

go phut
informal usually of something mechanical or electrical, to break or cease to function
Ⓘ Probably from the sound accompanying the breakdown

pick

have a bone to pick with someone *see* **bone**

pick and choose
to select or choose very carefully

pick holes in *see* **hole**

pick someone's brains *see* **brain**

pick something or **somewhere clean** *see* **clean**

pick (someone) off
to shoot (especially people in a group) one by one

pick on someone
informal
1 to choose them to do a (usually difficult or unpleasant) job
2 to speak to or treat them angrily or critically

pick up the pieces *see* **piece**

pick up the threads of something *see* **thread**

picnic

no picnic
informal no easy task

picture

be/put someone in the picture
to have or provide all the necessary information about something

get the picture
slang to understand the situation

one picture is worth a thousand words
a graphic illustration is much more valuable than a long verbal explanation in communicating something to someone

the pictures
Brit informal the cinema

pie

as easy as pie
extremely easy

have a finger in the pie *see* **finger**

pie in the sky
derogatory informal something good promised for the future but which one is not certain or likely to get
Ⓘ A quotation — in full, 'You'll get pie in the sky when you die' — from a poem by the American anarchist Joe Hill

piece

all of a piece
informal all the same; happening etc according to the same rules or principles
• *Their rudeness is all of a piece with their lack of respect for authority*

give someone a piece of one's mind *see* **mind**

go (all) to pieces
informal of a person, to collapse physically or nervously

a nasty piece of work *see* **nasty**

pick up the pieces
to put things right or in good order after some form of upset

a piece of the action
involvement in something, a share of something, particularly something exciting or profitable

pull something or **someone to pieces**
1 to criticize severely
2 to investigate thoroughly with a view to finding fault

a set piece *see* **set**

the villain of the piece *see* **villain**

pig

as happy as a pig in muck
blissfully happy

buy/get a pig in a poke
to buy, get something without knowing whether it is worth anything or not
Ⓘ Allegedly from a fairground trick which involved selling unwary customers a cat in a bag while assuring them it was a piglet. Whether this is true or not, selling a piglet in a bag would make it impossible to check its value

drive one's pigs to market
old to snore or breathe heavily and noisily

go to pigs and whistles
to become ruined or worthless
① *Pigs* here means 'pieces of earthenware' and *pigs and whistles* therefore means 'trifles'

make a pig of oneself
informal to eat greedily; to eat too much

make a pig's ear of something
informal to do it badly or clumsily; to make a mess of it

pig-in-the-middle
informal someone who is in a position between two people or groups who are fighting, who disagree etc
① From a child's game in which two people throw a ball etc from one to another and a third tries to intercept it

pigs might fly
an expression indicating that one believes that something is very unlikely to happen

sweat like a pig
to perspire profusely

pigeon

pigeon-toed
of a person or his manner of walking, with toes turned inwards

put the cat among the pigeons *see* **cat**

a stool-pigeon *see* **stool**

that's (not) my etc pigeon
that is not my affair or interest
① Strictly, **not my pidgin** — pidgin English for 'not my business'

pikestaff

as plain as a pikestaff
very clear or obvious
① Apparently originally a play on words, referring to the lack of ornamentation or subtlety of shape in the wooden shaft of a pike

pile

makes one's pile
informal to make one's fortune, to make a great deal of money

pile it on thick
informal to exaggerate greatly

pile on the agony
to exaggerate the painful or distressing details of an unfortunate incident

pill

a bitter pill to swallow *see* **bitter**

sugar the pill *see* **sugar**

pillar

from pillar to post
usually of a person in trouble, difficulty etc, from one place to another usually looking for help etc
① An idiom from the game of real tennis

a pillar of the community/society
someone who holds a position of importance or power in a community
① A reference to the pillars which support some buildings

pillow

pillow talk
conversation, often about confidential or secret matters, between husband and wife or between lovers when in bed

pin

as neat as a new pin
extremely neat and tidy

for two pins
informal if given the smallest reason, encouragement etc; very readily
• *For two pins I would cancel the meeting, since no-one wants to go!*

on pins and needles
waiting anxiously for something

pin back one's ears *see* **ear**

pin someone down
to make them give a definite answer, statement, opinion, or promise

pin one's hopes/faith on someone
to rely on them; to hope or expect that they will do or achieve something

pin money
a small sum of money earned by a woman or given to her by her husband for items of personal use
① In the Middle Ages pins were both expensive and scarce and for a time were sold only on the first two days of the year

pin something on someone
informal to prove or suggest that a person was responsible for something bad, especially a crime

pins and needles
a tingling feeling in one's hands, feet or legs

you could hear a pin drop
it is absolutely quiet; no-one is making a sound

pinch

at a pinch/if it comes to the pinch
informal in an emergency; if absolutely necessary

feel the pinch
informal to have problems because of lack of money

pinch and scrape
to live on very little money

take something with a pinch of salt *see* **salt**

pink

be tickled pink *see* **tickle**

in the pink (of health)
old or facetious very well; in good health

the pink of perfection
absolutely perfect
Ⓞ A quotation from Goldsmith's play *She Stoops to Conquer* (1773) — *pink* meaning 'the finest example'

pip

give someone the pip
informal to annoy, disgust or offend them
Ⓞ *The pip* is a disease of poultry, applied from very early on to vague and generally not very serious human illnesses

pipped at the post
informal beaten in the very final stages of a race, competition, etc
Ⓞ A term from horse-racing. *Pipped* became a slang term for 'defeated' by extension from the meaning 'blackballed', ie denied access to a club etc by a vote cast by placing a white (for) or black (against) ball in a box. The black ball was likened to a pip

pipe

pipe down
informal to stop talking; to be quiet

a pipe dream
an idea which can only be imagined, and which would be impossible to carry out
Ⓞ Originally, a vision induced by smoking opium

(you can) put that in your pipe and smoke it!
informal you can think about that and see how you like it! usually said of something unpleasant to the hearer

pipeline

in the pipeline
not formal in preparation; not yet ready
• *Our plans for expansion are still in the pipeline*
Ⓞ The reference is to crude oil piped from the well to the refinery

piper

pay the piper
to provide the money for something, and thus have some control over it, a reference to the saying **he who pays the piper calls the tune**

piping

piping hot
informal very hot

pistol

hold a pistol to someone's head
to force them to do as one wishes, usually by using threats

pitch

as black as pitch
very dark

pitch in
informal to begin to deal with, do etc something
• *If everyone pitches in, we'll soon get the job done*

queer someone's pitch *see* **queer**

pitcher

little pitchers have big ears
a proverb, meaning small children overhear things which they are not supposed to know about, simply because people tend to overlook their presence

place

fall into place
of happenings, facts etc, to become easily understood because seen in the proper relationship

give place to
very formal to be followed and replaced by something

go places
slang to be successful, especially in one's career

in the first place
at the very beginning

know one's place
to accept one's low rank or lack of importance and behave in a suitable manner

a place in the sun *see* **sun**

pride of place *see* **pride**

put someone in his etc **place**
to remind them, often in a rude or angry way, of their lower social position, or lack of importance, experience etc

put oneself in someone's place
to imagine what it would be like to be someone else

take place
formal to happen

take someone's place
to do something or go somewhere as a replacement for someone else

take the place of something
to be used instead of, or to be a substitute for, it

plague

avoid someone or **something like the plague**
to do one's very best not to come into contact with or be involved with them or it

plain

as plain as a pikestaff *see* **pikestaff**

as plain as the nose on your face *see* **nose**

plain sailing
progress without difficulty
Ⓣ Probably, by confusion between *plane* and *plain*, from *plane sailing*, a method of making navigational calculations at sea in which the earth's surface is treated as if it were flat

plan

go according to plan
to happen as arranged or intended

plank

as thick as two short planks
derogatory informal very stupid

plate

have something handed to one on a plate
informal to get something without having to do anything for it

on one's plate
waiting to be dealt with; occupying one's time
• *I'd like to help you but I've got too much on my plate at the moment*

platonic

platonic friendship/relationship
a relationship between a man and a woman which involves only friendship and not a sexual or romantic attachment
Ⓣ Named after the Greek philosopher Plato, who maintained that it was possible for two people to love each other deeply without sexual attraction

play

all work and no play makes Jack a dull boy *see* **work**

bring/come into play
formal to (cause to) be used or exercised

child's play *see* **child**

fair play *see* **fair**

make a play for something
to try and get it
Ⓣ An idiom from chess

make great play with something
rather formal to place great emphasis on something; to treat or talk of something as very important
• *She had just got engaged, and was making great play with her fiancé's wealth and aristocratic connections*

play along with someone or **something**
to work together with someone or towards an aim etc; to agree with and help someone, usually only for a short while

play a losing game *see* **losing**

play a part *see* **part**

play one's cards close, right *see* **card**

play something down
to try to make it appear less important

played out
informal
1 exhausted
2 no longer of any interest or influence
Ⓞ Literally, of theatrical performances, 'played to the end'

play fair
to act honestly and in an unbiased way; not to cheat

play fast and loose *see* **fast**

play for time *see* **time**

play gooseberry *see* **gooseberry**

play hard to get
deliberately to avoid someone or to avoid making a decision on a proposal or invitation, often with the purpose of making one seem more desirable or wanted

play havoc with *see* **havoc**

play (merry) hell with *see* **hell**

play it by ear *see* **ear**

play it cool *see* **cool**

play musical chairs *see* **musical**

play no part in something
not to be one of the people who are doing something
Ⓞ From acting in a play

play someone off against someone else
to set one person against another in order to gain an advantage

play on/upon someone's feelings, fears etc
to make use of someone's feelings, fears etc

a play on words
a joke, clever saying etc based on similarities, associations etc between words

play possum *see* **possum**

play safe
to take no risks
Ⓞ From billiards

play second fiddle *see* **second**

play the devil's advocate *see* **devil**

play the field
to spread one's interest, affections etc over a wide range of subjects, people etc rather than concentrating on any single one

play the fool *see* **fool**

play the game *see* **game**

play to the gallery *see* **gallery**

play one's trump card *see* **trump**

play up
to annoy, cause trouble for or be a nuisance to
• *The children are playing up today; I sprained my ankle last month and it still plays me up occasionally*
Ⓞ Originally used of horses behaving badly

play up to someone
to flatter or pretend to admire them for one's own advantage
Ⓞ Originally theatrical slang for supporting another actor in a play

play with fire *see* **fire**

please

as pleased as Punch *see* **Punch**

if you please
old or formal please

please yourself
informal do what you choose

small things please small minds *see* **small**

pleasure

have had the pleasure (of meeting)
formal or facetious to have been introduced to

take pleasure in
to get enjoyment from doing (something)

pledge

sign the pledge
to decide or promise not to take any alcoholic drinks
Ⓞ In former times members of

temperance societies signed a piece of paper to this effect

plot

the plot thickens
usually facetious the affair is becoming more complicated and interesting
ⓘ A quotation from a Restoration play, *The Rehearsal* (1671) by George Villiers, Duke of Buckingham

plough

plough a lonely furrow *see* **furrow**

plough something back
to put money, profits etc back into a business etc
ⓘ From ploughing an unimportant crop into the ground to act as fertilizer

put one's hand to the plough
to set about a task

pluck

pluck up courage *see* **courage**

plumb

plumb the depths *see* **depth**

plunge

take the plunge
to decide to start doing something new or difficult
ⓘ Literally 'to dive into water'

pocket

burn a hole in someone's pocket
facetious said of money when one is eager to spend it

in pocket, out of pocket
having gained, lost money over a business deal etc

in someone's pocket
influenced or controlled by them

line one's pockets
to make money dishonestly from one's job

out of pocket *see* **in pocket**

put one's hand in one's pocket
informal to pay, to bear the cost

poetic

poetic justice
the suitable but accidental punishing of wrong and, often, rewarding of right

poetic licence
the disregarding of some rules of form, grammar or of fact by creative writers to achieve a particular effect

point

be beside the point
to have no direct connection with, or to be unimportant to, the subject being discussed

be on the point of (doing something)
to be about to (do something)

be to the point
formal to be connected with what is being discussed; to be relevant
• *Her speech was very much to the point*

come to the point
to reach the most important matter, consideration in a conversation etc

in point of fact
actually; in reality

make a point of doing something
to be especially careful to do it

make one's point
to state an opinion etc so clearly and persuasively that it has been understood and accepted

not to put too fine a point on it *see* **fine**

the point of no return
the stage in a process etc after which there is no possibility of stopping or going back
ⓘ Originally the point in an aircraft's flight after which it does not have enough fuel to go back to its place of departure

a point of view
a way or manner of looking at a subject, matter etc

point taken!
a phrase indicating that one accepts as true or just the comment that someone has just made

point the finger at someone *see* **finger**

score a point against someone
to defeat or get the advantage of them in an argument, etc, especially by clever means

a sore point *see* **sore**

stretch a point *see* **stretch**

someone's strong point *see* **strong**

take someone's point
to understand and accept what they wish to say, especially during an argument, debate etc

up to a point
to a certain extent but not completely

when it comes to the point
at the moment when something must be done, decided etc
• *He always promises to help, but when it comes to the point, he's never there*

poison

name your poison *see* **name**

a poison-pen letter
an anonymous letter saying wicked things about a certain person etc

poke

buy a pig in a poke *see* **pig**

poke fun at someone
to laugh unkindly at them

poke one's nose into *see* **nose**

poker

as stiff as a poker
very stiff

a poker face
total lack of expression, a deadpan expression
⌚ A reference to the card game of poker where players try not to reveal the quality of their hand by remaining expressionless

pole

be poles apart
informal to be as different or as far apart as possible

in pole position
in a position of advantage
⌚ From the use of the expression in motor racing and horse-racing to describe the most favourable starting position on the line

up the pole
slang
1 in difficulties
2 crazy
3 pregnant

polish

polish something off
informal to finish it
⌚ From boxing slang

spit and polish *see* **spit**

pony

on shanks's pony *see* **shanks**

poor

like the poor
facetious always present, always in the vicinity
⌚ Short for **the poor are always with you**, a biblical reference to Matthew 26:11 — 'For the poor always ye have with you'

a poor thing but mine own
a phrase usually used in mock-modesty to describe something that one is actually rather proud of
⌚ A reference to Touchstone's speech in Shakespeare, *As You Like It* V, iv — 'A poor virgin, sir, an ill-favoured thing, sir, but mine own'

pop

pop the question *see* **question**

pop up
informal to appear
• *You never know where he'll pop up next!*

top of the pops
informal very much in favour at the moment
⌚ Originally used of those pop records which are selling best at any given time

port

any port in a storm
a saying, meaning that one has to accept any possible solution, way out etc when one has difficulties

pose

strike a pose *see* **strike**

possess

what possessed him etc?
why did he do such a thing
• *What possessed you to buy that hideous coat?*
⌚ Literally 'what evil spirit made him ...'

possession

possession is nine points of the law
a proverb, meaning that if there is a dispute about who should have something, the person who has it at the time is in the strongest position
Ⓞ The *nine points* are visualized as being out of a hypothetical ten available to be won in a lawsuit

possum

play possum
informal to pretend to be unavailable, ignorant of a fact etc or uninterested in order to protect oneself
Ⓞ From the reputed habit of the possum of pretending to be dead when attacked

post

as deaf as a post
very deaf

from pillar to post *see* **pillar**

keep someone posted
informal to give regular information to a person
Ⓞ Originally US, from a book-keeping expression meaning 'to keep ledgers etc fully made up to date'

pipped at the post *see* **pip**

pot

go to pot
informal to become bad; to get worse and worse
Ⓞ Literally, 'to be made into stew'

a pot-boiler
derogatory a book or other work by a writer, artist etc, produced for the sake of money only
Ⓞ From **keep the pot boiling**, which originally meant 'to earn one's living'

the pot calling the kettle black
someone who is criticizing someone else for doing something etc that he does himself
Ⓞ From the uniform black colour of all kitchen utensils used over an open fire

pot-hunting
derogatory entering a competition only in order to win a prize

a pot-shot
an easy or casual shot that doesn't need careful aim
Ⓞ Originally this term was slightly derogatory and implied that one was shooting birds etc solely for food and not in order to exercise one's skill

take pot-luck
informal to have a meal as someone's guest without their having prepared special food
Ⓞ Literally 'to accept whatever happens to be served to one from the cooking-pot'

a watched pot never boils
a proverb, meaning that when one is waiting for something to happen etc, the time seems even longer if one is continually watching and thinking about it

potato

couch potato
informal an inactive person who takes little exercise
Ⓞ From the fact that such a person spends a great deal of time sitting on a couch watching television

a hot potato
a subject, person etc which is extremely difficult and dangerous to handle

small potatoes
people or things regarded as being extremely unimportant

pound

get/have one's pound of flesh
to obtain everything one is entitled to have, especially if this causes difficulties or unhappiness to others
Ⓞ From the bargain between Shylock and Antonio in Shakespeare's *The Merchant of Venice* whereby Shylock was entitled to a pound of Antonio's flesh if he was unable to repay a loan

pour

it never rains but it pours
a proverb, meaning that when things go wrong, they go disastrously, or frequently, wrong

pour one's heart out *see* **heart**

pour oil on troubled waters *see* **oil**

powder

keep one's powder dry
not to take immediate action

ⓘ From gunpowder, which must be kept dry to be usable

powder one's nose *see* **nose**

power

do a power of good, harm etc
to do a lot of good, harm, evil etc

in one's power
under one's control and dependent on one's mercy

more power to his etc **elbow**
I wish him etc good luck
• *If he is really trying to reform the system, more power to his elbow — it badly needs to be reformed*
ⓘ Of Anglo-Irish origin — derivation unknown

the power behind the throne
the person who really runs an organization etc, while giving the impression that someone else is in charge

the powers that be
the people in authority
ⓘ A Biblical reference, to Romans 13:1

practical

a practical joke
a usually irritating joke consisting of an action done to someone, rather than a story told

practice

be out of practice
not having had a lot of practice recently

make a practice of doing something
to do it habitually

practice makes perfect
a proverb, meaning that if one practises one will eventually be able to do something well, and often said to encourage someone to try again

put something into practice
to do something, as opposed to thinking about it, planning it etc

sharp practice *see* **sharp**

practise

practise what one preaches
to act or behave oneself as one tells other people they should act or behave

praise

damn someone or **something with faint praise** *see* **damn**

praise someone to the skies *see* **sky**

sing someone's praises
to praise them with great enthusiasm
ⓘ A Biblical phrase

preach

practise what one preaches *see* **practise**

preach to the converted *see* **convert**

precious

precious few/little
informal very few/little

prejudice

without prejudice to something
formal without any possible harm or danger to a person's rights, position, prospects etc
• *You ought to be able to criticize your firm without prejudice to your chances of promotion*
ⓘ A legal term

premium

be at a premium
to be wanted by a lot of people and be therefore difficult to get
• *Tickets for the rugby match were at a premium*
ⓘ A financial term — 'sold at more than the nominal value' — the opposite of *at a discount*

prepare

be prepared to do something
to be willing to do it

presence

presence of mind
calmness and the ability to act sensibly in an emergency etc

present

at present
at the present time

for the present
as far as the present time is concerned

there's no time like the present *see* **time**

press

be pressed for (something)
informal to be short of (time, money etc)

press someone or **something into service**
formal or facetious to make use of a person or thing in an emergency
ⓘ *Press* here means 'to force'

press something on someone
formal to urge someone to accept something

pressgang

pressgang someone into doing something
to force them to do it
ⓘ The *pressgang* was a group of sailors under an officer formed, especially in the 18c, to seize and carry off seamen etc and force them to join the navy

pressure

bring pressure to bear on someone
formal to try to force them to do something

a pressure group
a group of people who try to get the government etc to take notice of certain matters

pretence

false pretences *see* **false**

pretty

a pretty kettle of fish *see* **kettle**

pretty much the same, alike etc
informal more or less the same, alike etc

a pretty pass
a bad state or condition
• *Things have come to a pretty pass when you cannot trust your friends*

a pretty penny
informal a large amount of money

pretty well
informal nearly
• *I've pretty well finished*

sitting pretty
informal in a very good position
• *These problems don't worry you — you're sitting pretty*

prevention

prevention is better than cure
action taken to prevent something bad or unfortune happening is preferable to action taken to remedy the situation since the latter is often difficult and time-consuming

prey

be prey to something
to be a sufferer from something

prey on/upon someone's mind
to cause distress or unhappiness to them
ⓘ Literally, *prey upon* means 'to hunt for food'

price

at a price
informal at a high price
• *We can get dinner at this hotel — at a price!*

beyond price
formal priceless

every man has his price
a proverb, meaning anyone will do something unlawful or questionable if they are offered sufficient inducement

a price on someone's head
a reward offered for their capture or killing

price something/oneself out of the market
to charge so much for something or one's services that no one can afford to pay

what price something?
informal what do you think of something?; what part does something play in all this?
• *I hear you've appointed yourself our leader — what price democracy, then?*

prick

kick against the pricks
to show opposition or protest to people who are in control or power
ⓘ From cattle kicking against being driven forward by a sharp stick

prick up one's ears
informal to start to pay attention
ⓘ Literally used of animals

pride

be someone's pride and joy
to be the object of their pride or admiration; said of someone or something they are responsible for

pride goes before a fall
a proverb, meaning that too much confidence and vanity is likely to be followed by misfortune

pride of place
the most important place
⌚ This is apparently a reference to falconry — the *place* was the point from which a hunting falcon begins its dive — coined from Shakespeare, *Macbeth* II, iv

pride oneself on something
to take pride in, or feel satisfaction with something one has done, achieved etc

swallow one's pride
to behave humbly, eg by making an apology

take pride in something
to feel pride about it

prime

be cut off in one's prime
to die or be killed in one's youth or during the most successful period in one's life

the prime mover
rather formal the original force that sets something in motion
⌚ In medieval astronomy, the *primum mobile* — 'prime mover' — was the ninth heaven, dividing the motionless, eternal domain of God from the eight spheres containing the stars and the planets, which rotated round the earth. This motion was believed to stem from the rotation of the *primum mobile*

primrose

the primrose path *see* **path**

principle

in principle
in general, as opposed to in detail
• *I think it is a good idea in principle*

on principle
because of one's principles or moral standards
• *They refused to do it, entirely on principle*

print

small print *see* **small**

private

a private eye
a private detective
⌚ From the trademark of the Pinkerton Detective Agency

pro

the pros and cons
the arguments for and against
⌚ Latin *pro* 'for' and *contra* 'against'

probability

in all probability
rather formal most probably; most likely

probation

be/put on probation
in certain jobs, to spend a period of time during which one is carefully watched to see that one is capable of the job
⌚ A legal term for a system of allowing offenders to go free provided they commit no more crimes

procrastination

procrastination is the thief of time
a proverb emphasizing the virtues of getting tasks done right away rather than delaying them as the delays waste time

profile

keep a low profile
informal to behave so that one's attitudes, opinions and actions are not made generally known

proof

the proof of the pudding is in the eating
a proverb, meaning that it is only possible to say whether something is a success or not when one has found out if it does what it was intended to do etc

promise

the promised land *see* **land**

prophet

a prophet of doom *see* **doom**

proportion

be, get out of (all) proportion to something
to cause to have an incorrect

relationship to each other or something else
• *The money they received was out of all proportion to the work they did*

a sense of proportion
the ability to judge what is important and what is not

proud

as proud as a peacock *see* **peacock**

do someone proud
informal to give a person good treatment or entertainment

public

in the public eye
well-known, often seen in public

Joe public *see* **Joe**

public enemy number one *see* **enemy**

public spirit
a desire to do things for the good of the community

puff

puffed out
informal exhausted and out of breath

puffed-up
derogatory conceited

pull

pull a face *see* **face**

pull a fast one *see* **fast**

pull a rabbit out of a hat *see* **rabbit**

pull something off
informal to succeed in doing it
• *He's pulled off a good business deal*

pull out
to abandon a place, situation or course of action which has become too difficult or dangerous

pull out all the stops *see* **stop**

pull one's punches *see* **punch**

pull one's socks up *see* **sock**

pull strings *see* **string**

pull the other one *see* **other**

pull oneself together
informal to control oneself; to regain one's self-control

pull through
to survive a difficult situation, illness etc by effort

pull someone through
informal to help them to survive a difficult situation, illness etc

pull up
of a driver or vehicle, to stop

pull one's weight *see* **weight**

pulse

keep one's finger on the pulse
to keep oneself informed about modern ideas, events etc
Ⓞ A medical idiom

pump

all hands to the pumps
everyone must set to and help, especially in some form of emergency
Ⓞ A reference to the pumps used to remove water from a sinking ship

Punch

as pleased as Punch
very happy or pleased
Ⓞ From the puppet-show character, who is depicted as gleefully triumphant in his antisocial behaviour

punch

cannot punch one's way out of a paper bag
informal to be totally ineffectual

pack a punch
slang to be very powerful

pull one's punches
to use less force in attacking than one is really capable of
Ⓞ Literally a boxing term for striking blows without using one's full strength

punch-drunk
dazed and confused
Ⓞ Literally, suffering from a form of concussion caused by blows to the head and causing one to behave as if drunk — a condition once often found in boxers

a punch-up
informal a fight using fists

punishment

a glutton for punishment *see* **glutton**

pup

sell someone a pup
slang to cheat someone

pure

pure and simple
nothing but
• *It was an accident pure and simple*

pure as the driven snow *see* **drive**

purple

a purple patch
an especially brilliant section of something, originally sometimes derogatory, an elaborate piece of writing
Ⓛ From a phrase — *purpureus pannus* — coined by the Latin poet Horace

purple prose
prose which is overwritten and too fluid
Ⓛ See above

purpose

accidentally on purpose *see* **accidentally**

at cross purposes *see* **cross**

serve a purpose
formal to be useful in some way

to good/some purpose
with useful results

to no purpose
formal with no useful results
• *We discussed the problem several times but to no purpose*

to the purpose
formal relevant; to the point
• *His reply was not really to the purpose*

purse

you can't make a silk purse out of a sow's ear *see* **silk**

push

be pushed for something
informal to be short of it; not to have enough of it
• *I'm a bit pushed for time/money*

give someone/get the push
slang to dismiss someone/be dismissed from a job etc

push one's luck *see* **luck**

push off
impolite informal to go away

a push-over
slang a very easy job or task

pushing

be pushing forty, fifty etc
informal to be nearly forty, fifty in age

put

put something across
to convey or communicate ideas etc to others

put a good face on it *see* **face**

put a stop to something *see* **stop**

put something down to something
to attribute eg a way of behaviour to a particular circumstance

put one's hand in one's pocket *see* **pocket**

put someone in his place *see* **place**

put someone in mind *see* **mind**

put oneself in someone's place *see* **place**

put someone in the picture *see* **picture**

put something into practice *see* **practice**

put one's finger on something *see* **finger**

put one's mind to *see* **mind**

put someone's nose out of joint *see* **nose**

put someone or **something off**
to postpone them

put someone off something
to cause someone to feel disgust etc for something

put something on
to make a false show of something; to feign something
• *She said she felt ill, but she was just putting it on*

put on an act *see* **act**

put one across someone *see* **across**

put someone out
informal to cause bother or trouble to them

put someone right *see* **right**

put something right *see* **right**

put the cat among the pigeons *see* **cat**

a put-up job
informal something done to give a false appearance, in order to cheat or trick someone

put upon someone
to make use of them for one's own benefit to an unreasonable extent
• *She is very helpful and tends to be put upon by the lazier membes of her family*

put someone up to doing something
to persuade them to do it

put up with something
to bear it patiently; to tolerate it

stay put *see* **stay**

putty

be putty in someone's hands
to be very easily influenced or manipulated by someone

pyjamas

the cat's pyjamas *see* **cat**

Pyrrhic

a Pyrrhic victory
formal a situation where one is successful but where the cost of winning is so great that it was not worth it
ⓘ From the costly victory of Pyrrhus, king of Epirus, over the Romans at Asculum in 279BC

Q

quantity

an unknown quantity
a person or thing whose characteristics, abilities etc cannot be predicted
Ⓛ A mathematical term — the definition of *x*, etc, in algebra

quarter

at close quarters
from or at a position nearby
Ⓛ A military term

queer

in Queer Street
in difficulties, especially in debt or very short of money
Ⓛ In the early 19c *queer* was an element in many slang terms for shady or criminal persons, activities, etc

a queer fish *see* **fish**

queer someone's pitch
informal to spoil their plans; to make it impossible for them to do something
Ⓛ A showman's term — a *pitch* is the place where a stall, circus etc is set up (from pitching tents) and anything that went wrong, especially interference from the police, was said to *queer* it

question

beg the question *see* **beg**

call something into question
formal to raise doubts about something

in question
formal being talked about
• *The matter in question can be left until our next meeting*

a loaded question *see* **load**

out of the question
not to be thought of as possible; not to be done

pop the question
informal to ask (a woman) to marry one

a rhetorical question *see* **rhetorical**

the sixty-four (thousand) dollar question *see* **sixty**

a vexed question *see* **vex**

queue

jump the queue
to move ahead of others in a queue without waiting for one's proper turn

qui

on the qui vive
alert, vigilant
Ⓛ From the standard challenge of a French sentry: *Qui vive?* — 'Long live who?', ie 'Which side are you on?'

quick

as quick as lightning *see* **lightning**

cut someone to the quick
to hurt their feelings very much
Ⓛ The *quick* is the living sensitive part of eg a fingernail

a quick one
informal a quick drink

quick on the uptake *see* **uptake**

quid

quids in
slang in a very good or favourable position

quit

be quits with someone
to be even with them, neither owing them anything nor being owed anything by them

call it/cry quits
informal to agree with someone that neither person owes the other person anything
• *This fight has been going on for years — why don't you two call it quits and be friends?*

quite

quite something
informal something special, remarkable or very good

R

R

the three Rs
reading, writing and arithmetic, thought of as the most necessary parts of a basic education
◷ From *r*eading *w*riting and a*r*ithmetic

rabbit

breed like rabbits
derogatory a phrase used to indicate that people have a great many children, usually close together in age

let the dog see the rabbit *see* **dog**

pull a rabbit out of a hat
to do something totally unexpected in order to produce a very pleasant surprise or some timely assistance
◷ From the stage magician's trick of pulling a live rabbit out of a seemingly empty hat

race

a one-horse race *see* **one**

the rat race *see* **rat**

slow and steady wins the race
a proverb indicating that success in anything is often achieved by continuous effort
◷ A reference to Aesop's fable about the hare and the tortoise in which the tortoise wins the race by slow and steady progress

rack

go to rack and ruin
to get into a state of neglect and decay
◷ *Rack* here means 'destruction'

rack one's brains *see* **brain**

rag

from rags to riches
from extreme poverty to wealth, usually through one's own efforts

from rags to rags
from extreme poverty back to relative poverty; used of a family who have achieved commercial success but lose it in a succeeding generation

glad rags *see* **glad**

like a red rag to a bull *see* **red**

lose one's rag
Brit informal to lose one's temper
◷ Origin uncertain

rage

(all) the rage
informal very much in fashion

rail

off the rails
Brit informal not sensible; slightly mad
◷ The reference is to a railway train

rain

as right as rain
informal perfectly all right; completely well
◷ A pun on the original meaning of *right* = straight

rain on someone's parade
to spoil their plans or special occasion
◷ US in origin — a reference to wet weather spoiling a celebratory parade of decorated floats, etc

rain or shine
whatever the weather is like

rain cats and dogs *see* **cat**

rainbow

chase after rainbows
to spend time in trying to achieve things that one cannot possibly obtain, to pursue illusory goals
◷ A reference to the legend that it was possible to find a crock of gold where the rainbow ended

the crock/pot of gold at the end of the rainbow *see* **gold**

raincheck

take a raincheck on something
informal to refuse an invitation to something but ask if one may accept it at a later date
◷ Originally US, a reference to the free pass given to future sports fixtures if bad weather cancels the present one

rainy

keep/save etc **something for a rainy day**
to keep something, especially money, until one needs it or in case one may need it
◷ The reference is to money-making activities only possible on days when the sun shines

raise

raise a stink *see* **stink**

raise Cain/hell etc
informal to make a great deal of noise

raise someone's hopes *see* **hope**

raise the wind *see* **wind**[1]

raise one's voice *see* **voice**

rake

as thin as a rake
very thin

rake something up
to find out and tell or remind people about something, usually something unpleasant that would be better forgotten
• *The newspaper reporters raked up a story about the politician stealing sweets from a shop when he was a boy*
◷ From *muckraking, see at* **muck**

rally

rally round
to come together for a joint action or effort, especially of support

ram

ram something down someone's throat *see* **throat**

rampage

be/go on the rampage
to rush about angrily, violently or in excitement

ranch

meanwhile back at the ranch
a catch phrase used to call the attention of one's listeners back to the central or original theme or point of one's conversation
◷ From a caption shown on silent Western films

random

at random
without any particular plan or system
• *The police were stopping cars at random and checking their tyres*

rank

break ranks
to cease to take united defensive action

close ranks
to act together as a defensive measure
◷ Literally used of soldiers etc, meaning 'to move closer together'

the rank and file
ordinary people
• *The rank and file in a trade union do not always agree with their officials*
◷ Literally, *ranks* and *files* are the horizontal and vertical lines in which battalions of soldiers were once drawn up in the field and on parade

rise through/from the ranks
to achieve a high position in an organization by one's own efforts, having worked one's way up from the bottom, rather than by means of privilege

ransom

hold someone to ransom
to use threats etc to try to persuade them to do as one wishes
◷ Literally, to keep someone as a prisoner until a sum of money is paid for his release

a king's ransom
a vast amount of money
◷ Literally, the amount of money that would be demanded as ransom for a king, if captured

rant

rant and rave
to talk angrily about something

rap

take the rap for something
slang to take the blame, punishment etc for a crime, mistake etc

rare

a rare bird
an unusual person or phenomenon
• *He is one of those rare birds who worries more about others than he does about himself*
Ⓣ A translation of Latin *rara avis*

raring

raring to go, rarin' to go
informal very keen to begin, go etc
Ⓣ A dialectal form of *rearing* — ie in eagerness

rat

like a drowned rat
soaking wet and bedraggled

rat on someone
to betray one's friends, colleagues etc

the rat race
informal a fierce, unending competition for success, wealth etc in business, society etc
Ⓣ A nautical phrase for a fierce tidal current — both *rat* and *race* are forms of the French *ras* = a tide-race

like rats deserting a sinking ship *see* **desert**

smell a rat
informal to have a feeling that something is not as it should be, but is wrong or bad
Ⓣ The reference is to a terrier hunting

rate

at any rate
1 whatever may happen or have happened
• *It's a pity it has started to rain, but at any rate we can still enjoy ourselves at the cinema*
2 that is to say; at least
• *The Queen is coming — at any rate, that's what John says*

at a rate of knots *see* **knot**

at this, at that rate
if this or if that is the case; if this or if that continues

rather

rather you than me
a phrase addressed to someone who is about to do something undesirable, dangerous, etc which the speaker is glad not to be doing

rattle

rattle someone's cage *see* **cage**

raw

in the raw
in the natural state; exactly as it is, without anything to make it look nicer

a raw deal
informal unfair treatment

raw material
something out of which something else can be made
Ⓣ Literally, the naturally-occurring products out of which manufactured goods are made

razor

as sharp/keen as a razor
1 very sharp
2 very quick-witted and intelligent

on a razor's/knife edge
in a critical or risky state
• *The future of the accident victim is on a razor's edge*

read

read between the lines *see* **line**

read something into something
to understand a statement etc to have a meaning which is not actually stated, and may not be intended

read the riot act *see* **riot**

read up on something
informal to learn it by study

take something as read
to assume something without checking it, doing it etc
Ⓣ Literally used of the minutes of a previous meeting which are accepted without being formally read over

real

for real
especially US: slang genuine; true

- *He says he's got a new bike, but I don't know if that's for real*

the real McCoy/Mackay
informal something genuine, especially of very good quality, as contrasted with all other inferior things called by the same name
- *I have been in many so-called 'Chinese restaurants', but this one is the real McCoy*

Ⓛ Origin unknown

reality

in reality
really; actually

rear

bring up the rear
formal to come last
Ⓛ A military term

rear its ugly head *see* **head**

reason

have (good) reason to believe, think etc
formal to feel justified in believing etc something

it stands to reason (that)
anyone who things about a subject will come to the conclusion that something is true, probable etc

listen to reason
to allow oneself to be persuaded to do something more sensible than what one was going to do; to pay attention to common sense

lose one's reason
formal to become mad or insane

see reason
to be persuaded to be more sensible than one is or has been

within reason
within the limits of good sense

rebound

on the rebound
informal soon after, and as the result of suffering, a great disappointment, especially the end of a love affair
- *His fiancée left him, and he married the girl next door on the rebound*

Ⓛ An idiom from ball-games

recall

beyond recall
unable to be changed, stopped etc

reckon

reckon on something
to depend on or expect it

reckon with
to expect trouble, difficulties etc from a person etc
- *He's a man to be reckoned with*

record

break the record
to do something better, faster, more often etc than anyone else has done

for the record
formal in order to be sure that the facts are recorded correctly

off the record
of information, statements etc, not intended to be repeated or made public

on record
written down or recorded for future reference
- *I wish to go/be put on record as disagreeing with all these decisions*

set the record straight
formal to put right a mistake or misunderstanding

someone's track record *see* **track**

red

catch someone red-handed
to find someone in the act of doing wrong
Ⓛ The reference is to finding a murderer with blood still on the hands

in the red
informal in debt
Ⓛ From the use of red ink to make entries on the debit side of a ledger

like a red rag to a bull
informal certain to make a person angry
Ⓛ From the widespread belief that the sight of the colour red makes bulls angry. In fact, bulls are colour-blind

on red alert
in a state of being warned and ready for an immediately approaching danger
Ⓛ Originally a military term for use

especially in mobilizing civilians during an air-raid etc. *Yellow, blue* and *red alerts* represented increasing degrees of readiness for an attack

paint the town red *see* **paint**

red-blooded
active; manly; full of strong, usually sexual desires

(the) red-carpet treatment
great respect and honour given to important guests or visitors
① From the practice of rolling out a red carpet for important guests to walk on

a red herring
a false clue intended or tending to mislead someone
① Red herring, a type of smoked herring, were occasionally used to lay trails for hunting dogs to follow. The scent of a red herring which had been dragged across the trail of genuine animal-scent, however, could also be used to mislead the dogs

red-hot
informal
1 very enthusiastic
2 erotic, sexy

a red-letter day
a day which will always be remembered because something particularly pleasant or important happened on it
① From the medieval custom of using red ink for saints' days when writing out a calendar

reds under the bed
derogatory the belief that everything bad that happens to one's country is caused by the secret activities of Communists

red tape
derogatory the strict attention to and following of annoying and unnecessary rules and regulations
① From the 'red' — actually pink — tape used by government offices etc to tie up bundles of papers

see red
informal to become angry
① Probably the same origin as **like a red rag to a bull**, *above*

redbrick

a redbrick university
sometimes derogatory any of the universities founded in England in the late nineteenth century, usually contrasted with Oxford and Cambridge

redeeming

a redeeming feature
something which compensates for something which is bad or wrong
• *It's an ugly house — its one redeeming feature is its position on the hill*

redress

redress the balance
very formal to make things, more nearly, equal again

reed

a broken reed *see* **broken**

reel

reel off something
to say or repeat it quickly and easily without pausing

refresh

refresh one's (someone's) memory
to (cause someone to) think about, read etc the facts or details of something again so that they are clear in the mind

refusal

first refusal
the opportunity to buy, accept etc or refuse something before it is offered, given, sold etc to someone else

refuse

make someone an offer which he or she can't refuse
to make a proposal, such as the offer of a job, which is so attractive or generous that it would be folly to turn it down

regard

as regards something
formal as far as something is concerned; turning our attention to something
• *That answers your first question. As regards your second question, I feel that it is ridiculous*

with regard to something
formal about; concerning
• *I have no complaints with regard to his work*

region
in the region of
formal about; near

regular
regular as clockwork *see* **clockwork**

rein
give (free) rein to something
formal to allow oneself, one's mind etc great freedom to act, think etc as one pleases
ⓘ From riding or driving horses

keep a tight rein on someone or **something**
formal to keep strict control of a person, thing etc
ⓘ As previous idiom

reinvent
reinvent the wheel *see* **wheel**

relieve
relieve someone of something
facetious to steal something from someone

repeat
repeat oneself
to say the same thing more than once

reputation
live up to one's reputation
to behave in the way that people say one behaves; to do what people expect one to do

repute
of repute
formal well thought of and respected by many people

reserve
have, keep etc **something in reserve**
formal to have or keep it in case or until it is needed

resort
as a/in the last resort
when all other methods etc have failed
ⓘ Originally a legal term referring to a hearing in a court from which there was no appeal

resource
leave someone to his etc **own resources**
to leave someone to amuse himself, or to find his own way of solving a problem etc

respect
in respect of something
formal as far as it is concerned

pay one's respects to someone
to visit them as a sign of respect to them

with respect to something
formal about or concerning it
• *With respect to your request, we regret that we are unable to assist you in this matter*

respecter
be no respecter of persons
not to be influenced by the importance, wealth etc of the people involved
ⓘ A Biblical reference, to Acts 10:34

rest
come to rest
to stop moving

for the rest
as far as everything else is concerned; when thinking of everything else

God rest his soul
a wish that a dead person's soul may be at peace
• *My father, God rest his soul, was out fishing on the very day he died*

lay someone to rest
formal euphemism to bury someone in a grave

no rest for the wicked
a saying used by someone, whether wicked or not, to indicate how busy they are

rest assured
formal to be certain
• *You may rest assured that we will take your views into consideration*

rest on one's laurels *see* **laurel**

rest on one's oars *see* **oar**

resting
someone's last resting-place
formal someone's grave

retreat
beat a (hasty) retreat
to leave or go away in a hurry

Ⓞ A military phrase, from the former practice in infantry regiments of transmitting orders by means of different drum signals

return

by return (of post)
formal of an answering letter etc, immediately; sent by the very next post

in return for something
as an exchange for it
• *We'll send them whisky and they'll send us vodka in return; They'll send us vodka in return for whisky*

many happy returns (of the day)
an expression of good wishes said to a person on his birthday

the point of no return *see* **point**

rhetorical

a rhetorical question
a question which the speaker answers himself, or which does not need an answer
Ⓞ From the use of such stylized questions as one of the commonest and most effective elements of formal speech-making

rhubarb

rhubarb, rhubarb
a phrase used to indicate to someone that he or she is talking nonsense in an effort to get them to be quiet
Ⓞ Actors in crowd scenes on stage mumble 'rhubarb, rhubarb' to give the impression of mumbled conversation

rhyme

without rhyme or reason
without sense, reason or a logical system

rich

rich as Croesus
having a great deal of wealth, phenomenally rich
Ⓞ Croesus was a ruler of Lydia, an ancient kingdom in Asia Minor, who was renowned for his wealth

strike it rich
informal to make a lot of money
Ⓞ An idiom from gold-mining

rid

be, get rid of someone or **something**
to have removed, to remove someone or something; to free oneself from a problem, worry etc; to make someone or something go away

riddance

good riddance to someone or **something**
informal I am happy to have got rid of someone or something
• *I've thrown out all those old books, and good riddance to the lot of them*

ride

be/come/go along for the ride
informal to join a group of people etc simply out of interest, not to take part oneself in what they are doing
Ⓞ Originally used of joining other people on a journey which they were obliged to make

let something ride
informal to do nothing about it; to let it continue as it is

ride off into the sunset
an expression indicating the end of something, usually a happy ending
Ⓞ A reference to the classic final scene of early Western films when the cowboy hero rides off into the sunset having defeated the villains

ride out something
to survive until a period of difficulty is past
Ⓞ Literally, of a ship, 'to keep afloat throughout a storm etc'

ride roughshod over someone *see* **roughshod**

ride shotgun
informal to sit in the passenger seat of a car
Ⓞ Originally US. From the armed guard who sat next to the driver on a stagecoach to provide protection against bandits, etc

ride up
of a skirt etc, to move gradually up out of its correct position

take someone for a ride
informal to trick, cheat or deceive them
Ⓞ Originally American gangsters' slang for killing someone, from a common

practice of doing so in a moving car to avoid attracting attention

riding

riding for a fall
behaving in a manner likely to cause a disaster to oneself
Ⓞ A hunting metaphor

riding high
very successful; in a high position etc
Ⓞ A phrase often used literally of the moon etc

rift

a rift in the lute
literary a small disagreement, problem etc that shows signs of developing into something which will destroy a project or relationship
Ⓞ A quotation from Tennyson's *Idylls of the King*

right

as right as rain *see* **rain**

be right up someone's street *see* **street**

by right(s)
rightfully

get, keep on the right side of someone
to make someone feel, or continue to feel, friendly or kind towards oneself

get something right
to understand, so, say etc something correctly

go right
to happen as expected, wanted or intended; to be successful or without problems

in one's own right
1 not because of someone else; independently
• *She is a baroness in her own right (= because she has inherited the title or has received it as an honour, not because she is married to a baron)*
2 because of one's own ability, work etc
• *She's married to a writer, but she is a novelist in her own right*
Ⓞ A medieval legal term

in one's right mind *see* **mind**

in the right
correct in what one says or does

keep someone right
to prevent them from making mistakes

Mr Right
often facetious the perfect man for someone to marry

not (quite) right in the head
informal slightly mad

on the right track *see* **track**

put someone right
1 to tell them the truth, the correct way of doing something etc
2 to make them healthy again
• *I used to think he was a fool but John put me right about him*

put something right
1 to repair something; to remove faults etc in something
2 to put an end to or change something that is wrong
• *He hasn't been paid for the last job he did, but we can soon put that right*

someone's right arm *see* **arm**

a right-hand man
a person's most trusted and useful assistant

right off
immediately; without delay

right you are
informal certainly; very well

serve someone right
to be what a person deserves, usually something bad

set something to rights
to put something into the correct order, place etc, or into a good or desirable state

strike the right note *see* **note**

take something in the right spirit *see* **spirit**

ring

ring a bell *see* **bell**

ring down the curtain *see* **curtain**

ring off
to end a telephone call
Ⓞ From the method of ending a call in the early days of the telephone, by alerting the operator by means of a bell

ring the changes *see* **change**

ring true, to have the ring of truth
to sound or seem to be true
• *His story does not ring true*
Ⓘ From the practice of testing the quality of metal or glass by striking it and listening to the resultant sound

ring someone or something up
1 to telephone someone
2 to record the price of something sold on a cash register

ringer
a dead ringer for someone or **something**
slang almost identical to some other person or thing
Ⓘ An American phrase probably connected with the use of the word *ringer* to mean a person sent to vote illegally in a district where they are not entitled to vote, and later to mean a horse substituted for another horse of less ability in a race

ringside
have a ringside seat
informal to be in a position where one can see clearly something which is happening
Ⓘ Probably from boxing

riot
read the riot act
to tell someone angrily that they have done wrong and warn them that their bad behaviour must stop
Ⓘ The Riot Act of 1715 decreed that when a group of twelve or more people assembled in one place were considered to be a threat to the peace, the magistrates should read part of the Act to them, commanding them to disperse in the King's name, after which action could be taken against them if they did not

run riot
to act, speak etc in an uncontrolled way
Ⓘ A hunting term for hounds which are following the scent of the wrong animal, from the Old French word for a dispute

riotous
riotous living
usually facetious living in a very extravagant and energetic manner
Ⓘ A Biblical reference, to the parable of the Prodigal Son, Luke 15:13

ripe
a ripe old age
a very old age
• *He lived to the ripe old age of ninety-five*

rise
give rise to something
formal to cause something

rise and shine!
informal: usually facetious an instruction to someone to get out of bed quickly, especially in the morning
Ⓘ The image is of the sun

rise through/from the ranks *see* **rank**

rise to the occasion *see* **occasion**

take/get a rise out of someone
informal to make someone angry etc by teasing or annoying them

rising
a rising tide
a powerful surge, a strong tide
• *He was aware of the rising tide of opposition against his plans*
Ⓘ A reference to the movement of the ocean's tides

risk
at someone's own risk
with the person concerned agreeing to accept any loss, damage etc involved

risk one's neck *see* **neck**

run/take the risk of doing something
to do something which involves a risk

river
sell someone down the river
to betray them
Ⓘ An American phrase, from the former custom of slave-owners in the upper Mississippi states of selling unsatisfactory household slaves to the much harsher life on the cotton and sugar plantations of Louisiana

road
get the show on the road *see* **show**

in, out of the/someone's road
informal in or out of the/their way

one for the road
informal a last alcoholic drink before leaving to go somewhere

on the road to recovery
getting better after an illness

a road-hog
a person who drives carelessly or selfishly, causing trouble and annoyance to other drivers
⏀ From the proverbial greediness and bad manners of pigs

roaring

do a roaring trade
informal to have a very successful business; to sell a lot of something

roaring drunk
informal very drunk

roast

a dripping roast *see* **dripping**

rob

rob Peter to pay Paul
to get enough money etc to pay one debt or get one thing done by using the money etc needed to pay another debt or do something else
⏀ Probably from the fact that St Peter and St Paul share the same feast-day, 29 July, and have alliterating names

robbery

daylight robbery
informal the charging of prices which are too high

rock

as steady as a rock
very steady and unmoving
• *Although he had quite a lot to drink, his hand was as steady as a rock*

between a rock and a hard place
in a situation in which one is faced with a choice between two equally unpleasant or unacceptable alternatives
⏀ A rock *is* a hard place

hit rock bottom
to reach the lowest possible level, to be as low as it is possible to get
• *House prices have hit rock bottom in the area near the new motorway; He's very successful now but a few years ago he was an alcoholic who hit rock bottom*

on the rocks
informal
1 of a marriage, into a state where the husband and wife wish to separate or be divorced
2 of a usually alcoholic drink, served with ice cubes
3 of a business firm, into a state of great financial difficulty, having no, or not enough, money

rock the boat *see* **boat**

rocker

off one's rocker
slang mad; crazy
⏀ The reference is to a broken rocking-chair

rod

make a rod for one's own back
to do something which is going to cause trouble for oneself
• *That child's mother is making a rod for her back by spoiling him like that*
⏀ Literally, 'to provide a stick for oneself to be beaten with' — a medieval image

rule with a rod of iron *see* **iron**

spare the rod and spoil the child
a proverb, once generally believed, meaning that it is a mistake to treat children too mildly

rogue

a rogue's gallery
slang a police collection of photographs of known criminals

roll

heads will roll *see* **head**

roll in
informal to come in or be got in large numbers or amounts

roll on (a time, day etc)
may a given time come soon
• *Roll on the day when I can afford to buy a new car!*

roll up
informal
1 to arrive
2 usually to a crowd eg in a market, an exhortation to come near

roll with the punches
informal to adapt one's attitude, actions, etc to suit adverse or disadvantageous

circumstances instead of confronting or opposing these
Ⓞ From boxing, in which a contestant who is in the path of a blow shifts his body to the side to deflect it

rolling

be rolling in the aisles
to laugh long and heartily
Ⓞ A reference to theatre aisles

be rolling in something
informal to have large amounts of it, usually money
• *He doesn't have to worry about money — he's rolling in it*

a rolling stone gathers no moss
a proverb, meaning that people who have never stayed in one place generally have no responsibilities and few possessions

Rome

fiddle while Rome burns *see* **fiddle**

Rome was not built in a day
a proverb, meaning that a difficult or important aim cannot be achieved quickly or all at once

when in Rome, do as the Romans do
a proverb, meaning that one is wise to copy the behaviour of people who are used to the circumstances, places etc in which one finds oneself
Ⓞ A saying of St Ambrose

Romeo

a Romeo
1 a young male lover
2 a young man who engages in a great many love affairs
Ⓞ A reference to the hero of Shakespeare's *Romeo and Juliet* (1595)

romp

romp home
informal to win easily

roof

go through the roof/hit the roof
informal to become very angry

have a roof over one's head
to have somewhere to live

shout something from the rooftops *see* **shout**

room

room to swing a cat *see* **cat**

roost

(chickens) come home to roost
of a usually bad action, to have an unpleasant effect on the person who did the action
• *Al his lies have come home to roost*
Ⓞ From the motto of Robert Southey's poem *The Curse of Kehama* — 'Curses are like young chickens, they always come home to roost'

rule the roost
to be the person in a group, family etc whose orders, wishes etc are obeyed
Ⓞ An alteration of the obscure **rule the roast**, of which the origin is unknown

root

be rooted in something
formal to have something as a cause; to originate in something
Ⓞ From plants

the grass roots *see* **grass**

root and branch
formal completely and absolutely
• *This evil system must be destroyed root and branch!*
Ⓞ A phrase derived from the Bible, Malachi 4:1, and much used in the early 1640s in connection with the attempt at that time to abolish episcopacy in the Church of England

rooted to the spot *see* **spot**

the root of the matter
the ultimate reason for something, the basic cause of something
• *They could not account for her illness and then they discovered that her diet was the root of the matter*

root something out
to destroy it completely
• *We must do our best to root out disease and poverty*

take root
to grow firmly; to become established
Ⓞ From plants

rope

give someone enough rope
in some situations, if one lets someone act as they please then they will bring

about their own downfall or misfortune. The full version of this phrase is **give someone enough rope and he/she will hang himself/herself**

know the ropes
to understand the detail and procedure of a job etc
Ⓞ A nautical idiom, from the practical implications of getting used to working on board ship

money for old rope *see* **money**

rope someone in
informal to include them; to persuade them to join in doing something
Ⓞ Originally US, from the use of lassoes to catch and collect cattle in the American West

rose

a bed of roses *see* **bed**

everything's coming up roses
not formal everything is proving to be successful, happy, lucky etc for a particular person

it was roses, roses all the way
it was a happy, carefree, or successful time or situation

look at/see something through rose-coloured spectacles
to have a very ideal, optimistic view of it

a rose by any other name
a saying indicating that the name of someone or something is unimportant and that it is the quality and nature of the person or thing that is important
Ⓞ The phrase is a shortened version of **a rose by any other name would smell as sweet**. This is a quotation from Shakespeare's *Romeo and Juliet* II, ii

rotten

a rotten apple
a bad or evil person who has a bad influence on other members of the group to which he or she belongs and is liable to corrupt the good or innocent members
Ⓞ A rotten apple in a container of apples quickly affects the sound ones

rough

be rough on someone
informal to be bad luck or unfortunate for them

cut up rough
slang to behave in an unpleasant, angry manner

rough-and-ready
1 not carefully made or finished, but good enough
2 of people, friendly enough but without politeness etc

rough-and-tumble
a usually friendly fight; a scuffle
Ⓞ Originally boxing slang for a kind of fight in which the normal rules did not apply

a rough diamond *see* **diamond**

rough it
informal to live primitively, without the usual comforts of life

rough something out
to draw or explain a rough sketch etc or idea
• *He roughed out the plan to the others*

sleep rough
to sleep out-of-doors

take the rough with the smooth
to accept the disadvantages of a person, situation etc with the advantages

roughshod

ride roughshod over someone
informal to treat them without any regard for their feelings
Ⓞ Literally, *roughshod* is used of a horse, and means 'provided with roughened horse-shoes' — to give better grip on roads

roulette

play Russian roulette *see* **Russian**

round

get round to something
informal to manage to do it; to find enough time to do it

go the rounds
informal to be handed from one person to another or from place to place
• *His first novel went the rounds for a year before he finally found a publisher for it*

in the round
formal visible from all sides
• *Sculpture should be seen in the round*

round figures/numbers
the nearest convenient or easily remembered numbers

round something off
to complete it successfully; to make a successful ending to it

round on someone
formal to attack them, usually in words

round the twist *see* **twist**

a round trip
a journey to a place and back again

round something up
1 to collect something together
2 to raise a number to the nearest convenient figure, usually ten, one hundred etc
• *The total came to £2.89, which we rounded up to £3.00 and divided among the six of us*

talk someone round *see* **talk**

rounder

an all-rounder
in games etc, a person who can play any position, eg who can bat as well as bowl in cricket

row

have a hard row to hoe
to have to lead a life full of difficulties and hardship

in a row
one after the other

rub

rub along with someone
informal to get on fairly well with them; to be fairly friendly with them

rub something in
informal to keep reminding someone of something unpleasant

rub someone's nose in it *see* **nose**

rub off on (to) someone
to pass to them through close contact etc

rub salt into the wound *see* **salt**

rub shoulders with *see* **shoulder**

rub someone (up) the wrong way
informal to annoy or irritate them
Ⓘ The reference is to an animal's coat

there's the rub
rather formal that is where the difficulty lies
Ⓘ A Shakespearian quotation, from *Hamlet* III, i

rubber

rubber-stamp
derogatory to give official approval to a decision actually made by somebody else
Ⓘ From the practice of using a rubber stamp instead of an individually written signature

Rubicon

cross the Rubicon
to do something which commits one to a particular course of action
Ⓘ See **the die is cast** at **die²**. As the Rubicon was the boundary between Cisalpine Gaul and Italy, into which generals were not permitted to bring their armies, Caesar's crossing of the river in 49BC committed him to war with the Senate

ruffle

ruffle someone's feathers *see* **feather**

rug

pull the rug (out) from under someone
to do something suddenly which leaves someone in a very weak position

ruin

go to rack and ruin *see* **rack**

rule

as a rule
usually

the exception proves the rule *see* **exception**

golden rule *see* **golden**

rule of thumb
a method of doing something based on experience rather than theory or careful calculation
Ⓘ From the use of one's thumb to make rough measurements

rule out something
to leave out or not to consider it
• *We mustn't rule out the possibility of bad weather*
ⓘ Literally, to judge officially that something is now allowable, possible etc

rule something out of court *see* **court**

rule the roost *see* **roost**

rule with a rod of iron *see* **iron**

run

an also-ran
derogatory informal an unsuccessful or unimportant person, especially compared with someone else
ⓘ A racing term for a horse which was not placed in a race

a dry run *see* **dry**

in the long run *see* **long**

on the run
escaping; running away

run across someone
informal to meet them by chance

run along
informal to go away

run a tight ship *see* **tight**

run away with something
to win a prize etc easily

run circles round *see* **circle**

run down
tired or exhausted because one has worked too hard

run for it
informal to try and escape

a (good) run for one's money
a good show or performance; something worth having in return for the effort, money etc one has spent
• *Our team did not win, but they gave the opposition a run for their money*
ⓘ A racing term, indicating that the horse one has bet on has actually raced, although it has not won, as opposed to being withdrawn and not running at all

run high *see* **high**

run someone or **something in**
informal
1 to get a new engine etc working properly
2 to arrest someone

run in the family *see* **family**

run-of-the-mill *see* **mill**

run out
1 of a supply, to come to an end; to finish
2 with **of**, to have no more

run out of steam *see* **steam**

run out on someone
slang to leave or abandon them

run something over
of a vehicle or driver, to knock down or drive over it

run riot *see* **riot**

run the gauntlet *see* **gauntlet**

run the show *see* **show**

run through something
to look at it, deal with it etc from beginning to end

run to something
to be or have enough of something, especially money, to do or have something
• *We can't run to a new car this year*

run to earth *see* **earth**

run something up
informal
1 to make something quickly or roughly
2 to make money increase; accumulate money
• *He ran up an enormous bill*

run wild *see* **wild**

run with the hare and hunt with the hounds *see* **hare**

a trial run *see* **trial**

runner

the runner-up
a person, thing etc that is second in a race or competition

running

in, out of the running
having a, no chance of success

take a running jump!
slang go away!

rush

be rushed off one's feet *see* **feet**

rush one's fences *see* **fence**

the rush hour
a period when there is a lot of traffic on the roads, usually when people are going to or leaving work

Russian

play Russian roulette
to engage in a highly risky undertaking the outcome of which is potentially ruinous or fatal

Ⓘ A reference to a game played by Russian officers at the court of the Czar in which each player, using a revolver that contained one bullet, spun the cylinder and aimed at his head. Since the cylinder contained six chambers there was one chance in six that he would kill himself

rustle

rustle something up
informal to get or make it quickly

rut

in(to) a rut
having a fixed, monotonous, firmly established way of life

Ⓘ The reference is to a cartwheel which is unable to change direction easily if it is running in a rut in the track

S

sabre

rattle one's sabre
to put on a show of fierceness or aggression without actually resorting to physical force in order to frighten someone

sack

get the sack
informal to be dismissed from one's job etc
Ⓘ A French idiom, probably from the bag in which a workman carried his tools from one job to another

give someone the sack
informal to dismiss them from their job etc
Ⓘ As previous idiom

hit the sack
slang to go to bed

sackcloth

sackcloth and ashes
a state of penitence or repentance
Ⓘ A reference to the ancient Hebrew custom of putting on a coarse material from which sacks were made and smearing oneself with ashes to demonstrate one's humility to God. The phrase is referred to in the Bible in Daniel 9:3

sacred

a sacred cow
derogatory a custom, tradition, body of people etc that is regarded, by a group of people etc, with so much respect that one is not allowed even to criticize it freely
Ⓘ From the fact that cattle are regarded as sacred by Hindus

sad

a sadder and a wiser man
a person who has learned from his own mistakes, a person who has had many unfortunate experiences but has benefited from these

saddle

in the saddle
in a position of power or control
Ⓘ From horse-riding

saddle someone with something
informal to give a person something annoying, difficult etc to deal with
• *I can't do very much shopping when I'm saddled with the children*

safe

as safe as houses *see* **house**

be on the safe side
to avoid risk or danger
• *I don't think we'll need much money but I'll take my cheque-book just to be on the safe side*

play safe *see* **play**

safe and sound
unharmed

safety

there's safety in numbers
a saying, meaning that it is fairly safe to do something, even if it may seem risky, if a large number of other people are also doing it

sail

sail close to the wind *see* **wind**[1]

sail under false colours *see* **false**

take the wind out of someone's sails *see* **wind**[1]

sailing

plain sailing *see* **plain**

saint

enough to try the patience of a saint *see* **patience**

salad

someone's salad days
the time when someone was young and inexperienced
Ⓞ A Shakespearian quotation, from *Antony and Cleopatra* I, v, from the association of greenness with youth

Sally

Aunt Sally *see* **Aunt**

salt

back to the saltmines
facetious an exhortation to resume work
Ⓞ A reference to the former Russian punishment of working in the saltmines of Siberia

below the salt
in a very humble or lowly position
Ⓞ In former times the salt container marked the division at a dinner table between the rich and important people and the more lowly people, the important people being near the top

go through something like a dose of salts *see* **dose**

salt into the wound/someone's wounds
to make their sorrow, shame, regret etc worse, often deliberately
Ⓞ Aboard ship etc, salt was often used as an antiseptic

something away
informal to store up, especially money, for future use
• *He has a pile of money salted away*
Ⓞ From preserving meat or fish in salt

the salt of the earth
a very good or worthy person or persons
Ⓞ A Biblical reference, to Matthew 5:13

take something with a grain/pinch of salt
to receive a statement, news etc with scepticism

worth one's salt
deserving the pay that one gets
Ⓞ The reference is to the salt eaten by a servant etc

Samaritan

a good Samaritan
someone who helps others who are in need
Ⓞ A Biblical reference to the parable in Luke 10

same

all/just the same
nevertheless; in spite of this

at the same time
nevertheless; still

be all the same to someone
informal to make no difference to, or be a matter of no importance to them
• *I'll leave now, if it's all the same to you*

much the same
not very much changed or different

not to be in the same street as *see* **street**

the same as always/ever
not at all changed

same here
informal I think, feel etc the same
• *'This job bores me.' 'Same here.'*

the same old story *see* **story**

sand

as happy as a sand-boy
informal very happy and cheerful
Ⓞ Apparently a *sand-boy* was a young seller of sand, although why such people should be particularly jolly is obscure

build on sand
to try to establish something without enough security or support
Ⓞ A Biblical reference, to Matthew 7:26

sardine

packed like sardines
crowded very close together
Ⓞ From the practice of selling sardines very tightly packed in tins

sauce

what's sauce for the goose is sauce for the gander
a proverb, meaning that a rule, method of treatment etc which applies to one person must also apply to others, especially to the person's wife or husband

sausage

not a sausage
informal nothing at all

savage

the noble savage *see* **noble**

save

saved by the bell *see* **bell**

save one's breath *see* **breath**

save one's/someone's face *see* **face**

save something for a rainy day *see* **rainy**

save one's skin *see* **skin**

save the day *see* **day**

scrimp and save *see* **scrimp**

saving

a saving grace *see* **grace**

say

have something, nothing etc **to say for oneself**
to be able, unable to explain one's actions etc
• *Your work is very careless — what have you to say for yourself?*

I say!
words expressing surprise or protest or used to attract someone's attention
• *I say! Look at those birds!*

I wouldn't say no to something
informal I would like something

it goes without saying (that) *see* **go**

it is said/they say
expressions used in reporting rumours, news that is not yet definite etc

say the word *see* **word**

say when
a phrase used when inviting someone to say when their glass or cup is full enough when one is pouring drinks

that is to say
in other words; I mean

to say nothing of *see* **nothing**

what would you say to something
informal would you like something
• *'What would you say to a cup of tea?' 'I'd love one!'*

you can say that again!
informal you're absolutely right!

saying

there's no saying
it is impossible to guess
• *There's no saying what will happen next*

scald

like a scalded cat *see* **cat**

scales

tip the scale(s)
to be the (usually small) fact, happening etc which causes events to happen in a certain way, a certain decision to be made etc

tip/turn the scales at (a certain weight)
informal to weigh a certain amount

scarce

make oneself scarce
informal to run away or stay away, especially in order to avoid trouble or difficulty

scare

scare someone out of his wits *see* **wit**

scare someone stiff *see* **stiff**

scarlet

a scarlet woman
facetious an immoral and dangerous woman, especially a prostitute
① A Biblical reference, to the woman in Revelation 17

scene

behind the scenes
out of sight of the audience or public
① A theatrical idiom: the *scenes* are the flat pieces of scenery etc forming the set on stage

come on the scene
to arrive
① A theatrical idiom

not to be someone's scene
informal not to be the kind of thing they like, are good at etc
• *I'm afraid politics is not my scene — I hate arguments*

set the scene
to discuss the background to an event etc
Ⓛ A theatrical phrase — 'to prepare the stage for the beginning of the action'

scent

put/throw someone off the scent
to give them wrong information so that they will not find the person, thing etc they are looking for
Ⓛ Literally used of dogs distracted while tracking a prey

schedule

according to schedule
as planned

ahead of, behind, on schedule
before, later than, or by, the arranged time

scheme

the best-laid schemes *see* **best**

school

the old school *see* **old**

the school of hard knocks
a way of life in which one's learning and education is gained from experience, especially experiences of misfortunes and setbacks, often contrasted with university or college life

score

know the score
informal to know the facts of the situation; to know exactly how difficult the situation is and what the risks are etc
Ⓛ Literally, 'to know how unlikely one is to win the game from one's present position'

on that score
for that reason
• *He's perfectly healthy, so you don't need to worry on that score*
Ⓛ A figurative use of *score* meaning 'a record or list'

score an own goal *see* **goal**

score off someone
informal to make someone appear foolish, especially in conversation
• *He's always scoring off his wife in public*

settle old scores
to get revenge from someone for past wrongs

scot

scot-free
derogatory unhurt or unpunished
• *The older of the two boys was fined but the younger got off scot-free*
Ⓛ An old legal term — literally 'free from tax'

scrape

bow and scrape
to behave in a very humble and respectful way — especially to people from whom one is hoping to gain some advantage

scraping

scraping the (bottom of the) barrel *see* **barrel**

scratch

scratch the surface *see* **surface**

start from scratch
to start an activity etc from nothing, from the very beginning, or without preparation or the advantage of previous experience
Ⓛ Literally, to begin a race from the starting-line, originally scratched on the track, rather than from a position further down the course determined by any handicap the competitor might have

up to scratch
not formal at or to the required or satisfactory standard
• *Your work does not come up to scratch*
Ⓛ From the mark up to which prize-fighters were once obliged to make their way at the beginning of each round

scratching

backscratching *see* **back**

scream

scream blue murder *see* **blue**

screen

the big screen
informal the cinema, as opposed to television

screw

have a screw loose
informal of a person, to be slightly mad

Ⓘ The reference is to unreliable machinery

put the screws on someone
informal to use force or pressure in dealing with them
Ⓘ *The screws* are thumbscrews, an old instrument of torture

screw up one's courage *see* **courage**

scrimp

scrimp and save
to be thrifty or very careful with money
Ⓘ *Scrimp* literally means 'to be mean with money'

Scrooge

a Scrooge
derogatory a person who is mean with money
Ⓘ From the main character in Dickens's *A Christmas Carol* (1843)

Scylla

between Scylla and Charybdis
faced with two equally undesirable choices
Ⓘ A reference to Homer's *Odyssey* (c.850BC) in which Odysseus has to sail down a narrow strait between Scylla, a monster on a rock and Charybdis, an extremely dangerous whirlpool

sea

at sea
puzzled or bewildered
• *Can I help you? You seem all/completely/ rather at sea*

get one's sea legs
informal to become accustomed to the motion of a ship
Ⓘ Originally, this phrase meant only 'to be able to walk steadily on a heaving deck'

seal

seal someone's fate *see* **fate**

my etc **lips are sealed** *see* **lip**

set one's seal on/to something
to give one's authority or agreement to something
Ⓘ Literally, to sign by attaching a wax seal to something

seam

come/fall apart at the seams
to become completely ruined, useless or unworkable
Ⓘ Literally, used of a garment etc which is badly sewn together

seamy

the seamy side (of life)
the roughest, most unpleasant side or aspect of human life
Ⓘ A Shakespearian metaphor, from *Othello* IV, ii, referring to the wrong side of a garment, on which the seams show

search

search me!
informal I really don't know!

season

the compliments of the season *see* **compliment**

a man for all seasons
a person with a wide range of talents or abilities; an adaptable, accommodating person
Ⓘ A quotation from a description of Thomas More (1478–1535) by Robert Whittington, one of his contemporaries and popularized in the title of Robert Bolt's play about Sir Thomas More (1960)

the off season *see* **off**

the silly season *see* **silly**

seat

by the seat of one's pants
using experience or instinct rather than calculations based on scientific or technological methods
Ⓘ Originally used by pilots in World War II to describe conditions in which their instruments were not working or were not effective

have a ringside seat *see* **ringside**

in the hot seat *see* **hot**

take a seat
rather formal to sit down

second

at second hand
through or from another person

come off second best
to be the loser in a struggle

get one's second wind
often fig to recover one's natural breathing after breathlessness

play second fiddle to someone
derogatory to be a supporter or follower of them in an activity, rather than a leader
⌚ From the roles of *first* and *second fiddle* in a chamber orchestra etc

someone's second childhood
derogatory the return to childish habits and behaviour that occurs in some elderly people

a second-class citizen
a member of a group, community etc who does not have full political rights, privileges etc

second nature
a firmly fixed habit
• *It was second nature to/with him to think carefully before spending even 50p*
⌚ From a Latin proverb, *consuetudo est secunda natura* = habit is a second nature

second-rate
derogatory inferior; not of the best quality
⌚ Originally applied literally to warships, which were graded in seven *rates* according to size, number of guns etc

second sight
the power of seeing into the future or into other mysteries

second thoughts
a change of opinion, decision etc; an opinion reached after thinking again about something
• *I'm having second thoughts about selling the piano; On second thoughts, I'd rather stay here*

second to none
better than every other person, thing etc

a split second *see* **split**

secret

an open secret *see* **open**

see

have seen better days *see* **better**

let me see
used to indicate that one is trying to find an answer, trying to remember something, made a decision or do a calculation etc
• *I think I could let you have the money in — let me see — ten days*

see about something
to attend to, or deal with a matter

see daylight *see* **day**

see double
to see two images of everything instead of only one

see eye to eye *see* **eye**

see further than the end of one's nose *see* **nose**

see here!
a phrase used, usually in anger, when telling a person what they ought not to do or have done

see how the land lies *see* **land**

see which way/how the wind blows *see* **wind[1]**

see life *see* **life**

see someone off
informal
1 to accompany someone starting on a journey to the airport, railway station etc from which they are to leave
• *He saw me off at the station*
2 to chase someone away
• *There were some children stealing my apples but my dog soon saw them off*

see someone out
informal
1 to lead or accompany someone to the door or exit of a building etc
2 to last longer than someone

see over something
to visit and inspect eg a house that is for sale

see red *see* **red**

see stars *see* **star**

see the last of *see* **last**

see things *see* **thing**

see something/someone through
to give support to a person, plan etc until the end is reached

see through someone or **something**
not to be deceived by a person, trick etc

see to someone or **something**
to attend to or deal with them or it

see to it that
formal to ensure or make certain that

see one's way to (doing) *see* **way**

see with half an eye *see* **eye**

see you later
informal goodbye

I etc **will see**
I shall wait and consider the matter later

I etc **will see what I can do**
I will do what I can to help

you see
1 a phrase used when giving an explanation
• *I can't meet you tomorrow — I'm going away, you see*
2 a phrase used to draw attention to the correctness of what one has said
• *You see! I told you he wouldn't help us*

seeing

(I'll) be seeing you
informal goodbye

seeing is believing
a proverb, meaning that it is only possible to believe fully in something which can be demonstrated and seen

seeing that
since; considering that

seed

go to seed
1 of a person, to become careless about one's clothes and appearance
2 of a place, to become rather shabby and uncared for
🕒 Literally, of a plant, to produce seeds after flowering and therefore, if a leaf vegetable, to become unfit for use as food

seek

seek and ye shall find
a saying, now usually used humorously, advising someone that if they want something then they must look for it or go out and try to obtain it
🕒 A Biblical reference, to Matthew 7:7–8

seize

seize on something
to accept an idea, suggestion etc with enthusiasm

seize up
of machinery etc, to get stuck and stop working

self

self-possessed
calm in manner or mind, and able to act confidently in an emergency

self-righteous
derogatory having too high an opinion of one's own goodness, and intolerant of other people's faults
🕒 A theological term

self-willed
derogatory determined to do, or have, what one wants

sell

sell someone a pup *see* **pup**

sell someone down the river *see* **river**

a sell-out
informal
1 an event, especially a concert, for which all the tickets are sold
2 a betrayal

send

send away/off for something
to order goods by post

send someone down
to expel a student from university

send someone packing *see* **packing**

send someone to Coventry *see* **Coventry**

send something up
informal to ridicule something, especially through satire or parody
• *In his latest play, he sends up university teachers*

sense

bring someone to his etc **senses**
to make them understand that they must behave, think etc more sensibly

come to one's senses
to realize that one must behave more sensibly, or that facts etc are not as one thought they were

horse sense *see* **horse**

in a sense
in a certain way, or to a certain extent, but not complete
• *What you said was right in a sense, but the problem is rather more complex than you seem to think*

out of one's senses
not in a normal or sane state of mind

a sense of proportion *see* **proportion**

a sixth sense *see* **sixth**

take leave of one's senses
to become slightly mad

separate

separate the men from the boys *see* **men**

separate the sheep from the goats *see* **sheep**

sepulchre

a whited sepulchre *see* **white**

servant

what did your last servant die of?
facetious an expression used in reply to a request for assistance in a task

serve

serve a purpose *see* **purpose**

serve its turn *see* **turn**

serve someone right *see* **right**

serve two masters *see* **master**

service

at your etc **service**
often facetious ready to help or be of use
• *I'm at your service if you want my help; My bicycle is at your service*

be of service to someone
formal to help them

have seen good service
to have been well used

press into service *see* **press**

sesame

open sesame *see* **open**

set

all set (to)
ready or prepared to do something; just on the point of doing something

be set on something
to want to do it very much; to be determined to do it

get set
of runners in a race
to get ready to start running

set about someone or **something**
1 to attack someone
2 to begin something

set someone against someone
formal to cause a person to dislike another person

set someone by the ears *see* **ear**

set someone by the heels *see* **heel**

set one's cap at *see* **cap**

set one's face against *see* **face**

set one's heart on *see* **heart**

set in
of weather, seasons, feelings etc
to begin or become established
• *Winter has set in early; Boredom soon set in among the children*

set something or **someone on someone**
to cause, eg dogs, to attack someone

a set piece
a carefully planned performance, series of events, etc
• *She wanted us to believe that her passionate speech was on the spur of the moment but to us it seemed very much a set piece*

set one's seal on *see* **seal**

set one's sights on *see* **sight**

set someone's teeth on edge *see* **teeth**

set the record straight *see* **record**

set the pace *see* **pace**

set the wheels in motion *see* **wheel**

set to
to start to do something vigorously
• *They set to, and finished the work the same day*

a set-to
informal an argument or fight

set something to rights *see* **right**

set to work *see* **work**

settle

settle down
to begin to work, live etc in a quiet, calm etc way

settle for something
to accept something that is not completely satisfactory

settle someone's hash *see* **hash**

settle old scores *see* **score**

settle something on someone
formal or legal to give money, property etc to a person

settle up with someone
to pay money owed to someone

seven

at sixes and sevens *see* **six**

in (the) seventh heaven *see* **heaven**

sew

sewn up
informal completely settled or arranged
• *We've definitely got the contract — it's all sewn up*

shack

shack up with someone
slang to live with someone one is not married to

shade

put someone or something in the shade
to cause a person, a piece of work etc to seem unimportant
Ⓛ Literally, to make someone etc appear dark by being much brighter oneself

shades of someone or something!
that reminds me of a particular person or thing!
• *Shades of school! We were all treated like children at the conference*
Ⓛ Originally a humorous calling up of the spirit of someone who is dead but who would have an interest in what is happening

shadow

be afraid of one's shadow
to be very timid and easily scared

be a shadow of one's former self
to be much reduced in size, strength or power as a result of age, illness, etc

worn to a shadow
made thin and weary through eg hard work

shaggy

a shaggy-dog story
informal a kind of joke which relies for its effect on being very long and having a sudden ridiculous ending
Ⓛ From the subject of many of the best-known jokes

shake

no great shakes
informal not very good or important
Ⓛ Perhaps from the shaking of dice

shake off someone or something
to rid oneself of someone or something unwanted

two shakes (of a lamb's tail)
in a very short time
Ⓛ 19c US

shaking

be shaking in one's shoes *see* **shoe**

shame

a crying shame *see* **crying**

put someone or something to shame
to make a person feel ashamed of their work or to make the work seem to be of poor quality by showing greater excellence

shame on you etc!
often facetious you should be ashamed!

shanks

on shanks's pony/mare
on foot
Ⓛ From *shank* = leg

shape

get/knock something into shape
informal to put something into the desired condition

in any shape or form
at all
• *I don't accept bribes in any shape or form*

in, out of shape
in good, bad physical condition

in the shape of
in the form of

• *Help arrived in the shape of a passing motorist*

lick into shape *see* **lick**

shape up
to develop or become formed
• *The team is shaping up well*

take shape
to develop or grow into a definite form

share

go shares with someone
informal to share expenses, profits etc with them

the lion's share *see* **lion**

share and share alike
to own, use, pay for etc something with everyone having an equal share

sharp

as sharp as a razor *see* **razor**

look sharp
informal to be quick or to hurry
• *Bring me the books and look sharp about it!*

sharp practice
derogatory dishonesty or cheating

a sharp tongue
derogatory the tendency to be bad-tempered or sarcastic in speech

shebang

the whole shebang
informal the whole lot
• *Don't bother sorting through those old clothes — just get rid of the whole shebang*
ⓘ US in origin but of uncertain derivation. *Shebang* once meant a hut or shack

sheep

as well be hanged for a sheep as a lamb
a proverb, meaning that if one is going to do something wrong, likely to be disapproved of etc, one might as well do something much worse which will benefit oneself more
ⓘ From the fact that at one time stealing a lamb was punishable by death

a black sheep *see* **black**

separate the sheep from the goats
to make it possible to distinguish good, useful etc people in a group from the bad, useless etc ones
ⓘ A Biblical reference, to Matthew 25:32

a wolf in sheep's clothing *see* **wolf**

sheet

as white as a sheet
very pale

come down in sheets
informal to rain very heavily

three sheets to the wind *see* **three**

shelf

on the shelf
derogatory of an unmarried woman, no longer likely to attract a man enough for him to want to marry her

shell

come out of one's shell
to become more confident and less shy
ⓘ The reference is to a tortoise, or a crab etc

shell out
informal derogatory to pay out money

shift

shift for oneself
formal to do as well as one can; to manage without help

shift one's ground *see* **ground**

shilling

cut someone off without a shilling
to disinherit them, to leave them little or no money in one's will
ⓘ A shilling is a former unit of currency equivalent to 10p today

take the king's shilling *see* **king**

shine

take a shine to someone
informal to become fond of them
ⓘ Originally US

take the shine off something
to cause something to appear less attractive, impressive, etc than it previously seemed

ship

run a tight ship *see* **tight**

ships that pass in the night
people who only meet once, by chance
Ⓛ An image from a poem by Longfellow

spoil the ship for a ha'porth of tar
to spoil something valuable by trying to save money etc and not buying or doing something very small but necessary
Ⓛ Presumably from the use of tar to make boats watertight

when my etc **ship comes in**
when I become rich

shipshape

shipshape (and Bristol fashion)
in good order; neat
Ⓛ A nautical term

shirt

in one's shirt-sleeves
without a jacket or coat

keep one's shirt on
informal not to become angry
• *Keep your shirt on — I'm not accusing you of anything*

put one's shirt on (a horse)
slang to bet everything one has on a racehorse

a stuffed shirt *see* **stuff**

shiver

the shivers
informal a feeling of horror
• *The thought of working for him gives me the shivers*

shoe

be shaking in one's shoes
to be very nervous or frightened

in someone's shoes
in someone's place

step into dead men's shoes *see* **dead**

shoestring

on a shoestring
with or using very little money

shoot

shoot a line *see* **line**

shoot something down in flames
to destroy or refute it completely, to expose it as false
• *We shot their argument down in flames*
Ⓛ A reference to aircraft warfare in World War I

shoot one's mouth off *see* **mouth**

the whole shoot, the whole shooting match
informal the whole lot

shop

all over the shop
spread out everywhere

set up shop
to begin doing something
• *She set up shop as a singing teacher*
Ⓛ Literally, to open a shop

shop around
to compare prices, quality of goods etc at several shops before buying anything

shut up shop
to stop doing something, working etc

a talking-shop *see* **talking**

talk shop
to talk about one's work

short

at short notice
without much warning time for preparation etc

be in short supply *see* **supply**

bring someone up short
to cause them suddenly to stop what they are doing

by a short head
by a very small amount
Ⓛ A racing term for the shortest distance by which a horse can be judged to have won a race — once under *a length*, the distances are *half a length*, *a neck*, *a head* and *a short head*

caught/taken short
informal having a sudden need to urinate

fall short *see* **fall**

for short
as an abbreviation
• *His name is Victor, but we call him Vic for short*

give someone or **something short shrift**
to waste little time or consideration on

someone or something, usually in an unpleasant or unfriendly way

Ⓘ *Short shrift* was the short time given to a criminal for confession and absolution before his execution

go short
to cause or allow oneself not to have enough of something, eg in order to allow someone else to have some

have someone by the short hairs *see* **hair**

in short
often used after listing complaints, reasons etc, in a few words

in short order *see* **order**

little/nothing short of something
almost the same as, or as bad as something else

• *Charging prices like that is little short of robbery; To do that would be nothing short of suicide!*

make short work of something
to settle, or dispose of it very quickly

run short
1 of a supply, to become insufficient
2 with **of**, not to have enough

sell someone or **something short**
to belittle a person or thing

• *Tell them about your achievements — don't sell yourself short*

Ⓘ Literally, not to sell the correct amount, ie enough, of something

short and sweet
ironic very short and emphatic

Ⓘ A 16c proverb, meaning in effect 'the shorter the better'

short for something
an abbreviation of something

short measure *see* **measure**

short of
1 not as far as or as much as

• *Our total came to just short of £1000; We stopped five miles short of London*

2 without doing something as bad, unpleasant etc as something else

• *Short of murdering her, I'd do anything to get rid of her*

short on something
informal lacking in a particular thing, quality etc

short-tempered
easily made angry

stop short of *see* **stop**

to cut a long story short *see* **story**

shot

a big shot
informal an important person

call the shots
informal to be in control of what is happening

Ⓘ Literally used of target shooting — to say, as a shot is fired, where on the target it will strike

get shot of something
to get rid of it

have shot one's bolt *see* **bolt**

like a shot
informal a guess, attempt etc unlikely to be right or succeed, but worth trying

a long shot
informal an unlikely or desperate expedient

not by a long shot
informal not by any means

a shot across the bows
something intended to be a warning

Ⓘ From naval warfare

a shot in the arm
the addition of new ideas, money etc to a failing business etc in the hope of reviving it

Ⓘ Literally, an injection in the arm

a shot in the dark
informal a guess based on little or no information

shotgun

a shotgun marriage/wedding
a forced marriage

Ⓘ From the idea that such a wedding might well be arranged solely because the bride's father threatened the bridegroom with a shotgun

shoulder

give someone the cold shoulder *see* **cold**

have a chip on one's shoulder *see* **chip**

have a (good) head on one's shoulders *see* **head**

have broad shoulders
to be able to accept a great deal of responsibility

put one's shoulder to the wheel
informal to begin to work very hard

rub shoulders with someone
to mix or associate with them

a shoulder to cry on
slightly derogatory a sympathetic listener

shoulder to shoulder
close together; side by side

straight from the shoulder
bluntly, in a outspoken manner
• *He told her what he thought of her work straight from the shoulder*
🕔 From boxing

shout

shout someone down
to make it impossible for a speaker to be heard, eg at a meeting, by shouting, jeering etc very loudly

shout something/it from the rooftops
to publicize something widely, to make sure that something is widely known

shouting

be all over bar the shouting
informal of a happening, contest etc, to be almost completely finished, over or decided
• *If you have decided to give up supporting us, then it's all over bar the shouting, I'm afraid*

shove

shove off
informal: sometimes impolite to go away
🕔 Literally a nautical term meaning 'to push a boat away from the shore'

show

for show
in order to give the appearance of something special
• *They did it just for show, to make themselves seem more important than they are*

get the show on the road
informal to get a plan, organization etc into operation; to begin a planned activity etc
🕔 Originally used of a theatre company etc going on tour

give the show away *see* **give**

good show!
informal that's good; I'm pleased

on show
obvious and able to be watched by a lot of people

run the show
to be in control or charge of a plan, organization etc
🕔 A theatrical idiom

show one's face *see* **face**

show one's hand *see* **hand**

show oneself in one's true colours *see* **colour**

the show must go on
no matter what misfortune or tragedy occurs everything must go on as usual
🕔 Originally used with reference to a stage performance

show off
informal derogatory to try to impress others with one's possessions, ability to do something etc

a show of hands
at a meeting, debate etc, a vote expressed by people raising their hands

show one's paces *see* **pace**

show one's teeth *see* **teeth**

show the flag *see* **flag**

show the white feather *see* **feather**

show up
informal
1 to make obvious (faults etc)
• *This light shows up the places where I've patched my coat*
2 to reveal the faults, mistakes etc of a person
• *Mary was so neat that she really showed me up*
3 to appear or arrive

steal the show
to attract the most admiration, attention etc during an event of some kind

Ⓛ A theatrical term for attracting the most applause during a performance

to show for something
having been got as a profit, advantage etc
• *I've worked for this firm for twenty years and what have I got to show for it? Nothing!*

shrift

give someone or something short shrift *see* **short**

shrug

shrug something off
to get rid of or dismiss it or treat it as unimportant
• *She shrugged off all criticism and calmly went on with the project*

shuffle

shuffle off this mortal coil *see* **mortal**

shut

shut someone's mouth *see* **mouth**

shut up
informal to stop speaking

shy

fight shy (of) *see* **fight**

sick

make someone sick
informal to make them feel very annoyed, upset etc

sick and tired/sick of the sight/sick to death of something
informal derogatory very tired of it; wishing to have, hear, see etc no more of it
Ⓛ **Sick to death** once literally meant 'suffering from a fatal illness'

sick as a dog
extremely sick, vomiting heavily

sick as a parrot
informal suffering from a disappointment

sick at heart *see* **heart**

worried sick
informal very worried

side

get, keep on the right side of *see* **right**

get on the wrong side of *see* **wrong**

let the side down
informal to disappoint and hinder one's associates by acting, performing etc less well than they have been done

on, from all sides
in, from all directions

on the long, short, tight etc **side**
informal rather too short, long, tight etc
• *This shirt is a bit on the small side for me*

on the side
slang in another way than through one's ordinary occupation
• *He is earning quite a lot on the side as a singer*

on the side of the angels *see* **angel**

pass by on the other side
not to help someone in trouble etc, especially to pretend one has not noticed them
Ⓛ A Biblical reference, to the action of the priest and the Levite in the parable of the Good Samaritan, in Luke 10

pick/choose sides
to select the people for each team etc before a game

put something on one side
to leave a plan, problem etc to be considered later

side by side
beside one another; close together

side with someone
to give support to a person, group etc in an argument etc

take sides
to choose to support a particular opinion, group etc against another

there are two sides to every question
a saying emphasizing the importance of being impartial and not making up one's mind to support something or someone until one has studied the evidence and arguments

sidekick

a sidekick
derogatory slang a partner, assistant or special friend

sieve

have a head/memory like a sieve
to be very forgetful

sigh

heave a sigh of relief
to express or show one's relief that something unpleasant, dangerous, etc is over or has been averted

sign

be signed, sealed and delivered
to reach a satisfactory stage of completion
Ⓞ Originally applied to legal documents

a sign of the times
an indication or example of current attitudes, opinions, fashions, etc

sign on the dotted line
to indicate one's acceptance of whatever is being offered
Ⓞ A reference to signing a contract

sign one's own death warrant *see* **death**

sight

catch sight of someone or **something**
to get a brief view of them; to begin to see them

have something in one's sights
to be preparing to try to get something
Ⓞ The reference is to the sights of a gun

have/set one's sights on something
to try to get something
Ⓞ As previous idiom

keep sight of someone or **something**
to remain close enough to see them or it

know someone by sight
to be able to recognize them without ever having spoken to them

lose sight of someone or **something**
1 to stop being able to see them or it
2 to forget about a purpose etc

not to be able to stand the sight of someone
informal to dislike them intensely

out of sight
no longer visible

out of sight, out of mind
a proverb, meaning that one ceases to think about someone who is absent or something that is no longer obvious

second sight *see* **second**

set one's sights on *see* **have one's sights on,** *above*

a sight for sore eyes
informal a most welcome sight

silence

an eloquent silence
a silence that is full of meaning so that it indicates more than the use of words would

silence is golden
a saying, usually meaning that it is better to say nothing in a particular situation — from the proverb **speech is silver, silence is golden** = it is good to speak and even better not to

silent

the silent majority
the people, making up most of the population, whose opinions are moderate and reasonable, but who do not make them known

silk

you can't make a silk purse out of a sow's ear
a proverb, meaning that one cannot make something good out of materials which are by nature bad and usually implying that a certain result is the best that can be expected

silly

the silly season
rather old: derogatory a time of year, usually late summer, when the newspapers, television etc spend a lot of time on unimportant things because there is a lack of important news

silver

be born with a silver spoon in one's mouth
to be born into a wealthy family
Ⓞ Probably from the custom of godparents giving a silver spoon to a child as a christening present

every cloud has a silver lining *see* **cloud**

thirty pieces of silver
the symbol of betrayal
Ⓞ A Biblical reference to Matthew 26:15 in which Judas betrayed Jesus for thirty pieces of silver

sin

as ugly as sin
very ugly

be more sinned against than sinning
to be less guilty or responsible than other people who have done wrong
• *Many people feel that prostitutes are more sinned against than sinning*
① A quotation from Shakespeare, *King Lear* III, ii

cover a multitude of sins *see* **multitude**

live in sin
usually facetious to live together without being married

sing

sing for one's supper *see* **supper**

sing someone's praises *see* **praise**

singing

all singing, all dancing
a description originally used of stage shows to indicate how splendid they were, now extended to other things such as machines, to indicate how elaborate they are

single

not a single
not even one

single-handed
working etc by oneself, without help

single-minded
of a person, having one aim or purpose only

single someone or **something out**
to pick them or it out for special treatment

sink

be sunk
slang to be defeated, in a hopeless position etc

have to sink or swim
to be in a situation in which one has to cope as best one can and in which one will either be a success or a failure

sink our, your etc **differences**
to forget mutual disagreements etc

sinking

desert a sinking ship *see* **desert**

have a sinking feeling
to have a feeling of dread or pessimism about some approaching event

sit

sit at someone's feet *see* **feet**

sit back
to rest and take no part in an activity

sit in on something
to be present at a meeting etc without being an actual member

sit on the fence *see* **fence**

sit tight *see* **tight**

sit something out
to remain inactive and wait until the end of an unpleasant episode

sit up
1 to remain awake, not going to bed
2 *informal* to pay attention
• *That'll make them all sit up!*

sit up and take notice
informal to start paying attention and taking note of what is going on after a period of apathy

sitting

a sitting duck
someone or something likely to be attacked and unable to put up a strong defence
① From shooting. A duck on the water or ground is easier to shoot than one in the air

sitting pretty *see* **pretty**

a sitting target
someone or something that is in an obvious position to be attacked
① As **a sitting duck** above

six

at sixes and sevens
informal in confusion; completely disorganized
① From playing dice, originally meaning 'having gambled on the high numbers only' and thus 'in disarray'

knock someone for six
informal to overcome or defeat them completely; to take them totally by surprise
① A cricketing idiom — literally to score six runs off a ball

six feet under
informal dead and buried
Ⓛ The traditional depth of a grave

six of one and half a dozen of the other
of two things, possibilities etc, equally to blame, responsible, important, relevant etc
Ⓛ From the fact that half a dozen = six

six of the best
old six strokes with a cane as a punishment at school etc

sixth

a sixth sense
an ability to feel or realize something apparently not by means of any of the five senses
Ⓛ From the fact that there are five normal senses: sight, hearing, touch, taste and smell

sixty

the sixty-four (thousand) dollar question
informal facetious a most important and/or difficult question
Ⓛ From a US quiz game in which the prize was $1 for answering the first question, $2 for the second, $4 for the third etc, up to the last question when the contestant won $64 or lost it all

size

cut someone down to size
informal to reduce someone's sense of their own importance

of a size
of the same size
• *Your coat should fit me — we're very much of a size*

that's about the size of it
informal that is a reasonable assessment of the state of affairs

size up someone or **something**
slightly informal to form an opinion about the worth, nature, etc of a person, situation etc

try that on for size!
informal what do you think of that!

skate

get one's skates on
informal to hurry up

skate over something
informal to pass over a subject, difficulty etc quickly, trying to avoid taking it into consideration

skeleton

the skeleton at the feast
someone or something that spoils the enjoyment of an occasion by reminding people of misfortune
Ⓛ A reference to a custom in ancient Egypt by which a seat was reserved for a skeleton at special feasts

a skeleton in the cupboard/closet
a closely-kept secret concerning a hidden cause of shame

skid

on skid row
slang destitute, down-and-out
Ⓛ US in origin — a term from the US timber industry where it first meant something down which felled logs were slid. It became the term for the part of a town occupied by people engaged in felling trees, and then to an area of town where vagrants and down-and-outs lived

put the skids under someone
informal to cause them to hurry

skin

be more than one way to skin a cat *see* **cat**

by the skin of one's teeth
very narrowly; only just

get under someone's skin
informal to annoy and upset them greatly

jump out of one's skin
informal to get a great fright or shock

no skin off one's nose
informal something about which one is not concerned, or does not care, because it is not inconvenient to one or benefits one

save one's skin
to save one's life

skin and bone
informal very thin

skin-deep
formal or literary on the surface only

thick-skinned *see* **thick**

thin-skinned *see* **thin**

skinflint

a skinflint
derogatory a very mean person

skull

the skull and crossbones
hist a design displayed on a pirate's flag

sky

pie in the sky *see* **pie**

praise someone to the skies
to praise them very highly

sky-high
very high

the sky's the limit
informal there is no upper limit eg to the amount of money that may be spent

slanging

a slanging-match
informal an angry quarrel or argument in which rude expressions are used by both sides

slap

slap and tickle
informal playful and not very serious lovemaking

a slap in the face
informal an insult or rebuff

a slap on the wrist
derogatory, usually facetious a mild scolding

slapstick
a kind of humour which depends for its effect on very simple practical jokes etc
Ⓛ From the double stick once carried by a harlequin and used to make a slapping noise on stage

slap-up
informal of a meal etc, splendid; excellent

slate

a clean slate *see* **clean**

on the slate
on credit

slave

a slave-driver
a person who expects too much work from his employees, pupils etc
Ⓛ Literally, a man in charge of getting slaves to work

sleep

beauty sleep
informal the amount of sleep which a person needs to look healthy and attractive

lose sleep over something
informal to worry about it
• *Don't lose any sleep over the problem!*

put someone or **something to sleep**
euphemism
1 to cause a person or animal to become unconscious by means of an anaesthetic; to anaesthetize
2 to kill an animal painlessly, usually by the injection of a drug

sleep around
informal, often derogatory to be in the habit of having sexual intercourse with a number of different people; to be promiscuous

sleep in
Brit to sleep late in the morning; to oversleep

sleep like a log *see* **log**

sleep like a top *see* **top**

sleep something off
to recover from something by sleeping

sleep on something
informal to put off making a decision about it
• *I can't decide whether to accept the job or not — I'm going to sleep on it*

sleep with someone
euphemism to have, or be in the habit of having, sexual intercourse with them

sleeping

let sleeping dogs lie *see* **dog**

sleeve

have/keep something up one's sleeve
to keep a plan etc secret for possible use at a later time
Ⓛ From cheating at cards by having extra cards hidden in one's sleeve

laugh up one's sleeve
to laugh secretly

slice

a slice of the cake
informal a share of something valuable which has been gained

slide

let something slide
informal to neglect and not to bother about it

slight

not in the slightest
not at all

sling

sling mud at *see* **mud**

slip

a Freudian slip *see* **Freud**

give someone the slip
informal to escape from or avoid them in a secretive manner

let something slip
1 to miss an opportunity etc
2 to say something unintentionally
• *She let slip some remark about my daughter*

let something slip through one's fingers *see* **finger**

slip someone something
informal to pass money etc, usually intended as a bribe to a person
• *I slipped the barman a fiver to serve us first*

slip one's mind *see* **mind**

a slip of the tongue
a word etc said by mistake when the speaker meant something else

slip up
to make a mistake; to fail to do something

there's many a slip 'twixt cup and lip
a proverb, meaning that a plan can easily go wrong before it is carried out and that it is therefore unwise to praise, depend on, etc anything before it is completed

slope

the slippery slope
informal the beginning of a course of action that might lead to disaster

slope off
slang to go away, especially secretively and without warning

slow

go slow
Brit of workers in a factory etc, to work less quickly than usual, eg as a form of protest

in slow motion
informal very much slower than normal
Ⓞ Literally used of movement in films made very slow by running the film very slowly

slow on the uptake *see* **uptake**

sly

on the sly
secretly, without informing others

smack

a smack in the eye
very informal an insult or rebuff

small

feel/look small
to feel or look foolish or insignificant

in a small way
1 with little money or stock
• *He is an antique-dealer in a small way*
2 quietly, without extravagance

it's a small world
a phrase used to indicate surprise, interest etc at some unexpected coincidence, contact between unconnected people one knows etc

small beer *see* **beer**

small fry *see* **fry**

the small hours
the hours immediately after midnight
Ⓞ From the fact that the numbers involved are small — one o'clock, two o'clock etc

small-minded
having, or showing, narrow interests or intolerant and unimaginative opinions

small potatoes *see* **potato**

the small print
the place in a document etc where important information is given without being easily noticed

small talk
polite conversation about very unimportant matters

small things please small minds
derogatory a proverb, meaning that mean and petty people are pleased by mean and petty subjects, victories etc

small-time
of a thief etc, not working on a large scale

small wonder
it is not really surprising

smart

look smart
to be quick

a smart Alec(k)/Alick
derogatory slang a person who thinks he is cleverer than others
① Originally US, c.1870, of unknown derivation

smash

a smash-and-grab (raid/robbery)
a robbery in which the window of a shop is smashed and goods grabbed from behind it

a smash hit
informal a song, show etc that is a great success

smear

a smear campaign
an attempt to damage someone's reputation by making a number of accusations in speech or writing

smell

smell a bit fishy *see* **fish**

smell a rat *see* **rat**

smell of the lamp *see* **lamp**

smile

be all smiles
to be, or look, very happy

smile on someone or **something**
rather literary to be favourable to them or it

wipe the smile off someone's face
to cause them to lose their smug or satisfied look

smoke

go up in smoke
informal
1 to vanish very quickly, leaving nothing behind
• *All his plans have gone up in smoke*
2 to lose one's temper
① *Literally, to burn*

smoke out something or **someone**
to discover them or it
① Literally, to drive an animal from a hiding-place with smoke or fire

there's no smoke without fire
a saying, meaning that there is always a basis for any rumours, talk etc however untrue they may appear

snail

at a snail's pace
very slowly

snake

a snake in the grass
derogatory informal a person who cannot be trusted
① An image from one of Virgil's *Eclogues*

snap

make it/look snappy
informal hurry up

snap out of it
informal to make oneself quickly stop being miserable, depressed etc

snap something up
to grab it eagerly

sneeze

not to be sneezed at
informal of a chance, opportunity etc, not to be ignored

sniff

sniff something out
informal to discover or detect it
① The reference is to a tracker dog

snook

cock a snook at someone *see* **cock**

snow

as pure as the driven snow *see* **drive**

snowed under
overwhelmed eg with a great deal of work

snowball

not to have a snowball's chance in hell *see* **hell**

so

so-and-so
derogatory
1 an unnamed, unidentified person
• *If I said I would meet so-and-so, I would do it*
2 used as a substitute for an offensive term for a person or thing
• *I've had another letter from those so-and-sos at the bank!*

so-so
informal neither very good nor very bad

so what?
impolite informal what of it?; does it really matter?

soap

a soap opera
usually derogatory a radio or television serial broadcast weekly, daily etc, especially one that continues from year to year, that concerns the daily life, troubles etc of the characters in it
🕐 From the fact that in the US they were often sponsored by soap manufacturers

sob

a sob-story
derogatory informal a story of misfortune etc told in order to gain sympathy

sober

as sober as a judge *see* **judge**

stone-cold sober *see* **stone**

sock

pull one's socks up
to make an effort to do better

put a sock in it!
slang be quiet!

sock it to someone
slang to speak to or behave towards someone in a very strong or impressive manner

soft

have a soft spot for someone or **something**
informal to have a weakness for someone or something because of great affection

soft in the head *see* **head**

a soft option
informal a choice, alternative etc which is easier or more pleasant than the others

soft-pedal
informal not to make evident or acknowledge the importance etc of something
🕐 From the action of the *soft pedal* on a piano, which makes it play more quietly

a soft touch/mark
slang a person who is easily deceived, used etc

soften

soften someone up
informal to weaken someone to make them less able to resist something which follows

softly

softly-softly
slang careful, cautious and gentle

sold

be sold on something
slang to be enthusiastic about it

be sold out
sometimes with **of**
1 to be no longer available, because all have been sold
2 to have no more of something available to be bought

soldier

soldier on
to keep going despite difficulties etc

something

be/have something to do with something
to be connected with it

make something of something
informal to understand it

make something of oneself
informal to become important or successful in some way
• *He's a clever boy — I hope he'll make something of himself*

or something
used when the speaker is uncertain or being vague
• *Her name is Mary or Margaret or something*

something tells me
I have reason to believe; I suspect

song

for a song
informal for a very small amount of money
ⓘ Probably derived from an image of Shakespeare's, in *All's Well that Ends Well* III, iii

make a song and dance about something
to make an unnecessary fuss about it
ⓘ From the expanding of an incident into a musical number in a stage or film musical

someone's swan song *see* **swan**

soon

no sooner said than done
of a request, promise etc, immediately fulfilled

sooner or later
eventually

the sooner the better
as quickly as possible

speak too soon
to say something that takes a result etc for granted before it is certain

sop

a sop to Cerberus *see* **Cerberus**

sore

a sight for sore eyes *see* **sight**

a sore point
a subject which it annoys or offends one to speak about
• *Gambling has been a sore point with him since he lost a fortune betting on horses*

stick out like a sore thumb
to be too noticeable, painful, awkward etc to be ignored

sorrow

drown one's sorrows *see* **drown**

more in sorrow than in anger
often facetious more disappointed and unhappy than angry at someone's bad behaviour etc

sorry

be/feel sorry for someone
to pity them

sort

it takes all sorts (to make a world)
a saying, meaning that one should be tolerant towards everyone, whatever their views, behaviour etc

not a bad sort
informal quite a nice person

of a sort/of sorts
of a (usually poor) kind
• *She threw together a meal of sorts but we were still hungry afterwards*

out of sorts
informal
1 slightly unwell
2 not in good spirits or temper
ⓘ Possibly from the use of the phrase as a printing term — literally, 'with some of the letters of the alphabet used up and unavailable'

sort of
informal rather; in a way; to a certain extent

sort something or **someone out**
informal
1 to separate one lot or type of things from a general mixture
• *I'll try to sort out some books that he might like*
2 to correct, improve, solve etc something
• *You must sort out your business affairs before you are forced to close down*
3 to attend to someone, usually by punishing or reprimanding

soul

God rest his soul *see* **rest**

not to be able to call one's soul one's own
to be organized and controlled by someone else

the soul of something
a perfect example of a quality etc

soul-searching
the examination of one's own

conscience to find out eg whether one's motives are genuine

would sell one's soul for something
would like very much to have it
Ⓘ A reference to the idea of people allowing the devil to take their souls in return for great wealth or power, as Faust did

sound

as sound as a bell *see* **bell**

sound off
derogatory slang to speak loudly and freely, especially while complaining

sound someone out
to try to find out their thoughts and plans etc
• *Will you sound out your father on this?*

soup

duck soup *see* **duck**

in the soup
slang in serious trouble
Ⓘ Originally US

souped-up
slang of a car etc, made more powerful
Ⓘ Originally US, c.1945

sour

sour grapes *see* **grape**

sow[1]

sow one's wild oats *see* **wild**

as you sow, so shall you reap
a saying indicating that you will get the treatment that you deserve
Ⓘ A Biblical reference, to Galatians 6:7

sow[2]

you can't make a silk purse out of a sow's ear *see* **silk**

space

in the space of (a minute, hour etc)
in as little as a minute, hour etc

spade

call a spade a spade
to say plainly and clearly what one means, not softening anything by trying to use polite words
Ⓘ From a 16c mistranslation of a passage in one of Plutarch's works

spadework
hard word done at the beginning of a project etc, serving as a basis for the future
Ⓘ From the fact that digging is a main constituent of the first stage of any building project

spanner

throw a spanner in the works
to frustrate or ruin a plan, system etc
Ⓘ A reference to engines

sparring

a sparring-partner
informal a person with whom one enjoys a lively argument
Ⓘ Literally, a person with whom a boxer practises

spare

go spare
slang to become angry or upset

spare the rod and spoil the child *see* **rod**

a spare tyre
informal a roll of fat around the middle of one's body

(and) to spare
in larger numbers or quantities than is needed; extra
• *Go to the exhibition if you have time to spare; She has enough to spare*

spark

sparks will fly
there is going to be an argument or row
Ⓘ A reference to a hammer striking a piece of metal and causing sparks to fly

speak

so to speak
if one may use such an expression; in a way; it could be said

speak for someone
to give an opinion etc on behalf of someone else

speak for itself/themselves
to have an obvious meaning; not to need explaining

speak one's mind *see* **mind**

speak out
to say boldly what one thinks

speak the same language *see* **language**

speak too soon *see* **soon**

speak up
to speak more loudly

speak up for someone
to say things in their favour; to support them

speak volumes *see* **volume**

speak with a forked tongue *see* **fork**

to speak of
informal worth mentioning
• *He has no talent to speak of*

to speak to
informal well enough to have a conversation with
• *I don't know him to speak to*

speaking

be on speaking terms with someone
to be friendly enough with them to speak to them

generally speaking
in general

spec

on spec
informal taking a chance in the hope of achieving something etc
Ⓣ An abbreviation of *on speculation* = as a gamble

spectacles

look at something through rose-coloured spectacles *see* **rose**

spell

spell something out
to give a highly detailed explanation of something

spend

spend a penny *see* **penny**

spend money like water *see* **money**

spice

variety is the spice of life *see* **variety**

spick

spick and span
neat, clean and tidy
Ⓣ The original phrase was **spick and span new**, literally, 'with even the nails and chips of wood brand-new'

spike

spike someone's guns *see* **gun**

spill

not cry over spilt milk
to avoid wasting time regretting an accident, loss etc that cannot be put right

spill the beans *see* **beans**

spin

in a flat spin *see* **flat**

spin a yarn *see* **yarn**

spin something out
to cause something to last a, usually unnecessarily, long or longer time
• *He spun out his speech for an extra five minutes*
Ⓣ The image is of spinning a long thread from a short bundle of fibres

spirit

be with someone in spirit
not to be with them in the flesh but to be thinking of them

out of spirits
formal or literary feeling depressed

public spirit *see* **public**

spirit someone or **something away**
to carry away or remove someone or something secretly and suddenly, as if by magic

the spirit is willing (but the flesh is weak)
a saying, meaning that it is not always physically possible to do everything one would like to, often used to explain one's failure to do something
Ⓣ A Biblical quotation, from Matthew 26:4

take something in the right spirit
not to be offended by it

spit

the dead spit/the spitting image of someone
informal an exact likeness of them

spit and polish
very careful cleaning of equipment, furniture etc
Ⓘ From the practice of using spit along with polish to clean boots etc, especially in the army

splash

make a splash
informal to attract a lot of notice, especially deliberately

splash down
of spacecraft etc, to land in the sea at the end of a trip

splash out on something
informal to spend a lot of money on it

spleen

vent one's spleen
to express the anger and frustration one feels, often by attacking someone innocent
Ⓘ In medieval medicine, the spleen was thought to be the source of spite, melancholy and resentment

splice

splice the mainbrace
old slang to serve out alcoholic drinks
Ⓘ Naval slang, originally a euphemism

splinter

a splinter group
a group, especially a political group, formed by breaking away from a larger one

split

do the splits
to sit down on the ground with one leg straight forward and the other straight back
Ⓘ From the gymnastic exercise

split hairs *see* **hair**

a split second
a fraction of a second

split the vote *see* **vote**

spoil

spoil the ship for a ha'porth of tar *see* **ship**

too many cooks spoil the broth *see* **cook**

spoiling

be spoiling for something
informal to be eager for, especially a fight

spoke

put a spoke in someone's wheel
to put difficulties in the way of what someone is doing
Ⓘ From a Dutch idiom deriving from the practice of jamming a cartwheel with a bar — in Dutch, *spaak* — to act as a brake when going downhill

sponge

throw up the sponge
to give up a struggle, argument etc
Ⓘ From a method of conceding defeat in a boxing match

spoon

be born with a silver spoon in one's mouth *see* **silver**

spoon-feed
derogatory to teach or treat a person in a way that does not allow him to think or act for himself
Ⓘ Literally, 'to feed with a spoon'

the wooden spoon
the prize which is given to the person or team that comes last in a contest
Ⓘ A reference to a former custom in Cambridge University of giving such a prize to the student with the lowest examination results

sport

make sport of someone or **something**
formal to make fun of or ridicule a person, efforts etc

sporting

a sporting chance
a reasonably good chance

spot

have a soft spot for *see* **soft**

hit the spot
to be exactly what is wanted or required, to be absolutely satisfactory
Ⓘ Probably originally a reference to archery but popularized by a commercial jingle for a popular soft drink on American radio in the 1930s and 1940s

in a spot
informal in trouble

knock spots off someone
informal to do something much better, faster etc than them
Ⓞ Originally US

on the spot
informal
1 at once; immediately
2 in the exact place referred to; in the place where one is needed
• *He felt that he was the best person to deal with the crisis as he was on the spot*

put someone on the spot
to place them in a dangerous, difficult or embarrassing position
Ⓞ 1920s US gangsters' slang for 'to decide to assassinate someone'

rooted to the spot
informal unable to move, because of fear, surprise etc

spot on
informal very accurate or exactly on target
Ⓞ World War II RAF slang

a tight spot *see* **tight**

spout

up the spout
slang
1 completely ruined, useless or damaged beyond repair
2 pregnant
Ⓞ Originally this phrase meant 'at the pawnbroker's', allegedly from a pawnbroker's method of checking articles in by passing them up a spout to the back shop

sprat

a sprat to catch a mackerel
something small granted, conceded etc in order to make a large gain

spread

spread like wildfire *see* **wild**

spread one's wings *see* **wing**

spring

spring something on someone
informal to tell or propose something suddenly to a person, so that he is surprised

spur

on the spur of the moment
suddenly; without previous planning

spur someone on
to cause them to make greater efforts
Ⓞ Literally, to urge a horse to go faster, using spurs

win one's spurs
to achieve something important; to become recognized
Ⓞ When a man was knighted in the Middle Ages, he was presented with a pair of spurs by his sponsor

spurt

put a spurt on/put on a spurt
informal to run or go faster eg towards the end of a race

spy

my spies are everywhere
a catch phrase, used as a humorous response to questions seeking information as to how something little known, secret, confidential, etc became known

spy on someone
to watch a person etc secretly

spy out the land
to investigate or examine, eg an area of land, a matter etc, before proceeding further

square

go back to square one
informal to start again at the beginning
Ⓞ From a common instruction on board games

a square deal
informal an honest bargain, transaction etc

a square meal
a good nourishing meal

a square peg in a round hole *see* **peg**

square up with someone
to settle an account with them

square up to something
to face it honestly and try to deal with it

squeak

a narrow squeak
a narrow escape

squeaky clean *see* **clean**

squib

a damp squib *see* **damp**

stab

have a stab at (doing) something
informal to try to do it

stab someone in the back
to behave treacherously towards them

a stab in the back
a treacherous act

stable

lock the stable door after the horse has bolted
to take action to stop something from happening after it is too late

stack

stack the cards against *see* **card**

staff

the staff of life
old or facetious bread

stage

set the stage for something
to make preparations for something; to prepare the way for it

stage fright
the nervousness felt by an actor etc when in front of an audience, especially for the first time

stage-manage
to be in charge of the organization of, eg a military operation, a large-scale robbery etc
Ⓛ Literally, to be in charge of the scenery and equipment for a play etc

a stage whisper
a loud whisper that is intended to be heard by people other than the one to whom it is addressed
Ⓛ From the fact that whispers on stage must be audible to the audience

stair

below stairs
old in the part of a house etc where the servants live and work

stake

at stake
1 to be won or lost
2 in great danger

have a stake in something
to have an investment in a business etc or an interest or concern in something

stake a claim
to assert or establish one's ownership or right to something
Ⓛ From gold and silver mining

stake someone or **something out**
slang to watch a person, place etc carefully
• *The police staked out the gang's headquarters and waited for them to appear*

stamp

stamp something out
to crush or subdue a rebellion etc
• *The new king stamped out all opposition to his rule*
Ⓛ Literally, to extinguish a fire by stamping on it

stamping

a stamping-ground
often facetious a place where a person or people can usually be found
Ⓛ Literally used of animals

stand

it stands to reason *see* **reason**

know where one stands
to know what one's position or situation is in some particular sense

make a stand
to resist something one believes to be wrong etc
Ⓛ A military phrase, literally 'to stop and offer resistance'

not to be able to stand the sight of *see* **sight**

on stand-by
informal ready for action if necessary

stand by
1 to watch something happening without doing anything
• *I couldn't just stand by while he was hitting the child*
2 to be ready to act
• *The police are standing by in case of trouble*
3 to support or maintain
• *She stood by him throughout his trial*

stand corrected
to agree that one has been wrong and accept the correction given to one

stand down
to withdraw from a contest

stand fast/firm
to refuse to yield
• *I'm standing firm on/over this issue*

stand for something
informal to tolerate it

stand one's ground *see* **ground**

stand in for someone
to take another person's place, job etc for a time

stand someone in good stead *see* **stead**

stand-offish
derogatory of a person or his manner etc, unfriendly
🕐 From the naval term *stand off* = 'to keep away from the shore' of a ship and thus of a person 'to keep away from other people'

stand on ceremony *see* **ceremony**

stand or fall by something
to be completely committed to an idea etc; to depend completely on something

stand out
1 to be noticeable because exceptional
• *They were all pretty, but she stood out among them*
2 to go on resisting or to refuse to yield
• *The garrison stood out against the besieging army as long as possible*

stand out a mile *see* **mile**

stand someone up
slang to fail to keep an appointment, especially a date

stand up and be counted
to make one's opinions public, especially if they are only held by a minority of people or are unpopular

stand up for someone or **something**
to support or defend them in a dispute etc

stand up to someone or **something**
to show resistance to them or it

standing

a standing joke
a subject that causes a laugh whenever it is mentioned

star

hitch one's wagon to a star *see* **wagon**

thank one's lucky stars *see* **lucky**

see stars
informal to see flashes of light as a result of a hard blow on the head

staring

be staring someone in the face *see* **face**

start

a false start *see* **false**

for a start
used in argument etc, in the first place, or as the first point in an argument

get off to a good, bad start
to start well or badly in a race, business etc

get a head/running start
make progress ahead of everyone else

get started on something
informal to start doing etc or talking about something

start from scratch *see* **scratch**

starter

for starters
informal in the first place; to begin with
🕐 Literally 'as the first course of a meal'

state

get into a state
informal to become very upset or anxious

the state of play
the position or stage reached in the course of an activity, situation, etc
• *What is the state of play in the salary negotiations with management?*

statistics

someone's vital statistics *see* **vital**

status

the status quo
formal or legal the situation as it now is, or as it was before a particular change

a status symbol
a possession which people are supposed to get in order to show their high social position

stay

stay put
informal to remain where placed

stay the course
to continue going to the end of a race, period of training etc

stay the pace *see* **pace**

stead

stand someone in good stead
formal to be useful to a person in a time of need

steady

as steady as a rock *see* **rock**

go steady
of a girl and boy not yet engaged to be married, to go out together regularly; to have a steady relationship

steady (on)!
informal don't be so angry, upset etc!
◷ Apparently a nautical term

steal

steal a march on *see* **march**

steal the show *see* **show**

steal someone's thunder *see* **thunder**

steam

full steam ahead
at the greatest speed possible
◷ Literally, an instruction for maximum forward speed conveyed to the engine-room of a steamship

get, be (all) steamed up
informal to get or be very upset or angry

get up steam
to collect energy to do something
◷ Literally, to increase the pressure of steam in an engine before putting it into operation

let off steam
informal to release or get rid of excess energy, emotion etc
◷ Literally, to release steam from an engine into the air and thus reduce the pressure

run out of steam
informal to lose energy, or become exhausted
◷ Literally used of a steam engine

under one's own steam
informal by one's own efforts, without help from others

steer

steer clear of someone or **something**
to avoid them

stem

from stem to stern
absolutely everywhere, completely
• *We searched the house from stem to stern for the lost watch*
◷ A reference to the front and back of a ship

stem the tide of something *see* **tide**

step

a false step *see* **false**

in, out of step with someone
able, unable to share their interests and attitudes

one step forwards, two steps back/ backwards
an expression indicating the negative nature of progress with regard to a project
• *We are not getting on very well with our request for planning permission. It's a case of one step forwards, two steps back*
◷ A reference to the title of a book by Lenin (1904)

step by step
gradually

step down
informal to give up a position, advantage etc in order to let someone else have it
• *Mr Grant, our chairman, has decided that it is time he stepped down in favour of a younger man*

step in
to intervene

step on it
informal to hurry
◷ Originally, to drive a car faster by pressing harder on the accelerator pedal

step out of line *see* **line**

step something up
to increase something, especially to raise it to a higher level
• *The firm must step up production this year*

take steps
to take action

watch one's step
to behave with care and caution so as not to make mistakes

stew

be, get in a stew
to be or become very anxious and worried

stew in one's own juice *see* **juice**

stick

the big stick
informal control or power based on the threat of punishment

get (hold of) the wrong end of the stick
to misunderstand a situation, something said etc

give someone stick
informal to punish, criticize or scold them
• *The Prime Minister got a lot of stick from Opposition MPs over the Government's failure to reduce unemployment*

in a cleft stick *see* **cleft**

stick around
slang to remain in a place, usually in the hope of some future advantage etc

stick at something
to hesitate, or refuse, eg to do especially something wrong

stick by someone
informal to support or be loyal to a person

a stick-in-the-mud
informal derogatory a person who can never be persuaded to do anything new

stick in someone's throat *see* **throat**

stick it out
informal to endure a situation for as long as necessary

stick one's neck out *see* **neck**

stick one's oar in *see* **oar**

stick out a mile *see* **mile**

stick out for something
informal to refuse to accept less than something

stick out like a sore thumb *see* **sore**

stick to one's guns *see* **gun**

stick up for someone
to speak in defence of a person etc

sticky

come to a sticky end
informal to have an unpleasant death or to end a period of one's life in an unpleasant way

on a sticky wicket
in difficult circumstances, especially in a position where one's actions may be illegal, immoral etc
① A cricketing idiom — *sticky* here meaning 'muddy'

sticky-fingered
derogatory informal in the habit of stealing things

stiff

as stiff as a board *see* **board**

as stiff as a poker *see* **poker**

bore, scare someone stiff
informal to bore or frighten a person very much
• *His driving scares me stiff; I was bored stiff at the lecture*

keep a stiff upper lip *see* **lip**

still

a still small voice *see* **voice**

still waters run deep *see* **water**

sting

take the sting out of something
to make a disappointment etc less painful

stink

like stink
slang very much; very strongly
• *You'll have to work like stink if you're going to win the prize!*

raise a stink
slang to cause trouble

stir

stir one's stumps *see* **stump**

stir up a hornet's nest *see* **hornet**

stitch

he etc **hasn't got a stitch on/isn't wearing a stitch**
informal he etc is completely naked

in stitches
informal laughing a great deal

a stitch in time saves nine
a proverb, meaning that one can save oneself a great deal of work by repairing something, putting something right etc as soon as the fault is noticed, and before it gets worse

stock

on the stocks
still being made, prepared, arranged etc
• *A new expansion plan for the car industry is now on the stocks*
Ⓞ Literally used of a ship, which is supported on *stocks* — a wooden framework — while being built

someone's stock-in-trade
the standard ideas, methods etc used by someone

stock up on something
to accumulate a supply of something

take stock
to form an opinion about a situation etc
• *He had no time to take stock of the situation*
Ⓞ Literally, 'to make a list of goods in stock'

stomach

have a strong stomach *see* **strong**

have no stomach for something
formal not to have any desire, enough courage etc for something
Ⓞ From the medieval belief that the stomach was the source of physical courage

turn someone's stomach
informal to make someone feel disgusted, sick or angry

stone

leave no stone unturned
to try every possible means

stone-cold sober
informal completely sober and not under the influence of alcohol

a stone's throw
a very short distance
• *They live only a stone's throw away from here*

stonewall
to obstruct or impede progress intentionally
Ⓞ A cricketing term for 'to play defensively'

stool

fall between two stools
to lose both of two possibilities by hesitating between them or trying to achieve both

a stool-pigeon
informal derogatory an informer or spy especially for the police
Ⓞ Originally US, a shooting term for a pigeon tied to a stool and used as a decoy

stop

come to a full stop
to stop completely
Ⓞ Literally, to arrive at the full stop at the end of a sentence

pull out all the stops
to act etc with as much energy, determination or emotion as possible
Ⓞ From the stops of an organ: pulling them all out makes the organ play at full volume

put a stop to something
to make sure that something does not continue

stop at nothing
to be willing to do anything unworthy, in order to get something
• *He'll stop at nothing to get what he wants*

stop dead
to stop completely

stop someone's mouth *see* **mouth**

stop off
informal to make a halt on a journey etc

stop over
informal to make a stay of a night or more during a journey

stop short of something
to be unwilling to go beyond a certain limit in one's conduct

storage

in/into cold storage
kept aside ready for use, but not used immediately

store

in store
coming in the future
• *There's trouble in store for her! If you've never been to York, that's a treat in store for you*

mind the store
to be in charge of the running of an organization, etc, often when the person who is usually in charge is temporarily absent
⏲ Originally US. *Store* literally means 'shop'

set great store by something
to value highly eg a person's approval, opinion etc

storm

any port in a storm *see* **port**

a storm in a teacup
a fuss made over an unimportant matter
⏲ The title of a farce written by William Bernard in 1854

a stormy petrel
someone whose presence indicates that there is likely to be some kind of trouble in the near future
⏲ A reference to a small bird that lives in areas where storms are common

take someone or **something by storm**
to impress someone or something greatly and immediately
⏲ Literally a military term, to capture a fort etc by making a sudden violent attack

weather the storm
to survive a difficult time

story

cut a long story short
to describe something etc briefly

the same old story
something that happens or has happened in the same way often

the story goes (that)
people say that

a success story *see* **success**

a tall story *see* **tall**

straight

get something straight
to get the facts right, so that a situation is fully understood
• *Let's get this straight — you gave her the message, but she forgot to give it to me*

go straight
informal of a former criminal, to lead an honest life

set the record straight *see* **record**

(on) the straight and narrow (path)
leading a good and admirable way of life
⏲ A variation on a Biblical reference, Matthew 7:4: 'Strait is the gate, and narrow is the way, which leadeth unto life'

straight away
immediately

straight from the horse's mouth *see* **horse**

straight from the shoulder *see* **shoulder**

straight off
informal without deliberation
• *I knew straight off that she was telling a lie*

straight out
informal frankly, directly
• *I told her straight out that she was talking nonsense*

straight talking
frank and honest conversation
⏲ From the idea that *straight*, like *level* and *square*, implies rightness and fairness

strait

strait-laced
derogatory strict and severe in attitude and behaviour
⏲ Literally, having one's corset laced up very tightly

strange

strange bedfellows
two people or things which are closely associated with each other in one area of activity although being completely dissimilar in most ways

strangely enough
it is strange that

strange to say/tell/relate
surprisingly

stranger

be no stranger to something
literary or formal to have had experience of a condition, quality etc
- *He is no stranger to misfortune*

straw

clutch at straws
to hope that something may happen to help one in a difficult, dangerous situation etc when this is extremely unlikely

the last straw *see* **last**

a man of straw *see* **man**

a straw in the wind
a small incident etc that shows what kind of thing may happen in the future

a straw poll
a vote taken unofficially, eg within a trade union, to get some idea of the general opinion

the straw that breaks the camel's back *see* **the last straw,** *at* **last**

streak

be on a winning streak
to have a series of successes in gambling etc

street

be on the street
informal to be homeless

be streets ahead of someone or **something**
informal to be much better than someone or something

be (right) up someone's street
informal to be exactly suitable for a person

go on the streets
slang to become a prostitute

in Queer Street *see* **queer**

the man in the street *see* **man**

not to be in the same street as someone or **something**
to be completely different, usually worse, in quality than someone or something

strength

go from strength to strength
to move forward successfully from one achievement, triumph etc to another

in strength
in large numbers

on the strength
informal included as a member of a staff, group etc

on the strength of something
relying on something

a tower of strength *see* **tower**

stretch

at a stretch
continuously
- *He can't work for more than three hours at a stretch*

at full stretch
using all one's powers, energy etc to the limit in doing something

stretch a point
to go further, in giving permission, than the rules allow

stretch one's legs
informal to go for a walk for the sake of exercise

stride

get into/hit one's stride
to reach one's normal or expected level of skill or success at something
ⓘ An idiom from running

make great strides
to progress well

take something in one's stride
to accept or cope with a matter successfully without worrying about it
ⓘ Literally used of a horse, runner etc jumping an obstacle without altering stride to do so

strike

strike a bad patch *see* **patch**

strike a balance
to find an acceptable and satisfactory compromise between two extremes

strike a bargain/an agreement
to make a bargain; to reach an agreement

strike a chord *see* **chord**

strike an attitude/pose
to place oneself in a particular usually rather showy pose, as an actor does, or to express an opinion etc strongly and usually insincerely

strike fear/terror etc **into someone**
to fill a person with fear etc
• *The sound struck terror into them/their hearts*

strike it rich *see* **rich**

strike (it) lucky *see* **lucky**

strike someone off
to remove or erase, eg a doctor's name, from a professional register etc for misconduct

strike oil *see* **oil**

strike terror into someone *see* **strike fear into someone,** *above*

strike the right note *see* **note**

strike up
1 to begin to play a tune etc
• *The band struck up with 'The Red Flag'*
2 to begin a friendship, conversation etc
• *He struck up an acquaintance with a girl on the train*
ⓘ The first meaning is the original one

strike while the iron is hot *see* **iron**

striking

come, be within striking distance of something
to get or have got reasonably close to something or doing something

string

have more than one string to one's bow *see* **bow**[2]

have someone on a string
informal to have a person under one's control

hold the purse strings
to control the spending of money, to be in charge of the budget of an organization or household

pull strings
informal to use one's influence or that of others to gain an advantage

pull the strings
informal to be the person who is really, though usually not apparently, controlling the actions of others
ⓘ The image is of manipulating a puppet

string someone along
slang to keep a person attached to oneself without being seriously committed to him/her

string someone up
slang to hang them

strung up
informal very nervous

with no strings attached
informal without any conditions being made

strip

strip off
informal to remove one's clothes

tear a strip off someone/tear someone off a strip
informal to rebuke a person very angrily

stroke

at a stroke
with a single effort

different strokes for different folks *see* **different**

on the stroke of (a time)
punctually at a time
ⓘ From the striking of a clock

put someone off his etc **stroke**
to make it impossible for someone to proceed smoothly with what they are doing
ⓘ A rowing idiom — to upset the rhythm with which a rower is completing each stroke

strong

be still going strong
informal to continue to be successful, healthy etc

be someone's strong suit
formal to be the thing in which they are expert or excel
ⓘ An idiom from card games

have a strong stomach
to be not easily made sick or disgusted

strong-arm methods/tactics
the use of violent methods to solve a problem etc

Ⓞ Originally US

strong language
formal or facetious swearing or abuse

someone's strong point
a quality etc in which someone excels

stubborn
as stubborn as a mule *see* **mule**

stuck
get stuck in
slang
1 to start working hard at a job etc
2 to start eating

stuck for something
informal unable to go on doing something because of the lack of something

stuck on something or **someone**
informal very fond of someone or something

stuck with something
informal unable to escape from or avoid a burden, task etc

stuff
a bit of stuff
derogatory slang a girl or woman

do one's stuff
informal to perform in the expected way, or show what one can do

get stuffed!
impolite slang an angry expression rejecting or dismissing someone or their opinions, requests etc

the green stuff *see* **green**

the hard stuff
informal spirits, such as whisky

hot stuff *see* **hot**

kid's stuff *see* **kid**

know one's stuff
informal to have skill and knowledge in one's chosen subject, job etc

stuff and nonsense!
slightly derogatory that's nonsense!

a stuffed shirt
derogatory informal a pompous person
Ⓞ Literally, a dummy

that's the stuff
informal that's just what is wanted
Ⓞ *Originally US, probably popularized in Britain as used in the song 'Boiled Beef an' Carrots' (c.1910)*

stuffing
knock the stuffing out of someone
informal to make them weak, less strong etc
Ⓞ From stuffed toys

stumbling
a stumbling-block
a difficulty that prevents progress
Ⓞ A Biblical reference, Romans 14:13

stump
on the stump
slang taking part in a political speech-making tour or campaign
Ⓞ Originally US, from the use of tree-stumps as impromptu platforms

stir one's stumps
informal to start moving
Ⓞ *Stumps* here = legs

stump up
informal to pay a sum of money, often unwillingly

style
cramp someone's style
usually facetious to prevent them from showing their ability to the full

do something, live etc **in style**
to do something, or live, in a luxurious, elegant way without worrying about the expense

subject
be subject to something
1 to be liable to or likely to suffer from, or have a tendency towards something
• *The programme is subject to alteration*
2 to depend on something
• *These plans are subject to your approval*

change the subject
to start talking about something different

success
nothing succeeds like success
a proverb indicating that someone who

has already achieved a degree of success is more likely to be successful than other people

a success story
the story of someone's rise to fame, wealth etc

such

such-and-such
used in discussing unreal or hypothetical situations, to refer to an unnamed person or thing
• *Let's suppose that you go into such-and-such a shop and ask for such-and-such*

such as it is, they are
ironic though it hardly deserves the name
• *You can borrow our lawnmower, such as it is*

suck

suck up to someone
derogatory informal: especially used by schoolchildren to try to gain a person's favour by flattery etc

sudden

all of a sudden
suddenly or unexpectedly

suffer

suffer fools gladly
usually in negative to be sympathetic and patient with foolish people
Ⓞ A Biblical reference, II Corinthians 11:19

sufferance

on sufferance
formal with permission but without welcome

suffice

suffice it to say
formal I need only say
• *Suffice it to say that the manager is on the whole pleased with the work*

sugar

a sugar daddy
derogatory slang an elderly man who has a young girlfriend to whom he gives generous presents

sugar the pill
to make an unpleasant experience as pleasant as possible

suit

be someone's strong suit *see* **strong**

follow suit *see* **follow**

suit one's actions to one's words
literary or formal to do immediately what one is promising or threatening to do

suit someone down to the ground *see* **ground**

suit oneself
informal to do what one wants to do, without considering other people etc

sum

the sum total
the complete or final total

summer

an Indian summer *see* **Indian**

one swallow doesn't make a summer *see* **swallow**[1]

sun

catch the sun
informal to become sunburnt

make hay while the sun shines *see* **hay**

a place in the sun
a highly advantageous position
Ⓞ Originated by French philosopher Blaise Pascal (1660) but popularized around the beginning of the twentieth century as a description of Germany's territorial ambitions

under the sun
informal in the whole world

Sunday

a month of Sundays *see* **month**

someone's Sunday best
the smart, formal garments that a person wears for going to church or for other special occasions

sundry

all and sundry
everybody

sunk

sunk *see* **sink**

sunset

ride off into the sunset *see* **ride**

supper

sing for one's supper
to do something, such as work, in return for one's food, entertainment or other service

supply

be in short supply
of goods etc, to be scarce

sure

as sure as eggs is eggs *see* **egg**

be/feel sure of oneself
to be confident

be sure to/and
informal don't fail to do something etc

for sure
definitely or certainly

make sure
to act so that, or check that, something is certain or sure

sure enough
in fact, as was expected

to be sure
old or dialect certainly; of course

surface

scratch the surface
only to deal with a very small part of a subject, problem etc

surprise

take someone by surprise
to catch them unawares
🕔 Literally a military term — to capture a fort etc by a sudden, unexpected attack

(much, greatly etc) to someone's surprise
causing someone great surprise

suspense

the suspense is killing me, etc
I etc cannot wait to know the result or outcome of something

survival

the survival of the fittest
the ability of people who are very strong, talented, etc to succeed in situations where weaker people fail
• *The university course is extremely difficult — it will be a case of the survival of the fittest*

suspicion

be above suspicion
formal to be too highly respected ever to arouse suspicion

swallow[1]

one swallow doesn't make a summer
a proverb, meaning that one should not be too quick to assume that a single success, opinion etc indicates that the success, opinion etc will be general
🕔 From the fact that swallows arrive in Britain at the beginning of summer

swallow[2]

swallow one's pride *see* **pride**

swan

swan around/off
informal derogatory to wander about or go travelling in a leisurely and rather irresponsible way

someone's swan song
formal or facetious the last work or performance of eg a poet, musician etc before his death or retirement
🕔 From the ancient legend that the swan, which is usually silent, sings only once in its life, as it is dying

sway

hold sway
formal to have control or influence; to rule

swear

swear by something
informal to put complete trust in a certain remedy etc
🕔 Literally, to use the name of something as an oath

swear someone in
to introduce a person into a post or office formally, by making them swear an oath
• *The new Governor is being sworn in next week*

swear like a trooper *see* **trooper**

sweat

a cold sweat
coldness and dampness of the skin

when a person is in a state of shock, fear etc

no sweat
slang no trouble
Ⓣ Originally US

sweat blood
informal to work hard; to use a great deal of effort

sweat it out
informal to endure or bear a difficult or unpleasant situation

sweat like a pig *see* **pig**

the sweat of one's brow
often facetious one's effort and hard work

sweep

make a clean sweep *see* **clean**

sweep someone off his etc **feet** *see* **feet**

sweep something under the carpet *see* **carpet**

sweet

have a sweet tooth
informal to like sweet things to eat

sweet nothings
rather old loving but unimportant things whispered to someone attractive of the opposite sex

the sweets of something
literary the delights of eg life, success etc

sweetness

be (all) sweetness and light
to appear to be gentle and reasonable

swim

be in the swim
informal to be involved in, or aware of, the latest fashion or trend of affairs, business etc

out of the swim of things
no longer playing a major part in an activity or organization

swim with the tide
to follow the opinions, attitudes or actions of the majority of people rather than think for oneself

swing

get into the swing (of things)
informal to begin to understand, and fit into, a routine or rhythm of work etc

in full swing
going ahead, or continuing, busily or vigorously

room to swing a cat *see* **cat**

the swing of the pendulum *see* **pendulum**

swing the lead *see* **lead**[2]

what you win on the swings you lose on the roundabouts
a saying, meaning that a gain in one place is usually cancelled out by a loss in another
Ⓣ The reference is to a fairground

switch

be switched on
slang
1 to be aware of and in sympathy with all the activities and developments that are up to date and fashionable
2 to take drugs for stimulation; to be under the influence of such drugs

switch over
to cause to change

swollen

swollen-headed
derogatory too pleased with oneself; conceited

swoop

at one fell swoop
all at the same time; in a single movement or action
Ⓣ A Shakespearian quotation, from *Macbeth* IV, iii. The reference is to a hawk swooping on its prey

sword

beat swords into ploughshares
to make peace after a period of war
Ⓣ A Biblical reference, to Isaiah 2:4

cross swords
to quarrel or disagree
Ⓣ From fencing

the sword of Damocles
a disaster which may happen at any moment
Ⓣ From the story of Damocles, who was forced by Dionysius of Syracuse to sit through a banquet with a sword suspended over him held up only by a single hair

symbol

a status symbol *see* **status**

system

all systems go

everything is active and functioning properly

ⓘ A phrase used by the controllers of a space flight to indicate that everything is ready for the spacecraft to be launched

get something out of one's system

to deal with a preoccupation or anxiety by acting on it or by expressing one's feelings about it

ⓘ A medical reference

T

T

to a T
informal exactly; very well
• *This job suits me to a T*
Ⓞ Origin obscure — possibly from *to a title* = to the last dot in writing etc

tab

keep tabs on someone or **something**
to keep a check on someone or something; to watch someone or something
Ⓞ Originally US, from an American use of *tab* to mean 'account'

pick up the tab
US informal to pay the bill for something
Ⓞ As previous idiom

table

drink someone under the table
informal to remain conscious after having drunk an amount of alcohol that makes someone else unconscious

turn the tables on someone
to reverse a situation etc and put someone in a totally different position, especially one where he has lost his previous advantage
Ⓞ From the medieval game of *tables* — of which backgammon is a form — in which turning the board round would exactly reverse the position of the players

tag

tag along
informal: sometimes derogatory to follow or go with someone, often when one is not wanted

tail

a case of the tail wagging the dog *see* **case**

tail-end Charlie
informal someone who is last in a competition, series or group of people etc
Ⓞ RAF slang for the rear-gunner in an aircraft and hence for the last aircraft in a group

with one's tail between one's legs
in a very miserable and ashamed manner
Ⓞ From the behaviour of an unhappy dog

take

be taken with something
informal to find it pleasing or attractive

take a back seat *see* **back**

take after someone
informal to be like someone, especially a parent or relation, in appearance or character

take something as gospel *see* **gospel**

take something as read *see* **read**

take one's cue from someone *see* **cue**

take someone for someone or **something**
to believe mistakenly that someone is someone or something else
• *I took you for your brother; I took him for an intelligent person*

take someone for a ride *see* **ride**

take heart *see* **heart**

take someone in
informal to deceive or cheat them

take it (*with* **can/could**)
to be able to bear suffering, trouble, difficulty etc
• *Tell me the bad news. Don't worry, I can take it*

take it easy *see* **easy**

take it from me (that)
you can believe me when I say that

take it from there
informal to deal with events as they happen, not following any plan of action
• *I think we should offer him the job and take it from there*

take it or leave it
to accept something or refuse to accept it, without trying to alter what one is being offered

take something on the chin *see* **chin**

take it out of someone
informal to tire or exhaust them

take it out on someone
informal to be angry with or unpleasant to someone because one is angry, disappointed etc oneself

take someone's mind off *see* **mind**

take off
informal to begin suddenly to improve or get bigger
Ⓛ From the launching of rockets

take someone off
informal to imitate someone, often unkindly
• *He used to take off his teacher to make his friends laugh*

take place *see* **place**

take someone's place *see* **place**

take sides *see* **side**

take steps *see* **step**

take the edge off something *see* **edge**

take the floor *see* **floor**

take the place of *see* **place**

take the risk *see* **risk**

take one's time *see* **time**

take up arms *see* **arm**

take someone up on something
informal to accept their offer etc

take something upon oneself
to take responsibility for something

take up the cudgels *see* **cudgel**

take up with someone
informal to become friendly with or associate with them

take something up with someone
formal to discuss with them (especially a complaint)

tale

an old wives' tale
a story or statement which is based on folklore, superstition, etc

tell its own tale
to show clearly what has happened

tell tales/tell tales out of school
derogatory to give away secret or private information about the, usually wrong, actions of others

thereby hangs a tale
there is a story connected with that which could be told
Ⓛ A pun on *tail*, a favourite of Shakespeare's which appears in several of his plays

talk

money talks *see* **money**

talk about something
this is an excellent example of something
• *Talk about bad manners! She left the party without saying a word to the hostess!*

talk back to someone
derogatory to answer them rudely

talk big
informal to talk as if one is very important; to boast

talk down to someone
to speak to them as if they are much less important, clever etc

talk one's head off
to talk a great deal

talk someone into, out of doing something
to persuade them to do, not to do something

talk nineteen to the dozen *see* **dozen**

the talk of the town
someone or something that everyone in society is talking about

talk something over
to discuss it

talk someone round
to persuade them

talk shop *see* **shop**

talk through one's hat *see* **hat**

talk through the back of one's head/neck *see* **back**

talk turkey *see* **turkey**

talking

now you're talking
informal at last you are saying something important or to the point

straight talking *see* **straight**

talking of something
informal while we are on the subject of something

a talking-shop
derogatory informal a place or meeting where things are discussed but no action is ever decided on or taken

tall

a tall order
something very difficult to do
ⓘ Originally US, from a slang use of *tall* = large

a tall story
a story which is hard to believe
ⓘ Originally US

tan

tan someone's hide *see* **hide**

tangent

go off at a tangent
to go off suddenly in another direction or on a different line of thought, action etc
ⓘ A *tangent* is a line which touches a curve at one end — the reference is to something which is rotating in a circle round a point and which suddenly breaks loose and flies out of the circle into space

tango

it takes two to tango *see* **two**

tap

on tap
ready for immediate use
ⓘ Literally used of beer etc which is in a cask fitted with a tap and thus ready to be drawn off as required

tape

have someone or **something taped**
1 to understand something, especially a person's character and abilities, very clearly
2 to have got a matter arranged as one wants
ⓘ The implication is probably 'measured with a tape'

red tape *see* **red**

tar

be tarred with the same brush
to have the same faults as someone else
ⓘ From the use of tar to cover sores on sheep, especially considered as members of a flock

spoil the ship for a ha'porth of tar *see* **ship**

target

a sitting target *see* **sitting**

tart

tart someone or **something up**
derogatory slang to make a person, thing etc more attractive, especially in a showy or tasteless way

task

take someone to task
formal to blame or criticize a person
• *She took him to task for his rudeness to her mother*
ⓘ Literally, 'to accept, the correction of someone etc, as one's allotted task'

taste

to taste
used in recipes etc, in whatever quantity is desired
• *Add salt and pepper to taste*

to one's taste
in a way that is pleasing to one

tea

someone's cup of tea *see* **cup**

not for all the tea in China
certainly not; not at all
ⓘ From the fact that for a long time China was the source of all the world's tea

teacup

a storm in a teacup *see* **storm**

teach

teach one's grandmother to suck eggs *see* **egg**

I, that etc **will teach someone to be, do** etc (*something bad*)

I, that etc will punish a person, or be a person's punishment, for doing something bad
• *I'll teach you to be rude to me!; That'll teach you to disobey me*

you can't teach an old dog new tricks
a proverb indicating that it is difficult for people who have held certain attitudes, opinions, etc for a long time, or have been doing something in the same way for a long time, to adapt to change

tear[1]

tear a strip off someone *see* **strip**

tear one's hair *see* **hair**

tear[2]

crocodile tears *see* **crocodile**

teeth

armed to the teeth
old or facetious carrying all the weapons, armour, equipment etc possible for a fight or struggle
ⓘ A medieval idiom

by the skin of one's teeth *see* **skin**

cut one's teeth on something
to get valuable experience from something
ⓘ Literally, of a child, to use something to chew on in order to help new teeth to break through the gum

draw the teeth of someone or **something**
to make someone or something no longer dangerous, especially to oneself
ⓘ Literally, to remove an animal's teeth

fed to the back teeth *see* **fed**

get one's teeth into something
to tackle something serious in a determined manner

gnash one's teeth
rather facetious to be angry and disappointed
ⓘ A Biblical reference, to Matthew 8:12

grit one's teeth
to try not to show one's feelings

in the teeth of something
formal against or in opposition to something

lie in one's teeth *see* **lie[1]**

set someone's teeth on edge
to cause them to experience an unpleasant feeling of discomfort etc
• *That shrill bell set everyone's teeth on edge*

show one's teeth
to show one's anger and power to resist; to act decisively etc

teething

teething troubles
problems experienced at the beginning of a new plan, operation etc
ⓘ From the fact that a baby is often unwell and uncomfortable for a short time very early in its life while its teeth are developing

tell

all told
rather formal altogether; including everything or everyone
• *There was an audience of nine all told*
ⓘ *Told* here means 'counted'

I told you so
I told or warned you that this would happen, had happened etc, and I was right

tell its own tale *see* **tale**

tell someone off
informal to scold them
ⓘ Probably from the older meaning, 'to separate or detach from others for a purpose', and its use in the army

tell on someone
informal
1 to have a bad effect on
2 to give information about a person, usually if they are doing something wrong

tell tales *see* **tale**

tell that to the marines *see* **marine**

tell someone where to get off *see* **get**

to tell the truth *see* **truth**

you never can tell
it is possible

you're telling me!
informal certainly; that is definitely true
• *'It's cold today.' 'You're telling me it is!'*
ⓘ Originally US, probably from Yiddish idiom

telling

take a telling
not to do what one is told, warned etc not to do

there's no telling
it is impossible to know

temper

keep, lose one's temper
not to show, to show, anger

tempt

tempt fate *see* **fate**

tender

leave someone to someone's tender mercies
to leave someone to be dealt with by someone hostile, unattractive, inefficient etc
Ⓛ A Biblical reference, to Psalm 25:6

tenterhooks

be on tenterhooks
informal to be uncertain and anxious about what is going to happen
Ⓛ *Tenterhooks* were hooks for stretching newly-woven cloth on a frame or *tenter* — the idiom thus means 'very tense or tightly-stretched'

term

be on speaking terms *see* **speaking**

come to terms with something
to find a way of living with or tolerating some personal trouble or difficulty
Ⓛ A phrase from diplomacy — 'to reach an agreement with'

in terms of something
using something as a terminology, a means of expression, a means of assessing value etc
• *He thought of everything in terms of money; Give the answer in terms of a percentage*

terror

strike terror into someone *see* **strike**

test

put someone or **something to the test**
to test someone or something

tether

at the end of one's tether *see* **end**

thank

be thankful for small mercies *see* **mercy**

have only oneself to thank for something
to be the cause of something unfortunate which has happened to one

I'll thank you etc **to do something**
impolite please do something, used to indicate that the speaker is angry
• *From now on I'll thank you to keep your nose out of my business!*

no thanks to
informal in spite of a person's help, lack of help etc

thank one's lucky stars *see* **lucky**

thanks to
because of

thank you for nothing
informal, ironic an expression indicating that the speaker is not pleased by the information he has been given, the job he has been asked to do etc

a vote of thanks *see* **vote**

that

and all that
informal and all the rest of that kind of thing
• *He said he was sorry and didn't want to hurt anyone, and all that, but I didn't think he really meant it*

at that
in addition; when everything has been considered
• *He's a novelist, and a good one at that; It wasn't such a bad idea at that, but it didn't work*

(just) like that
informal immediately, without further thought, discussion etc

that's/there's a (good) boy, girl, dog etc
informal an expression used to praise or encourage a child, animal etc

that's that
an expression used to show that a decision has been made, that something has been completed, made impossible etc

- *He has said that we can't do it, so that's that*

then

then and there/there and then
informal at that very time or moment

there

so there
informal an expression used, especially by children, to indicate that the speaker thinks he has an advantage of some kind over the person he is speaking to and wishes to make it obvious
- *The teacher says my spelling is better than yours, so there*

there and then *see* **then**

there's a (good) boy, girl, dog etc *see* **that**

there you are
1 used to express satisfaction when something one said would happen does happen
- *There you are! I told you you would fall in!*

2 used to indicate that something is a feature of life that cannot be changed
- *We can't really afford to run a car, but there you are — when you live in the country, you need one*

thick

as thick as thieves
informal very friendly

as thick as two short planks *see* **plank**

a bit thick
informal more than a person can tolerate; not just or fair

give someone a thick ear
to strike a child etc on the ear, usually as a punishment

lay it on thick
to go beyond the truth in what one is saying, especially in praising something

the plot thickens *see* **plot**

thick and fast
frequently and in large numbers

thick-skinned
not easily hurt by criticism or insults

through thick and thin
informal whatever happens; in spite of all difficulties
Ⓞ An idiom from hunting — the reference is to thick and thin vegetation

thief

a den of thieves
a place, organization or group of people who are thought to be dishonest or have criminal tendencies

as thick as thieves *see* **thick**

procrastination is the thief of time *see* **procrastination**

set a thief to catch a thief
a saying, meaning that the best way to outwit a deceitful person is to employ another deceitful person to do it

thin

as thin as a rake *see* **rake**

be thin on top
informal to be becoming bald

on thin ice *see* **ice**

thin air
nowhere
Ⓞ A Shakespearian quotation, from *The Tempest* IV, i

the thin end of the wedge *see* **wedge**

thin on the ground
rare

thin-skinned
sensitive; easily hurt or upset

a thin time
informal a difficult or not very pleasant time, eg because of a lack of money

thing

all things being equal
if none of the other facts of the matter make/made any difference

be all things to all men
slightly derogatory to be able to fit in with the attitudes etc of whoever one is with, especially by constantly changing one's opinions to agree with one's companions
Ⓞ A Biblical reference, to I Corinthians 9:22

do one's (own) thing
slang to behave in a way which is natural to one or to do something which one is good at

first thing *see* **first**

for one thing
used to introduce the first reason for not doing something

have a thing about something or **someone**
informal to be especially fond of, keen on, annoyed by, frightened by something or someone etc
• *I've got a thing about men in uniforms; She's got a thing about spiders*

hear things *see* **see things,** *below*

know a thing or two
informal to be wise and show good practical judgement

make a thing of something
informal to make a fuss about something

a near thing *see* **near**

no such thing
1 something quite different
• *He said he was a lawyer, but he turned out to be no such thing*
2 no, not at all
• *I expected him to be waiting for us, but no such thing — he'd gone*

not to know the first thing about *see* **first**

(just) one of those things
something that must be accepted

a poor thing but mine own *see* **poor**

see, hear things
to see or hear something that is not there

a stupid, wise etc **thing to do**
a stupid, wise etc action

a thing of beauty is a joy forever
now often ironic a saying indicating that something beautiful, such as a piece of furniture or a painting, will give pleasure for a very long time
Ⓞ A line from *Endymion* (1818), a poem by John Keats

the thing is ...
informal the important fact or question is; the problem is

the very thing *see* **very**

think

have (got) another think coming
derogatory informal to be mistaken in what one thinks

I should think so, not
that is, is not what one should do etc; certainly not
• *'I've come to apologize for being rude to you.' 'I should think so, too!'; 'I never drink when I'm going to be driving.' 'I should think not'*

not think much of *see* **think little of,** *below*

put on one's thinking cap
informal to think about, and try to solve, a problem etc

I etc **shouldn't think of**
I etc would certainly not want to (do something under consideration)
• *They said they wouldn't think of asking me to pay*

think better of someone or **something**
1 to think again and decide not to do something; to reconsider something
• *He was going to ask for more money, but he thought better of it*
2 to think that someone would not be so bad etc as to act in a certain way
• *I thought better of you than to suppose you would lie to me*

think little of/not think much of something
to have a very low opinion of something

think nothing of it *see* **nothing**

think something out
to plan something; to work something out in the mind
• *I haven't thought out the details of the operation yet*

think something over
to think about something carefully; to consider all aspects of an action, decision etc

think the world of *see* **world**

think twice *see* **twice**

think something up
to invent or devise something
• *He thought up a new way of making polythene*

third

give someone the third degree *see* **degree**

third time lucky
a saying, expressing the belief that one usually succeeds in something the third time one tries, and usually said to encourage a third attempt, as one begins a third attempt, or to draw attention to a success at the third attempt

thirty

thirty pieces of silver *see* **silver**

this

this and that/this, that and the other
various unimportant objects, actions etc

Thomas

a doubting Thomas *see* **doubting**

thorn

a thorn in someone's flesh/side
something or someone that continually irritates someone
ⓘ A Biblical reference, to II Corinthians 12:7

thought

food for thought *see* **food**

perish the thought *see* **perish**

second thoughts *see* **second**

train of thought *see* **train**

thrash

thrash something out
to discuss a problem etc thoroughly and solve it
ⓘ Literally, to separate the grains of corn from the stalk by threshing

thread

hang by a thread
to be in a very precarious, dangerous state
ⓘ Probably a reference to the story of Damocles — *see* **Sword of Damocles** at **sword**

lose the thread
to cease to understand the connection between the details of a story etc

pick up the threads of something
to continue to do something or be involved in something after a period of not so doing
• *After she recovered from her long illness she had to pick up the threads of her life again*
ⓘ A reference to weaving

three

the three Rs *see* **R**

a three-ring circus
a state of utter confusion
ⓘ A reference to a circus with three arenas in which performances are taking place simultaneously

three sheets to the wind
informal drunk, tipsy
ⓘ A nautical term. The sheet is the rope that holds the sail and if the sheets are allowed to flap freely the ship proceeds on an erratic course

thrill

thrilled to bits
very greatly delighted and excited

throat

at each other's throat
quarrelling violently
ⓘ The reference is to fighting dogs

cut one's own throat
to act in a way which damages oneself

have a frog in one's throat *see* **frog**

jump down someone's throat
informal to attack someone verbally in a violent way before they can explain themselves

ram something down someone's throat
derogatory informal to try to force someone to believe or accept a statement, idea etc, especially one they are unwilling to believe or accept

stick in someone's throat
informal to be impossible to believe, accept etc
ⓘ Literally, to be impossible to swallow

throe

in the throes of something
formal or facetious in the difficult process of

Ⓛ Literally, 'in labour' — the reference is to producing something new with difficulty and effort, but the emphasis has shifted from the creativity to the suffering involved

throne

the power behind the throne *see* **power**

through

fall through *see* **fall**

pull through *see* **pull**

see through *see* **see**

through and through
completely
• *He was a gentleman through and through*

through with someone or **something**
informal finished with someone or something
Ⓛ From US usage, although existent also in older and dialectal British English

throw

throw cold water on/over *see* **cold**

throw down the gauntlet *see* **gauntlet**

throw dust in someone's eyes *see* **dust**

throw good money after bad *see* **money**

throw something in
informal to include or add something as a gift or as part of a bargain
• *When I bought his car he threw in the radio and a box of tools*

throw in one's hand *see* **hand**

throw in the towel *see* **towel**

throw something off
to get rid of something
• *She finally managed to throw off her cold; They were following us, but we managed to throw them off*

throw someone over
informal to leave, abandon a girlfriend, boyfriend etc

throw out the baby with the bathwater *see* **baby**

throw the book at someone *see* **book**

throw someone to the lions *see* **lion**

throw up
informal
1 to vomit
2 to give up or abandon

throw up the sponge *see* **sponge**

throw one's weight about *see* **weight**

thumb

rule of thumb *see* **rule**

stick out like a sore thumb *see* **sore**

thumb a lift
to ask for or get a lift in someone's car etc by signalling to the driver with one's thumb

thumb one's nose at someone
to express defiance or contempt towards someone, originally by means of a rude gesture

thumbs down
a sign indicating disapproval or failure
Ⓛ From the signal made by a Roman crowd voting for the death of a gladiator, although the form of the signal was probably not as traditionally supposed

thumbs up
a sign indicating hope of, or wishes for, success
Ⓛ See **thumbs down**, *above*

twiddle one's thumbs
informal to do nothing
Ⓛ Literally, to rotate one's thumbs round each other, a pointless activity indicating boredom

under someone's thumb
controlled or greatly influenced by someone

thunder

steal someone's thunder
to prevent someone from receiving congratulations, getting publicity etc for something, by using it, making it public etc before they do
Ⓛ From an incident in the 17c theatre when a machine invented by the playwright John Dennis for simulating thunder on stage was pirated and used in a rival play

tick

on tick
Brit informal on credit, promising to pay later
Ⓛ From *on ticket* once being the usual

name for a formal acknowledgement of money owed

tick someone off/give someone a ticking-off
informal to scold someone, usually mildly
① Army slang

tick over
to run quietly and smoothly at a gentle pace
① Literally used of a car engine

ticket

just the ticket
slightly old, informal exactly right, ideal etc
① Possibly from the US use of this word to mean 'a party's list of candidates for an election'

a meal ticket *see* **meal**

tickle

be tickled pink, be tickled to death
informal to be very pleased by something

tickle someone's fancy
informal to attract someone mildly in some way

tide

a rising tide *see* **rise**

stem the tide of something
to stop the course or spread of something such as a trend, opinions, etc
• *The government tried to stem the tide of opposition against the bill*

tide someone over
informal to help someone for a time
① Literally, to carry someone over an obstacle, as the tide does

tie

be tied up
informal
1 to be busy; to be involved with
• *I can't come to the party this evening — I'm a bit tied up tonight; I can't discuss this matter just now —I'm tied up with other things*
2 connected with

tie someone down
1 to limit someone's freedom etc
2 to make someone come to a decision
• *He managed to tie them down to a definite date for the meeting*

tie (up) in knots *see* **knot**

tie in with something
informal to be linked or joined logically to something

tiger

have a tiger by the tail
to be involved in a situation that turns out to be extremely difficult or dangerous

paper tiger *see* **paper**

ride a tiger
to be in a very precarious or dangerous situation

tight

keep a tight rein on *see* **rein**

run a tight ship
to be in control of an efficient, well-run organization or group
① A nautical idiom

sit tight
informal to keep the same position or be unwilling to move or act

a tight corner/spot
a difficult position or situation

tighten one's belt *see* **belt**

tile

have a tile loose
informal to be a little mad
① The reference is to a roof

on the tiles
slang away from home drinking, dancing etc
① The reference appears to be to cats spending the night out on the roof

tilt

(at) full tilt
at full speed
① From the flat-out gallop at which knights competed in a joust or *tilt*

tilt at windmills *see* **windmill**

time

about time
not too soon; the correct time or rather late to do something

• *Here comes John — and about time too. I was beginning to think he was lost*

ahead of one's time
having ideas etc which are too advanced to be acceptable at the time

all in good time
soon enough

one, two etc **at a time**
singly, or in groups of two etc

at one time
at a time in the past

at the same time *see* **same**

behind the times
not modern; old-fashioned

bide one's time
to wait for a good opportunity
◷ *Bide* means literally 'to await'

the big time
slang the top level in any kind of activity
• *She was a struggling actress for many years before she finally made the big time*
◷ Originally US

do time
slang to be in prison

for the time being
meanwhile

from time immemorial *see* **immemorial**

from time to time
occasionally; sometimes

gain time
to cause something to be delayed in order to give oneself more time to do something else

half the time
informal frequently; very often
• *I hate going to parties — half the time I don't even know the host very well*

have a time of it
informal to have to deal with problems, difficulties etc

have no time for someone or **something**
to despise someone or something

have the time of one's life
informal to enjoy oneself very much

have time on one's hands
to have a great deal of spare time so that one is idle or bored

in good time
informal early enough; before a set time for an appointment etc

in someone's own good time
slightly derogatory at whatever time or however quickly is convenient to someone

in someone's own time
1 in someone's spare time, when not at work
2 at the speed which is natural to one

in the fullness of time *see* **full**

in the nick of time *see* **nick**

in one's time
at some past time in one's life, especially when one was at one's best

in time
early enough
• *He arrived in time for dinner; Are we in time to catch the train?*

keep time
of a clock etc, to show the time accurately

keep time with someone
to perform an action in the same rhythm as someone else

kill time
informal to find something to do to use up spare time, such as a period of waiting

live on borrowed time
to live longer than is expected or is thought likely
• *He has cancer and was given a few months to live a few years ago — he's living on borrowed time*

make good time
to travel as quickly or more quickly than one had expected or hoped

mark time
to allow time to pass without making any progress
◷ Literally, of soldiers, to move the feet up and down as if marching but without going forwards, in order to retain marching rhythm

move with the times
to adapt to changes in fashions, changing social attitudes and opinions, etc

not before time
informal not too soon; rather late

no time (at all)
informal a very short time indeed

an old timer *see* **old**

on time
at the right time

play for time
to delay an action, decision etc in the hope or belief that conditions will be better at a later time
⌚ Literally, to play a game, such as cricket, in such a way as to avoid defeat by playing defensively until the game ends

procrastination is the thief of time *see* **procrastination**

stand the test of time
to last or survive, to prove to be of lasting value
• *Their relationship has stood the test of time*

a stitch in time saves nine *see* **stitch**

take one's time
to do something as slowly as one wishes, often more slowly than someone else wishes
• *Take your time — there's no hurry; I wish he would hurry up — he's rather taking his time about making a decision*

there's no time like the present
a proverb, meaning that if an action has been decided on, it is best to do it immediately
⌚ A quotation from a play of c.1700

a thin time *see* **thin**

time and (time) again/time after time
again and again; repeatedly

time and tide wait for no man
a proverb meaning that life moves on without any delay for people to make decisions, plans etc and that therefore opportunities must be taken when they arise because they may not be available for long

time flies
a saying, meaning that time passes very quickly — usually expressing surprise at the amount of time that has passed without one noticing it
⌚ From the Latin *tempus fugit*, a quotation from one of Virgil's *Georgics*

time is getting on
informal time is passing; it is getting late

time is money
a saying indicating that spending an unnecessary amount of time in an activity, discussion, etc is expensive as either salaries have to be paid for the people involved or else they are losing money by being concerned with the activity or discussion instead of performing their usual paid tasks

time out of mind
formal during the whole time within human memory
⌚ A translation of **time immemorial**, *see* **immemorial**

time was
rather formal there was once a time when
• *Time was when I would have come sailing with you, but I'm too old now*

time will tell
a saying indicating that one will have to wait for some time to elapse before one can judge or see the effects of a situation
• *The drug may cure her illness — only time will tell*

tin

put the tin lid on something *see* **lid**

a tin god
derogatory informal a person who thinks he is very important and orders other people about

tinker

not to give a tinker's cuss/damn for something
informal not to care anything at all about something
⌚ It has been suggested that this phrase originated in a pun, from the fact that tinkers used a *dam* made from a pellet of bread to keep the solder from escaping while they mended a hole in a pan, and that the dam — which was worthless and expendable — was discarded when the repair was complete

tinkle

give someone a tinkle
Brit informal to call someone on the telephone

ⓘ A humorous variant of *give someone a ring* from the sound made by early telephone bells

tip

be on the tip of one's tongue
to be almost, but usually not, spoken or said
• *Her name is on the tip of my tongue (*= I can't quite remember it)*; It was on the tip of my tongue to tell him (*= I almost told him*)*

just/only the tip of the iceberg *see* **ice**

tip someone off
slang to give information or a hint to someone; to warn someone

tip the scales *see* **scales**

tip someone the wink *see* **wink**

tit

tit for tat
informal blow for blow; repayment of injury with injury
ⓘ This phrase may represent *tip for tap* — 'blow for blow', the Dutch *dit voor dat* — 'this for that', or the French *tant pour tant* — 'equal for equal'

to

to and fro
backwards and forwards

toing and froing
going backwards and forwards in an anxious way, or without apparently achieving anything

toast

as warm as toast
very warm

tod

on one's tod
informal alone
ⓘ From Cockney rhyming slang *on one's Tod Sloan* — on one's own. Tod Sloan was an American jockey

toe

be on one's toes
informal to be ready; to be prepared for action

toe the line
informal to act according to the rules

tread on someone's toes
informal to offend or upset someone

toffee

not for toffee
informal not at all
• *I can't sing for toffee*

token

by the same token
formal also; in addition

told

told *see* **tell**

Tom

any/every Tom, Dick or/and Harry
anybody at all
ⓘ From the fact that all three have always been common English names

a peeping Tom
derogatory a man who spends his time watching women who are naked, undressing etc, usually through the windows of their houses
ⓘ From the story of Lady Godiva, who is said to have ridden naked through the streets of Coventry in 1040 as part of a bargain made with her husband Leofric, Earl of Mercia, to persuade him to lift a tax he had imposed on his tenants. A late addition to the legend says that only one citizen of Coventry — 'Peeping Tom' — looked out to see her pass, and he was immediately struck blind

too

too many cooks spoil the broth *see* **cook**

too close for comfort *see* **close**[1]

tone

tone something down
to make something softer, less harsh etc
• *The painters added white to tone down the colour of the green paint*

tongue

be on the tip of one's tongue *see* **tip**

hold one's tongue
informal to remain silent or stop talking
ⓘ An idiom which existed in Old English

a sharp tongue *see* **sharp**

a slip of the tongue *see* **slip**

speak etc **with/have one's tongue in one's cheek**
to say something that one does not intend literally or seriously

tonight

not tonight, Josephine *see* **not**

tooth

be, get etc **long in the tooth**
informal of a person or animal, to be, become etc, old
Ⓛ From the receding gums of elderly horses and the practice of assessing the age of horses by examining their teeth

have a sweet tooth *see* **sweet**

tooth and nail
fiercely and with all one's strength
• *They fought tooth and nail*

top

at the top of one's voice *see* **voice**

be thin on top *see* **thin**

be top dog
informal to be the most important or powerful person
Ⓛ From the hierarchical structure of dog packs

blow one's top
informal to become very angry
Ⓛ Originally US. The reference is probably to an oil-well

off the top of one's head *see* **head**

on top of the world *see* **world**

out of the top drawer *see* **drawer**

over the top
informal too much, too strong or too great

sleep like a top
to sleep very soundly
Ⓛ A pun on the specialized meaning of *sleep* when applied to a top = 'to spin steadily without wobbling'

the top brass *see* **brass**

the top of the ladder/tree
informal the highest point in one's profession

top of the pops *see* **pop**

top something up
to fill a cup etc that has been partly emptied

torch

carry a/the torch for someone
to be in love with someone who does not appear to be in love with oneself
Ⓛ The reference is to love as a flame

torn

be torn between (one thing and another)
to have a very difficult choice to make between two things

that's torn it
informal that has spoilt everything!; that's most unfortunate!

toss

argue the toss
informal to dispute a decision
Ⓛ The image is of someone arguing about the result of having tossed a coin

it's a toss-up (whether)
informal it is a matter of uncertainty (whether)
Ⓛ Literally, as uncertain as tossing a coin

toss something off
informal
1 to drink something quickly
• *He tossed off a pint of beer*
2 to produce something quickly and easily
• *He tossed off a few verses of poetry*

toss up
informal to toss a coin to decide a matter

win, lose the toss
to guess rightly, or wrongly, which side of the coin will fall uppermost

touch

the common touch
the ability to get on well with a wide range of ordinary people

finishing touches *see* **finish**

in touch
in communication with; able to talk to

it's touch-and-go (whether)
it's very uncertain whether

lose touch
to stop communicating with

the Midas touch *see* **Midas**

out of touch
1 not in communication with
• *We have been out of touch for years*
2 not sympathetic or understanding towards
• *Older people sometimes seem out of touch with the modern world*

touch a chord *see* **chord**

touch down
of aircraft, to land

touch someone for something
informal to persuade someone to lend money

touch something off
to cause something to begin to happen vigorously
• *His remark touched off an argument*
Ⓛ Literally, to ignite gunpowder etc by touching with a flame

touch something up
to improve, eg paintwork, a photograph etc, by small touches

touch wood *see* **wood**

tough

a tough customer
informal a person who is difficult to deal with

tough luck
bad luck

tow

have someone in tow
informal to have someone in one's charge

towel

throw in the towel
informal to give up and admit defeat
Ⓛ From a method of conceding defeat in a boxing match

tower

an ivory tower *see* **ivory**

a tower of strength
someone who is a great help or encouragement
Ⓛ A Shakespearian metaphor, from *Richard III* V, iii

town

go out on the town
informal to have a good time eating, drinking, dancing etc

go to town
informal to do something very thoroughly or with great enthusiasm or expense
• *He really went to town on preparing the meal*
Ⓛ Originally US, probably implying that to go to town on some business was to take a great deal of trouble over it

paint the town *see* **paint**

the talk of the town *see* **talk**

track

be on someone's track/be on the track of someone or **something**
to be following, pursuing, or looking for someone or something

have a one-track mind *see* **one**

in one's tracks
informal where one stands or is
• *He stopped dead in his tracks*

keep, lose track of someone or **something**
informal to keep, not to keep, oneself informed about the progress or whereabouts of someone or something

make tracks (for)
informal to depart, or set off towards

on the right, wrong track
progressing in a way which is, is not, going to achieve what one wants; working, not working, correctly

on the wrong side of the tracks
on the poorer or less desirable part of a town or area
Ⓛ Originally US. When railways were built they often divided an area into two sharply divided districts

track someone or **something down**
to pursue or search for someone or something until it is caught or found
• *I managed to track down an old copy of the book*

someone's track record
the history of someone's success or lack of success in an activity, especially their job

Ⓞ From athletics

trade

trade something in
to give something as part-payment for something else
• *We decided to trade in our old car and get a new one*

trade on something
derogatory to take usually unfair advantage of something

trail

blaze a trail
formal to lead or show the way towards something new
Ⓞ Literally, to mark a trail by *blazing*, ie stripping sections of bark from trees

train

train of thought
a process of reasoning, a series of connected ideas
• *I lost my train of thought when someone asked an irrelevant question*

tread

tread on someone's corns *see* **corn**

tread on eggs *see* **egg**

tread on someone's toes *see* **toe**

tread water *see* **water**

tree

a family tree *see* **family**

not to be able to see the wood for the trees *see* **wood**

tremble

be/go in fear and trembling (of)
especially facetious to be very afraid
Ⓞ A Biblical reference, to Philippians 2:12

trial

trial and error
the trying of various methods, alternatives etc until the right one happens to appear or be found
Ⓞ The name of a method of solving mathematical problems

a trial run
a rehearsal, first test etc of anything, eg a play, car, piece of machinery etc

triangle

the eternal triangle *see* **eternal**

tribute

be a tribute to something
to be the praiseworthy result of

trice

in a trice
rather old in a very short time; almost immediately
Ⓞ From an old word meaning 'to tie up' — literally 'in the time taken to make a single tug'

trick

a bag of tricks *see* **bag**

a confidence trick *see* **confidence**

do the trick
informal to do or be what is necessary

how's tricks
slang how are you

never miss a trick
to be very alert and not to miss any opportunities to profit
Ⓞ From card games

a trick of the trade
sometimes derogatory one of the ways of being successful in a job etc

up to one's tricks
informal, often derogatory behaving in one's usual deceitful, amusing etc way

tried

tried and true
tested and found to be effective

trigger

trigger-happy
informal too ready or likely to use guns or general violence

trip

trip the light fantastic
now usually facetious to dance
Ⓞ A reference to a line from *Allegro* (1632) by John Milton — 'Come, and trip it as ye go, On the light fantasticic toe'

trolley

off one's trolley
slang insane, extremely foolish

trooper

swear like a trooper
derogatory to swear very often or very strongly
Ⓘ A trooper was an ordinary cavalry soldier

trot

on the trot
informal
1 one after the other
• *He ate four ice-creams on the trot*
2 continually moving about; busy

trot something out
derogatory, informal to bring something out, usually to show to someone
• *He is always trotting out the same excuses for being late*
Ⓘ Literally to make a horse trot that one is attempting to sell, in order to show how it moves

trouble

be asking for trouble *see* **ask**

fish in troubled waters *see* **fish**

trousers

wear the trousers
derogatory informal of a wife, to be the person who makes the decisions etc in her household

(be caught) with one's pants/trousers down *see* **pants**

trowel

lay it on with a trowel
informal to say very obviously flattering things
Ⓘ From a remark made by Charles Dickens

truck

have no truck with something
formal to have nothing to do with something; not to take part in something
Ⓘ From *truck* = bartering, ie business dealings

true

come true
of a dream, hope etc, to really happen

out of true
not straight or not properly positioned etc

ring true *see* **ring**

trump

play one's trump card
to use something powerful and influential which one has saved in order to use it when really necessary
Ⓘ From certain card games, in which a *trump* is a card of whichever suit has been declared to be the higher-ranking than any of the others for the purposes of the hand being played

turn up trumps
informal to behave or do one's work well when things are difficult, especially unexpectedly
Ⓘ As above — the reference is to drawing a trump from the pack in the course of one's turn

trumpet

blow one's own trumpet
informal to boast, praise oneself greatly etc
Ⓘ From the herald who formerly would announce the arrival of an important person with a fanfare on a trumpet

trust

take someone or **something on trust**
to accept or believe someone or something without checking

truth

be economical with the truth
a euphemism used to refer to someone who is not being completely honest about something
Ⓘ Popularized by, although not originated by, Sir Robert Armstrong, the British Cabinet Secretary, who used it when being cross-examined in the Supreme Court of New South Wales in 1986 when the British government were trying to prevent publication in Australia of a book about MI5, the British Secret Service, "Spycatcher" by Peter Wright

a home truth *see* **home**

the naked truth
the plain facts without any embellishment or any attempt to disguise the true nature of the facts

to tell the truth
informal really; actually

truth is stranger than fiction
a proverb indicating that facts are often more remarkable and less plausible than invented stories

truth will out
a saying, meaning that it is impossible to conceal the truth about something for ever

the unvarnished truth
same as **the naked truth**, *see above*

try

try one's hand at *see* **hand**

try it on
informal to attempt to do something; to indulge in a certain kind of behaviour etc in order to see whether it will be allowed

try something on
to put on clothes etc to see if they fit

try something out
to test something by using it
• *He tried out the bicycle; We are trying out new teaching methods*

try that on for size! *see* **size**

tuck

tuck in
informal to eat greedily or with enjoyment

tuck into something
informal to eat something eagerly

tug

tug at the heartstrings *see* **heartstring**

tumble

tumble to something
informal to understand or realize something suddenly

tune

call the tune
informal to be the person who gives the orders
ⓘ From the saying **he who pays the piper calls the tune** = the person who is paying has a right to choose what is done with his money — *see also* **pay the piper** at **piper**

change one's tune
informal to change one's attitude, opinion etc

dance to a different tune
to change one's attitude, opinion, or behaviour completely
ⓘ A reference to the necessity of changing dance steps to accord with a change of tune or rhythm

in tune with something or **someone**
agreeing or fitting in with something or someone
ⓘ A musical idiom — literally 'adjusted so as to be at the same pitch as'

to the tune of
informal amounting to the sum or total of

tune in
to tune a radio to a particular station or programme

turkey

cold turkey *see* **cold**

talk turkey
especially US to talk honestly and openly, especially about business
ⓘ Originally US, of unknown derivation

turn

at every turn
formal or literary everywhere, at every stage etc

do someone a good turn
to do something helpful for someone

done to a turn
informal cooked to exactly the right degree
ⓘ This phrase originally applied to meat roasted on a spit, and implied that if the spit had been turned once more the meat would have been overcooked

in turn/by turns
one after the other; in regular order

one good turn deserves another
a proverb indicating that if someone does one a favour or helps one in some way one should undertake a similar act in return

on the turn
informal
1 of the tide etc, in the process of turning
2 of milk etc, on the point of going sour

out of turn
out of the correct order or not at the correct time

serve its turn
to be useful or good enough to achieve a particular result, help to do a particular job etc

take a turn for the better, worse
of things or people, to become better, or worse

take turns
of two or more people, to do something one after the other, not at the same time
• *We took turns at pushing the pram*

turn a blind eye to *see* **eye**

turn (and turn) about
one after the other, each taking his turn

turn against someone or **something**
to become dissatisfied with or hostile to people or things that one previously liked etc

turn an honest penny *see* **penny**

turn one's coat *see* **coat**

turn something down
to say 'no' to something; to refuse something
• *He turned down her offer/request*
Ⓞ Originally US slang

turn one's hand to *see* **hand**

turn someone's head *see* **head**

turn in
informal
1 *Brit* to go to bed
2 to hand over a person or thing to people in authority
• *They turned the escaped prisoner in to the police*

turn in one's grave *see* **grave**

turn someone off
slang to create feelings of dislike, repulsion, disgust etc in someone

turn of phrase
a way of expressing things

a turn of speed
an ability to move fast for a short period

the turn of the month, year, century
the end of one month or year or century and the beginning of the next

turn someone on
slang to create feelings of excitement, interest, lust, pleasure etc in someone

turn on one's heel *see* **heel**

turn on the heat *see* **heat**

turn out
1 of a crowd, to come out; to get together for a public meeting, celebration etc
2 to happen or prove to be

turn over a new leaf *see* **leaf**

turn someone's stomach *see* **stomach**

turn tail
to run or walk away

turn the corner *see* **corner**

turn the other cheek *see* **cheek**

turn the scales at *see* **scales**

turn the tables *see* **table**

turn to (good) account *see* **account**

turn turtle *see* **turtle**

turn up
informal
1 to appear or arrive
2 to be found
3 to discover facts etc
• *The police have apparently turned up some new evidence*

a turn-up for the book(s)
informal something which happens unexpectedly
Ⓞ 19c racing slang

turn up one's nose (at) *see* **nose**

turn up trumps *see* **trump**

a U-turn *see* **U**

turtle

turn turtle
of a boat etc, to turn upside down; to capsize
Ⓞ Literally, to make a turtle easy to kill by turning it on its back

twice

think twice
to be very careful about considering doing something
• *We thought twice about travelling in bad weather; I wouldn't think twice about sacking him*

twiddle
twiddle one's thumbs *see* **thumb**

twinkle
in the twinkling of an eye/in a twinkling
in a moment; immediately
◷ A Biblical image, from I Corinthians 15:51

twist
get one's knickers in a twist *see* **knickers**

round the twist
slang slightly mad

twist someone's arm *see* **arm**

twist someone round one's little finger *see* **finger**

two
as (a)like as two peas in a pod *see* **pea**

for two pins *see* **pin**

in two minds *see* **mind**

it takes two to tango
a saying indicating that certain activities require the participation of two people, the implication being that both participants are equally responsible or equally to blame for the activity in question, often an illicit love affair
◷ Tango is the name of a dance

put two and two together
informal to realize or work out something from what one sees, hears etc
• *You won't be able to keep the deal a secret — people will soon put two and two together*
◷ Literally, to be able to solve the sum 2 + 2 = ?

serve two masters *see* **master**

there are no two ways about it *see* **way**

two a penny *see* **penny**

two heads are better than one *see* **head**

two of a kind
often derogatory of the same type, similar in character, outlook etc

two's company (three's a crowd)
a saying, meaning that a third person who joins a couple to do something is often unwanted

two shakes (of a lamb's tail) *see* **shake**

two ticks
informal a very short time
◷ The reference is to a clock

two-time
slang to deceive a boyfriend or girlfriend by having a relationship with another person

tyre
a spare tyre *see* **spare**

U

U

a U-turn
a turn, in the shape of a letter U, made by a motorist etc in order to reverse his direction

ugly

ugly as sin *see* **sin**

an ugly duckling
a member of a family who at first lacks beauty, cleverness etc but later becomes the most beautiful or successful
Ⓞ From the story by Hans Andersen of the duckling who is rejected by ducks for being ugly by their standards, but turns out eventually to be not a duck but a swan

umbrage

take umbrage
to feel, and show that one is, offended by another person's action etc
Ⓞ Originally 'to feel overshadowed and thus threatened', from Latin *umbra* = shade

uncle

like a Dutch uncle *see* **Dutch**

Uncle Sam

informal the United States of America
Ⓞ Coined in Troy, NY in 1812, probably from the initials U.S. which were stamped on government supplies etc and possibly also because someone actually called Uncle Sam was employed in handling such supplies

under

take someone under one's wing *see* **wing**

under a cloud *see* **cloud**

under one's belt *see* **belt**

under someone's (very) nose *see* **nose**

under one's breath *see* **breath**

under one's own steam *see* **steam**

under the weather *see* **weather**

under someone's thumb *see* **thumb**

under way *see* **way**

understand

give someone to understand
formal to cause someone to think (that)
• *I was given to understand that you were coming at two o'clock*

unkind

the unkindest cut of all
the utmost disloyalty or treachery
Ⓞ A quotation from Shakespeare, *Julius Caesar* in the description of the assassination of Caesar by his friends — 'This was the most unkindest cut of all'

unknown

an unknown quantity *see* **quantity**

unsound

of unsound mind
especially legal insane

unstuck

come unstuck
informal to fail

unsung

unsung heroes
people who deserve to be recognized for their bravery, talent, etc but are not famous or well-known
Ⓞ Ancient heroes were 'sung' about in the epic poems of Homer and Virgil

unvarnished

the unvarnished truth *see* **truth**

unwashed

the great unwashed

now often facetious the common people, the working classes

unwritten

an unwritten law *see* **law**

up

be in something up to one's neck *see* **neck**

be one up on *see* **one**

be on the up-and-up
informal to be progressing very successfully especially financially

be up with someone
informal to be wrong with someone

be/come up against something
to be faced with difficulties etc

be (well) up in/on something
informal to know a lot about a subject

be up in arms *see* **arm**

be up to someone
to be the duty or privilege of
• *It's up to you to decide; The final choice is up to him*

be up to something
informal
1 to be busy or occupied with an activity etc
• *What is he up to now?; I'm sure that man is up to no good*
2 to be capable of
• *She wasn't up to cooking a meal; He isn't quite up to the job*
3 to reach the standard of

be up to no good *see* **good**

be up to the hilt in something *see* **hilt**

be up to the mark *see* **mark**

have/keep something up one's sleeve *see* **sleeve**

it is all up with someone
there is no hope for the survival of someone

not up to much *see* **much**

his etc **number is up** *see* **number**

up-and-coming
of eg a person starting a career, progressing well
Ⓞ Originally US

up and doing
informal to be active and occupied

up for grabs *see* **grab**

ups and downs
informal times of good and bad luck

up in the air *see* **air**

the upshot
informal the result or end of a matter
Ⓞ Literally, the last shot in an archery competition

upstage
informal to take people's interest or attention away from someone or something
Ⓞ A theatrical term, from the fact that an actor who is *upstage of* — further towards the back of the stage than — another has the advantage, as his companion, in order to face him, has to act with his back to the audience

up the creek *see* **creek**

up the pole *see* **pole**

up the wall *see* **wall**

up to a point *see* **point**

up to one's ears (in) *see* **ear**

up to scratch *see* **scratch**

up to the minute *see* **minute**

upper

have, get the upper hand (of/over someone)
informal to have or win an advantage over someone

keep a stiff upper lip *see* **lip**

on one's uppers
informal very short of money
Ⓞ Literally, with the soles completely worn off one's shoes so that one is walking on the uppers

upper-crust
derogatory informal of the upper classes
Ⓞ The population is pictured as a closed pie with a lower and upper crust and a filling in the middle

upset

upset the applecart *see* **apple**

upside

be, get upsides with someone
informal to be or become level or equal with someone

Ⓛ Originally a Scots dialect phrase

turn something upside down
to put something into confusion

upstairs

kick someone upstairs
to promote someone to a seemingly higher position in an organization but one which has less responsibility in order to get him or her out of the way

uptake

quick, slow on the uptake
quick, or slow, to understand
Ⓛ Originally a Scots phrase

Uriah

Uriah Heep
a sycophant, a person who always shows undue humility to others
Ⓛ A reference to a character in *David Copperfield* by Charles Dickens

use

come in useful
to become useful *see* **come in handy,** *at* **handy**

have no use for someone or **something**
informal to despise someone or something

in, out of use
able, or not able, to be used

it's no use
it's impossible or useless

make (good) use of something/put something to (good) use
to use something to one's advantage

V

vain
take someone's name in vain
formal or facetious to use someone's, especially God's, name in an insulting or blasphemous way
Ⓞ From the phraseology of the Ten Commandments in the Bible, Exodus 20

value
at face value *see* **face**

variety
variety is the spice of life
a proverb, meaning that the many different things, situations, opportunities etc that occur, and the constant changes, are what make life interesting
Ⓞ A quotation from a poem by William Cowper

veil
draw a veil over something
often facetious not to discuss, mention etc something, or to hide a fact etc, because one feels it is better forgotten

velvet
the velvet glove *see* **the iron hand, at iron**

vengeance
with a vengeance
in a very great or unexpected degree; violently; thoroughly

vent
give vent to something
to express an emotion etc freely
vent one's spleen *see* **spleen**

venture
nothing ventured, nothing gained *see* **nothing**

very
the very thing
exactly what is wanted or needed

vessel
empty vessels make most noise *see* **empty**

vested
a vested interest
a biased and usually personal interest in continuing or suggesting a particular scheme etc
• *She has a vested interest in suggesting that we sell our shares in the company, since she would make a huge profit if we did*
Ⓞ A legal term

vex
a vexed question
a problem that is discussed a great deal, without being solved

vicious
a vicious circle
informal a bad situation whose results make it worse
Ⓞ In logic, the term for the fallacy of proving one statement by the evidence of another which itself is only valid if the first statement is valid

victory
a landslide victory *see* **land**

a Pyrrhic victory *see* **Pyrrhic**

view
in view of something
formal taking something into consideration; because of something

a point of view *see* **point**

take a serious, kindly etc **view of something**
to adopt a serious, kindly etc attitude to something

with a view to something
formal with the aim of doing something

villain
the villain of the piece
formal or facetious the person or thing responsible for some evil
Ⓞ A theatrical idiom

vine
a clinging vine *see* **cling**

vino
in vino veritas
a phrase indicating that people who have had too much to drink often reveal information that they would otherwise want to keep secret
Ⓞ Latin, literally 'there is truth in wine'

violet
a shrinking violet
a very timid or shy person

viper
nurse a viper in one's bosom
to have a friend whom one thinks is loyal but who turns out to be treacherous
Ⓞ A reference to one of Aesop's fables in which a peasant nurses a snake who is dying from cold and gets fatally bitten by it when it recovers

virtue
by virtue of something
formal because of something
• *She is allowed to do as she wishes by virtue of the fact that she is the manager's daughter*

make a virtue of necessity
to make the best of things

vital
vital statistics
facetious informal a woman's chest, waist and hip measurements
Ⓞ Originally statistics dealing with population — eg births, marriages and deaths

vive
vive la difference
a catch phrase humorously praising the difference between men and women
Ⓞ French for 'long live the difference'

voice
at the top of one's voice
very loudly

in good voice
not informal having one's voice in good condition for singing or speaking

lose one's voice
to be unable to speak eg because of having a cold, sore throat, etc

raise one's voice
to speak more loudly than normal especially in anger

a still small voice
one's conscience, the voice of reason
• *He went ahead and borrowed the car without permission although a still small voice told him it was wrong*

with one voice
formal simultaneously or unanimously

volume
speak volumes
rather literary to have a great deal of meaning
• *She said nothing but her face spoke volumes*

vote
put something to the vote
to decide a matter by voting

split the vote
to cause an opponent etc to be elected by giving supporters a choice of two things, people etc to vote for instead of only one

a vote of confidence
a vote taken to establish whether the government or other body or person in authority still has the majority's support for its/his policies

a vote of thanks
an invitation, usually in the form of a short speech, to an audience etc to show gratitude to a speaker etc by applauding etc

vulture
culture vulture *see* **culture**

W

wade

wade in/into someone or **something**
informal to attack someone, a task etc, with enthusiasm and without hesitation

wages

the wages of sin
the consequences which follow wickedness or wrongdoing
Ⓞ A biblical reference to Paul's letter to the Romans 'The wages of sin is death'

wagon

hitch one's wagon to a star
to aim extremely high in one's ambitions
Ⓞ Originally US, invented in 1870 by Ralph Waldo Emerson

on the wagon
not allowed or prepared to take alcoholic drink
Ⓞ Originally US, in full **on the water wagon**

wait

waiting in the wings *see* **wing**

wait on someone hand and foot
to look after someone to such an extent that he or she does nothing

wake

in the wake of something
immediately after and usually caused by something
• *He made several valuable business deals in the wake of his appearance on television*
Ⓞ From the strip of disturbed water left by the passage of a ship

in someone's wake
close behind someone more noticeable or important
Ⓞ As previous idiom

walk

cock of the walk *see* **cock**

walk all over someone
derogatory informal to pay no respect to a person's rights, feelings etc

walk away/off with something
informal to win prizes etc easily

a walking encyclopedia, a walking dictionary
facetious a very knowledgeable or intellectual person

walk it
informal to win or succeed easily

a walk of life
formal a way of earning one's living; an occupation or profession

walk on air
informal to feel extremely happy etc

walk out on someone
derogatory to abandon someone

walk tall
to feel and show that one is self-confident and proud of one's achievements

wall

climb the wall
to be extremely bored or frustrated
Ⓞ The implication is that one might start climbing the wall as a diversion from the boredom

go to the wall
to be defeated in, especially business, competition
Ⓞ An old phrase of obscure origin

have one's back to the wall *see* **back**

off the wall
slang unusual, weird
• *Their style of music is really off the wall*

send/drive etc **someone up the wall**
informal to make someone angry, confused etc

walls have ears
a saying, meaning that a secret conversation may still be overheard even if it seems impossible

I etc **would like to be a fly on the wall** *see* **fly**

the writing on the wall *see* **write**

Walter

a Walter Mitty
derogatory a person who makes up stories to make his life seem more exciting than it really is
Ⓛ From the main character in a short story by James Thurber

wane

on the wane
formal becoming less
Ⓛ Literally used of the moon

want

be found wanting in something
formal to be seen to be lacking certain things
Ⓛ A Biblical idiom: *see* **weigh**

want for something
to lack something

war

carry the war into the enemy's camp
to proceed with an argument etc by attacking one's opponent strongly
Ⓛ A military reference

have been in the wars
informal facetious to have been injured, usually slightly, in some rough activity

an old warhorse
someone who is very experienced in some area of activity and has been involved in it for a long time
Ⓛ A reference to the time when horses were used in battle

on the warpath
informal in a very angry mood
Ⓛ An expression associated with Native Americans = going to war

a war of nerves
a conflict or dispute that employs psychological methods rather than physical aggression or violence

war to the knife
a fierce, pitiless struggle
Ⓛ From the Spanish phrase *guerra al cuchillo*

warm

as warm as toast *see* **toast**

warm the cockles of the heart *see* **cockle**

wart

warts and all
including all the faults, disadvantages or unattractive parts
Ⓛ From the story that Oliver Cromwell instructed Sir Peter Lely, who was commissioned to paint his picture, that he wanted the portrait to show him as he really was, and to include the warts which disfigured his face

wash

come out in the wash
to work out satisfactorily in the end
• *Never mind, these problems will all come out in the wash*
Ⓛ Literally, of a stain etc, to be removed by washing

wash one's dirty linen *see* **linen**

washed-out
informal completely lacking in energy etc
Ⓛ Literally, of garments, having lost colour as a result of washing

wash one's hands of *see* **hand**

wash something out
especially of rain, to ruin, prevent etc something
• *Heavy rain washed out twenty football matches today in southern England*

washed-up
slang defeated, finished, failed etc
Ⓛ The reference is apparently to a shipwreck

waste

go/run to waste
to be allowed to be wasted

lay waste
formal or literary to destroy or ruin a town, country etc by force

waste one's breath *see* **breath**

waste not, want not
a proverb, meaning that if one is careful not to waste anything, one is unlikely ever to find oneself short of anything

watch

be on the watch for something or **someone**
to stay alert in order to notice something or someone; to look out for something or someone

a watched pot never boils *see* **pot**

watch it!
informal be careful!

watch someone like a hawk *see* **hawk**

watch out
to be careful of

watch over someone or **something**
formal to guard or take care of someone or something

watch one's step *see* **step**

water

be like water off a duck's back
to have no effect
Ⓛ From the fact that water runs straight off a duck's oily feathers without wetting them

hold water
formal to be correct or accurate and bear examination
• *His version of the facts doesn't hold water*

in deep water *see* **deep**

like a fish out of water *see* **fish**

milk and water *see* **milk**

of the first water *see* **first**

pour oil on troubled waters *see* **oil**

spend money like water *see* **money**

still waters run deep
a proverb indicating that people who do not say very much often do a great deal of thinking and are often very complicated, and sometimes devious

throw cold water on/over *see* **cold**

tread water
to keep oneself afloat in an upright position by moving the legs and arms

water something down
to make something less strong
• *He watered down his comments so that they became less offensive*
Ⓛ Literally, to dilute with water

water under the bridge
something that is past and cannot now be altered, is not worth worrying about or regretting etc
Ⓛ From the saying **a lot of water has passed the bridge** (= a lot has happened) *since* ...

Waterloo

meet one's Waterloo
rather facetious to be finally defeated
Ⓛ From the Battle of Waterloo (1815) in which Napoleon was defeated for the last time. The phrase was coined by Wendell Phillips

wave

make waves
to cause trouble or disturbance in what had been a calm or peaceful situation
Ⓛ Waves are a sign of a disturbed sea

on the same wavelength
having the same attitude of mind, opinions, sympathies etc

way

by the way
incidentally, in passing, while I remember etc

by way of something
for, or as if for, the purpose of doing something
• *He did it by way of helping me*

come someone's way
to become available to, possible for etc someone
• *Very few chances have come my way this year*

get into, out of the way of (doing) something
to become accustomed to doing, not doing something; to get into, out of the habit of doing something

get/have one's own way
to do, get etc what one wants

go a long way to(wards) something
to help greatly in achieving something

go out of one's way
to do more than is really necessary

go one's own way
to act as one likes, especially in a manner different from others

go the way of all flesh
usually facetious to die or disappear finally
Ⓘ A Biblical reference, to the dying words of David, in II Kings 2:2, in a medieval mistranslation

have a way with someone or **something**
to be good at dealing with or managing someone or something

have a way with one
formal or facetious to have an attractive manner

have everything/it (all) one's own way
to get one's own way in everything/something

have it both ways
to get the benefit from two actions, situations etc, each of which excludes the possibility of the other

in a bad way
informal unhealthy or in a poor state

in a big way
informal strongly and with enthusiasm

in a way
from a certain point of view
• *In a way I think this book is her biggest success, although it has serious faults*

in, out of the/someone's way
blocking, not blocking someone's progress, or occupying, not occupying, space that is needed by someone

lead the way *see* **lead**[1]

look the other way
to ignore or pretend not to notice something wrong, illegal etc

lose one's way
to stop knowing where one is, or in which direction one ought to be going

make one's way
1 to go
2 to get on in the world

make way for something
to stand aside and leave room for something

mend one's ways
old or formal to improve one's behaviour

no two ways about it
no alternative, no possible room for dispute or disagreement
• *There's no two ways about it — we'll have to cut our expenditure*

no way *see* **no**

one way and another
when one considers various qualities, features etc of something
• *This has been a very trying week, one way and another*

on the way
coming; about to happen; being prepared

the parting of the ways *see* **part**

pave the way *see* **pave**

pay one's way
to pay one's own expenses; never to owe money

see one's way to (doing) something
to be able and willing to do something

the way to a man's heart is through his stomach
a recommendation given to a woman trying to attract a man, indicating that men are more likely to be attracted by someone who can cook, since they appreciate good food

under way
moving, in progress etc

ways and means
methods, especially of providing money

wayside

fall by the wayside
to fail to continue with something until the end
Ⓘ A Biblical reference, to the parable of the Sower, Luke 8:5

weak

as weak as a kitten *see* **kitten**

have a weakness for something
informal to have a liking for something

a weak moment
a moment of weakness

wear

wear one's heart on one's sleeve *see* **heart**

wear off
of effects etc, to become less

wear the trousers *see* **trousers**

weather

keep a weather eye (open)
to remain alert or watchful
⌚ A nautical term — one's weather eye is the eye one keeps on the weather

lovely weather for ducks
a humorous phrase indicating that the weather is very wet

make heavy weather *see* **heavy**

under the weather
informal in poor health; unwell
⌚ Literally, affected by thundery weather — originally US

weave

get weaving
slang to start working or moving quickly

wedding

a shotgun wedding *see* **shotgun**

wedge

the thin end of the wedge
a small beginning, usually of something bad, that will certainly lead to greater and worse things

weed

weed something out
informal to remove things which are unwanted from a group or collection
• *We'll weed out all the unsuitable candidates and then interview the rest*

weep

weep buckets *see* **bucket**

weigh

weigh one's words *see* **word**

be weighed in the balance and found wanting
to be found to be defective or unsatisfactory in some way
⌚ A Biblical reference, to David 5:27

weight

carry weight *see* **carry**

pull one's weight
informal to take one's fair share of work, duty etc

throw one's weight about
derogatory informal to use one's power in an unsubtle way; to be bossy or domineering

weigh in
to join in a discussion, project etc with enthusiasm

weigh something up
to calculate or assess a probability etc
• *He weighed up his chances of success; She weighed the situation up and decided she could win easily; She's good at weighing up people*

worth its/one's weight in gold
extremely valuable

welcome

be welcome to (do, have) something
to be gladly given permission to do, have something
• *You're welcome to stay as long as you wish; (ironic) You're welcome to marry him — I don't want him!*

make someone welcome
to welcome someone; to put them at their ease

outstay one's welcome
to stay too long
⌚ Literally 'to remain after one's welcome has gone'

well[1]

all very well
apparently satisfactory, but really not satisfactory for some reason

as well
informal in addition; too

as well as
in addition to

be as well (to)
to be advisable or sensible to do something

be just as well (that)
it is fortunate or advantageous that; it is no cause for regret that

be well out of something
to be lucky because one has got out of an unfortunate situation etc

do well out of something
informal to make a profit or get some other advantage from something

well and good
that is quite acceptable, usually as opposed to something else which is not
• *If you want to come, well and good, but you mustn't interfere*

well-heeled
wealthy, prosperous
① A person who is well-heeled can afford to be well shod and is not down at heel

well off
informal
1 rich
2 in a fortunate position

well up in/on something
informal knowing a great deal about something

well²

the well has run dry
a source of something that was formerly very plentiful but has now been used up or is no longer available

west

go west
slang to become useless; to be destroyed
① World War I airmen's slang

wet

be wet behind the ears
derogatory to be young, inexperienced and easily fooled
① The reference is to a young animal washed by its mother

a wet blanket *see* **blanket**

wet one's whistle *see* **whistle**

whale

have a whale of a time
informal: slightly old to enjoy oneself very much

what

give someone what for
informal to scold or punish someone severely

know what something is
to have experienced something, an emotion, etc
• *If you had lived in our town in the 1930s, you would know what poverty is*

know what's what
to be able to tell what is important
• *He'll make a sensible decision — he knows what's what*

or whatever
informal or something of that sort
• *You can practise singing while you wash the dishes, clean the house or whatever*

so what? *see* **so**

what about?
informal used in asking whether the listener would like to do something
• *What about a glass of milk?; What about going to the cinema?*

what all/what have you/whatnot
informal and similar things; and so on
• *He told me all about publishing and whatnot; The cupboard was full of books, boxes and what all*

what in the world? *see* **world**

what of it?
informal used in replying, to suggest that what has been done, said etc is not important
• *'You've offended him.' 'What of it?'*

what price something? *see* **price**

what's the odds? *see* **odd**

what with
informal because of
• *What with having no exercise and being overweight, he had a heart attack*

wheel

a fifth wheel
a person or thing that is not needed
• *She feels like a fifth wheel when she goes out with the two couples*
① A fifth wheel on a vehicle is unnecessary unless it is the spare wheel

oil the wheels *see* **oil**

put a spoke in someone's wheel *see* **spoke**

put one's shoulder to the wheel *see* **shoulder**

reinvent the wheel
to fail to take advantage of available information, experience, etc and start from scratch when there is no need to do so

set the wheels in motion
to arrange for the beginning of a process etc
Ⓒ The reference is to a large piece of machinery

wheeling and dealing
making intelligent but possibly immoral business deals etc

wheels within wheels
circumstances which create a very complicated situation affected by several different influences
Ⓒ A Biblical reference, to Ezekiel 1:16

when

when in Rome, do as the Romans do *see* **Rome**

whet

whet someone's appetite for something
to make someone eager to have more of something
Ⓒ Literally, to increase someone's desire for food

while

once in a while *see* **once**

worth someone's while
worth someone's time and trouble

whip

crack the whip
to behave in a very stern and severe way
Ⓒ A reference to someone in charge of a team of slaves or animals cracking a whip as a threat

have the whip hand over someone
to have control, or hold an advantage over someone
Ⓒ The reference is to driving coach-horses

a whipping-boy
someone punished because of someone else's mistakes
Ⓒ Literally, a boy once educated with a royal prince and punished for the prince's mistakes because it was not permitted for the tutor to strike a member of the royal family

whirl

give it a whirl
informal to have a try at something
• *He doesn't know if he will like being a salesman but he's willing to give it a whirl*

whisker

the cat's whiskers *see* **cat**

do something by a whisker
to barely manage to do something

whisper

a stage whisper *see* **stage**

whistle

as clean as a whistle
very clean or cleanly

blow the whistle on someone
slang to expose or make public someone's illegal or deceitful schemes

wet one's whistle
old informal to have a drink

whistle for something
slang to ask for something with no hope of getting it
• *If you want me to give you fifty pounds, you can whistle for it*
Ⓒ Probably a reference to the sailors' superstition that a wind can be summoned by whistling

white

as white as a sheet *see* **sheet**

show the white feather *see* **feather**

a whited sepulchre
rather formal someone who is bad, but who pretends to be very good and moral
Ⓒ A Biblical reference, to Matthew 23:27

a white elephant *see* **elephant**

a white lie
a trivial or unimportant lie

whizz

a whizz-kid
informal: sometimes derogatory a very bright person who gains quick promotion
Ⓒ Originally US

whole

go the whole hog *see* **hog**

on the whole
taking everything into consideration
• *I think our trip was very successful on the*

whole; On the whole I am quite satisfied with the experiment

the whole shebang *see* **shebang**

the whole shoot *see* **shoot**

whoop

whoop it up
slang: slightly derogatory to celebrate or enjoy oneself in a noisy, extravagant manner

why

the whys and the wherefores
informal all the reasons for an action etc or details of a situation etc

wick

get on someone's wick
slang to annoy someone greatly

wicket

on a sticky wicket *see* **sticky**

widow

a grass widow *see* **grass**

wild

run wild
to behave without control or discipline

sow one's wild oats
usually of young men, to live a life of wild enjoyment before settling down to a quieter, more serious and respectable life

spread like wildfire
of eg news, to spread extremely fast
◷ *Wildfire* was probably originally a furious fire caused by lightning

a wild-goose chase
an attempt to catch or find something one cannot possibly obtain, especially because it does not exist or is not there
◷ From a kind of 16c horse race in which each horse had to follow exactly the erratic course of the leader, forming a string like that of geese in flight

wild horses would not do something etc
certainly nothing at all would be able to do something etc
• *Wild horses would not drag his secret from him; Wild horses would not get me to go there again!*

wilderness

crying in the wilderness
giving opinions or making suggestions that are not likely to be followed
◷ A Biblical reference, to Isaiah 40:3

will

at will
as or when one chooses; freely

a willing horse *see* **horse**

with a will
formal eagerly and energetically

with the best will in the world
however hard one tries or wishes to do something

willies

give someone the willies, get the willies
slang to give someone or get an uncomfortable, eerie or fearful feeling

win

be on a winning streak *see* **streak**

win hands down *see* **hand**

win someone over
to succeed in gaining the support and sympathy of someone

win some, lose some
a saying indicating a philosophical view of life which recognizes the fact that some enterprises end in success and some in failure

win one's spurs *see* **spur**

win the day *see* **day**

win the toss *see* **toss**

win through
to succeed in getting to a place, the next stage etc
• *It will be a struggle, but we'll win through in the end*

wind[1]

cast/throw caution etc **to the wind(s)**
to abandon caution etc, often recklessly

get one's second wind *see* **second**

get/have the wind up
informal to become nervous or anxious

get/have wind of something
informal to get a hint of or hear indirectly about something

ⓘ Literally 'to smell something in the wind'

in the wind
about to happen
• *Government officials seem to think that a change in policy is in the wind*

it's an ill wind (that blows nobody any good) *see* **ill**

like the wind
very quickly

put the wind up someone
to cause someone to become nervous or anxious

raise the wind
old informal to get enough money to do something

sail close to the wind
nearly to break a rule of acceptable behaviour etc
ⓘ Literally, in a sailing boat, to sail as nearly straight into the wind as possible

see which way/how the wind blows
to wait before making a decision etc to find out what the situation is going to be
ⓘ A nautical idiom

a straw in the wind *see* **straw**

take the wind out of someone's sails
to take an advantage away from someone; to make someone feel silly, embarrassed etc
ⓘ A nautical idiom — a ship takes the wind out of another's sails by passing close to it on the windward side

a wind of change
a new current of opinion bringing changed policies, attitudes, etc
ⓘ A phrase popularized by Harold Macmillan in his speech to the South African Parliament (1960) with reference to the social and political unrest in the continent

wind^2

wind up *see* **wound^2**

windmill

tilt at windmills
to struggle against imaginary opponents or imaginary opposition
ⓘ From an episode in Cervantes's *Don Quixote*, in which the hero mistakes a row of windmills for giants and attacks them

window

out the window
slang gone for good

window-dressing
derogatory the giving to something of an appearance which makes it seem more favourable, good etc than it really is
ⓘ Literally, the arranging of goods in a shop window

window-shopping
looking at things in shop windows, but not actually buying anything

wine

put new wine in old bottles
to put forward new ideas, policies, etc within the framework of an old system

wine and dine someone
to give someone expensive meals

wine, women and song
a catch phrase describing what is popularly supposed to be the good life as envisaged by men

wing

clip someone's wings
to take away from someone the power of doing something
ⓘ From a method of preventing domestic birds from flying away

spread one's wings
to try to carry out one's plans and ideas for oneself etc

take someone under one's wing
to take someone under one's protection and/or guidance
ⓘ From the way in which birds protect their offspring

waiting in the wings
ready to do something, especially to take over someone's else's job
ⓘ Literally, in a theatre, waiting at the side of the stage ready to go on

wing it
informal to improvise, to do something without preparation and sometimes without proper resources
• *He hadn't studied for the exam but he was hoping to wing it*

ⓘ US in origin. The phrase originally referred to an actor studying his or her part in the wings of the theatre because of being called upon to stand in for another actor at short notice

wink

a nod is as good as a wink to a blind horse *see* **nod**

forty winks *see* **forty**

tip someone the wink
informal to give someone information privately or secretly
• *He tipped me the wink that the house was for sale*
ⓘ Originally criminals' slang

wipe

wipe someone or **something out**
1 to remove or get rid of someone or something
• *You must try to wipe out the memory of these terrible events*
2 to destroy someone or something completely
• *They wiped out the whole regiment in one battle*

wipe the floor with someone *see* **floor**

wipe the slate clean *see* **clean**

wire

have one's wires crossed
to misunderstand one another

live wire *see* **live²**

wise

be wise after the event
to know what one should have done etc after a situation has passed

be wise to something
informal to be aware of or know the purpose of something
ⓘ Originally US

none the wiser
not knowing any more than before

put someone wise
informal to let someone know or give someone information about
ⓘ Originally US

a wise guy
derogatory informal a person who shows that he thinks that he is smart, knows everything etc
ⓘ Originally US

wish

wishful thinking
the belief or hope that something unlikely will happen merely because one wishes that it should

wish someone joy of something
usually ironic to wish that something will be a pleasure or advantage to someone

wit

at one's wits' end
utterly confused and desperate

frighten/scare someone out of someone's wits
to frighten someone greatly, almost to the point of madness

have/keep one's wits about one
to be cautious, alert and watchful

live by one's wits
formal to live by cunning rather than by regular employment

witch

a witch-hunt
a search for, and persecution of, people whose views are regarded as being evil
ⓘ Originally US, from the organized hunts for witches which took place in America and in Britain, especially in the 17c

with

be with someone
informal
1 to understand someone
• *Are you with me so far?*
2 to support someone
• *I'm with you all the way in your effort to be elected*

with it
slang, sometimes facetious fashionable

without

without rhyme or reason *see* **rhyme**

without so much as *see* **much**

wives

an old wives' tale *see* **tale**

woe

woe betide him etc
literary or facetious he will regret it

• *Woe betide you if you forget!*
Ⓛ *Betide* = happen to

woe is me
usually facetious I am unhappy, unlucky etc

wolf

cry wolf
to give warning of an imaginary danger
Ⓛ A reference to the fable of the shepherd boy who amused himself by rousing his village to beat off attacks on his sheep from non-existent wolves. He did this so often that at last, when the sheep were indeed attacked by wolves, no-one would come to help him and all his sheep were killed

keep the wolf from the door
to keep away poverty or hunger

a lone wolf *see* **lone**

a wolf in sheep's clothing
a dangerous, ruthless person who appears to be gentle and harmless
Ⓛ A Biblical reference, to Matthew 7:15

wonder

the eighth wonder of the world
usually ironic someone or something marvellous or extraordinary, often applied to a conceited or opinionated person
Ⓛ A reference to the Seven Wonders of the World in ancient times

a nine days' wonder *see* **nine**

no wonder
informal it isn't surprising that
• *No wonder you couldn't open the door — it was locked!; 'He says he feels sick.' 'No wonder, after eating all that ice-cream!'*

small wonder *see* **small**

wonders will never cease
a phrase indicating that something is extremely surprising and unusual
• *You say he's working? Wonders will never cease!*

wood

this, that etc **neck of the woods** *see* **neck**

the nigger in the woodpile *see* **nigger**

not to be able to see the wood for the trees
not to understand exactly the nature and purpose of a situation etc because of too much concern with the details of it

out of the wood(s)
out of danger
Ⓛ From a proverb — **do not shout until you are out of the wood** = do not celebrate prematurely

touch wood
used as an interjection to touch something made of wood superstitiously, in order to avoid bad luck

wooden

the wooden spoon *see* **spoon**

wool

pull the wool over someone's eyes
to deceive someone
Ⓛ Originally US

wool-gathering
absentmindedness or daydreaming
Ⓛ From collecting tufts of wool from hedges, which obliges one to wander to and fro in a haphazard manner

word

be as good as one's word *see* **good**

break, keep one's word
to fail to keep, keep one's promise

by word of mouth
by one person telling another in speech, not in writing

eat one's words
to admit humbly that one was mistaken in saying something
• *I'll make him eat his words!*

famous last words *see* **last**

fine words butter no parsnips
a proverb indicating that the use of unduly elegant language is unlikely to produce practical results

from the word go *see* **go**

get a word in edgeways
informal to break into a conversation etc and say something
• *She couldn't get a word in edgeways — those two kept shouting at each other*

hang on someone's (every) word
to listen attentively, and often ingratiatingly, to what someone says

have a word in someone's ear
to tell someone something confidentially

have a word with someone
to have a short conversation with someone

have words
informal to argue or quarrel

in a word
to sum up briefly

in so many words
stating very clearly or bluntly
• *He said in so many words that he was sick to death of me'; 'Did he tell you to leave?' 'Not in so many words, but that was what he meant'*

keep one's word *see* **break one's word,** *above*

the last word *see* **last**

a man of his word *see* **man**

mum's the word *see* **mum**

not the word for something
informal not a strong enough word to describe something

(a man, woman etc**) of few, many words**
someone who talks little, a lot

one picture is worth a thousand words *see* **picture**

the operative word *see* **operative**

a play on words *see* **play**

put in/say a good word for someone
to say something pleasant to someone about someone else

put words into someone's mouth
to say or suggest that someone has said something which they did not

say the word
informal I'm ready to obey your wishes

take someone at his etc **word**
to believe someone without question and act accordingly

take the words out of someone's mouth
to say something which is exactly what someone was about to say or would have said if asked

take someone's word for it
to assume that what someone says is correct without checking

weigh one's words
to consider carefully what one says

word for word
in the exact, original words; verbatim

words fail me
I cannot describe my feelings

work

all in a/the day's work
not causing extra or unusual effort or trouble

all work and no play makes Jack a dull boy
a proverb, meaning that it is not good for people to work, or do something disagreeable, all the time and that they should not do so

give someone the works
informal to give someone the full treatment
① Originally US gangsters' slang for 'to kill someone'

go to work on something
to begin work on something

gum up the works *see* **gum**

have one's work cut out
to be faced with a difficult task
① Literally, to have a lot of work already prepared for one to start

in working order *see* **order**

a nasty piece of work *see* **nasty**

out of work
having no employment

set to work
to start work

throw a spanner in the works *see* **spanner**

worked-up
excited, nervous, annoyed etc

work one's fingers to the bone *see* **finger**

a work of art
a painting, sculpture etc

work something off
to get rid of something unwanted or unpleasant by taking physical exercise etc

• *He tried to work off some of his excess weight by doing exercises every day*

work out
1 to happen successfully
2 to take exercise

work something out
to solve or calculate something correctly
• *I can't work out how many should be left*

work the oracle *see* **oracle**

world

all the world and his wife
old informal a very large number of people

dead to the world *see* **dead**

do someone a world of good
to have a very good effect on someone, to be of great benefit or advantage to someone

for all the world
exactly, quite etc

have the best of both worlds *see* **best**

it's a small world *see* **small**

it takes all sorts to make a world *see* **sort**

a man of the world *see* **man**

the New World *see* **new**

not long for this world *see* **long**

on top of the world
feeling very well and happy

out of this world
informal unbelievably marvellous

think the world of someone
to be very fond of someone

what in the world?
often derogatory used for emphasis when asking a question

with the best will in the world *see* **will**

the world is his etc **oyster** *see* **oyster**

worm

the worm turns
a patient, long-suffering person decides not to be patient and long-suffering any longer
◷ From a saying, **tread on a worm's tail and it will turn**

worn

worn(-)out
1 so damaged by use as to be unfit for further use
2 very tired

worn to a frazzle
utterly exhausted

worn to a shadow *see* **shadow**

worse

none the worse for something
not in any way harmed by something

the worse for wear
1 *informal* tired and untidy etc
2 *facetious* drunk

worse luck! *see* **luck**

worship

worship the ground someone walks on
to regard someone with great admiration and reverence

worst

be one's own worst enemy *see* **enemy**

do one's worst
to do the most evil etc thing that one can do

get the worst of something
to be affected more unpleasantly etc than someone else by something; to lose something

if the worst comes to the worst
if the worst possible thing happens

the worst of it is (that)
the most unfortunate etc aspect of the situation is that

worth

for all one is worth
using all one's efforts, strengths etc

for what it is worth
used to suggest that what is being said is doubtful or does not deserve consideration
• *For what it's worth, John told me that quite the opposite was true; For what it's worth, I like it even if nobody else does*

worth one's salt *see* **salt**

worth its/one's weight in gold *see* **weight**

worth someone's while *see* **while**

worthy of the name *see* **name**

wound[1]

rub salt into the wound *see* **salt**

wound[2]

be, get wound up
informal to be, or get, in a very excited or anxious state
Ⓞ The reference is to winding up a spring

wrap

keep something under wraps
informal to keep something secret

wrapped up in something
informal giving all one's affection or attention to something

wrap something up
informal to finish something completely
• *I went to Aberdeen to wrap up my firm's deal with the oil companies*
Ⓞ Originally US

wrist

a slap on the wrist *see* **slap**

write

write something off
informal
1 to regard something as lost for ever
2 to destroy something completely or damage it beyond repair
Ⓞ A term from finance — to deduct the value of something from an account etc as being a complete loss

the writing on the wall
something which shows that a disaster or failure is about to happen
• *The criminal saw the writing on the wall and left the country just before the police arrived to arrest him; I'd like to think our company can survive, but I'm afraid this year's sales figures are the writing on the wall*
Ⓞ From the Biblical story of Balshazzar's Feast in Daniel 5:5–31, at which a mysterious hand appeared and wrote words on the wall which Daniel interpreted as foretelling Belshazzar's death and the downfall of his kingdom. The words the hand actually wrote were *Mene, Mene, Tekel, Upharsin*

wrong

get off on the wrong foot *see* **foot**

get on the wrong side of someone
to make someone dislike one or be hostile to one

get (hold of) the wrong end of the stick *see* **stick**

get something wrong
informal to misunderstand something

go wrong
1 to go astray, badly, away from the intended plan etc
2 to stop functioning properly
3 to make a mistake

if anything can go wrong it will
a pessimistic comment on the number of problems that arise in life and how often things seem to go wrong, often illustrated by the fact that if a piece of buttered bread falls it usually seems to fall on the buttered side — often called **Murphy's Law**

in the wrong
guilty of an error or injustice

not to put a foot wrong *see* **foot**

on the wrong side of the blanket *see* **blanket**

on the wrong side of the tracks *see* **track**

on the wrong track *see* **track**

put someone in the wrong
formal to cause someone to seem to be in the wrong

wrongfoot someone
informal to cause someone to be unprepared to deal with an unexpected problem; to attack someone in an unexpected manner
Ⓞ Literally a sporting term — to attack in such a way that one's opponent has his weight on the wrong foot to defend effectively

Y

yarn

spin a yarn

to tell a long story, especially one that is not true

year

year in, year out

all the time, every year without exception

yesterday

not born yesterday

informal experienced and wise, not stupid or easily fooled

yet

as yet

up to the time referred to, usually the present

yours

yours truly

informal I, me

• *He didn't cook the meal — it was yours truly*

⌚ From a closing formula for an informal letter

Z

zero

zero hour

informal the time at which something is fixed to begin

zero in on something

informal to aim accurately for something one wants etc

① From target-shooting

SUBJECT INDEX